Classroom Assessment

Principles and Practice for Effective Standards-Based Instruction

James H. McMillan

Virginia Commonwealth University

FIFTH EDITION

Boston   Columbus   Indianapolis   New York   San Francisco   Upper Saddle River
Amsterdam   Cape Town   Dubai   London   Madrid   Milan   Munich   Paris   Montreal   Toronto
Delhi   Mexico City   Sao Paulo   Sydney   Hong Kong   Seoul   Singapore   Taipei   Tokyo

Editor: *Paul Smith*
Editorial Assistant: *Matt Buchholz*
Director of Marketing: *Margaret Waples*
Marketing Manager: *Joanna Sabella*
Production Editor: *Mary Beth Finch*
Editorial Production Service: *TexTech International*
Maufacturing Buyer: *Megan Cochran*
Electronic Composition: *TexTech International*
Interior Design: *TexTech International*
Cover Designer: *Linda Knowles*

Library of Congress Cataloging-in-Publication Data

McMillan, James H.
   Classroom assessment : principles and practice for effective standards-based instruction / James H. McMillan. — 5th ed.
     p. cm.
   ISBN-13: 978-0-13-209961-5
   ISBN-10: 0-13-209961-6
   1. Educational tests and measurements.   2. Examinations.   3. Examinations— Validity.   4. Examinations—Interpretation.   I. Title.
   LB3051.M462499 2011
   371.26—dc22

2010027308

10 9 8 7 6 5 4 3 2 1   RRD-VA   14 13 12 11 10

Allyn & Bacon
is an imprint of

www.pearsonhighered.com   ISBN-10: 0-13-209961-6
ISBN-13: 978-0-13-209961-5

CONTENTS

CHAPTER 3

High-Quality Classroom Assessment   60

CHAPTER 4

Formative Assessment I: Gathering Evidence   98

CHAPTER 5

Formative Assessment II: Feedback and Instructional Adjustments   133

CHAPTER 6

Planning and Implementing Classroom Summative Assessments   156

CHAPTER 12

Assessing Special Needs and ELL Students   326

When I took my first "tests and measurements" course I remember it well because I was fairly apprehensive—what would this have to do with teaching? Would I have to use complex mathematics and learn about the technical aspects of standardized testing that really had little to do with what I wanted to do day in and day out in the classroom? Well, the course met my negative expectations! It was interesting, but not really very helpful when applied to teaching. I have written this book to be directly relevant to instruction so that teaching and student learning are enhanced.

Over the past few years, the assessment field has changed so that much more emphasis is placed on how *student assessment is an integral part of teaching,* not just something that's done after instruction to measure what students have learned. In recent years there has also been a dramatic change in instruction and assessment throughout the United States as a result of No Child Left Behind (NCLB) legislation. NCLB has led to standards-based classrooms at every level of education and nearly every subject. Finally, there is renewed interest in the importance of "scientific" research and "empirical data" as sources of knowledge about what works in education. These three influences—assessment as part of instruction, standards-based teaching, and data-driven evidence—form the foundation for this book. All are essential factors in understanding how classroom assessments can improve targeted student outcomes.

This book, then, is designed to provide prospective and practicing teachers with (a) a *concise presentation* of assessment principles that clearly and specifically relate to standards-based instruction, (b) *current research and new directions* in the assessment field, and (c) *practical and realistic* examples, suggestions, and case studies. I have tried to keep the writing *nontechnical, easy to understand, and interesting.*

The approach I have taken to meet these criteria is to build assessment into the instructional process, focusing on assessment concepts and principles that are essential for effective teacher decision making. The emphasis throughout is on helping teachers to understand the importance of establishing credible performance standards (learning targets), communicating these standards to students, and providing feedback to students on their progress. There is much less emphasis on technical measurement concepts that teachers rarely find useful, though there is extensive discussion of aspects of assessment that result in high quality and credibility, such as fairness, matching assessment to clearly and publicly stated standards, positive consequences, and practicality.

There have been several significant changes for the fifth edition. The most important change is adding a new chapter on practicing formative assessment, so there are now two formative assessment chapters. The first formative assessment chapter (Chapter 4) shows how to gather formative evidence, the second chapter (Chapter 5) examines how teachers give feedback and make instructional adjustments. This enhanced coverage of formative assessment is justified with new research on formative assessment that has burgeoned in the last few years.

A second important change for the fifth edition is that chapters are now organized by type of assessment rather than type of learning target. This provides a clearer, more complete summary of each technique, while still focusing on how each approach to assessment is used for different types of learning targets. Chapters 1 through 3 present the fundamental principles of assessment and instruction, with an emphasis on the importance of the teacher's professional judgment and decision making as integral to making useful and credible assessments.

Chapter 6 is now focused solely on what teachers need to plan for summative assessment—how to put summative assessments together and to administer them. Chapters 7 through 10 then present types of assessments, divided generally into selected-response items (Chapter 7) and three types of constructed-response assessments (completion, short answer, and essay in Chapter 8, performance assessment in Chapter 9, and portfolio assessment in Chapter 10). Chapter 11 presents so-called noncognitive assessments that are used to measure attitudes, interests, beliefs, student self-assessment and other affective traits. Chapter 12 reviews the assessment of students who have disabilities and are included in the regular classroom as well as English language learners. Chapter 13 examines what teachers do with assessment information in the form of grading and reporting the results. Finally, Chapter 14 summarizes important information concerning the administration, interpretation, and use of standards-based and standardized tests.

Several instructional aids have been included to facilitate understanding and applying the material. These include *cognitive maps* at the beginning of each chapter to provide graphic overviews; *boldface key terms*; *quotes from National Board Certified teachers* throughout to illustrate practical applications; *chapter summaries* to review essential ideas; *self-instructional review exercises*, with answers, to provide opportunities for practice and application; *suggestions for conducting action research*; extensive use of *examples, diagrams, charts,* and *tables*; *case studies for reflection*; a *glossary* of key terms; and an expanded Companion Website (www.ablongman. com/mcmillan_assessment5e) that provides further exercises to enhance student learning, including links to helpful websites on the Internet.

Several additional changes have been made to improve the fifth edition:

- Greater emphasis on formative assessment, especially providing feedback.
- Greater emphasis on student motivational consequences of different assessment and grading practices.
- More emphasis on student self-assessment.
- More emphasis on how state standards influence classroom assessment.
- More in-depth coverage of formative assessment, including new coverage of instructional adjustments following feedback.
- Added coverage of the assessment of English language learners.
- Substantially revised chapter on grading, with emphasis on electronic grading software.
- Added coverage of electronic portfolios.

- Simplification of types of cognitive learning outcomes.
- New chapter on summative assessment.
- Greater emphasis on benchmark assessments.
- New coverage of Classroom Response Systems.
- New coverage of learning progressions.

Acknowledgments

Throughout the development and writing of this book, I have been fortunate to have the support and assistance of classroom teachers who have provided quotations, practical examples, and suggestions. I am very grateful for their willingness to help, for their patience in working with me, and, most of all, for keeping me grounded in the realities of teaching. They include Susan Pereira, Marie Wilcox, Carole Fokey, Beth Carter, Tami Slater, Arleen Reinhart, Patricia Harris, Ann Marie Seeley, Andrea Ferment, Terri Williams, Steve Myran, Suzanne Nash, Steve Eliasek, Daphne Patterson, Craig Nunemaker, Judy Bowman, Jeremy Lloyd, Marc Bacon, Mary Carlson, Michelle Barrow, Margie Tully, Rixey Wilcher, Judith Jindrich, Dan Geary, Joshua Cole, Christy Davis, Elizabeth O'Brien, Beth Harvey, Rita Truelove, Rita Driscoll, Dodie Whitt, Joe Solomon, and Leslie Gross. I am very fortunate that Angela Wetzel assisted me in several ways for this fifth edition—editing, checking references, and offering suggestions, and always doing exceptional work.

I would also like to express my appreciation to the following college and university professors who offered insightful and helpful comments and suggestions: For the first edition, Cheri Magill, Virginia Commonwealth University; H. D. Hoover, University of Iowa; Kathryn A. Alvestad, Calvert County Public Schools; John R. Bing, Salisbury State University; John Criswell, Edinboro University of Pennsylvania; George A. Johanson, Ohio University; Catherine McCartney, Bemidji State University; and Anthony Truog, University of Wisconsin, Whitewater; for the second edition, Lyle C. Jensen, Baldwin-Wallace College; Cathleen D. Rafferty, Indiana State University; Gerald Dillashaw, Elon College; Daniel L. Kain, North Arizona University; Charles Eiszler, Central Michigan University; Betty Jo Simmons, Longwood College; for the third edition, Gyu-Pan Cho, University of Alabama; Saramma T. Mathew, Troy University; E. Michael Nussbaum, University of Nevada; and Kit Juniewicz, University of New England; for the fourth edition, Sally Blake, University of Texas at El Paso; Roberta Devlin-Scherer, Seton Hall University; Carla Michele Gismondi Haser, Marymount University; Saramma T. Mathew, Troy University; and for the fifth edition, Rondall R. Brown, Eastern Oregon University; Carolyn Burns, Eastern Michigan University; Candyce Chrystal, Mount Marty College; Stephanie Kotch, University of Delaware; Alan L. Neville, Northern State University; and Tasha Almond Reiser, The University of South Dakota.

Finally, I am very grateful for the encouragement and direction of my editor, Paul Smith, as well as the support of others at Pearson.

The Role of Assessment in Teaching

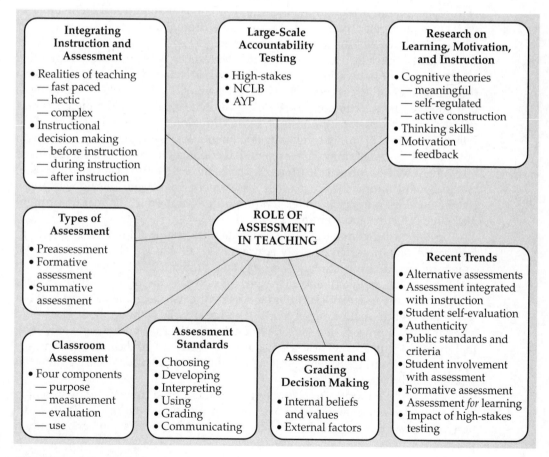

Integrating Instruction and Assessment
- Realities of teaching
  — fast paced
  — hectic
  — complex
- Instructional decision making
  — before instruction
  — during instruction
  — after instruction

Large-Scale Accountability Testing
- High-stakes
- NCLB
- AYP

Research on Learning, Motivation, and Instruction
- Cognitive theories
  — meaningful
  — self-regulated
  — active construction
- Thinking skills
- Motivation
  — feedback

Types of Assessment
- Preassessment
- Formative assessment
- Summative assessment

ROLE OF ASSESSMENT IN TEACHING

Classroom Assessment
- Four components
  — purpose
  — measurement
  — evaluation
  — use

Assessment Standards
- Choosing
- Developing
- Interpreting
- Using
- Grading
- Communicating

Assessment and Grading Decision Making
- Internal beliefs and values
- External factors

Recent Trends
- Alternative assessments
- Assessment integrated with instruction
- Student self-evaluation
- Authenticity
- Public standards and criteria
- Student involvement with assessment
- Formative assessment
- Assessment *for* learning
- Impact of high-stakes testing

CHAPTER 1 Concept Map

Allow me to begin with a story about my daughter. When Ryann was 11, she was heavily into gymnastics, working out most days of most weeks. During this particular year, the gym where she worked out hired new coaches, both from Russia. Immediately, the review of her work (performance) changed dramatically. What she was once praised for now received detailed, critical feedback (e.g., "No, put your hands in this position, not like this"). When the girls were "tested," doing their routines, they were judged with high expectations and only received praise when well deserved. Instead of hearing "good" all the time, they heard "wrong" most of the time. Negative comments, though, were accompanied by suggestions for doing something different and practice that would help them. The gym and training assessment environment changed, and with it the level of performance. The end of the story is happy. As a team, they were the best in the state, and Ryann made significant positive contributions!

This case shows how important assessment is for learning, whether in the gym or classroom. It shows how the right kind of assessment, and the manner in which it is integrated with teaching, can have dramatic effects on how much is learned and how well something is performed.

Over the past 20 years or so, research on teacher decision making, cognitive learning, student motivation, and other topics has changed what we know about the importance of assessment for effective teaching. For example, one finding is that good teachers continually assess their students relative to learning goals and adjust their instruction on the basis of this information. Another important finding is that assessment of students not only documents what students know and can do but also influences learning. Assessment that enhances learning is as important as assessment that documents learning. As a result of this research, new purposes, methods, and approaches to student assessment have been developed. These changes underscore a new understanding of the important role that assessment plays in instruction and learning.

In the past decade large-scale accountability testing ("high-stakes" testing) has had a significant impact on education at all levels. These two areas of influence—research on student learning and motivation, and teacher decision making, on the one hand, and high-stakes testing on the other—have created a complex context in which classroom assessment exists as a key element in what teachers do and what students learn. It is important to think about classroom assessment as a process that *supports and enhances student learning,* not something that merely documents what students know, understand, and can do. This means that teaching and assessment coexist in dynamic interaction, each feeding and influencing the other.

This chapter introduces classroom assessment by summarizing the research on teacher decision making to show how assessment is integrated with instruction and how teachers make decisions about their assessment and grading practices.

Integrating Instruction and Assessment

The Realities of Teaching

Classroom life is fast paced, hectic, and complex. To illustrate this reality, I have summarized some of what Michelle Barrow does during a typical day in her first-grade classroom. She has 10 boys and 11 girls in her class, 4 of whom are from racial minority groups and 6 of whom are from single-parent families. As many as 4 of her students will participate in the gifted/talented program, and 4 students were retained from the previous year. See how easy it is for you to get through this list of disparate tasks.

Before school begins in the morning, Michelle:

- Reviews what was learned/taught the previous day
- Goes over student papers to see who did or did not grasp concepts
- Prepares a rough agenda for the day
- Speaks with aide about plans for the day
- Puts journals on student desks

As soon as students enter the classroom, Michelle:

- Greets students at the door
- Reminds students to put away homework
- Speaks with Brent about his expected behavior for the day
- Reminds Anthony about what he is to do if he becomes bothered or frustrated by others

During the morning, Michelle:

- Calls students to the table to go over the reading assignment
- Has Dawn read a column of words and then goes back and randomly points to words to see whether Dawn knows them or simply has them memorized
- Comments to Lucy that she has really improved since the first day of school
- Discusses with Kevin the importance of doing homework every night
- Listens as Tim attempts to sound out each word and gradually blends them together
- Reminds Maggie that she is to be working in her journal rather than visiting and talking with others
- Gives Jason, Kory, and Kristen a vocabulary sheet to do because they have completed their journals
- Observes students in learning centers before calling reading groups to tables
- Verbally reinforces correct answers, gives each student a copy of the week's story, goes through the book and points out action words
- Calls up the low reading group and focuses on letters m and f

- Notices that Kevin has poor fine-motor skills and makes a mental note to send a message to his parents telling them that he should practice his handwriting
- Checks on Anthony to see how many centers he has completed
- Notices that students in the writing center are not doing as they were instructed
- Walks beside Anthony down the hall, verbally praising him for following directions
- Notices that Sarah has some difficulty answering higher-level thinking questions
- Makes a mental note to split gifted group up into two smaller groups

After lunch, Michelle's day continues as she:

- Begins math lesson on beginning addition with hippo counter
- Walks behind Scott and gives the next problem to the class
- Punches cards of students who have followed directions
- Notices that another table immediately stops talking and starts paying attention
- Tells students to rewrite sloppy copies
- Reminds Kevin and Brent to use guidelines on the paper
- Praises and gives punches on cards to Sarah and a few other students for good handwriting and concentration
- Notices that Tim is watching others, asks him if he needs help
- Gives 5-minute warning for music time, notices students working more intensely
- While students are in music, looks over their writing, arranges the papers into groups

After students leave for the day, Michelle continues to teach by:

- Grading student papers
- Making sure materials are ready for the next day
- Making notes in her gradebook about notes sent home and how the day went
- Checking portfolios to see progress
- Calling some parents

And so it goes for most classrooms. There is a hectic immediacy while multitasking. Many decisions are made, continuously, about students, instruction, and assessment. What is represented here is just a small sample of Michelle's actions, all of which are based on decisions that in turn depend on how well she has assessed her students. How did she decide to discuss with Kevin the importance of homework? What evidence did she use to decide that she needed to check Dawn's reading? In each of these cases, Michelle had to conduct some kind of assessment of the student before making her decisions. The role of an effective teacher is to reach these decisions reflectively, based on evidence gathered through assessment, reasoning, and experience.

Each decision is based on information that Michelle has gathered through a multitude of student interactions and behavior. Research indicates that a teacher may have as many as 1,000 or even 1,500 interactions with students *each day* (Billups & Rauth, 1987; Jackson, 1990). Often these interactions and decisions occur with incomplete or inaccurate information, making the job of teaching even more difficult.

Consider how the following aspects of Michelle's and other teachers' classrooms affect decision making (Doyle, 1986).

1. *Multidimensionality:* Teachers' choices are rarely simple. Many different tasks and events occur continuously, and students with different preferences and abilities must receive limited resources for different objectives. Waiting for one student to answer a question may negatively influence the motivation of another student. How can the teacher best assess these multiple demands and student responses to make appropriate decisions?
2. *Simultaneity:* Many things happen at once in classrooms. Good teachers monitor several activities at the same time. What does the teacher look for and listen for so that the monitoring and responses to students are appropriate?
3. *Immediacy:* Because the pace of classrooms is rapid, there is little time for reflection. Decisions are made quickly. What should teachers focus on so that these quick decisions are the right ones that will help students learn?
4. *Unpredictability:* Classroom events often take unanticipated turns, and distractions are frequent. How do teachers evaluate and respond to these unexpected events?
5. *History:* After a few weeks, routines and norms are established for behavior. What expectations for assessment does the teacher communicate to students?

It is in these complex environments that teachers must make some of their most important decisions—about what and how much students have learned. Accurate and appropriate student assessment provides the information to help teachers make better decisions. In the classroom context, then, **assessment** *is the gathering, interpretation, and use of information to support teacher decision making.* Assessment is an umbrella concept that encompasses different techniques, strategies, and uses. It is much more than simply "testing."

Instructional Decision Making and Assessment

It is helpful to conceptualize teacher decision making by *when* decisions are made—before, during, or after instruction—and then examine how assessment affects choices at each time. Preinstructional decisions are needed to set learning goals, select appropriate teaching activities, and prepare learning materials. As instructional activities are implemented, decisions are made about the delivery and pace in presenting information, keeping the students' attention, controlling students' behavior, and making adjustments in lesson plans. At the end of instruction, teachers evaluate student learning, instructional activities, and themselves to know what to teach next, to grade students, and to improve instruction.

Thinking about teaching as phases that occur before, during, and after instruction is aligned with three major types of assessments—*preassessment, formative assessment,* and *summative assessment.* **Preassessment** is done by the teacher before instruction to ascertain students' knowledge, attitudes, and interests. This information is then used as a starting point for designing instruction (Chapman & King, 2009). For example, a government teacher who wants to begin a unit on the 2009 recession might want to know how well students are prepared by examining scores on a previous test that demonstrate their knowledge of supply and demand. If students show weak understanding, these concepts need to be reviewed. **Formative assessment** occurs during teaching. It is a way of assessing students' progress, providing feedback, and making decisions about further instructional activities. **Summative assessment** is conducted after instruction primarily as way to document what students know, understand, and can do.

Table 1.1 presents examples of the types of questions teachers ask themselves at these different points in the instructional process. Table 1.1 also offers examples of the type of assessment information needed to make these decisions.

Figure 1.1 illustrates further how assessment is involved in each stage of the instructional process. This figure shows how preassessment is used to provide information to transform general learning goals and objectives into specific

TABLE 1.1 **Examples of Questions for Decision Making and Assessment Information**

When Decisions Are Made	Questions	Assessment Information
		Preassessment
Before Instruction	How much do my students know?	Previous student achievement; test scores; observations of student performance
	Are my students motivated to learn?	Observations of student involvement and willingness to ask questions
	Are there any exceptional students? If so, what should I plan for them?	Student records; conference with a special education teacher
	What instructional activities should I plan? Are these activities realistic for these students?	Overall strengths and needs of students; comments from previous teachers; evaluations of previous teaching
	What homework assignments should I prepare?	Student progress and level of understanding
	What is acceptable evidence that students have attained desired proficiencies?	Determine which assessment methods will provide needed evidence

When Decisions Are Made	Questions	Assessment Information
		Formative Assessment
During Instruction	What type of feedback should I give to students?	Quality of student work; type of student
	What question should I ask?	Observation of student understanding
	How should a student response to a question be answered?	Potential for this student to know the answer
	Which students need my individual attention?	Performance on homework; observations of work in class
	What response is best to student inattention or disruption?	Effect of the student on others
	When should I stop this lecture?	Observation of student attention
		Summative Assessment
After Instruction	How well have my students mastered the material?	Achievement test results in relation to a specified level
	Are students ready for the next unit?	Analysis of demonstrated knowledge
	What grades should the students receive?	Tests; quizzes; homework; class participation
	What comments should I make to parents?	Improvement; observations of behavior
	How should I change my instruction?	Diagnosis of demonstrated learning; student evaluations

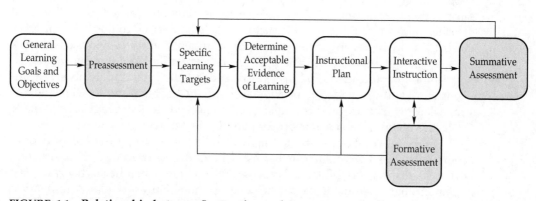

FIGURE 1.1   Relationship between Instruction and Assessment

learning targets. You will usually be provided with general state, district, or school learning goals for a particular grade level or subject. These goals are used as a starting point to develop more specific learning targets that take into account the characteristics and needs of the students and your style and beliefs. Preassessment is an absolutely essential step for effective instruction. If you can't identify what specific knowledge, skills, attitudes, and other learning targets are important, it is unlikely that students, parents, or the teacher will know when they have been successful. In other words, you must determine what it is that students should know, understand, and be able to do at the end of an instructional unit.

The next step in instructional decision making is to specify the evidence that is needed to document student learning. This evidence is identified up front, *before* determining instructional plans, because it should influence the nature of instruction. This approach to planning is known as "backward design" (McTighe & Wiggins, 2004; Wiggins, 1998; Wiggins & McTighe, 2005). It is called "backward" because conventional instructional planning typically considers assessment an activity that is done after instruction. But it is very helpful to think like an assessor before planning learning activities. This helps accomplish a true integration of assessment and instruction.

Once acceptable evidence is identified, the teacher selects instructional strategies and activities to meet the targets. This is often operationalized as a lesson plan or instructional plan. It consists of what teachers will do and what they will have their students do for a specific period of time. During instruction, there is interaction between the teacher and students that constantly involves making assessments about how to respond to students appropriately and keep them on task. During this time, formative assessment information is used to monitor learning, check for progress, and diagnose learning problems and specify instructional adjustments.

After instruction, more formal summative assessment of learning targets is conducted, which loops back to inform subsequent learning targets, instructional plans, and interactive instruction. Assessment at the end of an instructional unit also provides information for grading students, evaluating teaching, and evaluating curriculum and school programs.

The point is that assessment is not only an *add-on* activity that occurs after instruction is completed. Rather, assessment is integrally related to all aspects of teacher decision making and instruction. Michelle Barrow did assessment *before* instruction by reviewing the performance of students on the previous day's work to see who did and who did not grasp the concepts. She used this information to plan subsequent instruction. *During* instruction Michelle constantly observed student work and responded to provide appropriate feedback and to keep students on task. *After* instruction she graded papers, checked student progress, and made decisions about the focus of instruction for the next day.

In the first of the case studies that will appear in each of the chapters, teacher comments are made about whether assessment drives instruction or instruction drives assessment (McMillan & Workman, 1999). From what the teachers said, is it apparent that assessment should drive instruction? How would you respond to this question?

Case Study
for Reflection

In one of my classroom assessment studies, teachers were asked whether assessment drives instruction or instruction drives assessment. Here is what a few of them said:

"I would say my plan determines my assessments. What I teach is what I assess."

"I guess a little bit of both but I guess assessment comes from your lesson plans. You can't have the test made up if you have some unforeseen circumstance or you don't get to teach something during the week. It wouldn't be fair to have that on the test."

"In the remedial class, assessment somewhat dictated lesson plans."

"Assessments absolutely drive lesson plans. I'll introduce it, assess what students know, and how fast they pick it up and then adjust my plans or write my plans accordingly."

"What we teach determines the assessment."

"It's both, really. For instance, the writing rubric sometimes comes first because I know a certain skill that I want to teach them. So I'll design whatever final product I want them to come up with. Then I'll do my lesson plan to lead up to that."

With this introduction, we will now consider in more detail what is meant by such terms as *test* and *assessment* and how current conceptualizations enhance older definitions of *measurement* and *evaluation* to improve teaching and learning.

What Is Classroom Assessment?

Classroom assessment can be defined as the collection, evaluation, and use of information to help teachers make decisions that improve student learning. Conceptualized in this way, assessment is more than *testing* or *measurement,* which are familiar terms that have been used extensively in discussing how students are evaluated.

There are four essential components to implementing classroom assessment: purpose, measurement, evaluation, and use. These components are illustrated in Figure 1.2, with questions to ask yourself at each step. The figure shows the sequence of the components, beginning with identification of purpose.

Purpose

Whether done before, during, or after instruction, the first step in any assessment is to clarify the specific purpose or purposes of gathering the information. A clear

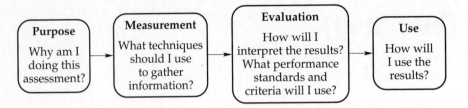

FIGURE 1.2   **Components of Classroom Assessment**

vision is needed of what the assessment will accomplish. Why are you doing the assessment? What will be gained by it? What teacher decision making is enhanced by the information gathered through the assessment process?

There are many reasons for doing classroom assessments, some of which are traditional (such as the first four listed next [Popham, 2011]), and others that have become important with changes in learning and motivation theory, curriculum alignment, and the current context of high-stakes testing.

- To diagnosis students' strengths and weaknesses
- To monitor student progress toward achieving objectives
- To assign grades
- To determine instructional effectiveness
- To provide students feedback
- To prepare students for high-stakes tests
- To motivate students

Knowing the reason for the assessment is crucial because this will determine what the assessment should look like, how it is administered and scored, and how the results will be used.

It is also helpful to understand that classroom assessments, for both individual students and whole classes, differ with respect to the nature of the information gathered for program and institutional evaluations (Stiggins, 2008a). At the program level, the emphasis is on what standards are met by groups of students (e.g., all fifth graders; students in the gifted program). At this level data are gathered periodically and aggregated for all students to design instruction for all students in each program. These data are typically used for changing programs that are not adequately meeting established standards. At the institutional level, the information is aggregated for the school or district as a whole. These data are used to inform policy that affect such factors as leadership roles, resource allocation, and parental involvement.

Measurement

The term *measurement* has traditionally been defined as a systematic process of assigning numbers to behavior or performance. It is used to determine how much of a trait, attribute, or characteristic an individual possesses. Thus, **measurement** is the process by which traits, characteristics, or behavior are *differentiated*. The process of differentiation can be very formal and quantitative, such as using a thermometer to measure temperature, or can consist of less-formal processes, such as observation ("It's very hot today!"). Typically, measurement is used to assign numbers to describe attributes or characteristics of a person, object, or event. A variety of techniques can be used to measure a defined trait or learning target, such as tests, ratings, observations, and interviews.

Evaluation

Once measurement is used to gather information, you will need to place some degree of value on different numbers and observations, based on a specific frame of reference. This process is identified in Figure 1.2 as *evaluation*, the making of judgments about quality—how good the behavior or performance is. **Evaluation** involves an *interpretation* of what has been gathered through measurement, in which value judgments are made about performance. For example, measurement often results in a percentage of items answered correctly. Evaluation is a judgment about what each percentage correct score means. That is, is 75% correct good, average, or poor? Does 75% indicate "proficiency"?

Teachers' professional judgments play a large role in evaluation. What is a "good" student paper to one teacher may be only an "adequate" paper to another teacher. Assessment is more than *correctness*; it is also about value.

An important determinant of how you evaluate a performance is the nature of the performance standards you employ. **Performance standards** are used to determine whether a performance is "good" or "bad." Increasingly, such standards refer to high, specific, and valued measurable results that indicate a specific level of performance.

Criteria also play an important part of the evaluation process. **Criteria** are the specific behaviors or dimensions that are evidenced to successfully attain the standard. These criteria may be the most important influences on evaluation. They may be called *scoring criteria, scoring guidelines,* or *rubrics*. For example, take as a standard that students know all state capitals in the United States. The criteria are what the teacher uses to conclude that the student does, indeed, know the capitals. For one teacher this may mean giving the students a map and having them write in the capital for each state; for another teacher it may mean answering 20 multiple-choice questions correctly. Often teachers use criteria for scoring tests and papers without a clear standard. In fact, if only informally, teachers must have some type of criteria in mind to make assessment evaluations.

Both standards and criteria communicate to students the teacher's expectations of them. The nature of questions and feedback, the difficulty of assignments, and the rigor of the criteria tell students what the teacher believes they are capable of achieving. These expectations are important in motivating students and in setting an academic achievement climate in the classroom.

As you can see, setting standards and criteria is a critical component of assessment, one that we will consider in much greater detail in Chapter 2.

Use

The final stage of implementing assessment is how the evaluations are used. The use of test scores and other information is closely tied to the decisions teachers must make to provide effective instruction, to the purposes of assessment, and to the needs of students and parents. As indicated in Figure 1.1, these decisions depend on *when* they are made; they can also be categorized into three major classroom uses: diagnosis, grading, and instruction.

Diagnosis.   Diagnostic decisions are made about individual students as well as about group strengths, weaknesses, and needs. Typically, information is gathered that will allow the teacher to diagnose the specific area that needs further attention or where progress is being made. The diagnosis includes an assessment of *why* a student may be having difficulty so that appropriate instructional activities can be prescribed. For example, teachers use homework diagnostically to determine the extent of student understanding and to identify students who do not understand the assignment. A pretest may be used to diagnose specific gaps in student knowledge that need to be targeted. Students are closely monitored to check motivation, understanding, and progress.

Grading.   Grading decisions are based on measurement-driven information. Although most teachers must adhere to grading scales and definitions, there is a great amount of variability in what teachers use to determine grades, how they use the process of grading to motivate students, and the standards they use to judge the quality of student work. Some teachers, for example, use grading to *control* and *motivate* (e.g., "This assignment will be graded"), and often teachers use completed work as a basis for giving privileges and otherwise rewarding students (e.g., "good" papers are posted). Grades and associated written comments also provide *feedback* to students and parents.

Instruction.   Teachers constantly make instructional decisions, and good teachers are aware that they must continuously assess how students are doing to adjust their instruction appropriately. One type of decision, termed a *process* instructional decision, is made almost instantaneously, such as deciding to end a lecture or ask a different type of question. *Planning* instructional decisions are made with more reflection; they might include changing student seating arrangement or grouping patterns, spending an extra day on a particular topic, or preparing additional worksheets for homework. It is hoped that teachers will use credible measurement information with clear standards to evaluate student behavior accurately.

Finally, assessment processes can be used *as* instruction. For example, performance and authentic assessments are long term and provide opportunities for student learning. As we will see in later chapters, such assessments are useful as teaching tools as well as methods to document student learning. As such, they educate and improve student performance, not merely audit it (Wiggins, 1998).

Research on Learning, Motivation, Instruction, and Curriculum: Implications for Assessment

As summarized in Table 1.2, recent research on learning, motivation, instruction, and curriculum has important implications for the nature and use of classroom assessments. It is becoming increasingly clear that effective instruction usually does much more than present information to students. Rather, good instruction

TABLE 1.2   Implications for Assessment from Cognitive Learning Theories

Theory	Implications for Classroom Assessment
Knowledge is constructed; learning involves creating personal meaning that connects new information with prior knowledge.	• Use multiple modes of assessment that allow flexibility in how students demonstrate knowledge and understanding. • Assess current state of knowledge to target instruction and subsequent assessments. • Use assessments that require application of knowledge. • Individualize feedback so that it is meaningful for each student.
There is variety among students on learning styles, language, memory, aptitudes, attention, and developmental pace.	• Provide choices in how to show mastery/competence. • Provide sufficient time for all students to demonstrate knowledge. • Provide students opportunities to revise and retest. • Use multiple modes of assessment.
Students perform best when they know the goal, see examples or exemplars, and know how their performance compares with established standards.	• Make standards explicit before beginning instruction. • Give students examples of performance at different levels. • Provide specific feedback that links performance with standards. • Use formative assessment. • Use student self-assessments.
Students need to know when to use knowledge, how to adapt it to new situations, and how to manage their own learning.	• Use performance assessment with actual "real-life" problems and issues. • Use student self-assessment. • Use formative assessment. • Avoid objectively scored assessments.
Motivation and effort are important components of learning and performance.	• Use "real-life" tasks and examples. • Use formative assessment. • Provide individualized feedback to see the connection between effort and performance. • Provide feedback that encourages internal attributions.

provides an environment that engages the student in active learning that connects new information with existing knowledge. Contemporary cognitive theories show that learning is *meaningful* and *self-regulated* (Schunk, 2004). Learning is an ongoing process in which students actively receive, interpret, and relate information to what they already know, understand, and have experienced. Effective assessment, in turn, promotes this process by documenting the attainment of progressive levels of more knowledge and understanding that eventually leads to mastery.

There is a growing awareness that it is essential for students to develop thinking skills (e.g., skills in problem solving and decision making). Students need to be able to apply what they learn to real-world demands and challenges, work with others to solve problems, and be self-regulated learners who have an awareness and willingness to explore new ideas and develop new skills. Instruction and curriculum as well as assessment need to be designed and delivered to enhance these skills.

Research on motivation suggests that teachers must constantly assess students and provide feedback that is informative. By providing specific and meaningful feedback to students and encouraging them to regulate their own learning, teachers encourage students to enhance their sense of self-efficacy and self-confidence, important determinants of motivation (Brookhart, 2008). Meaningful learning is intrinsically motivating because the content has relevance. The implication here is that assessment does not end with scoring and recording the results. Motivation is highly dependent on the nature of the feedback from the assessment. Thus, in keeping with the integration of assessment with instruction, feedback is an essential component of the assessment process.

There have also been significant recent changes in curriculum theory that have clear implications for classroom assessment. Due in part to the standards-based movement, curriculum is now based on the premise that all students can learn, that standards for learning need to be high for all students, and that equal opportunity is essential. Curriculum needs to show students how learning is connected to the world outside school.

Shepard (2000) has nicely illustrated the shared principles of contemporary curriculum theories, cognitive and constructivist learning theory, and recent trends in classroom assessment (Figure 1.3). Her overlapping circles signify that the changes we have seen from older behavioristic theories of learning and motivation, curriculum designed for social efficiency, and principles derived from scientific measurement overlap to provide a new set of ideas to guide classroom assessment. Although the changes in principles of curriculum, learning, and motivation are now fairly well established, classroom assessment practices are only beginning to change. Furthermore, recent high-stakes testing at the state level has nudged many educators back toward behavioristic and scientific (e.g., objective) measurement theories.

The research from cognitive learning and curriculum theories has laid the foundation for significant changes in classroom assessment. As we discover more about how students learn, we realize that assessment practices, as well as instructional practices, need to change to keep pace with this research.

**Reformed Vision
of Curriculum**

- All students can learn.
- Challenging subject matter aimed at higher-order thinking and problem solving
- Equal opportunity for diverse learners
- Socialization into the discourse and practices of academic disciplines
- Authenticity in the relationship between learning in and out of school
- Fostering of important dispositions and habits of mind
- Enactment of democratic practices in a caring community

**Cognitive and Constructivist
Learning Theories**

- Intellectual abilities are socially and culturally developed.
- Learners construct knowledge and understandings within a social context.
- New learning is shaped by prior knowledge and cultural perspectives.
- Intelligent thought involves "metacognition" or self-monitoring of learning and thinking.
- Deep understanding is principled and supports transfer.
- Cognitive performance depends on dispositions and personal identity.

**Classroom
Assessment**

- Challenging tasks to elicit higher-order thinking
- Addresses learning processes as well as learning outcomes
- An ongoing process, integrated with instruction
- Used formatively in support of student learning
- Expectations visible to students
- Students active in evaluating their own work
- Used to evaluate teaching as well as student learning

FIGURE 1.3   Shared Principles of Curriculum Theories, Psychological Theories, and Assessment Theory Characterizing an Emergent, Constructivist Paradigm

Source: From Shepard, L. A. (2000). The role of assessment in a learning culture. *Educational Researcher, 29*(10), 4–14. Reprinted by permission of Sage Publications.

Recent Trends in Classroom Assessment

In the past decade, some clear trends have emerged in classroom assessment. More established traditions of focusing assessment on "objective" testing at the *end* of instruction are being supplemented with, or in some cases replaced by, assessments *during* instruction—to help teachers make moment-by-moment decisions—and with what are called "alternative" assessments. **Alternative assessments** include authentic assessment, performance assessment, portfolios, exhibitions, demonstrations, journals, and other forms of assessment that require the active construction of meaning rather than the passive regurgitation of isolated facts. These assessments engage students in learning and require thinking skills, and thus they are consistent with cognitive theories of learning and motivation as well as societal needs to prepare students for an increasingly complex workplace.

Another trend is the recognition that knowledge and skills should not be assessed in isolation. Rather, it is necessary to assess the application and the use of knowledge and skills together. More emphasis is now placed on assessing thinking skills and collaborative skills that are needed to work cooperatively with others. Newer forms of assessment provide opportunities for many "correct" answers, rather than a single right answer and rely on multiple sources of information.

One of the most important advances in both instruction and assessment is the emphasis on **authenticity** (Wiggins, 1993, 1998). Authentic instruction and assessment focus on knowledge, thinking, and skills exhibited in real-life settings outside school that produce the student's best, rather than typical, performance. To accomplish this, students need multiple "authentic" opportunities to demonstrate the knowledge and skills and continuous feedback. This kind of emphasis results in greater student motivation and improved achievement. In this way authenticity effectively integrates instruction, assessment, and motivation.

Another important trend is to involve students in all aspects of assessment, from designing tasks and questions to evaluating their own and others' work. Engaging students in developing assessment exercises, creating scoring criteria, applying criteria to student products, and self-assessment all help students understand how their own performance is evaluated. This understanding, in turn, facilitates student motivation and achievement. Students learn to confidently evaluate their performance as well as the performance of other students. For example, if students are taught to internalize the key elements of what should be included in comprehending a short story, they are better able to monitor their progress toward achieving learning targets. Likewise, when students generate lists of the ways good essay answers differ from weak ones, they learn the criteria that determines high student performance. Thus, there is a change of emphasis from the teacher providing all assessment tasks and feedback to promoting student engagement in the assessment process. This is best accomplished when there is "a continuous flow of information about student achievement . . . to advance, not merely check on, student learning" (Stiggins, 2002, p. 761). That is, assessment *for* learning becomes as important as assessment *of* learning.

The distinction between assessment *of* learning and assessment *for* learning is critical for understanding the influences of recent theories of learning and motivation on the one hand (*for* learning), and external accountability testing on the other (*of* learning). These differences are summarized in Table 1.3. Note, too, that assessment *as* learning is also important.

Stiggins (2002, pp. 761–762) identifies eight ways that assessment *for* learning can be facilitated:

1. Understanding and articulating targets in advance of teaching/learning
2. Informing students about learning goals in terms that students understand, from the very beginning of the teaching and learning process

TABLE 1.3 Characteristics of Assessment *of* Learning, *for* Learning, and *as* Learning

Assessment *of* Learning	Assessment *for* Learning	Assessment *as* Learning
• Summative	• Formative	• Nature of assessment engages students in learning
• Certify learning	• Describes needs for future learning	• Fosters student self-monitoring of learning
• Conducted at the end of a unit; sporadic	• Conducted during a unit of instruction; ongoing	• Conducted during a unit of instruction
• Often uses normative scoring guidelines; ranks students	• Tasks allow teachers to modify instruction	• Emphasizes student knowledge of criteria used to evaluate learning
• Questions drawn from material studied	• Suggests corrective instruction	• Student selects corrective instruction
• General	• Specific	• Specific
• Used to report to parents	• Used to give feedback to students	• Fosters student self-monitoring
• Can decrease student motivation	• Enhances student motivation	• Enhances student motivation
• Highly efficient, superficial testing	• In-depth testing	• Testing teaches students
• Focus on reliability	• Focus on validity	• Focus on validity
• Delayed feedback	• Immediate feedback	• Immediate feedback
• Summary judgments	• Diagnostic	• Diagnostic

Source: Adapted from Earl, L. M. (2003). *Assessment as learning: Using classroom assessment to maximize student learning.* Thousand Oaks, CA: Corwin Press; and LeMahieu, P. G., & Reilly, E. C. (2004). Systems of coherence and resonance: Assessment for education and assessment of education. In M. Wilson (Ed.), *Toward coherence between classroom assessment and accountability. 104th Yearbook of the National Society for the Study of Education.* Chicago: National Society for the Study of Education.

3. Becoming assessment literate and able to transform expectations into assessment exercises and scoring procedures that accurately reflect student achievement
4. Using classroom assessment to build students' confidence in themselves as learners and help them take responsibility for their own learning
5. Translating classroom assessment results into frequent descriptive feedback, providing students with specific insights as to how to improve
6. Continuously adjusting instruction based on the results of classroom assessment
7. Engaging students in regular self-assessment, with standards held constant so that students can watch themselves grow over time
8. Actively involving students in communicating with their teacher and parents about their achievement status and improvement

Student engagement in assessment is closely related to another recent trend: a greater emphasis on formative assessment. It involves both formal and informal methods of gathering information with the sole purpose of improving student motivation and learning. In contrast, summative assessment documents what students have learned at the end of an instructional unit. Summative assessment is more formal and occurs after instruction is completed. Effective teaching requires the use of both formative and summative assessments. The greater emphasis on formative assessment in recent years, which integrates nicely with recent theories of motivation and cognition, suggests a continuing focus on improving student learning with assessments that are integrated with instruction.

In the first of many Teacher's Corner inserts, Susan Pereira makes a strong case for the integration of assessment with instruction. Note how she uses assessment to know "where" student are in their learning to know what subsequent instruction will be most effective.

These and other recent trends in classroom assessment are summarized in Figure 1.4 with some arrows back to indicate the influence of high-stakes testing. In presenting these trends, I do not want to suggest that what teachers have been doing for years is inappropriate or should necessarily be changed. Much of what we have learned about evaluating students from previous decades is very important and useful. For example, properly constructed multiple-choice tests are excellent for

Teacher's Corner

Susan Pereira

National Board Certified Elementary Teacher

In my classroom, instruction and assessment are always integrated. In fact, it's difficult for me to even think about them as separate entities. Assessment happens prior to any teaching, during teaching, and after teaching. Before the learning, sometimes this is done formally through standardized testing. Other times, it occurs informally, in discussions with my students. Through both informal and formal assessments, I gather a "picture" of their previous learning and where they currently are in the learning process. After this initial data is gathered, I can analyze the group as a whole, and organize the students into learning groups according to where they are in their learning.

I can also use the data I have gathered to sit down and plan appropriate, engaging lessons for each small group of students. During the actual teaching, more assessment occurs. This assessment can look different—it may be a pencil-and-paper task, or it may be information gathered through questioning my students, watching their body language, noticing how often they volunteer to answer questions, and how they communicate their learning to me and to others. Quality assessment during the teaching guides me in how long I need to spend on a topic, when I need to reteach, and when students need enrichment activities. My ongoing assessments drive the lesson, not me as the teacher.

FIGURE 1.4   Recent Trends in Classroom Assessment

From	To
Sole emphasis on outcomes	Assessing of process
Isolated skills	Integrated skills
Isolated facts	Application of knowledge
Paper-and-pencil tasks	Authentic tasks
Decontextualized tasks	Contextualized tasks
A single correct answer ◄———	Many correct answers
Secret standards	Public standards
Secret criteria	Public criteria
Individuals ◄———	Groups
After instruction	During instruction
Little feedback	Considerable feedback
"Objective" tests ◄———	Performance-based tests
Standardized tests	Informal tests
External evaluation	Student self-evaluation
Single assessments	Multiple assessments
Sporadic	Continual
Conclusive	Recursive
Assessment *of* learning ◄———	Assessment *for* and *as* learning
Summative	Formative

efficiently and objectively assessing knowledge of a large content domain. What is needed is a *balanced* approach to assessment, in which appropriate techniques are administered and used in a credible way for decision making. Just because the assessment focuses on complex thinking skills or uses portfolios does not mean it is better or more credible. Assessment technique must be matched to purpose and must be conducted according to established quality standards. Some of the recent trends, such as making standards and criteria public, are helpful procedures regardless of the assessment employed, and they will improve traditional as well as newer types of measurement by engaging students in the entire assessment process.

The Influence of Large-Scale Accountability Testing

Like it or not, it is abundantly clear that externally mandated high-stakes accountability tests have a profound impact on teaching and classroom assessment. For most teachers, there is no escaping this reality. What you do in the classroom will be influenced by both the content and the nature of these tests.

Students, teachers, and administrators have always been held accountable, primarily at a local school or district level, and sometimes at the state level. In the last decade unprecedented federal and state accountability testing policy initiatives have increased the pressure on schools to show positive test results. The first step toward this change was the establishment of state content standards and curriculum frameworks in the 1990s (more about these in Chapter 2). Accountability was tied to these standards in the form of "high-stakes" testing. **High-stakes tests** are ones that have important consequences. This is the case for tests that determine whether a student can graduate from high school and when school accreditation is tied to test scores. There are now statewide (large-scale) high-stakes tests that are used to hold students, teachers, and schools accountable.

Then, in 2002, the No Child Left Behind (NCLB) Act was passed, with federal-level pressure for demonstrating consistently improving student test scores. The heart of NCLB was to ensure that states had "challenging" content standards and extensive testing of the standards to hold schools accountable. By the 2005–2006 school year, all states tested reading and mathematics annually in grades 3–11 (once in grades 10–12). Science tests were required in 2008–2009. To hold schools accountable with these tests, each state was required to establish a "starting point" target for the percentages of students that need to be classified as "proficient" in 2002. Then, using a concept called **adequate yearly progress (AYP),** states established increasingly high percentages of students reaching the proficient level at each grade each year, until 2014, when 100% of students must be at the proficient level. What makes AYP difficult is that it must be demonstrated for several subgroups of students as well as for the whole school; subgroup size is determined by each state. Thus, separate percentages are calculated and reported for Blacks and Hispanics, as well as for students with disabilities and economically disadvantaged students. In addition, at least 95% of students in each group must be tested.

Although the specifics of NCLB and AYP may change, there is little doubt that some kind of federal pressure will ensure that large-scale accountability tests will have high stakes and negative sanctions, resulting in some cases with state takeover of schools. The more recent Race-to-the-Top initiative is focused on national standards and testing in math and English. It is also clear that administrators and local boards of education, as well as state-level policy makers, want these measures of student performance to be as high as possible. The latest "standard" is to make sure students have skills to succeed in college and the workplace. The public opinion of schools and of teachers will be influenced by the test results (annual school report cards are required). In fact, these tests will provide the primary source of evidence used to judge our schools. The pressure is on, and administrators and teachers are reacting.

With these new accountability requirements, large-scale testing has significantly influenced what teachers do in the classroom, including what they do in the construction and use of their student assessments. There is a great amount of emphasis on "test prep," on "teaching to the test," on aligning classroom tests with large-scale tests, and on using classroom test formats that are like the ones used in the state accountability tests. Almost all high-stakes tests use multiple-choice questions, and teachers are increasingly asked to use the same item format in their classroom assessments.

Like many aspects of teaching, teachers will be most effective by balancing the demands of high-stakes tests with what they know about best practices of teaching and assessment that maximize student motivation and learning. Clearly, classroom assessment must be considered in the current climate that emphasizes high-stakes testing. One purpose of this book, then, is to incorporate these account-ability demands and influences with classroom assessment procedures that we know can enhance student learning. Unfortunately, for many, teaching to external standards and high-stakes tests conflicts with classroom assessment methods that have changed to be more consistent with contemporary theories of learning and motivation. But here is the silver lining: It turns out that classroom assessments, especially of the formative type, that are selected and implemented on the basis of promoting student learning, rather than showing student performance, will result in higher state-level test results. The key is focusing on *how classroom assessments will maximize student motivation and learning,* rather than on what will result in the highest percentages of students judged at least "proficient."

Teachers' Classroom Assessment and Grading Practices Decision Making

Every teacher makes many decisions about the types of assessments that will be used, when these assessments are used, and grading. Consistent with previous research, a recent survey of over 1,000 teachers showed that these decisions result in highly individualized and idiosyncratic practices (McMillan, Workman, & Myran, 1998). Each teacher creates his or her own practices. This suggests that you, too, will develop your own assessment and grading practices.

To better understand the decision-making process teachers use, I participated in a study in which in-depth, individual interviews were conducted with 28 teachers to investigate the reasons teachers gave for the assessment decisions they made (McMillan, 2003; McMillan & Workman, 1999). The results have interesting implications because of the strong connection between this decision-making process and instruction.

We found that two major sources of influence affect assessment and grading practices decision making. One source lies within the teacher and consists of beliefs and values about teaching, and learning more generally, that provide a basis for explaining how and why specific assessment and grading practices are used. A second source lies external to the teacher, consisting of pressures that need to be considered, such as high-stakes testing. We found that these two sources of influence are in constant tension. Although internal beliefs and values that reflect a desire to enhance student learning are most influential, external pressures cause teachers to engage in certain practices that may not be in the best interests of student learning.

These influences are depicted in Figure 1.5 to show the nature of the internal and external factors and how these factors are in tension. Internal beliefs and values include a philosophy of teaching and learning, and assessment practices are con-sistent with that philosophy. For example, if teachers believe that all students can

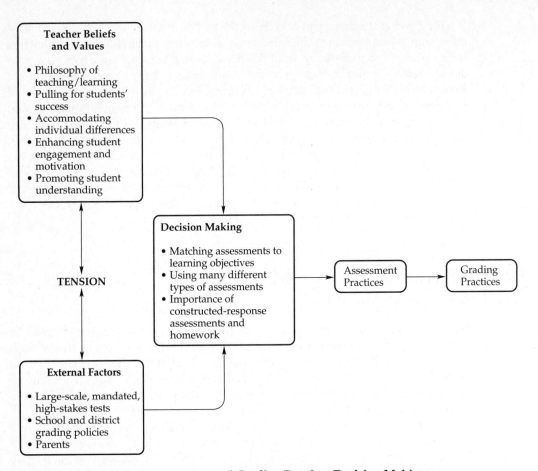

FIGURE 1.5   A Model of Assessment and Grading Practices Decision Making

succeed and that individual differences among students should be accommodated, then the teacher uses multiple types of assessment to allow sufficient opportunities to show success. If teachers believe it is important to get students involved, engaged, and motivated, they may use performance assessments and give points for student participation and effort. To better understand how much students know and can do, most teachers rely on assessments in which students show their work.

External pressures include school or school district assessment and grading policies that must be followed, parental demands, and large-scale, high-stakes testing. Teachers want to collect assessment information that will show parents why specific grades were given. Externally mandated large-scale testing of students can be very influential, as well as in direct contradiction to teachers' internal beliefs and values. For example, if statewide testing consists of multiple-choice items covering a great amount of material, and student performance will have important consequences, teachers feel pressure to use the same kinds of tests for classroom assessments. This may be in direct conflict with wanting to use performance assessments that are more engaging and informative about what students really understand.

Think about the model in Figure 1.5 in relation to your own beliefs and values and in relation to external pressures you may need to consider. Your decision making should consider these sources of influence so that the assessment and grading practices you implement reflect the relative importance of each. The most important question is this: To what extent are your assessment and grading practices consistent with principles of good instruction, and to what extent will the right kinds of student learning be enhanced?

Assessment Standards for Teachers

Before closing this chapter, I want to familiarize you with important sets of assessment standards for teachers. In 1990, the American Federation of Teachers, the National Council on Measurement in Education, and the National Education Association published a set of standards for teacher competence in educational assessment.

The standards organize the teacher's professional role and responsibilities into activities occurring before, during, and after the appropriate instructional segment. The standards also include responsibilities of the teacher for involvement in school and district decision making and involvement in the wider professional roles of teachers. These roles and responsibilities, which emphasize teacher activities that are directly related to assessment, are outlined in Appendix A. Throughout these roles and responsibilities, instruction is integrated with assessment. This is consistent with newer trends in assessment, and it forms the basis for the assessment content that is presented in this book.

The standards also indicate seven specific areas of assessment knowledge or skills that a teacher should possess to perform assessment roles and responsibilities. Specifically, teachers should be skilled in:

1. Choosing assessment methods appropriate for instructional decisions
2. Developing assessment methods appropriate for instructional decisions
3. Administering, scoring, and interpreting the results of both externally produced and teacher-produced assessment methods
4. Using assessment results when making decisions about individual students, planning teaching, developing curriculum, and making recommendations for school improvement
5. Developing valid pupil grading procedures
6. Communicating assessment results to students, parents, other lay audiences, and other educators
7. Recognizing unethical, illegal, and otherwise inappropriate assessment methods and uses of assessment information

Three additional documents summarize important assessment knowledge and skills for teachers: the *Code of Professional Responsibilities in Educational Measurement* (National Council on Measurement in Education, 1995, www.ncme.org/about/docs.cfm), *Principles and Indicators for Student Assessment Systems* (National Forum on Assessment, 1995, www.fairtest.org), and the *Student Evaluation Standards* (Gullickson, 2003). Appendix B summarizes the most recent standards, which were developed with the assistance of sixteen major educational organizations and reflect an international consensus about assessment skills needed by teachers.

Summary

This chapter introduced assessment as an integral part of teacher decision making and instruction. As a systematic method of collecting, interpreting, and using information, good assessment improves student learning. Major points in the chapter are the following:

- Assessment includes four major components: purpose, measurement, evaluation, and use.
- Measurement consists of differentiating behavior and performance.
- Evaluation involves professional judgment of the value or worth of the measured performance.
- Recent research on learning, motivation, and instruction suggests the need to use more alternative forms of measurement, such as performance assessments, portfolios, and authentic assessments.
- Student involvement in assessment promotes student engagement and achievement.
- The current trend is for more emphasis on formative assessment and assessment *for* learning rather than *of* learning.
- State and federal accountability requires high-stakes objective testing, which influences classroom assessments.
- Teacher assessment and grading decision making is influenced by internal beliefs and values and external factors.
- Professional standards have been developed to provide a framework for what teachers need to know about classroom assessment.

What's Coming

You have now been introduced to classroom assessment and some of the directions such assessment is taking. I want to give you an overview of the rest of this book—how it is organized, what you can expect, and how you can make the most of the application exercises at the end of each chapter.

The sequence of topics followed in the book reflects the steps teachers take in using assessment as part of instruction. The next two chapters present fundamental principles of any type of assessment. In Chapter 2 we consider how purpose is clarified through the development of appropriate learning targets. Chapter 3 reviews criteria that enhance the quality and credibility of assessments. With this background, methods of assessment are presented in the sequence teachers use when planning and delivering instruction. Two chapters are devoted to formative assessment. Chapter 4 examines how formative assessment data are gathered. In Chapter 5 there is discussion of how teachers provide effective feedback and make instructional adjustments. Chapters 6–11 then present major methods of assessment, aligned with different types of learning targets being assessed. In this book, the method of assessment follows from what needs to be assessed to emphasize that teachers first determine purpose and learning targets and then select and implement appropriate assessments. Chapter 12 focuses on issues concerning the assessment of students with special needs and ELL students in inclusive settings. Chapter 13 examines what teachers do with assessment information in the form of grading and reporting information. The last chapter summarizes important information concerning the administration, interpretation, and use of standardized tests.

Self-Instructional Review Exercises

Each chapter contains self-instructional exercises. They are intended to check your understanding of the content of the chapter. An answer key is provided to give you immediate feedback. Remember that you will learn most if you don't look at the key before you answer the question.

1. What is the relationship between teacher decision making, complex classroom environments, and assessment?

2. What does it mean when we say that assessment is not an "add-on" activity?

3. What is the difference between a *test* and an *assessment*?

4. Refer to Table 1.1. Identify each of the following examples as preassessment (P), formative assessment (F), or summative assessment (S).

   a. Giving a pop quiz
   b. Giving a cumulative final exam
   c. Giving students praise for correct answers
   d. Using homework to judge student knowledge
   e. Reviewing student scores on last year's standardized test
   f. Changing the lesson plan because of student inattention
   g. Reviewing student files to understand the cultural backgrounds of students

5. Identify each of the following quotes as referring to one of the four components of classroom assessment: purpose (P), measurement (M), evaluation (E), and use (U).

   a. "Last week I determined that my students did not know very much about the Civil War."
   b. "This year I want to see if I can assess student attitudes."
   c. "The test helped me to identify where students were weak."

d. "I like the idea of using performance-based assessments."

e. "I intend to combine several different assessments to determine the grade."

6. How do assessments communicate expectations for student learning?

7. Why, according to recent research on learning, is performance assessment well suited to effective instruction?

Answers to Self-Instructional Review Exercises

1. Complex classroom environments influence the nature of teacher decision making, and assessment is needed to make good decisions.

2. "Add-on" means assessment that occurs at the end of an instructional unit, for example, the midterm or final exam. However, the teacher also assesses students before and during instruction. Assessment should not be thought of as testing only at the end of instruction.

3. A test is only one part of assessment. Assessment refers to measuring something, evaluating what is measured, and then using the information for decision making. A test is one way to measure.

4. a. F, b. S, c. F, d. F, e. P, f. F, g. P.

5. a. E, b. P, c. E, d. M, e. U.

6. Expectations are set by the nature of the standards and criteria used in the assessments and the way teachers provide feedback and otherwise respond to students.

7. Recent learning research has shown the importance of connecting new to existing information, of applying knowledge, and of thinking skills. Performance assessments foster these behaviors by relating content and processes to problem solving in meaningful contexts.

Suggestions for Action Research

At the end of each chapter are suggestions for action research. The intent of these suggestions is to help you apply what you are learning from the book to practical situations. By conducting this type of informal research, the principles and ideas presented will have greater relevance and meaning to you.

1. Investigate the time that is taken for assessment in the classroom by observing some classes. Compare your results to how much time the teacher believes is devoted to assessment. Also note in your observations the nature of teacher decision making. What kinds of decisions are made? How, specifically, does information from assessment contribute to this decision making?

2. Conduct an interview with two or three teachers and ask them some questions about assessment. For example, you could take Figure 1.4 and ask the teachers if

they believe the so-called recent trends are actually evident. You could ask about the relationship between assessment and teaching/learning to see the extent to which assessment and teaching are integrated. Use Figure 1.5 to ask about "internal" and "external" factors that affect their assessment, grading practices, and decision making.

3. Interview a school administrator about what teachers need to know about assessment. Ask about the assessment standards to get a perspective on the reasonableness of the standards.

Cognitive Learning Targets and Standards

Good classroom assessment begins with appropriate *learning targets* and *standards*. How else will you know what to teach, what to assess, and how to judge student performance? In recent years there has been much controversy about what the learning targets should be and who should set them, evidenced

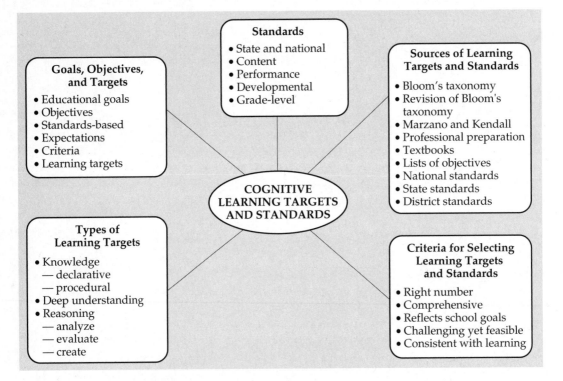

Goals, Objectives, and Targets

- Educational goals
- Objectives
- Standards-based
- Expectations
- Criteria
- Learning targets

Standards

- State and national
- Content
- Performance
- Developmental
- Grade-level

Sources of Learning Targets and Standards

- Bloom's taxonomy
- Revision of Bloom's taxonomy
- Marzano and Kendall
- Professional preparation
- Textbooks
- Lists of objectives
- National standards
- State standards
- District standards

COGNITIVE LEARNING TARGETS AND STANDARDS

Types of Learning Targets

- Knowledge
  — declarative
  — procedural
- Deep understanding
- Reasoning
  — analyze
  — evaluate
  — create

Criteria for Selecting Learning Targets and Standards

- Right number
- Comprehensive
- Reflects school goals
- Challenging yet feasible
- Consistent with learning

CHAPTER 2 Concept Map

most visibly by standards-based school reform. In this chapter we review the complex nature of cognitive learning targets and standards and present a framework that will help you to determine them for your students. Affective, product, skill, disposition, and motivational targets will be covered in later chapters.

Knowing Where Your Students are Going

As pointed out in Chapter 1, sound classroom assessment begins with a clear description of intended student competencies that result from student learning, a clear statement of student outcomes. Although there is much history and established practice in the labels that are used to identify these outcomes (e.g., goals, objectives, standards, or "what students should know and be able to do") the exact terminology used may indicate something somewhat different. It is important to review these differences because we need to be precise in our descriptions. I favor the term "learning target" because it represents more than any of the aforementioned labels. In the end, the label is not as critical as making sure the outcomes are clear, appropriate, and drive effective instruction.

Educational Goals

An **educational goal** is a very general statement of what students will know and be able to do. Goals are written to cover large blocks of instructional time, such as a unit, semester, or year, and indicate in broad terms what will be emphasized during that time period. Some examples of educational goals require that students will be able to:

Know how to think critically and solve problems
Work collaboratively with others
Understand the scientific method
Appreciate cultural differences
Develop an appreciation for fine arts
Learn to think independently
Become good citizens

Goals provide a starting point for more specific learning objectives. By beginning with goals, you will have a general outline that can be validated by parents, teachers, and other school officials. In most school systems, educational goals are listed as defining the mission of the system, but these are usually too broad to be of much practical help in your classroom. Goals will also be found in district curriculum guides, textbooks, and teaching materials.

Objectives

Educational objectives are usually relatively specific statements of student performance that should be demonstrated at the end of an instructional unit. However, over the years, the term **objective** has been used in many different ways, depending on words that specify the type of objective and the intent of the user. The term *global objective* means essentially the same thing as *educational goal.* Gronlund (1995) uses the term *instructional objective* to mean "intended learning outcomes" (p. 3). Gronlund emphasizes that instructional objectives should be stated in terms of specific, observable, and measurable student responses. Instructional objectives are sometimes referred to as *behavioral, performance,* or *terminal* objectives. These types of objectives are characterized by the use of action verbs such as *add, state, define, list, contract, design, categorize, count,* and *lift.* Action verbs are important because they indicate what the students actually do at the end of the unit. Here are some examples of instructional objectives.

The student will:

Summarize the main idea of the reading passage
Underline the verb and subject of each sentence
Write a title for the reading passage
List five causes of the Civil War
Identify on a map the location of each continent
Explain the process of photosynthesis

Proponents of instructional objectives emphasize that teachers should learn to write them at an appropriate level of generality—not so narrow that it takes much too long to write and keep track of the objectives, and not so general that the objectives provide little guidance for instruction. Ideally, objectives should be stated in terms that are specific enough to inform teaching and assessment but not limit the flexibility of the teacher to modify instruction as needed. Also, it is best to focus on *unit* rather than daily lesson plan instructional objectives. These intermediate-level objectives help keep the focus of student learning on the main understandings, learning processes, attitudes, and other learning outcomes of the unit as a whole. Writing objectives that are too specific results in long lists of minutiae that are time consuming to monitor and manage. Some examples of instructional objectives that are too specific, too broad, and about the right level of specificity (intermediate) are shown in Table 2.1.

Whether you focus on general or specific objectives, the main point is to describe what students will know and be able to do and what constitutes sufficient evidence that students have learned, and not what you will do as a teacher to help students obtain the knowledge and skills identified. What you plan to do as a teacher may be called a **teaching objective** or *learning activity* and may include such things as lecturing for a certain amount of time, asking questions, putting students in groups, giving feedback to students individually, conducting experiments, using a map to show where certain countries are located, asking students to solve math problems on the board, having students read orally, and so on. These teaching objectives describe the activities students will be engaged in and what you need to do to be sure that the activities occur as planned.

TABLE 2.1 Specificity of Instructional Objectives

Too Specific	About Right	Too Broad
Given a two-paragraph article from the newspaper, the student will correctly identify 10 statements that are facts and 5 statements that are opinions in less than 10 minutes without the aid of any resource materials.	Students will state the difference between facts and opinions.	Students will learn how to think critically.
Based on reading the content of Lincoln's and Douglas's debates over 1 week, the student will, without any aids, write four paragraphs in 1 hour that summarize, with at least 80% accuracy, their areas of agreement and disagreement.	Students will identify areas of agreement and disagreement in the debates between Lincoln and Douglas.	Compare and contrast the Lincoln/Douglas debates.
The student, given grid paper, will analyze data on the frequency of student birthdays in each month and construct a bar graph in 1 hour in teams of two of the results that show the two most frequent and two least frequent months.	Given frequency data and grid paper, students will construct bar graphs of selected variables.	Students will construct bar graphs.

Standards

During the 1990s the idea of "standards" became ubiquitous and powerful, fueling reform by advocating specific "high-level" student outcomes. Although the standards movement mostly concerns what have been called student outcomes or objectives, the reframing of how these outcomes would be judged was needed to stress three points: (a) this is not business as usual, not like "outcome-based" education; (b) standards apply to *all* students; and (c) the student achievement goals are much higher than what has been used in the past. The intent is to frame the idea of standards in such a way that no one could refute its importance. This is how Popham (2008) describes it:

> *Standards,* of course, is a warmth-inducing word. Although perhaps not in the same league with *motherhood, democracy,* and *babies,* I suspect that standards ranks right up there with *oatmeal, honor,* and *excellence.* It's really tough not to groove on standards, especially if those standards are *high.* Everyone wants students to reach high standards. (p. 109)

Standards-based education occurred first at the national level with content-oriented organizations, such as the National Council of Teachers of Mathematics or the Center for Civic Education. Today, all major subject-matter associations have **standards** that describe "what students should know and be able to do." In addition, each state has now developed its own standards, according to both grade level and subject, and national standards are being developed. This has led to a dizzying array of many standards statements from which to choose, particularly when considered along with school district, school, and classroom objectives. For example, there are different *types* of standards. We'll consider four that are most common (Table 2.2): content, performance, developmental, and grade-level standards.

Content standards (not to be confused with *curriculum* standards) are statements about what students should know, understand, and be able to do. Content standards describe "the knowledge and skills that students should attain" (Kendall & Marzano, 1997, p. 20). The way in which content standards are presented differs, depending on the source. One format, for example, may describe content as information:

> The constitution sets forth the organization of the government and describes powers of different branches of national government, states, and the people.

More typically, a content standard includes a description of the nature of the knowledge:

> Students will demonstrate an understanding of the purposes of the constitution.

Content standards can also vary greatly in specificity. Note the generality of the following content standard:

> Students will understand how immigration has influenced American society.

A more specific content standard would be:

> Students will compare the contributions of Socrates, Plato, and Aristotle to Greek life.

TABLE 2.2   Types of Educational Standards

Type of Standard	Description
Content	Desired outcomes for the content area
Performance	Desirable proficiency levels for student skills; what students should be able to do
Developmental	Desired sequences of growth and change
Grade-level	Desirable outcomes of a particular grade

Source: Adapted from Conley, M. W. (2005). *Connecting standards and assessment through literacy.* Boston: Allyn & Bacon.

Content standards may also differ with respect to the nature of the learning or performance. Some standards use the term *knows* to describe student attainment, and others emphasize *understanding* or reasoning skills. As we will see, these important differences influence how students are assessed.

Keep in mind that content standards are similar to what have been called general objectives. In both, the emphasis is on what students can demonstrate after instruction. The value of the standards movement is that the extensive amount of work that has been done to identify standards enables you to draw on the work of others to identify what outcomes are best for your students.

A **performance standard** indicates the level of proficiency that must be demonstrated to indicate the degree to which content standards have been attained. Performance standards address issues of attainment and quality. By indicating *degree* of attainment, performance standards are able to distinguish different levels of accomplishment. This is quite different from a behavioral objective, which typically has a single level. In other words, a performance standard describes what students must *do* and how different levels of proficiency on the content standards result. As described by McTighe and Ferrara (1998), performance standards "set expectations about how much students should know and how well students should perform" (p. 34).

You will probably find that what are called performance standards contain a description of what students must do but do not include levels of attainment. For example, consider the following content standard:

The student will understand the right of free speech.

A performance standard that contains a description of what the student must do to demonstrate this competency might be the following (Glatthorn, 1998):

Examines issue of right to free speech, explaining importance of that right in a democracy and noting limitations established by the courts. (p. 23)

Another example is found in standards that first indicate what students should know and understand (content standards) and then indicates what students should be able to do (performance standard; *National Standards for United States History: Exploring the American Experience,* Grades 5–12, 1996):

What students should know: The student understands causes of the American Revolution.

What students should be able to do: Demonstrate understanding of the causes of the American Revolution by:

- Explaining the consequences of the Seven Years War and the overhaul of English imperial policy following the Treaty of Paris in 1763.
- Compare the arguments advanced by defenders and opponents of the new imperial policy on the traditional rights of English people and the legitimacy of asking the colonies to pay a share of the costs of empire.
- Reconstructing the chronology of the critical events leading to the outbreak of armed conflict between the American colonies and England.
- Analyze political, ideological, religious, and economic origins of the Revolution.

■ Reconstruct the arguments among patriots and loyalists about independence and draw conclusions about how the decision to declare independence was reached.

What is not indicated with this performance standard is any degree of attainment. To do this, it is necessary to establish *criteria* and then use descriptors of different levels with these criteria (e.g., *not proficient, proficient, advanced,* or *complete, partial,* or *none*).

Developmental (age-appropriate) **standards** describe sequences of growth in learning over time. These standards may cover a single grade level or several grades. They are helpful because they provide **benchmarks** to monitor progress and record improvements in knowledge and skills. The focus is on what is developmentally appropriate. Standardized achievement tests provide scaled scores that can document growth over several years.

Grade-level standards are closely related, but here the emphasis is on what students should know and be able to do *at each grade.* Each state has established these kinds of standards because NCLB requirements are organized by grade level. State standards are grade-level specific and may not reflect what is developmentally appropriate. One thing is for sure, these standards are the ones that are most important in driving instruction to meet the demands of high-stakes accountability testing. Grade-level standards for one state may be different from another state's, which makes it difficult to compare states on measures of student performance.

Criteria

One of the most frustrating experiences for students is not knowing "what the teacher wants" or "how the teacher grades." Perhaps you can recall being in a class in which you did an assignment with little guidance from the teacher about how he or she would grade it. Once your assignment was returned with comments, your reaction might well have been, "If I had only known what the teacher was looking for I could have provided it!" Essentially, this issue is concerned with the criteria the teacher uses for evaluating student work and whether students know, *in advance,* what those criteria are. Here is a poignant illustration of how a lack of clear criteria can be unfair. The following actually happened to a sixth grader:

> [The student] was given the following problem to solve: "Three buses bring students to school. The first bus brings 9 students, the second bus brings 7 students, and the third bus brings 5 students. How many students in all do the buses bring? The student answered "21 kids," and the answer was marked wrong. After encouragement by my colleague the student asked the teacher "Why?" The reason was that the student said "kids" instead of "students." (Arter, 1996, p. VI-1:1)

Criteria, then, are clearly articulated and public descriptions of facets or dimensions of student performance that are used for judging the level of achievement. As pointed out in Chapter 1, criteria may be called *scoring criteria, rubrics, scoring rubrics,* or *scoring guidelines.* (The term *performance criteria* may also be used.)

Although criteria have been promoted most for more recent alternative and performance assessments, the issue of how student responses will be evaluated lies at the heart of any type of assessment. The key component of criteria is making your professional judgments about student performance clear to others. All methods of assessment involve your professional judgment. If you use multiple-choice testing, judgment is used to prepare the items and decide which alternative is correct. In an essay test, judgment is involved in preparing the question and in reading and scoring answers. Clearly articulated criteria will help you in many ways, including

- Defining what you mean by "excellent," "good," or "average" work
- Communicating instructional goals to parents
- Communicating to parents, students, and others what constitutes excellence
- Providing guidelines for making unbiased and consistent judgments
- Documenting how judgments are made
- Helping students evaluate their own work

When specifying criteria, it is necessary to summarize the dimensions of performance that are used to assign student work to a given level. The dimensions are what you consider to be essential qualities of the performance. They can be identified by asking yourself some questions: What are the attributes of good performance? How do I know when students have reached different levels of performance? What examples do I have of each level? What do I look for when evaluating student work? Criteria are best developed by being clear on what constitutes excellence as well as proficiency in the performance area of interest. By identifying and prioritizing key elements, the most important aspects of the performance will be utilized.

Once the dimensions have been identified, you can develop a quantitative or qualitative scale to indicate different levels of performance. Label each level as "good," "excellent," "poor," and so on. Examples are presented in Chapters 8 and 9.

Although it is very helpful for students to know the criteria as communicated in a scoring rubric, it is even more helpful if students can see an example of a finished student product or performance and your evaluation of it. These examples are called **exemplars** or **anchors**. For example, if you have established four levels of performance, an exemplar of work at each level will make the criteria more clear. To emphasize once again, you should share the exemplars with students *before* they begin their work. This will help students internalize the standards that you use and know what constitutes excellence. The exemplars could be as simple as giving students examples of the type of math word problems that will be on a test and how their answers will be graded. Of course you don't want to give students something that they will memorize or copy, but you do need to give them a sense of the difficulty of the task.

Expectations

It is important to distinguish expectations from standards and learning targets. An **expectation** is what you communicate to your students about the level of performance that you think they will be able to demonstrate. This is different from the learning target because it is based on students' previous achievement, aptitude, motivation, and other factors. It may be reasonable to think that most, if not all, of your students will not be able to attain the standard or the highest level of performance. For example, we set a high standard for what constitutes a good play in football, but our expectations for middle school students differ from what we expect of professionals. In school you may have a high standard for a research paper, but your expectations of the students, because of their lack of previous learning, may not meet this high standard. If your expectations are the same as your standards, it is likely that either your standards will drop to accommodate most students or your expectations will not be consistent with the reality of how students can perform. In either case, you are not doing what is in the best interests of the students. If your standards are lowered, students may attain a false sense of competency; if your expectations are too high, students may be frustrated at what they see as impossible demands. What you need to do is make high standards clear and then teach in a way that is consistent with realistic, yet challenging, expectations. You want students to go the extra step, so be explicit with them about why the standards are high.

Learning Targets

What, then, is a learning target? In this book **learning target** is defined as a statement of student performance that includes *both* a description of what students should know, understand, and be able to do at the end of a unit of instruction *and* something about the criteria for judging the level of performance demonstrated (see Figure 2.1).

The word *learning* is used to convey that targets emphasize the importance of how students will *change*. Learning implies a focus on the demonstrated competence of students, not on what you do as a teacher. Change reflects where students are in relation to the target before instruction as well as at the end of instruction.

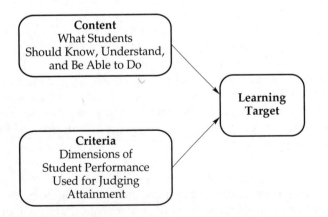

FIGURE 2.1   Components of Learning Targets

It is essential to include something about the criteria for judging levels of performance in the target. Think for a moment about a target at which one would shoot an arrow. The performance might be stated as "the student will hit the target with an arrow." But you need to communicate more than simply "hit the target." How far away is the target? How large is the target? Does it matter where the arrow hits the target? In other words, you need to indicate something about the dimensions of the performance that translate into qualitatively different levels of performance. Two teachers can state the same learning objective, but if different criteria are used to evaluate the performance, then in reality students in each class are learning something different.

A similar case can be made for learning subjects in school. The target "students will know state capitals in the United States" means something different if the student has to recall all 50 capitals from memory rather than if the student can correctly match half of the names of capitals with states. You must be able to articulate, as part of the target, the criteria you will use to judge performance, and remember, students should know these criteria *before* instruction. This does not need to be done in a single sentence. It is easier, in fact, to think about targets as a description of what will be assessed and how it will be judged. These two aspects of the target can be separated into different sentences. For example, this describes what students need to know:

> Students will demonstrate an understanding of the effect of the sun on seasons, length of day, weather, and climate.

Information about criteria could be added with another sentence:

> Students will demonstrate their understanding by correctly answering short-answer questions about each relationship.

If a matching test is used, try this description:

> Students will demonstrate their understanding by correctly matching all effects with the four elements discussed.

In practice, you would not be so wordy in describing the target. It is understood that "students will demonstrate" so you can simply say "understand effect of sun on seasons, length of day, weather, and climate." The information about criteria can be shortened by simply referring to "matching" or "short answer."

Learning targets for units of instruction in Figure 2.2 include both what students should know or be able to do and some aspects of the criteria. Note that some are written as one sentence and some are more detailed than others in aspects of criteria. The intent is not to worry about including specific aspects of criteria. Rather, the hope is that you will be aware of the effect of the criteria on the nature of the learning that occurs and your evaluation of it.

FIGURE 2.2   Examples of Unit Learning Targets

Students will demonstrate their knowledge of the parts of a plant by filling in words on a diagram for all parts studied.

Students will demonstrate their understanding of citizenship by correctly identifying whether previously unread statements about citizenship are true or false. A large number of items is used to sample most of the content learned.

Students will be able to explain why the American Constitution is important by writing an essay that indicates what would happen if we abolished our Constitution. The papers will be graded holistically, looking for evidence of reasons, knowledge of the constitution, and organization.

Students will know the difference between components of sentences by correctly identifying verbs, adverbs, adjectives, nouns, and pronouns is seven of eight long, complex sentences.

Students will be able to multiply fractions by correctly computing eight of ten fraction problems. The problems are new to the students; some are similar to "challenge" questions in the book.

Taxonomies of Educational Objectives

Several popular taxonomies of educational objectives are used by teachers to categorize the nature of the content that is learned and the mental processes that are used to learn the content. That is, the taxonomies show the types of cognition that students need to engage in. These taxonomies are widely used because they indicate what instruction and assessment needs to look like, they provide a structure that shows how the content is learned, and they provide a common language for describing student learning. There are many different taxonomies, some of which are published and widely available, and others that may be specific to an individual teacher or school. Although three major taxonomies are summarized in this chapter, remember that they don't need to be followed exactly as presented. You need to use the taxonomies to categorize different learning outcomes that make the most sense, given your overall goals for students.

Bloom's Taxonomy of Objectives

Perhaps the best-known source for conceptualizing learning targets is the *Taxonomy of Educational Objectives I: Cognitive Domain* (Bloom, 1956). As implied in the title, this initial taxonomy covered cognitive learning objectives. Later publications of the taxonomy focused on the affective and psychomotor areas. Thus, "Bloom's taxonomy," as it has become known, consists of three domains—cognitive, affective, and psychomotor.

TABLE 2.3   Bloom's Taxonomy of Educational Objectives: Cognitive Domain

Level	Illustrative Verbs
Knowledge: Recalling and remembering previously learned material, including specific facts, events, persons, dates, methods, procedures, concepts, principles, and theories	Names, matches, lists, recalls, selects, retells, states, defines, describes, labels, reproduces
Comprehension: Understanding and grasping the meaning of something; includes translation from one symbolic form to another (e.g., percent into fractions), interpretation, explanation, prediction, inferences, restating, estimation, generalization, and other uses that demonstrate understanding	Explains, converts, interprets, paraphrases, predicts, estimates, rearranges, rephrases, summarizes
Application: Use of abstract ideas, rules, or generalized methods in novel, concrete situations	Changes, demonstrates, modifies, produces, solves, constructs, applies, uses, shows
Analysis: Breaking down a communication into constituent parts or elements and understanding the relationship among different elements	Distinguishes, compares, subdivides, diagrams, differentiates, relates, classifies, categorizes
Synthesis: Arranging and combining elements and parts into novel patterns or structures	Generates, combines, constructs, assembles, formulates, forecasts, projects, proposes, integrates
Evaluation: Judging the quality, worth, or value of something according to established criteria (e.g., determining the adequacy of evidence to support a conclusion)	Justifies, criticizes, decides, judges, argues, concludes, supports, defends, evaluates, verifies, confirms

Bloom's taxonomy of the cognitive domain has received considerable attention and has been used to specify action verbs to accompany different types of cognition learning (see Table 2.3). The cognitive domain contains six levels. Each level represents an increasingly complex type of cognition. Although the cognitive domain is often characterized as having "lower" and "higher" levels, only the knowledge level is considered by authors of the taxonomy to be lower; all other levels are higher. The first level describes several different types of knowledge. The remaining five levels are referred to as "intellectual abilities and skills."

Bloom's taxonomy can be very helpful when formulating specific learning targets, even though this categorization of cognitive tasks was created more than 50 years ago. Since that time there have been significant changes in the educational and psychological theories that formed the basis for the taxonomy. The taxonomy, in comparison, was based on a focus on outcomes or objectives, learners as an object and as a reactor in the learning situation, and broad, single organizing principles that cut across different domains (Tittle, Hecht, & Moore, 1993). The taxonomies are still valuable, however, in providing a comprehensive list of possible learning objectives with clear action verbs that operationalize the targets.

Bloom's Revised Taxonomy of Objectives

A revision to Bloom's original taxonomy was proposed in 2001 "to refocus educators' attention on the value of the original *Handbook* . . . and to incorporate new knowledge and thought into the framework" (Anderson & Krathwohl, 2001, p. xxi–xxii). The revised taxonomy uses a two-dimensional model as a framework for identifying and writing learning objectives. The knowledge dimension includes four levels that describe different types of knowledge with a number of subcategories (see Figure 2.3). The cognitive process dimension includes six major categories and numerous subcategories that describe increasingly complex thinking. The reason for dividing the original single list into two dimensions is to create a matrix in which educators can identify the specific nature of the learning that is targeted.

For each learning objective, there would be a noun that describes the type of knowledge and a verb that indicates the level of cognitive processing that is needed. The advantage of this, according to the authors, is that teachers and administrators will be able to be more precise than they could be with the older taxonomy. Figure 2.3 shows how an educational objective could be classified according to the two dimensions.

Only time will tell if the new two-dimensional taxonomy will take hold. It is clear that a revised taxonomy was needed, but this version is more complicated for teachers to work with and may not be practical.

Marzano and Kendall's *New Taxonomy*

Marzano and Kendall (2007) present a taxonomy that is organized along the same approach to cognition that is used in Bloom's revision. The two dimensions used in the revision, a "knowledge" and a "cognitive process" dimension, are very similar to the two used in the *New Taxonomy*—"domain of knowledge" and "levels of processing." Both of these taxonomies recognize that learning outcomes need to be classified according to both type of knowledge and type of cognitive process.

The Domains of Knowledge in the *New Taxonomy* include information, mental procedures, and psychomotor procedures. In any given subject the knowledge represented can be described according to these three types. Information (declarative knowledge) consists of vocabulary terms, facts, and time sequences, as well as principles and generalizations. Mental procedure is what has been described as "procedural knowledge." It is knowledge that is needed to carry out an action or solve a problem. Psychomotor procedures include physical activities such as finger dexterity, posture, and strength.

The *New Taxonomy* Levels of Processing includes a "cognitive system" consisting of a hierarchical set of four cognitive operations—retrieval, comprehension, analysis, and knowledge utilization. Retrieval is simple recall or recognition. Comprehension is a type of understanding in which knowledge may be translated, classified, and interpreted. Analysis involves elaboration of and extension of knowledge, generalization, and application. Knowledge utilization

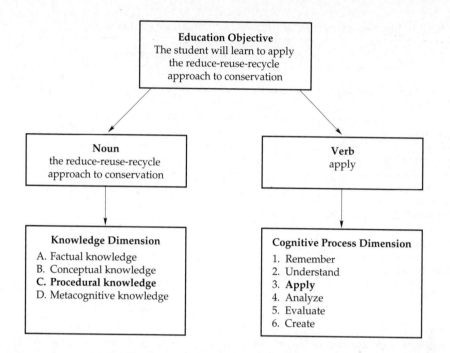

Education Objective
The student will learn to apply
the reduce-reuse-recycle
approach to conservation

Noun
the reduce-reuse-recycle
approach to conservation

Verb
apply

Knowledge Dimension
A. Factual knowledge
B. Conceptual knowledge
C. **Procedural knowledge**
D. Metacognitive knowledge

Cognitive Process Dimension
1. Remember
2. Understand
3. **Apply**
4. Analyze
5. Evaluate
6. Create

The Knowledge Dimension	Cognitive Process Dimension					
	1. Remember	2. Understand	3. Apply	4. Analyze	5. Evaluate	6. Create
A. Factual						
B. Conceptual						
C. Procedural			✗ ← The student will learn to apply the reduce-reuse-recycle approach to conservation			
D. Metacognitive						

FIGURE 2.3 How an Objective (the Student Will Learn to Apply the Reduce-Reuse-Recycle Approach to Conservation) Is Classified in the Taxonomy Table

Source: Adapted from Lorin W. Anderson & David R. Krathwohl, *A taxonomy for learning, teaching, and assessing: A revision of Bloom's taxonomy of educational objectives.* Published by Allyn & Bacon, Boston, MA. Copyright © 2001 by Pearson Education. Reprinted by permission of the publisher.

FIGURE 2.4   **Representation of Marzano & Kendall's** *New Taxonomy.*

	Domains of Knowledge		
Levels of Processing	Information	Mental Procedures	Psychomotor Procedures
Retrieval			
Comprehension			
Analysis			
Knowledge Utilization			
Metacognitive System			
Self-System			

consists of decision making, problem solving, experimenting, and investigating. The New Taxonomy also includes metacognition and self-system thinking as additional levels of processing.

A graphic representation of the New Taxonomy is presented in Figure 2.4. Like Bloom's revision, a matrix results to show how learning consists of different types of knowledge across various cognitive operations that begin with retrieval and extend to knowledge utilization. Thus, it would be possible to select procedural knowledge that is simply retrieval or is used to solve problems (knowledge utilization).

Types of Knowledge Targets

The phrase "what students should know" is used frequently as a concept for inclusion of important learning outcomes and standards. But this phrase is also pretty vague. We need to be much more specific about what is meant by "know" and "knowledge." Once this is accomplished, appropriate assessment methods can be selected to foster as well as measure the type of learning that is desired.

Knowledge Representation

Until recently, Bloom's taxonomy provided a definition of *knowledge* for many educators. In this scheme, knowledge is the first, and "lowest," level of categories in the cognitive domain, in which knowledge is defined as remembering something. All that is required is that the student recall or recognize facts, definitions, terms, concepts, procedures, principles, or other information.

In the revision of Bloom's taxonomy, the original knowledge category is divided into two categories: a knowledge dimension and remembering as a cognitive process. There is a distinction between "factual knowledge" that is remembered and other types of knowledge (conceptual, procedural, and metacognitive). Factual knowledge encompasses basic elements about a discipline, including knowledge of terminology (specific verbal and nonverbal labels and symbols such as words, numerals, pictures, and signs) and knowledge of specific details and elements (events, locations, sources of information, dates, and other information pertaining to a subject). Further details with examples of factual knowledge remembering are shown in Tables 2.4 and 2.5. Regardless of the classification scheme, though, the important point is that when students are required to remember something, whether facts, concepts, or procedures, this represents the most basic and elementary form of learning.

TABLE 2.4   Part of Knowledge Dimension of New Taxonomy

Major Types	Definition	Subtypes	Examples
Factual Knowledge	Basic elements of a discipline	Knowledge of terminology	Vocabulary; symbols
		Knowledge of specific details and elements	
			Major facts important to good health
Conceptual Knowledge	Interrelationships among basic elements that enable them to function together	Knowledge of classifications and categories	Forms of business ownership
		Knowledge of principles and generalizations	Law of supply and demand
		Knowledge of theories, models, and structures	Theory of evolution
Procedural Knowledge	How to do something, methods of inquiry, and skills, algorithms, and methods	Knowledge of subject-specific skills and algorithms	Painting skills; division algorithm
		Knowledge of subject-specific techniques and methods	Scientific method
		Knowledge of criteria for determining when to use appropriate procedures	Knowing when to apply Newton's second law

Source: Adapted from Lorin W. Anderson & David R. Krathwohl, *A taxonomy for learning, teaching, and assessing: A revision of Bloom's taxonomy of educational objectives.* Published by Allyn and Bacon, Boston, MA. Copyright © 2001 by Pearson Education. Reprinted by permission of the publisher.

TABLE 2.5   Part of Cognitive Process Dimension of New Taxonomy

Major Types	Defintion	Subtypes	Illustrative Verbs	Examples
Remember	Retrieval of knowledge from long-term memory	Recognizing	Identifying	Recognize dates of important events
		Recalling	Retrieving	Recall dates of important events
Understand	Construct meaning from oral, written, and graphic communication	Interpreting	Representing, translating	Paraphrase meaning in important speeches
		Exemplifying	Illustrating	Give examples of painting styles
		Classifying	Categorizing, subsuming	Classify different types of rocks
		Summarizing	Abstracting, generalizing	Write a summary of a story
		Inferring	Concluding, predicting	Draw a conclusion from data presented
		Comparing	Contrasting, mapping	Compare historical events to contemporary events
		Explaining	Constructing models	Show cause-and-effect of pollution affected by industry
Apply	Carry out a procedure	Executing Implementing	Carrying out Using	Divide whole numbers
				Apply procedure to an unfamiliar task

Source: Adapted from Lorin W. Anderson & David R. Krathwohl, *A taxonomy for learning, teaching, and assessing: A revision of Bloom's taxonomy of educational objectives.* Published by Allyn and Bacon, Boston, MA. Copyright © 2001 by Pearson Education. Reprinted by permission of the publisher.

The contemporary view of knowledge is that remembering is only part of what occurs when students learn. You also need to think about how the knowledge is represented in the mind of the student. *Knowledge representation* is how information is constructed and stored in long-term and working memory (Gagne, Yekovich, & Yekovich, 1993). We will examine two types of knowledge representation that have direct application to assessment: declarative and procedural. These are major types of knowledge in the revision to Bloom's taxonomy (Table 2.4).

Declarative Knowledge and Understanding

Declarative knowledge is information that is retained about something, knowing that it exists. The nature of the information learned can be ordered hierarchically, depending on the level of generality and degree of understanding that is demonstrated (Marzano, Pickering, & McTighe, 1993; Marzano & Kendall, 2007; Marzano, 1996) and the way the knowledge is represented. At the "lowest" level, declarative knowledge is similar to Bloom's first level—remembering or recognizing specific facts about persons, places, events, or content in a subject area. The knowledge is represented by simple association or discrimination, such as rote memory. At a higher level, declarative knowledge consists of concepts, ideas, and generalizations that are more fully understood and applied. This type of knowledge involves *understanding* in the form of comprehension.

The nature of the representation moves from rote memorization and association of facts to generalized understanding and usage. This is a critical distinction for both learning and assessment. As pointed out in Chapter 1, constructivist views contend that students learn most effectively when they connect new information meaningfully to an existing network of knowledge. Constructivists believe that new knowledge is acquired through a process of seeing how something relates, makes sense, and can be used in reasoning. This notion is quite different from memorized learning that can be demonstrated for a test. Although I don't want to suggest that some rote memorization is not appropriate for students, I do want to point out that your learning targets can focus on recall or understanding types of declarative knowledge and that your choice of assessment method and test items will be different for each of these.

Let's look at an example of different types of declarative knowledge. One important type of information students learn about is geometric shapes. Each shape is a concept (mental structures that use physical characteristics or definitions to classify objects, events, or other things into categories). If students learn the concept of "rectangle" at the level of *recall* or *recognition,* then they simply memorize a definition or identify rectangles from a set of different shapes that look like the ones they studied in class. If students *understand* the concept of rectangle, however, they will be able to give original examples and identify rectangles of different sizes, shapes, and colors they have never seen before. Each of these levels of learning is "knowing something," but the latter is much closer to true student mastery and what constructivists advocate. Also, because these levels are hierarchical, understanding requires recall. Thus, it may be better to state learning targets that require understanding but teach and test for recall as well because one is a prerequisite to the other.

Procedural Knowledge and Understanding

Procedural knowledge is knowing how to do something. It is knowledge that is needed to carry out an action or solve a problem. What is demonstrated is knowledge of the strategies, procedures, and skills students must engage in; for example, how to tie shoes, how to divide fractions, or how to check out library books. Like declarative knowledge, procedural knowledge can be demonstrated at different levels. At the level of recall, students simply identify or repeat the needed steps. Simple understanding is indicated as students summarize in their own words (comprehension) and actually use the steps in executing a solution (application).

Deep Understanding and Reasoning

Like other taxonomies, *Bloom's Revision* separates simple cognitive acts such as remembering, conceptual understanding, and application from "higher-level" cognition with which students analyze, evaluate, and create. These are generally regarded as "deep" understanding and reasoning skills, in which students mentally manipulate information to solve a problem or come up with an answer. The difference between remembering and understanding, on the one hand, and deep understanding and reasoning on the other, is a matter of degree. With knowledge and comprehension you are able to make sense out of something, and with further involvement and more detailed information, you deepen your understanding to eventually use information in new ways; to think about what is known in a systematic, integrated, holistic manner; and to explain relationships. This continuum is represented in Figure 2.5 with terms that are associated with knowledge and different levels of understanding. The terms are meant to describe the nature of

FIGURE 2.5 **The Knowledge/Understanding Continuum**

Remembering	Understanding	Deep Understanding and Reasoning
Fragmented	Comprehend	Penetrating
Ritualized	Apply	Elegant
Fragile	Rudimentary	Sophisticated
Literal	explanations	explanations
Superficial	Think about	Justify
Surface	Interpret	Compare and contrast
Temporary	Illustrate	Construct
Recall	Describe	Expert
Recognize		Critical thinking
Novice		Reasoning
Inflexible		Grasp structure
Formulaic		Rethinking
		Revising
		Reflective
		Enduring
		Infer

Source: Adapted in part from McTighe & Wiggins (2004), Perkins (1993), and Bruner (1960).

knowledge and the relative degree of understanding that is demonstrated, showing the spectrum from shallow to sophisticated.

Deep understanding implies that students know the "essence" of something, that they can think about and use knowledge in new and sophisticated ways and grasp the idea of relativity and significance (McTighe & Wiggins, 2004; Wiggins, 1998; Wiggins & McTighe, 2005); they can discover and interpret new relationships, construct novel explanations, and reason with what they comprehend. They are able to understand the complexity of knowledge. As pointed out by Borich and Tombari (2004), when we initially learn about something, our understanding is undeveloped and not very sophisticated. As we have more experience with it, our understanding deepens. For example, you may have had a surface or simple understanding of the meaning of the term *performance assessment* before reading this book. Initially, you may be able to provide a definition and simple understanding by recognizing performance assessments. Your understanding will be richer and more developed after you study performance assessments, use some in the classroom, and discuss their strengths and weaknesses with others.

It is important to realize that deep understanding targets are needed to help students internalize what they are able to do with their knowledge and construct meaningful connections with what they already know. At the very least, distinguish between surface recall and recognition knowledge, and deep understanding. As we will see, the implication for assessment is significant. Assessments that work well with knowledge and simple understanding are different from those that should be used for deep understanding.

Reasoning is something students do with their knowledge, a kind of cognitive or mental operation that employs their understanding to some end. Of course, knowledge and simple understanding, like reasoning, involve some type of thinking skill. Thinking occurs in the most fundamental process of remembering something, just as it does in demonstrating understanding and reasoning. It is in the nature of the thinking, however, that knowledge is distinguished from reasoning.

Reasoning, as I have conceptualized here, involves some kind of mental manipulation of knowledge. The task is to *employ* knowledge to interpret and draw inferences, solve a problem, make a judgment or decision, or engage in creative or critical thinking. Thinking is not normally content-free. Thus, I find it helpful to indentify three ingredients to reasoning. One is the mental skill needed to perform the task; a second is the declarative or procedural knowledge or simple understanding needed; and the third is the task itself. These ingredients differentiate cognitive skills such as analysis, comparison, and discrimination from the problem-solving or interpretation task (see Figure 2.6). The mental skills are used in conjunction with knowledge to perform the task. Even though we are sometimes interested in teaching and assessing students on their ability to perform certain types of mental operations, such as analysis or deductive logic, we don't normally test these skills directly. Rather, we are usually interested in the *use* of these skills to demonstrate deep understanding or to perform a problem-solving task in subject-matter domains.

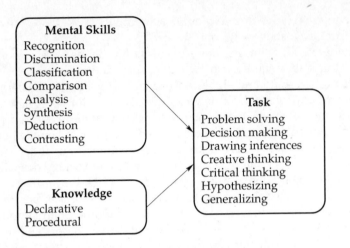

FIGURE 2.6   Major Components of Reasoning

I want to emphasize that selecting a way to operationalize thinking skills is up to you—there is no single right or best way. But assessing reasoning or thinking skills, no matter how one defines them in general, requires close attention to the nature of the specific mental operation involved.

In the revision of Bloom's taxonomy, three cognitive processes apply to deep understanding and reasoning: *analyze, evaluate,* and *create.* Analyze is essentially the same as *analysis* in other frameworks, whereas evaluate is similar to critical thinking and problem solving. The create process is similar to *inquiry* and emphasizes synthesis of information and problem solving. The three cognitive processes, with definitions and examples, are summarized in Table 2.6.

Sources for Learning Targets

Professional Preparation

Throughout your professional preparation you have been exposed to essential principles and methods of different disciplines. As you master each discipline you will be able to identify what is most important for learning. Perhaps you have heard that the best way to learn something is to teach it. Put yourself in the role of teacher even as you take courses. What specific knowledge is most important? What do you need to be able to do with the knowledge? What are *you* doing as a student? Do you *really know* the subject, inside and out, so you can do more as a teacher than simply read notes or do exactly what the curriculum guide says? You will find that the quality of your assessments will follow from the depth of your understanding of what you teach. The more you understand, the better the assessments. It is also important to keep current with the professional literature in both the subjects you teach and education in general. This literature will keep you

TABLE 2.6   Deep Understanding and Reasoning Parts of the Revision of Bloom's Taxonomy

Cognitive Process	Definition	Subtypes	Illustrative Verbs	Example
Analyze	Break material into its constituent parts and determine how the parts relate.	Differentiating	Discriminating, distinguishing, focusing, selecting	Distinguish between relevant and irrelevant numbers in a math word problem.
		Organizing	Finding coherence, integrating, outlining	Structure historical evidence for and against a particular historical explanation.
		Attributing	Deconstructing	Determine the point of view of an author based on his or her political perspective.
Evaluate	Make judgments based on criteria and standards	Checking	Coordinating, detecting, monitoring, testing	Determine if conclusions follow from observed data.
		Critiquing	Judging	Judge which of two methods is the best way to solve a problem.
Create	Pull elements together to form a whole; reorganize elements into a new structure or pattern.	Generating	Hypothesizing	Generate hypothesis to account for observed phenomenon.
		Planning	Designing	Plan a research paper.
		Producing	Constructing	Build habitats for a specific purpose.

Source: Adapted from Lorin W. Anderson & David R. Krathwohl, *A taxonomy for learning, teaching, and assessing: A revision of Bloom's taxonomy of educational objectives*. Published by Allyn and Bacon, Boston, MA. Copyright © 2001 by Pearson Education. Reprinted by permission of the publisher.

up-to-date and will give you many ideas about the kinds of learning targets that are appropriate.

Textbooks

Most textbooks for students are accompanied by an instructor's guide or a teacher's edition that provides information to help you plan lessons, deliver appropriate instruction, and assess student learning. The teacher's edition typically includes "objectives" for each lesson.

Although the objectives in a teacher's edition can be useful, keep in mind that textbook authors tend to emphasize limited, lower-level objectives that are applicable to a wide range of different classes and locations. Furthermore, textbook objectives are neither the *only*, nor necessarily the *best*, source for your learning targets. The objectives need to be reviewed in relation to your specific teaching situation and approach.

Three major criteria can be used to evaluate the appropriateness of textbook objectives (Brophy & Alleman, 1991). First, are the objectives stated with clear descriptions of what students will know or be able to do following instruction? Even if the behavior is clearly stated, the textbook probably will not indicate what criteria should be used to complete the learning target. Second, are the objectives appropriate for your students? Have your students learned the prerequisite knowledge and skills? Is the level of learning that is required appropriate for your students? Third, do the objectives include most of the student outcomes? How complete and comprehensive are the objectives? Are important areas overlooked? Using these three criteria, you can appraise the appropriateness and completeness of the objectives as a basis for your learning targets. You will probably need to modify and expand the objectives to meet unique characteristics of both yourself and your students.

The influence of standards-based education has led textbook publishers to show how their books are aligned with the grade-level standards. Remember, though, that these judgments are from the publisher, and of course, the greater the match the more likely a state or district will select the book as recommended, approved, or required.

Existing Lists of Objectives

You will find it helpful to locate and review lists of objectives that have already been developed. A number of sources can be used to locate these lists. Most methods of teaching textbooks, particularly those in each subject area, contain illustrative objectives as well as references that can be consulted. Yearbooks and handbooks in different disciplines sometimes contain objectives. Special reports issued by professional groups, such as the National Council of Teachers of Mathematics, the National Council of Teachers of English, the National Council for the Social Studies, and the National Science Teachers Association, contain extensive lists of objectives that emphasize thinking skills and applications to real-life problems. For example, the report *Science for All Americans: Project 2061*, prepared by the American Association for the Advancement of Science, recommends four goals for science education: understanding scientific endeavors, developing scientific perspectives about the world, developing historical and social views on science, and developing scientific "habits of mind." (For reasoning and critical thinking skills see Ennis [1987] and Quellmalz & Hoskyn [1997].)

An excellent source is state- or local-level curriculum guides. Although these guides may present objectives at different levels of specificity, they are very helpful in their comprehensive nature of critical objectives. In whatever state you are teaching, it would be worthwhile to contact your state department of education and inquire about existing curriculum guides or frameworks. If you are in a large school or school district, there will probably be a list of instructional objectives for you that you should consult as a starting point. In addition, most states will be responding to the national standards movement by developing a set of state-level core standards for all students.

National and State Standards

I have already pointed out that national content and performance standards have been developed in most areas. These standards will be excellent sources for your learning targets because they set general expectations for what will be emphasized. States set fairly specific objectives for student learning, and curriculum is organized to focus on these standards. Often state standards will include introductory information that provides further clarification of the nature of what student outcomes are expected. For example, Virginia's grade 5 Mathematics Standards of Learning introduction includes the following:

> Problem solving has been integrated throughout the six content strands. The development of problem-solving skills should be a major goal of the mathematics program at every grade level. Instruction in the process of problem solving should be integrated early and continuously into each student's mathematics education. Students must be helped to develop a wide range of skills and strategies for solving a variety of problem types.

Obviously it will be important for Virginia mathematics teachers to include problem-solving and reasoning targets. The actual standards make this more specific. The following is one of 22 Virginia mathematics grade 5 standards.

Computation and Estimation Strand

5.3. The student will create and solve problems involving addition, subtraction, multiplication, and division of whole numbers, using paper and pencil, estimation, mental computation, and calculators.

In the last decade state standards have improved considerably and become increasingly specific. Because they are the foundation for high-stakes accountability testing, teachers need to take them very seriously. Each standard, and accompanying text, tells what student competencies are tested. Here is another example of state standards, from high school history in Missouri:

> Describe the historical foundations of the United States governmental system as reflected in the following documents
> - **a.** Magna Carta
> - **b.** Enlightenment writings of Hobbes, Locke, Rousseau, Montesquieu, and the Social Contract Theory

    c. Mayflower Compact
    d. Declaration of Independence
    e. Articles of Confederation

In Missouri each standard is characterized by a "depth-of-knowledge" indicator, based on a four-point continuum: recall, basic reasoning, complex reasoning, and extended reasoning. This history standard is identified as requiring complex reasoning.

    This is a good illustration about the variety of schemes, labels, descriptions, and language used in standards-based education. State and local guidelines are critical. If you teach in Missouri, you need to study carefully what is meant by the different types of reasoning.

    Although the state materials will convey much information about the relative importance of different standards, teachers can also apply three criteria that will enable them to prioritize the standards so that instruction is focused on learning that is most important for success on high-stakes tests: "endurance, leverage, and the necessity for the next level of instruction" (Reeves, 2003, p. 110). Endurance is a trait that indicates the lasting value of the standard. Leverage refers to whether the standard applies to different disciplines. Necessity is self-evident. When standards are judged to have endurance and leverage, and are prerequisites to subsequent learning, they are the ones to emphasize.

    One last and very important point about state standards is that they often express "minimum" levels of competency. As expressed in the following Teacher's Corner, it is wise not to depend solely on state standards, even if they are the ones that are tested on high-stakes tests. Your best guide is to use whatever levels of competency are appropriate to enhance student learning. This is often reflected in teacher standards and learning targets that go beyond state standards.

Teacher's Corner

Marie Wilcox

National Board Certified Middle School Mathematics Teacher

Standards-based education has changed the look of education. An accomplished teacher knows what skills need to be mastered in order for the students to be prepared for higher level learning in future years. Teaching just to the standards shortchanges students' education. If teachers teach concept and application rather than just procedure and state standards, students will pass the standard tests (SOLS in Virginia). The SOL test is a minimum proficiency assessment, educating students for their future is clearly more important. I charge all teachers to teach to a higher level and preparedness for SOL testing will fall in place.

TABLE 2.7 **Strengths and Limitations of Different Sources for Establishing Learning Targets**

Source	Strengths	Limitations
Bloom's Taxonomy	Established; well known; comprehensive; contains action verbs; hierarchical design	Dated; based on behavioristic learning theories; not consistent with recent cognitive theories of learning
Revision of Bloom's Taxonomy; The New Taxonomy	Consistent with recent learning theory; contains action verbs	New; untested; may be overly complex
Professional Preparation	Focus on essentials of a discipline; personal experience	Difficult to translate into targets and keep up-to-date; may be confined to a specific type of target
Textbooks	Directly related to instruction; easily adapted	Tend to emphasize lower-level targets; lacks criteria; need to be modified
Existing Lists of Objectives	Comprehensive; good ideas for targets	May not relate well to a local situation; need to be modified
National Standards	High standards; comprehensive; reflects national expertise; reflects current research on learning; discipline specific	May not relate well to local situation; need to be modified; may not be politically acceptable
State Standards	Comprehensive; tested; tied to curriculum and pacing guides; accompanied by instructional aids	May not cover or may conflict with local learning targets; may eliminate or minimize content areas not covered; requires locality to adapt its targets and standards
District Standards	Based on state standards; consistent with local needs and priorities; closely tied to aligned instruction	May be too provincial; may not reflect national standards; may make instruction too proscribed

The strengths and limitations of these seven sources of objectives for establishing learning targets are summarized in Table 2.7. Initially you may find that textbooks and existing lists of objectives contain ideas that will be most easily translated into practice.

Criteria for Selecting Learning Targets and Standards

After you have consulted existing sources of objectives and begun the task of selecting your learning targets and standards, you will need to make some choices about which ones to keep, which need revision, and which are not feasible. The following criteria will help you judge the adequacy of your learning targets and standards. They are summarized in Figure 2.7 in the form of a checklist.

FIGURE 2.7 **Checklist for Selecting Learning Targets and Standards**

✓ Are there too many or too few targets?
✓ Are all important types of learning included?
✓ Do the targets reflect school goals?
✓ Will the targets and standards challenge students to do their best work?
✓ Are the targets consistent with research on learning and motivation?
✓ Are the targets and standards established before instruction?

1. Establish the right number of learning targets. The number of different learning targets will vary, depending on the length of the instructional segment and the complexity of the target. Obviously, the longer the instructional period, the more targets are needed. Also, more complex targets, such as those requiring reasoning, take more time. I have found the following general rules of thumb appropriate: 40–60 targets for a year; 8–12 for a unit; 1–3 for a single lesson. Hundreds of targets for a year are clearly too many.

2. Establish comprehensive learning targets. It is essential that the targets represent all types of important learning from the instructional unit. Be careful not to overemphasize knowledge targets. Try to maintain a balance among the five areas (knowledge and simple understanding, deep understanding and reasoning, skills, products, and affect). Higher priority may be given to targets that integrate several of these areas. Do not rely too heavily on textbook objectives or teacher's guides.

3. Establish learning targets that reflect school goals. Your targets should be clearly related to more general school, district, and state learning goals. Priority may be given to targets that focus on school improvement plans or restructuring efforts.

4. Establish learning targets and standards that are challenging yet feasible. It is important to challenge students and seek the highest level of accomplishment for them. You will need to develop targets that are not too easy or too hard. It is also important to assess the readiness of your students to establish these challenging targets and standards. Do they have necessary prerequisite skills and knowledge? Are they developmentally ready for the challenge? Do they have needed motivation and attitudes? Will students see the standards as too easy? As we will see in the next chapter, these questions need to be answered through proper assessment before your final selection of learning targets, standards, instructional activities, and your assessment of student learning.

5. Establish learning targets and standards that are consistent with current principles of learning and motivation. Because learning targets are the basis for learning and instruction, it is important that what you set as a target will promote learning that is consistent with what we know about how learning occurs and what motivates students. For example, will the targets promote long-term retention in a meaningful way? Do the targets reflect students' intrinsic interests and needs? Do the targets represent learning that will be applicable to life outside the classroom? Will the targets encourage a variety of instructional approaches and activities?

After you identify the targets, it is best to write them out before teaching. This will allow a ready reference throughout the lesson and free you to concentrate on the fast-paced and complex activities in the classroom. From year to year you will find it necessary to revisit your targets and make appropriate modifications depending on changes in your students, curriculum, textbooks, and state requirements. It will also be helpful to identify performance standards as well as criteria, with examples of student work that illustrate different levels of performance.

Summary

Learning targets and standards—what students should know and be able to do and the criteria for judging student performance—are contrasted in this chapter with more traditional terms such as *goals, objectives,* and *expectations.* The major points include the following:

- Goals are broad statements about student learning.
- Instructional or behavioral objectives are specific statements that indicate what students should know and be able to do at the end of an instructional unit.
- Expectations are the teacher's beliefs about what students are capable of achieving.
- Goals, objectives, and expectations focus on what students do rather than on what the teacher does in instruction.
- It is not practical to write very specific behavioral objectives that include all aspects of the criteria and testing conditions.
- Learning targets need to contain as much about criteria as possible and feasible, because criteria are critical in establishing the standards on which performance toward the learning target is judged.
- Criteria are clearly stated dimensions of student performance that the teacher examines in making judgments about student proficiency. These criteria should be public and explained to students before each instructional unit.
- Exemplars and anchors are important examples that help students understand how teacher evaluations are made.
- Five types of learning targets are introduced: knowledge and simple understanding, deep understanding and reasoning, skill, product, and affect.
- Sources for constructing learning targets and standards include Bloom's taxonomy, the revision of Bloom's taxonomy, your professional preparation, textbooks, existing lists of objectives, and national, state, and district standards.
- Four kinds of standards are used: content, performance, developmental, and grade-level.

- States have established grade-level standards that have ubiquitous implications for teachers, instruction, and classroom assessments.
- Criteria to be used in selecting targets and standards were indicated. You should strive for the right number of comprehensive, challenging targets that will reflect school goals and will be consistent with current principles of learning and motivation.

Self-Instructional Review Exercises

1. Identify each of the following as a goal (G), behavioral objective (BO), or expectation (E).

   a. My students will pass all their exams.
   b. Students will be familiar with global geography.
   c. It is unlikely that Tom will finish his test.
   d. Students will answer 10 of 12 questions about ancient Egypt in 15 minutes without use of notes.

2. What does the term *criteria* have in common with behavioral objectives? How is it different from what is contained in objectives?

3. Suppose a teacher pulls out a graded paper that was handed in by a student from a previous year's class and distributes it to the class. What would the paper be called in relation to assessment?

   a. Rubric
   b. Anchor
   c. Scoring criteria
   d. Performance criteria

4. Give at least three reasons why using public criteria that are shared with students before instruction is an effective teaching/learning tool for evaluating student work.

5. Why is it important to include criteria in learning targets and standards?

6. Identify each of the following as a knowledge target (K) or a deep understanding/reasoning target (DU).

   a. Recalling historical facts from the Revolutionary War
   b. Comparing vertebrates to invertebrates
   c. Identifying the organs in a dissected frog
   d. Explaining how and why recent United States recessions affect the world economy

7. Why may Bloom's original taxonomy of educational objectives *not* be the best source for identifying classroom learning targets?

8. Give original examples of at least one knowledge and one deep understanding learning target that could be stated for you concerning the content of this chapter.

9. What is the primary difference between content and performance standards?

10. Give an example of each kind of standard (content, performance, developmental, grade-level) as related to teachers' knowledge of classroom assessment.

11. Identify each of the following descriptions as declarative (D) or procedural (P) and as knowledge (K) or understanding (U).

    a. Define procedural knowledge.
    b. What is the sequence of steps in preparing an objective test?
    c. Give an example of a multiple-choice item that measures application.
    d. List three suggestions for constructing matching items.
    e. Predict whether students will have questions about how to answer the items in the test.
    f. Review the strategy a teacher has used to construct binary-choice test items to determine if they can be improved.

12. Identify the thinking or reasoning skill illustrated by each of the following examples, using this key:

A analysis	P problem solving
S synthesis	I inference
C critical thinking	E evaluation
D decision making	

    a. Suppose you were President Obama and had to decide whether to send more troops to Afghanistan. What would you do? Why would you do it?
    b. State your reasons for agreeing or disagreeing with the following statement: Religious people are more likely to help others.
    c. Given what you know about sailing, what would most likely occur if a novice sailor tried to sail directly into the wind?
    d. Examine three different human cultures. What is common in all three cultures, and what principle about being human does this suggest?
    e. Examine four recent presidential speeches. Is any part of the speeches the same?
    f. How can the United States reduce the rate of teenage pregnancies?
    g. Suppose you had to choose between increasing taxes to reduce the U.S. budget deficit or decreasing federal spending to reduce the deficit. Which would you choose? Why? How would your choice affect retired persons?
    h. Examine the data on birthrates. What is likely to happen to the birthrate by the year 2020? Why?

Answers to Self-Instructional Review Exercises

1. a. E, b. G, c. E, d. BO.

2. Criteria are part of what would be included in a behavioral objective. Criteria, in contrast to objectives, contain descriptions of different levels of performance.

3. b.

4. Could have selected from communicating goals and different levels of work to parents, documenting judgments, helping students evaluate their own work, motivating students.

5. Criteria are needed to completely understand the nature of the target and what it takes to achieve different levels of performance. Without criteria, targets are statements similar to simple behavioral objectives (without conditions, criteria, and audience).

6. a. K, b. DU, c. K, d. DU,

7. Bloom's taxonomy is not aligned very well with more recent research on learning and motivation.

8. For example,

   Knowledge: Students are able to recall and write accurately 80% of the definitions of key terms in the chapter.
   Deep Understanding and Reasoning: Students are able to analyze five examples of learning targets and modify them in writing so that they correspond better to the criteria in the chapter.

9. Content standards describe the nature of the material that is to be learned, whereas performance standards indicate levels of achievement on the content that must be met.

10. For example,

    Content Standard: Teachers will understand how measurement differs from evaluation.
    Performance Standard: Teachers will be able prepare a classroom assessment that includes measurement of student simple and deep understanding.
    Developmental Standard: Student teachers will be able to construct classroom assessments illustrating principles in the book; teachers with 2 years of experience will be able to critique and improve classroom assessments used by other teachers.
    Grade-Level Standard: Entering students will be able to describe the difference between validity and reliability. Student teachers will be able to identify reliability and validity evidence for assessments given by their supervising teachers.

11. a. DK; b. PK; c. DU; d. DK; e. DU; f. PU

12. a. D; b. C; c. I; d. S; e. A; f. P; g. C; h. I

Suggestions for Action Research

1. Obtain some examples of student work from teachers that demonstrate different levels of performance on the same assessment. How easy is it to see how the examples are different? See if the criteria you use to differentiate the examples are the same as the criteria the teacher used.

2. In small groups, generate some examples of student performance on the same learning target that would demonstrate qualitatively different levels of achievement concerning the content of this chapter or Chapter 1.

3. Examine textbook objectives and national standards in your area of expertise. How are they similar, and how are they different?

4. Interview a teacher and ask about using textbook objectives. How useful are these objectives? What determines whether the teacher will use them?

5. In a group of three or four other students, develop a scoring rubric that could be used for judging the performance of a student on an assignment, project, or test that was used in a school setting. Find or generate examples of student work that illustrate different levels of performance.

High-Quality Classroom Assessment

Classroom assessment consists of determining purpose and learning targets related to standards, systematically obtaining information from students, interpreting the information collected, and using the information. In Chapter 2, establishing learning targets was identified as the first step in conducting assessments. Once you have determined *what* to assess, you will probably be concerned

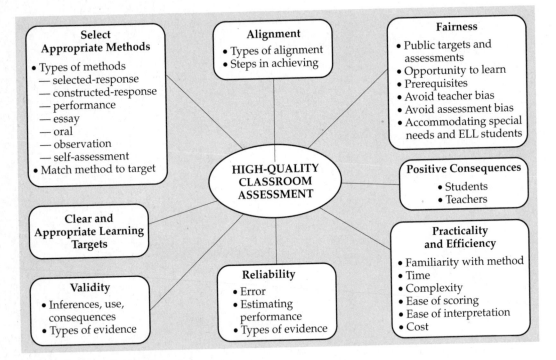

Select Appropriate Methods
- Types of methods
  — selected-response
  — constructed-response
  — performance
  — essay
  — oral
  — observation
  — self-assessment
- Match method to target

Alignment
- Types of alignment
- Steps in achieving

Fairness
- Public targets and assessments
- Opportunity to learn
- Prerequisites
- Avoid teacher bias
- Avoid assessment bias
- Accommodating special needs and ELL students

HIGH-QUALITY CLASSROOM ASSESSMENT

Positive Consequences
- Students
- Teachers

Clear and Appropriate Learning Targets

Practicality and Efficiency
- Familiarity with method
- Time
- Complexity
- Ease of scoring
- Ease of interpretation
- Cost

Validity
- Inferences, use, consequences
- Types of evidence

Reliability
- Error
- Estimating performance
- Types of evidence

CHAPTER 3 Concept Map

with *how* to assess it. That is, what methods of data collection will you use to gather the information? At this point it is important to keep in mind several criteria that determine the quality and credibility of the assessment methods you choose. In this chapter, we review these criteria and provide suggestions for practical steps you can take to keep the quality of your assessments high.

What Is High-Quality Classroom Assessment?

Obviously, it's best if classroom assessment demonstrates principles and criteria so that its quality is high. Traditionally, assessment quality has been determined by the extent to which specific psychometric standards, such as validity and reliability, were met. These standards were originally derived for large-scale, published, standardized objective tests. However, for published tests the emphasis is on highly technical, statistically sophisticated standards. Thus, complex statistical procedures are used to provide estimates of validity, reliability, and measurement error. To interpret standardized tests properly, it is necessary to have a basic understanding of these properties.

But in most classrooms such technical qualities have little relevance because the purpose of the assessment is different. This is not to say that the *ideas* of validity and reliability are not important criteria for classroom assessment. High-quality classroom assessment involves many other criteria as well, substituting technically pleasing types of validity and reliability with concerns about how the assessments influence learning and provide fair and credible reporting of student achievement. For teachers the primary determinant of quality is how the information influences students. Thus, the focus is on the use and consequences of the results and what the assessments get students to do, rather than on a detailed inspection of the test itself. This means that judgments about quality are made *after* students' performance on the assessment is summarized and analyzed.

High-quality classroom assessments, then, provide results that verify and promote targeted student learning. High-quality assessments also inform instructional decision making. As pointed out in Chapter 1, our understanding of learning and motivation, and our realization that much more is demanded of students than demonstrating simple knowledge, has changed how we define high-quality classroom assessments. Eight criteria of high-quality classroom assessment are presented in Figure 3.1.

Clear and Appropriate Learning Targets

As discussed in Chapters 1 and 2, sound assessment begins with clear and appropriate learning targets. Are the targets at the right level of difficulty to motivate students? Is there adequate balance among different types of targets? Are the targets consistent with your overall goals and the goals of the school and district? Are the

FIGURE 3.1   **Criteria for Ensuring High-Quality Classroom Assessments**

- Clear and appropriate learning targets
- Alignment of assessment methods and learning targets
- Validity
- Reliability
- Fairness
- Positive consequences
- Alignment
- Practicality and efficiency

targets comprehensive, covering all major dimensions that you hope to change and need feedback about? Are the criteria for judging student performance clear? Answers to these questions help ensure high-quality assessment. Clear targets means that both students and teachers understand the nature of learning that is expected, and what student proficiencies will result. Appropriate targets are those that are reasonable and aligned with student characteristics, instruction, and standards.

Alignment of Assessment Methods and Learning Targets

As you are well aware, a number of different types of assessment methods can be used in the classroom. Although your ultimate choice of an assessment method will depend on how well all the criteria in Figure 3.1 are met, the match between type of target and method is very important. Even though most targets may be measured by several methods, the reality of teaching is that certain methods measure some types of targets better than other methods do. Thus, one of your first tasks, once you have identified the targets, is to match them with methods.

Types of Assessment Methods

Many different approaches or methods are used to assess students. I have categorized them in Figure 3.2 according to the nature and characteristics of each method. A brief description of the methods is presented here to facilitate an understanding of how the methods should be matched to targets. They are covered in much more detail in later chapters.

Figure 3.2 divides different methods of assessment into four major categories: selected-response, constructed-response, teacher observation, and student self-assessment. The major distinguishing characteristic of most classroom assessments is whether the items use selected-response or constructed-response formats. In the **selected-response** format students are presented with a question that has two or more possible responses. Students then select an answer from the possible choices. Common selected-response items include multiple-choice, true/false, and matching. These kinds of items may also be called *objective*, referring to the way the

FIGURE 3.2 Classification of Assessment Methods

Selected-Response	Constructed-Response				Teacher Observation	Student Self-Assessment
	Performance Tasks		Essay Items	Oral Questioning		
	Products	*Skills*				
• Multiple-choice • Binary-choice (e.g., true/false) • Matching • Interpretive *Brief Constructed-Response Items* • Short answer • Completion • Label a diagram • "Show your work"	• Paper • Project • Poem • Portfolio • Video/audiotape • Spreadsheet • Web page • Exhibition • Reflection • Journal • Graph • Table • Illustration	• Speech • Demonstration • Dramatic reading • Debate • Recital • Enactment • Athletics • Keyboarding • Dance • Readings	• Restricted-response • Extended-response	• Informal questioning • Examinations • Conferences • Interviews	• Formal • Informal	*Self-Report Inventories* • Attitude survey • Sociometric devices • Questionnaires • Inventories *Self-Evaluation* • Ratings • Portfolios • Conferences • Self-reflection • Evaluate others' performances

answers are scored. A single correct or best answer is identified for each item, and scoring is simply a matter of checking to determine whether the correct choice was made.

A **constructed-response** format requires students to create or produce their own answer in response to a question or task. Brief constructed-response items are those in which students provide a very short, clearly delineated answer, such as filling in a blank at the end of a sentence, writing a few words or a sentence or two, or answering a mathematics problem by showing how they arrived at the answer. Although many constructed-response assessments require considerable subjectivity in judging an answer, brief constructed-response items are objectively scored in one sense because there is typically a single correct answer that is easily identified.

Performance assessments require students to construct a more extensive and elaborate answer or response. A well-defined task is identified, and students are asked to create, produce, or do something, often in settings that involve real-world application of knowledge and skills. Proficiency is demonstrated by providing an extended response. Performance formats are further differentiated into products and performances. The performance may result in a product, such as a painting, portfolio, paper, or exhibition, or it may consist of a performance, such as a speech, athletic skill, musical recital, or reading. (Be aware that many use the term *performance assessment* to refer to both performances and products, and others use *performance-based*.)

Essay items allow students to construct a response that would be several sentences (restricted-response) to many paragraphs or pages in length (extended-response). Restricted-response essay items include limits to the content and nature of the answer, whereas extended-response items allow greater freedom in response.

Oral questioning is used continuously in an informal way during instruction to monitor student understanding. In a more formalized format, oral questions can be used as a way to test or as a way to determine student understanding through interviews or conferences.

Teacher observations, like oral questions, are so common that we often don't think of them as a form of student assessment. But teachers constantly observe students informally to assess student understanding and progress. Teachers watch students as they respond to questions and study, and teachers listen to students as they speak and discuss with others. Often nonverbal communication, such as squinting, inattention, looks of frustration, and other cues, is more helpful than verbal feedback. Observation is used extensively as well in performance assessments, and other formal observational techniques are used to assess classroom climate, teacher effectiveness, and other dimensions of the classroom.

Student self-assessment refers to students' reporting on or evaluating themselves. In *self-evaluation of academic achievement*, students rate their own performance in relation to established standards and criteria. In *self-report inventories*, students are asked to complete a form or answer questions that reveal their attitudes and beliefs about themselves or other students.

Matching Targets with Methods

Figure 3.3 presents the Matching Targets with Methods Scorecard. This figure summarizes the relative strengths of different methods in measuring different targets. Notice that several methods may be used for some targets. This is good in that it provides more flexibility in the assessments you use, but it also means there is no simple formula or one correct method.

      The scorecard gives you *general* guidelines about how well particular assessment methods measure each type of target. The numbers (1 = poor, 5 = excellent) represent the relative strength of the method to provide a high-quality assessment for specific targets. Variations to what is presented in the figure should be expected. For example, good selected-response items *can* provide a high-quality measure of reasoning, but such items are difficult and time-consuming to prepare. What I have considered in assigning the numbers are both technical strengths and practical limitations. When each method is described in greater detail in later chapters, the variations will become more obvious. For now, however, the scorecard will give you a good overview and provide some preliminary information to use in selecting methods that are appropriate.

Knowledge and Simple Understanding.   Well-constructed selected-response and brief constructed-response items do a good job of assessing subject matter, procedural

FIGURE 3.3   **Matching Targets with Methods Scorecard**

	Assessment Methods					
	Selected-Response and Brief Constructed-Response	*Essay*	*Performance*	*Oral Question*	*Obervation*	*Student Self-Assessment*
Targets						
Knowledge and Simple Under-standing	5	4	2	4	3	3
Deep Under-standing and Reasoning	2	5	4	3	2	3
Skills	1	3	5	2	5	3
Products	1	1	5	2	4	4
Affect	1	2	4	4	4	5

Note: Higher numbers indicate better matches (e.g., 5 = excellent, 1 = poor).

knowledge, and simple understanding, particularly when students must recognize or remember isolated facts, definitions, spellings, concepts, and principles. The questions can be answered and scored quickly, so it is efficient for teachers. These formats also allow you to adequately sample from a large amount of knowledge. Asking students questions orally about what they know is also an effective way to assess knowledge, but this takes much more time, and the results are difficult to record. It also takes advance planning to prepare the questions and a method to record student responses. Thus, assessment by oral questioning is best in situations in which you are checking for mastery or understanding of a limited number of important facts or when you are doing informal diagnostic assessment. This is usually done during instruction to provide feedback about student progress.

Essays can be used effectively to assess knowledge and understanding when your objective is for students to learn large chunks or structures of knowledge that are related.

Using performance assessments presents some difficulties for determining what students know. Because performance assessments are time intensive for teachers and students, they are usually not the best choice for assessing vast amounts of knowledge. Much of the preparation for the performance often takes place out of class, and the final paper or product typically does not provide opportunities for demonstrating that the student has mastered specific facts. When the performance involves a demonstration of a process or series of steps, knowledge of the process or steps can be assumed when they are demonstrated.

Deep Understanding and Reasoning.   Deep understanding and reasoning skills are best assessed in essays and performance assessments. Essays can focus directly on specific reasoning skills by asking students to compare, evaluate, critique, provide justification for, organize, integrate, defend, and solve problems. Time is provided to allow students to use reasoning before answering the question. When oral questions require deep understanding and reasoning for an answer, they are excellent, though inefficient, for systematic assessment of all students at the end of a unit.

Performance assessments are also effective in measuring deep understanding and reasoning skills. For example, by observing students demonstrate how to go about planning a budget for a family of four, you can draw inferences about how the student used all the information provided and balanced different priorities. Science projects illustrate the ability to interpret results and make conclusions.

Selected-response and brief constructed-response questions *can* be a good method for assessing certain aspects of deep understanding and reasoning. When the item demands more than simply recalling or recognizing a fact, reasoning may be needed. For example, if an item requires the student to interpret a chart, analyze a poem, or apply knowledge to solve a problem, thinking skills can be measured.

Student self-evaluations of the reasoning they used in answering a question or solving a problem can help you diagnose learning difficulties. Students can be given sample graded answers and then asked to compare these to their responses.

Students can also be involved in scoring teams to actually provide evaluations of student answers.

Skills.   Performance assessments are clearly the preferred method to determine systematically whether a student has mastered a skill. Whether the student is demonstrating how to shoot a basketball, give a persuasive speech, sing a song, speak in a foreign language, or use a microscope, the skill is best assessed by observing the student perform the task. On a more informal basis, teachers use observation extensively to assess progress in demonstrating skills.

Selected-response and brief constructed-response tests and oral questioning can be used to assess student knowledge of the skills, such as knowing the proper sequence of actions or recognizing the important dimensions of the skill. But this represents prerequisite knowledge and is not the same as measuring the extent to which the student can actually *do* it.

As with essays, student self-evaluations can be used to focus students on how well their demonstration of skill meets stated criteria. Student evaluations of others' demonstrations are also useful.

Products.   The best way to assess student products is to have students complete one through a performance assessment (e.g., to write persuasively, write a letter that argues for something; if you want students to be able to act, have them participate in a play).

Like skills, you can use objectively scored items, essay items, and oral questions to determine whether students know the components of the product or to evaluate different products. But there is no substitute for actually creating the product.

Student self-evaluations are very effective with performance assessment because students need to focus on the performance criteria and make judgments about their own performance in relation to the criteria. It is also effective to have students judge each others' performances.

Affect.   Affective outcomes are best assessed by either observing students or using student self-reports. The most direct and efficient way to assess affect is to ask the students directly through self-report surveys and questionnaires. Direct oral questioning can be revealing if the right relationship exists between teacher and student and if the atmosphere is conducive to honest sharing of feelings.

Observation can be effective in determining, informally, many affective traits (e.g., motivation and attitudes toward subjects and student self-concept are often apparent when the student shows negative feelings through body posture, a reluctance to interact with others, and withdrawal). Some performance assessments provide ample opportunities for teachers to observe affect, though like other observations, this is usually nonsystematic, and inferences are required. Because you are both the observer and the one making the inference, you need to be careful to avoid bias.

Validity

What Is a Valid Assessment?

Classroom assessment is a process that includes gathering, interpreting, and using information. This conceptualization has important implications for how we define a familiar concept that is at the heart of any type of high-quality assessment—validity. **Validity** is a characteristic that refers to the appropriateness of the inferences, uses, and consequences that result from the assessment. Validity is concerned with the soundness, trustworthiness, or legitimacy of the claims or inferences that are made on the basis of obtained scores. In other words, is the interpretation made from test results reasonable? Is the information gathered the right kind of evidence for the decision that needs to be made or the intended use? How sound is the interpretation of the information? Validity has to do with the consequences of the inferences, not the test itself. Thus, it is an inference or use that is valid or invalid, not the test, instrument, or procedure that is used to gather information. Often we use the phrase "validity of the test," but it is more accurate to say "the validity of the interpretation, inference, or use of the results."

You probably have or will come across a somewhat different definition of validity, something like "the extent to which a test measures what it is supposed to measure." Although this notion is important to many decisions and uses, it suggests that validity is a characteristic that the instrument always possesses. In reality, the same test or instrument can be valid for one purpose and invalid for another. Actually, validity is always a matter of degree, depending on the situation. For example, a social science test may have high validity for inferring that students know the sequence of events leading up to the American Revolution, less validity for inferring that students can reason, even less validity for inferring that students can communicate effectively in writing, and virtually no validity for indicating a student's mathematical ability. An assessment is not simply valid or invalid, it is valid to some degree in reference to specific inferences or uses.

How Is Validity Determined?

Validity is determined primarily by professional judgment. For classroom assessment, this judgment is made by the teacher. An analysis is done by accumulating evidence that would suggest that an inference or use is appropriate and whether the consequences of the interpretations and uses are reasonable and fair.

The process of determining validity is illustrated in Figure 3.4. Traditionally, the validity of the inference has come from one of three types of evidence: content-related, criterion-related, and construct-related evidence. However, these categories do not adequately address the consequences and uses of the results. Thus, we will consider how classroom teachers can use these three types of evidence, as well as consideration of consequences and uses, to make an overall judgment about the degree of validity of the assessment. Table 3.1 summarizes the major sources of information (evidence) that can be used to establish validity.

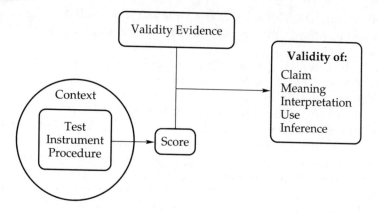

FIGURE 3.4   Determining Validity

Content-Related Evidence.   One feature of teaching that has important implications for assessment is that often a teacher is unable to assess everything that is taught or every instructional objective. Suppose you wanted to test for everything sixth-grade students learn in a 4-week unit about insects. Can you imagine how long the test would be and how much time students would take to complete the test? What you do in these situations is select a *sample* of what has been taught to assess, and then you use student achievement on this sample to make inferences about knowledge of the entire universe or domain of content, reasoning, and other objectives. That is, if a student correctly answers 85% of the items on your test of a sample of the unit on insects, then you infer that the student knows 85% of the content in the entire unit. If your sample is judged to be representative of the universe or domain, then you have **content-related evidence** for validity. The inference from the test is that the student demonstrates knowledge about the unit.

Adequate sampling of content is determined by professional judgment. This judgment process can be haphazard or very systematic. In a superficial review of the target, objectives, and test, validity is based only on *appearance*. This is sometimes referred to as face validity. *Face validity* is whether, based on a superficial examination of the test, there seems to be a reasonable measure of the objectives and domain.

TABLE 3.1   Sources of Information for Validity

Content-Related Evidence	The extent to which the assessment is representative of the domain of interest
Criterion-Related Evidence	The relationship between an assessment and another measure of the same trait
Construct-Related Evidence	The extent to which the assessment is a meaningful measure of an unobservable trait or characteristic

Does the test, on the face of it, look like an adequate measure? Although it is important to avoid face *in*validity, it is much better if the evidence is more structured and systematic.

Once the complete domain of content and targets is specified, the items on the test can be reviewed to be certain that there is a match between the intended inferences and what is on the test. This process begins with clear learning targets. Based on the targets, a **test blueprint** or **table of specifications** is sometimes prepared to further delineate what objectives you intend to assess and what is important from the content domain. The table of specifications is a two-way grid that shows the content and types of learning targets represented in your assessment. Constructing this type of **blueprint** may seem like an imposing task, but once completed it can be revealing. For example, suppose I'm constructing a test on assessment, and I have four major topics. These topics can be listed, as illustrated in Figure 3.5, with different types of learning targets to get an overall view of what is being emphasized. In this case, I have only 12% of the test related to what could arguably be the most important concepts, validity and reliability. Seventy-five percent of the test contains items that measure knowledge and application, so this looks like a test that is getting, for the most part, at comprehension and simple understanding. If there was encouragement to test at higher levels of cognition, I'd need to change the items so that a higher percentages are in the deep understanding and evaluate categories.

I want to emphasize that the goal of a blueprint is to systematize your professional judgment so that you can improve the validity of the assessment. As illustrated in Table 3.2, your judgment is used to determine what types of learning targets will be assessed, what areas of the content will be sampled, and how the assessment measures both content and type of learning. At this point, you are making decisions about the importance of different types of targets, the content assessed, and how much of the assessment is measuring each target and area of content. If the assessment does, in fact, reflect an actual or modified table of specifications, then there is content-related evidence of validity.

FIGURE 3.5 **Table of Specifications for a Test on Assessment**

Major Content Areas	Knowledge	Application	Deep Understanding	Evaluate	Totals
Validity	4/(12%)	2/(6%)	2/(6%)	0	8/(24%)
Reliability	2/(6%)	1/(3%)	1/(3%)	0	4/(12%)
Fairness	6/(18%)	2/(6%)	2/(6%)	2/(6%)	12/(35%)
Practicality	2/(6%)	6/(18%)	2/(6%)	0	10/(29%)
Totals	14/(41%)	11/(32%)	7/(21%)	2/(6%)	34/(100%)

(Header spanning: **Types Learning Targets**)

TABLE 3.2 Professional Judgments in Establishing Content-Related Evidence for Validity

Learning Targets	Content	Instruction	Assessment
What learning targets will be assessed? How much of the assessment will be done on each target area?	What content is most important? What topics will be assessed? How much of the assessment will be done in each topic?	What content and learning targets have been emphasized in instruction?	Are assessments adequate samples of students' performance in each topic area and each target?

Another consideration related to this type of evidence is the extent to which an assessment can be said to have *instructional* validity. **Instructional validity** is concerned with the match between what is taught and what is assessed. How closely does the test correspond to what has been covered in class and in assignments? Have students had the opportunity to learn what has been assessed? Again, *your* professional judgment is needed to ensure that what is assessed is consistent with what was taught. One way to check this is to examine the table of specifications after teaching a unit to determine whether the emphasis in different areas or on different targets is consistent with what was emphasized in class.

Criterion-Related Evidence.   Another way to ensure appropriate inferences from assessments is to have evidence that a particular assessment is providing the same result as another assessment of the same thing. **Criterion-related evidence** provides such validity by relating an assessment to some other valued measure (criterion) that either provides an estimate of current performance (concurrent criterion-related evidence) or predicts future performance (predictive criterion-related evidence). Test developers and researchers use this approach to establish evidence that a test or other instrument is measuring the same trait, knowledge, or attitude by calculating a correlation coefficient to measure the relationship between the assessment and the criterion (see Chapter 14 for a discussion of correlation).

Classroom teachers do not conduct formal studies to obtain correlation coefficients that will provide evidence of validity, but the *principle* is very important for teachers to employ. The principle is that when you have two or more measures of the same thing, and these measures provide similar results, then you have established, albeit informally, criterion-related evidence. For example, if your assessment of a student's skill in using a microscope through observation coincides with the student's score on a quiz that tests steps in using microscopes, then you have criterion-related evidence that your inference about the skill of this student is valid. Similarly, if you are interested in the extent to which preparation by your students, as indicated by scores on a final exam in mathematics, predicts how well they will do next year, you can examine the grades of previous students and determine informally if students who scored high on your final exam are getting high grades and students who scored low on your final are obtaining low grades. If a

FIGURE 3.6   Criterion-Related Evidence for the Validity of Classroom Assessments

Source of Evidence	Jack	Jim	Jon
Teacher observation	A-	C+	B+
Quiz	90%	77%	84%
Student self-assessment	Advanced	Proficient	Proficient
Overall Grade	A-	C	B

correlation is found, then an inference about predicting how your students will perform, based on their final exam, is valid. Based on this logic, an important principle is to conduct several assessments of the learning targets; try not to rely on a single assessment.

Figure 3.6 shows how different assessments suggest consistency of evaluations for each of the students.

An excellent illustration of the need to give a variety of assessments is voiced in the following Teacher's Corner. Note how Carole uses different methods of instruction. She also matches targets with methods of assessment and stresses the importance of using a variety of assessment tools.

Construct-Related Evidence.   Psychologists refer to a *construct* as an unobservable trait or characteristic that a person possesses, such as intelligence, reading comprehension, honesty, self-concept, attitude, reasoning ability, learning style, and anxiety. These characteristics are not measured directly, in contrast to performance

Teacher's Corner

Carole Fokey

National Board Certified Secondary Science Teacher

I believe that the essential elements that would make an assessment high quality are varied. Consistency and fairness in questioning is key to ensure student success. In designing assessment questions, I ask myself, will learning be achieved? I include a combination of basic knowledge questions, comprehension, application, and synthesis-level questions. In addition, the use of a variety of assessment tools is important, including paper/pencil assessments as well as lab assignments.

such as spelling or how many push-ups a person successfully completes. Rather, the characteristic is *constructed* to account for behavior that can be observed. Whenever constructs are assessed, the validity of our interpretations depends on the extent of the **construct-related evidence** that is presented. This evidence can take many forms, any one of which is probably insufficient by itself.

The three types of construct-related evidence are theoretical, logical, and statistical. One important type of evidence derives from a clear theoretical explanation or definition of the characteristic so that its meaning is clear and not confused with any other construct. For example, suppose you want to assess students' attitudes toward reading. What is your definition of *attitude*? Do you mean how much students *enjoy* reading, *value* reading, or *read* in their spare time? Are you interested in their *desire* to read or their perception of *ability* to read? None of these traits is necessarily correct as a measure of attitude, but you need to provide a clear definition that separates your construct from other similar, but different constructs.

Logical analyses can be one or more of several types. For some reasoning constructs, you can ask students to comment on what they were thinking when they answered the questions. Ideally their thinking reveals an intended reasoning process. Another logical type of evidence comes from comparing the scores of groups who, as determined by other criteria, should respond differently. These groups can be taught students compared to untaught students, before being taught and after being taught groups, age groups, or groups that have been identified by other means to be different on the construct.

Statistical procedures can be used to correlate scores from measures of the construct with scores from other measures of the same construct and measures of similar, but different constructs. For example, self-concept of academic ability scores from one survey should be related to another measure of the same thing but less related to measures of self-concept of physical ability. These statistical approaches are used for many standardized, published surveys and questionnaires. For a teacher, however, it will be most practical to use clear definitions and logical analyses as construct-related evidence.

Figure 3.7 summarizes suggestions for enhancing the validity of classroom assessments.

Reliability

What Is a Reliable Score?

Like validity, the term *reliability* has been used for many years to describe an essential characteristic of sound assessment. **Reliability** is concerned with the consistency, stability, and dependability of the scores. Suppose Mrs. Hambrick is assessing her students' addition and subtraction skills. She decides to give the

FIGURE 3.7   Suggestions for Enhancing Validity

- Ask others to judge the clarity of what you are assessing.
- Check to see if different ways of assessing the same thing give the same result.
- Sample a sufficient number of examples of what is being assessed.
- Prepare a detailed table of specifications.
- Ask others to judge the match between the assessment items and the objective of the assessment.
- Compare groups known to differ on what is being assessed.
- Compare scores taken before to those taken after instruction.
- Compare predicted consequences to actual consequences.
- Compare scores on similar, but different traits.
- Provide adequate time to complete the assessment.
- Ensure appropriate vocabulary, sentence structure, and item difficulty.
- Ask easy questions first.
- Use different methods to assess the same thing.
- Use *only* for intended purposes.

Case Study for Reflection

Ms. Pollard teaches middle school mathematics. In a typical week she gives several mini-quizzes for quick assessments of student understanding and an end-of-week test. She also has a weekly problem-solving question. Homework is checked, and she also collects a great deal of anecdotal evidence focused on student effort and achievement in their daily work. Although Ms. Pollard is an experienced teacher, she wasn't sure how she should respond to her principal when asked about the "validity" of her classroom assessments.

QUESTIONS FOR CONSIDERATION

1. From the information she collects, what kind of validity evidence should she say she has obtained?
2. How should Ms. Pollard respond to the principal's query?
3. What possible pitfalls should she avoid so that her inferences about student learning will be valid?

students a 20-point quiz to determine their skills. Mrs. Hambrick examines the results but wants to be sure about the level of performance before designing appropriate instruction, so she gives another quiz 2 days later on the same addition and subtraction skills. The results for some of her students are as follows:

Student	Addition		Subtraction	
	Quiz 1	Quiz 2	Quiz 1	Quiz 2
Rob	18	16	13	20
Carrie	10	12	18	10
Ryann	9	8	8	14
Felix	16	15	17	12

The addition quiz scores are fairly consistent. All four students scored within one or two points on the quizzes; students who scored high on the first quiz also scored high on the second quiz, and students who scored low did so on both quizzes. Consequently, the results for addition are reliable. For subtraction, on the other hand, there is considerable change in performance from the first to the second quiz. Students scoring high on the first quiz score low on the second one, and students scoring low on the first quiz score high on the second. For subtraction, then, the results are unreliable because they are not consistent. The scores contradict one another.

So what does Mrs. Hambrick make of the mathematics scores? Her goal is to use the quiz to accurately determine the defined skill. She cannot know the *exact* level of the skills, but, as in the case of addition, she can get a fairly accurate picture with an assessment that is reliable. For subtraction, on the other hand, she cannot use these results alone to estimate the students' real or actual skill. More assessments are needed before she can be confident that the scores are reliable and thus provide a dependable result. But even the scores in addition are not without some degree of error. In fact, *all* assessments have error; they are never perfect measures of the trait or skill. Let's look at another example to illustrate this point.

Think about the difference between a measure of attitude toward science and time required to run a mile. The measure of attitude will have a relatively high degree of error, but the measure of time will be precise, with little error (highly reliable). This is because there are many more influences on how students answer questions about their attitudes (such as the student's mood that day, the heat in the room, poorly worded items, and fatigue) than there are on a timekeeper's ability to press the stopwatch and read the time elapsed. This is not to say that the measure of time is without any error. It's just that measuring time will have much less error than measuring attitudes.

Assessment Error

The concept of error in assessment is critical to our understanding of reliability. Conceptually, whenever we assess something, we get an *observed* score or result. This observed score is a product of what the *true* or *real* ability or skill is *plus* some degree of *error:*

Observed Score = True Score + Error

Reliability is directly related to error. It is not a matter of all or none, as if some results are reliable and others unreliable. Rather, for each assessment there is some *degree* of error. Thus, we think in terms of low, moderate, or high reliability. It is important to remember that the error can be positive or negative. That is, the observed score can be higher or lower than the true score, depending on the nature of the error. Sometimes you will know when a student's score is lower than it should be based on the behavior of the student at the time of the assessment. For example, if the student was sick, tired, in a bad mood, or distracted, the score may have negative error and underestimate the true score.

Figure 3.8 shows how different sources of error influence assessment results. Notice how reliability is influenced by factors within the student (internal sources of error), such as mood and physical condition, as well as external factors, such as the quality of the test, scoring errors, and test directions. The actual or true knowledge, reasoning, skill, or affect is captured to some extent by the assessment, but the internal and external sources of error also contribute to the score. In the end, you get an observed score that is made up of the actual or true performance plus some degree of error.

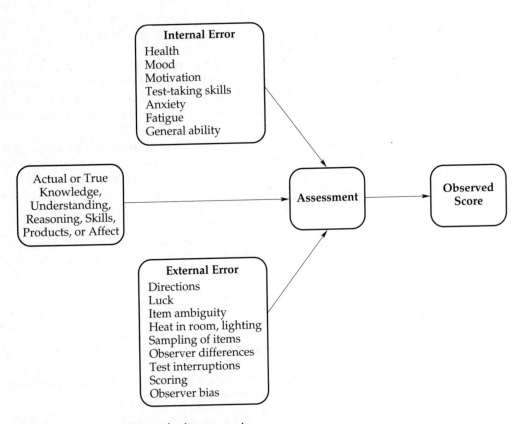

FIGURE 3.8   Sources of Error in Assessment

An important practical implication of knowing about error in testing is that small differences between scores of different students should be treated as if they were the same. Typically, your interpretation of a score of 75 should be the same as your interpretation of a score of 77. These observed scores are so close that, when we consider error that can be positive or negative, the true scores of the students should be considered equal (e.g., 75, plus or minus 3, or 77, plus or minus 3).

How Is Reliability Determined?

Reliability is determined by estimating the influence of various sources of error. If there is little error, then the reliability is high. If there is much error, the reliability is low. How, then, is this "amount of error" estimated? In large-scale and standardized testing, estimating error is done statistically with correlation procedures that produce reliability coefficients. These coefficients are then used to estimate the precise amount of random error that should be used in interpreting the results. This index is called the **standard error of measurement (SEM)**. It will be discussed in further detail in Chapter 14. In classroom assessment, there is rarely any statistical estimate of reliability (although software programs make this very easy for objective tests). Rather, in the classroom, reliability is determined by noting some sources of error, such as those in Figure 3.6, by using logic associated with different measures of the same thing and by observing the consistency with which students answer questions on the same topic. For example, if Ms. Lopez knows that Susan is distracted by a family problem and has difficulty concentrating, a reasonable conclusion is that a low score is being influenced by this problem. In other words, there is considerable error in Susan's observed performance. If it seems like different students score highest on different measures of the same skill, this lack of consistency points to low reliability. If one subgroup of students always scores well each time a quiz is given, whereas another subgroup always scores low, this consistency is logical evidence of good reliability.

Sources of Reliability Evidence

Like validity, making good judgments about reliability is based on using one or more sources of evidence to justify score interpretations. We will consider the five most common types of reliability evidence (summarized in Table 3.3).

Evidence Based on Stability.   A stability estimate of reliability refers to consistency over time. It is produced by administering an assessment to a group of individuals, waiting for a specified amount of time (typically a week or more), and then readministering the same assessment to the same group of individuals. A correlation between the two sets of scores is calculated as an indicator or reliability. This type of estimate is also called **test-retest** reliability.

Evidence Based on Equivalent Forms.   An estimate of equivalence is obtained by administering two forms of the same assessment to a group of students and correlating the scores. In classroom assessment, teachers rarely use equivalence evidence because it would be too time-consuming to make and administer two

TABLE 3.3   Sources of Evidence in Estimating Reliability

Source of Evidence	Description
Stability	Scores from two administrations of the same assessment to the same group of individuals with a time interval between the assessments
Equivalence	Two forms of the same assessment given at about the same time
Internal Consistency	A single administration of the assessment
Scorer or Rater Consistency	Agreement between two or more scorers or raters on the same performances
Decision Consistency	Percentage of decisions that are the same

similar assessments of the same thing. But, again from a logical standpoint, the *idea* of equivalence is relevant if students are offered makeup tests or if teachers want to use a pretest-posttest design to conduct action research.

Equivalent forms evidence is used extensively in standardized testing and high-stakes testing because several forms of the same test are needed to allow retakes and makeup testing. These estimates are statistical, reported as reliability coefficients.

Evidence Based on Internal Consistency. Internal consistency evidence is based on the degree of homogeneity of the scores on items measuring the same trait.[1] Only a single form of the assessment is needed for this kind of evidence. This approach assumes that the scores of items measuring the same trait should give consistent results. Suppose a teacher has a 20-item test on the parts of a flower. If students who truly master this knowledge get all or almost all the items correct, whereas students who knew nothing about flowers got all or almost all the items wrong, then there would be internal consistency. In other words, are the items functioning together in a consistent manner?

From a practical standpoint, internal consistency evidence is relatively easy to obtain. There is no need to develop a second form, nor is it necessary to give the assessment more than once. There are some limitations, however. First, there needs to be a sufficient number of items. One rule of thumb is that five items are needed to measure a single trait or skill. Second, internal consistency is not appropriate for tests with a time limit (called "speeded" tests). Third, it is somewhat limiting if all you know is that students answer consistently *at one time*. Typically, teachers need to make inferences about student knowledge over time. After all, we want students to remember what they have learned, and we want them to retain skills over time. That is a more complete and accurate indication of student learning than what can be demonstrated within only a short time frame. This is consistent with using quizzes during a unit and then a larger, more comprehensive assessment at the end of the unit.

Teacher's Corner

Elizabeth O'Brien

National Board Certified Secondary mathematics teacher

In determining if classroom assessments are high quality, I take several factors into consideration. First, I work collaboratively with the other teachers in my department who teach the same subjects that I do. By working together we are able to check each other and offer suggestions and feedback on questions that each of us creates. Second, I look at each of the objectives that I have taught and match questions accordingly.

Not only do I make sure that each objective has been assessed, but I also make sure that it has been assessed at several different levels of difficulty. For example, I want to ensure that students not only recall material but also can apply it and even evaluate others' work in some situations. Finally, over time I have determined that some questions are unfair and not suitable based on students' responses.

Evidence Based on Scorer or Rater Consistency. Whenever student responses need to be judged, rated, or scored, such as when teachers grade essays, writing samples, performance assessments, and portfolios, error can be contributed because of characteristics of the person doing the evaluation (e.g., halo effect, biases, fatigue, expectations, other idiosyncrasies). To take account of this kind of error, evidence can be gathered concerning the extent to which two or more raters agree in their evaluations. For example, if two teachers score 20 student essays and give 15 of them the same score, then the percentage of agreement, 75%, indicates rater consistency. It is also possible to use correlations between two raters. Scorer or rater evidence is best when there is good variation of products to be judged, when the criteria for scoring are clear, and when there is training for the scorers or raters.

Evidence Based on Decision Consistency. A final kind of evidence is particularly important in making judgments about whether students are "proficient" or whether they "pass." These kinds of decisions or classifications are used as the basis for reliability, rather than the scores themselves. Consistency is estimated as the percentage of same classifications on two or more administrations of the same test. For example, suppose a group of 20 students takes the same "minimum competency" test twice. On the first testing, 10 students were judged "competent" and 10 students were judged to be "not competent." On the second testing all "competent" students were again classified as "competent," but only 8 of 10 "not competent" students were judged that way. Thus, of the 20 classifications, 18 matched, which can be converted to a percentage—90% in this example. This approach can also be used in conjunction with rater consistency. Of the total number of decisions made, what percentage were the same?

FIGURE 3.9 **Suggestions for Enhancing Reliability**

- Use a sufficient number of items or tasks. (Other things being equal, longer tests are more reliable.)
- Use independent raters or observers who provide similar scores to the same performances.
- Construct items and tasks that clearly differentiate students on what is being assessed.
- Make sure the assessment procedures and scoring are as objective as possible.
- Continue assessment until results are consistent.
- Eliminate or reduce the influence of extraneous events or factors.
- Use shorter assessments more frequently than fewer long assessments.

Factors Influencing Reliability Estimates

Although a number of different sources of error will contribute to estimates of reliability, a few factors that affect results should be kept in mind. One important factor is the number of items in the assessment. The greater the number of items, the greater the reliability. The number of students also makes a difference—the higher the number of students, the stronger the reliability. Difficulty of items also affects reliability. The best reliability coefficients are obtained when items are not too easy or too hard. Items that are carefully constructed will improve reliability. Poorly worded or unclear items lead to poor reliability. The more objective the scoring, the greater the reliability. Typically, multiple-choice tests obtain better estimates of reliability than do constructed-response, performance, or portfolio assessments.

Figure 3.9, summarizes suggestions for developing and implementing highly reliable classroom assessments. The degree of reliability needed is dependent on the type of decision that will be made on the basis of the results. Higher reliability is needed when the decision has important, lasting consequences for individual students (e.g., placement to receive special education services). When the decision is about groups and is less important, the reliability does not need to be as high (e.g., whether to repeat a part of a unit of instruction).

Fairness

A *fair* assessment is one that provides all students an equal opportunity to demonstrate achievement and yields scores that are comparably valid from one person or group to another (Heubert & Hauser, 1999). We want to allow students to show us what they have learned from instruction. If some students have an advantage over others because of factors unrelated to what is being taught, then the assessment is not fair. Fair assessments are *unbiased* and *nondiscriminatory*, uninfluenced by irrelevant or subjective factors. That is, neither the assessment task nor scoring is differentially affected by race, gender, ethnic background, handicapping condition,

FIGURE 3.10   **Key Components of Fairness**

- Student knowledge of learning targets and assessments
- Opportunity to learn
- Prerequisiste knowledge and skills
- Avoiding student stereotyping
- Avoiding bias in assessment tasks and procedures
- Accommodating special needs and English Language Learners

or other factors unrelated to what is being assessed. Fairness is also evident in what students are told about the assessment and whether students have had the opportunity to learn what is being assessed. The following criteria, summarized in Figure 3.10, represent potential influences that determine whether an assessment is fair.

Student Knowledge of Learning Targets and Assessments

How often have you taken a test and thought, "Had I only known the teacher was going to test *this* content, I would have studied it!"? A fair assessment is one in which it is clear what will and will not be tested. Your objective is not to fool or trick students or to outguess them on the assessment. Rather, you need to be very clear and specific about the learning target—what is to be assessed and how it will be scored. And this is very important: Both the content of the assessment and the scoring criteria should be *transparent*. Being transparent means that students know the content and scoring criteria before the assessment and often before instruction. When students know what will be assessed, they know what to study and focus on. By knowing the scoring criteria, students understand much better the qualitative differences the teacher is looking for in student performance. One way to help students understand the assessment is to give them the assessment blueprint, sample questions, and examples of work completed by previous students and graded by the teacher.

When students know the learning targets and scoring criteria in advance, it is likely that they will be more intrinsically motivated and involved to obtain true mastery, rather than mere performance. It helps to establish a *learning* goal orientation for students, in which the focus is on mastering a task, developing new skills, and improving competence and understanding. In contrast, when a *performance* goal orientation is established, in which students perform to get a grade, recognition, or reward, motivation is extrinsic and less intense, and students are not as engaged or involved.

Opportunity to Learn

Opportunity to learn is concerned with sufficiency or quality of the time, resources, and conditions needed by students to demonstrate their achievement. It concerns the adequacy of instructional approaches and materials that are aligned with the assessment. Fair assessments are aligned with instruction that provides adequate time and opportunities for all students to learn. This is more than simply telling students, for example, that a test will cover certain chapters. Ample instructional time and resources are needed so that students are not penalized because of a lack of opportunity.

Prerequisite Knowledge and Skills

It is unfair to assess students on things that require prerequisite knowledge or skills that they do not possess. This means that you need to have a good understanding of prerequisites that your students demonstrate. It also means that you need to examine your assessments carefully to know what prerequisites are required. For example, suppose you want to test math reasoning skills. Your questions are based on short paragraphs that provide needed information. In this situation, math reasoning skills can be demonstrated only if students can read and understand the paragraphs. Thus, reading skills are prerequisites. If students do poorly on the assessment, their performance may have more to do with a lack of reading skills than with math reasoning.

Avoiding Student Stereotyping

Stereotypes are judgments about how groups of people will behave based on characteristics such as gender, race, socioeconomic status, physical appearance, and other characteristics. It is your responsibility to judge each student on his or her performance on assessment tasks, not on how others who share characteristics of the student perform. Although you should not exclude personal feelings and intuitions about a student, it is important to separate these feelings from performance. It is difficult to avoid stereotypes completely because of our values, beliefs, preferences, and experiences with different kinds of people. However, we *can* control the influence of these prejudices.

Stereotypes can be based on groups of people, such as "jocks have less motivation to do well," "boys do better in math," "students from a particular neighborhood are more likely to be discipline problems," and "children with a single parent need extra help with homework." You can also label students with words such as *shy, gifted, smart, poor, learning disabled, leader,* and *at-risk.* These labels can affect your interactions and evaluations by establishing inappropriate expectations. The nature of teacher expectations is discussed in greater detail in the next chapter.

Avoiding Bias in Assessment Tasks and Procedures

Another source of bias can be found in the nature of the actual assessment task—the contents and process of the test, project, problem, or other task. Bias is present if the assessment distorts performance because of the student's ethnicity, gender, race, religious background, and so on. Popham (2008a) has identified two major forms of assessment bias: offensiveness and unfair penalization.

Offensiveness occurs if the content of the assessment offends, upsets, distresses, angers, or otherwise creates negative affect for particular students or a subgroup of students. This negative affect makes it less likely that the students will perform as well as they otherwise might, lowering the validity of the inferences. Offensiveness occurs most often when stereotypes of particular groups are present in the assessment. Suppose a test question portrayed a minority group in low-paying, low-status jobs and white groups in high-paying, high-status jobs. Students who are members of the minority group may understandably be offended by the question, mitigating their performance. Here is an example of a biased mathematics test question that may result in offensiveness:

> Juan Mendez gathers lettuce for his income. He receives 15 cents for every head of lettuce he picks. Juan picked 270 heads of lettuce on Tuesday. How much money did he make?

Unfair penalization is bias that disadvantages a student because of content that makes it more difficult for students from some groups to perform as compared to students from other groups because of gender, socioeconomic status, race, language, or other characteristic. Suppose you take an aptitude test that uses rural, farm-oriented examples. The questions deal with types of cows and pigs, winter wheat, and farm equipment. If you grew up in a suburban community, do you think you will score as well as students who grew up on a farm? Do test items containing sports content unfairly advantage boys? Here is a reading comprehension test question that is biased with unfair penalization:

> Write a persuasive essay about the advantages of sailing as recreation. Include in your essay comparisons of sailing with other types of recreation such as hiking, swimming, and bowling.

Teachers don't *deliberately* produce biased assessments. It is most often unconscious and unintended. For these reasons, bias can be minimized by having others review your assessments, looking specifically for the types of bias presented here and, of course, by your own sensitivity to bias when creating the assessments. It should be noted that assessment tasks are not necessarily biased solely on the basis of differential performance by minority groups or other groups students may be members of. For example, just because Asian Americans score higher on the SAT than Native or African Americans does not mean that the SAT is biased to give an unfair advantage to Asian Americans.

Cultural differences that are reflected in vocabulary, prior experiences, skills, and values may influence the assessment. These differences are especially important in our increasingly diverse society and classrooms. Consider the following examples of how cultural background influences assessment:

- Knowledge from the immediate environment of the student (e.g., large city, ethnic neighborhood, rural, coastal) provides a vocabulary and an indication of the importance or relevance of assessment tasks.

- Depending on the culture, rules for sharing beliefs, discussion, taking turns, and expressing opinions differ.
- Respect and politeness may be expressed differently by students from different backgrounds (e.g., not looking into another's eyes, silence, squinting as a way to say no, looking up or down when asked a question).
- Learning style differences—which are exhibited in preferences for learning alone or in a group, for learning by listening or reading, for reflective or impulsive responses, and in the ability to think analytically or globally—influence a student's confidence and motivation to complete assessment tasks.

The influence of these differences will be minimized to the extent that you first understand them and then utilize multiple assessments that will allow all students to demonstrate their progress toward the learning target. If an assessment technique or approach advantages one type of student, another technique may be a disadvantage to that type of student. By using different types of assessments, one provides a balance to the other. Students who are unable to respond well to one type of assessment will respond well to another type. This reinforces the admonition that you should *never rely solely on one method of assessment*. This does not mean, however, that you should arbitrarily pick different methods. You need to select your assessments on the basis of what will provide the fairest indication of student achievement for *all* your students.

Accommodating Special Needs and English Language Learners

Another type of assessment task bias that has received a lot of attention recently is the need to accommodate the special abilities of exceptional children. An assessment is biased if performance is affected by a disability or other limiting characteristic when the student actually possesses the knowledge or skill being measured. In other words, when assessing exceptional students, you need to modify the assessment task so that the disabling trait is not a factor in the performance. For example, students with hearing loss may need written directions to complete an assessment that you give orally to other students.

With the increasing number of students with different languages teachers need to be aware of how these ELL students (English language learners) may make it difficult to obtain fair assessments. Teachers should consult with appropriate ELL specialists to ensure fair assessment. More about special needs and ELL students in Chapter 12.

A Model of Fairness in Classroom Assessment

In Figure 3.11 a model of fairness in classroom assessment is illustrated (McMillan & Tierney, 2009). The model captures important aspects of fairness, organized by the sequence of steps teachers take in their instruction and assessment. At each step

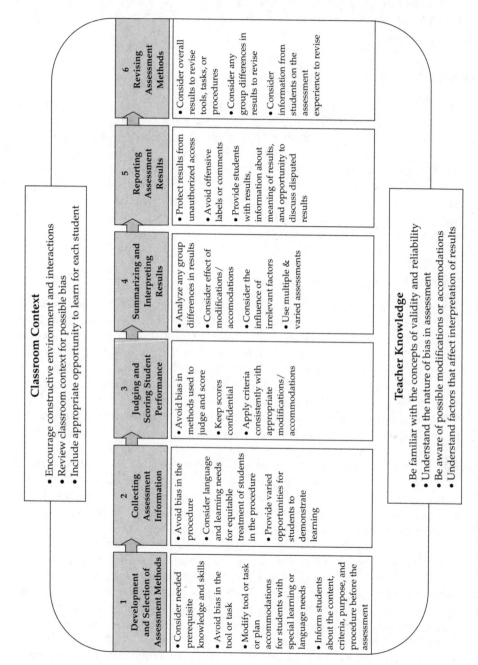

FIGURE 3.11 Model of Fairness in Classroom Assessment

Classroom Context

- Encourage constructive environment and interactions
- Review classroom context for possible bias
- Include appropriate opportunity to learn for each student

1 Development and Selection of Assessment Methods

- Consider needed prerequisite knowledge and skills
- Avoid bias in the tool or task
- Modify tool or task or plan accommodations for students with special learning or language needs
- Inform students about the content, criteria, purpose, and procedure before the assessment

2 Collecting Assessment Information

- Avoid bias in the procedure
- Consider language and learning needs for equitable treatment of students in the procedure
- Provide varied opportunities for students to demonstrate learning

3 Judging and Scoring Student Performance

- Avoid bias in methods used to judge and score
- Keep scores confidential
- Apply criteria consistently with appropriate modifications/ accommodations

4 Summarizing and Interpreting Results

- Analyze any group differences in results
- Consider effect of modifications/ accomodations
- Consider the influence of irrelevant factors
- Use multiple & varied assessments

5 Reporting Assessment Results

- Protect results from unauthorized access
- Avoid offensive labels or comments
- Provide students with results, information about meaning of results, and opportunity to discuss disputed results

6 Revising Assessment Methods

- Consider overall results to revise tools, tasks, or procedures
- Consider any group differences in results to revise
- Consider information from students on the assessment experience to revise

Teacher Knowledge

- Be familiar with the concepts of validity and reliability
- Understand the nature of bias in assessment
- Be aware of possible modifications or accomodations
- Understand factors that affect interpretation of results

there are factors teachers should consider, given the context and teacher understanding of fairness. Note the importance of confidentiality. This issue has become more important in recent years.

Positive Consequences

The nature of classroom assessments has important consequences for teaching and learning. Ask yourself these questions: How will the assessment affect student motivation? Will students be more or less likely to be meaningfully involved? Will their motivation be intrinsic or extrinsic? How will the assessment affect how and what students study? How will the assessment affect my teaching? How much time will the assessment take away from instruction? Will the results allow me to provide students with individualized feedback? What will the parents think about my assessments? High-quality assessments have consequences that will be positive for both students and yourself.

Positive Consequences for Students

The most direct consequence of assessment is that students learn and study in a way that is consistent with your assessment task. If the assessment is a multiple-choice test to determine the students' knowledge of specific facts, then students will tend to memorize information. If the assessment calls for extended essays, students tend to learn the material in larger, related chunks, and they practice recall rather than recognition when studying. Assessments that require problem solving, such as performance-based assessments, encourage students to think and apply what they learn. A positive consequence, in this sense, is the appropriate match between the learning target and the assessment task.

Assessments also have clear consequences on student motivation (McMillan & Hearn, 2008). Student motivation is best conceptualized in the context of student learning as a "process whereby goal-directed activity is instigated and sustained" (Pintrich & Schunk, 2002, p. 5). Defined in this way, motivation involves three key elements: goals, making a commitment to put forth effort to learn, and putting forth continued effort to succeed. Students are motivated when they believe that their effort will result in meaningful success. In relation to assessment, think about how these factors are influenced. Does the nature of learning targets determine whether success is meaningful? (yes!) Do the types of test items influence student effort in studying and trying to learn? (yes!) Does teacher feedback to students affect their conceptions of whether they can succeed? (yes!) Does the structure of the assessment determine whether students are able to show their best performance? (yes!) Table 3.4 shows the positive and negative effects of classroom assessment practices on motivation. Obviously we want positive motivational consequences. It is clear that the nature of the assessments affects this motivation. If students

TABLE 3.4 Motivational Consequences That Result from Different Assessment Practices

Motivation *Decreased* by Assessments That:	Motivation *Increased* by Assessments That:
Are irrelevant to students' lives	Are relevant to students' lives
Are summative	Are designed around student interests
Are closed-ended	Are open-ended
Use feedback to manage students	Use immediate and specific feedback
Disclose or display student performance publicly	Are aligned with learning goals set by students
Emphasize quantity rather than quality	Show how mistakes are essential to learning
Compare students to each other	Use learning goals that incorporate specific performance standards
Are artificial and abstract	Are meaningful and authentic
Use tasks that only some students can be successful with	Use tasks that are challenging but attainable
Use long-term goals	Use short-term goals
Provide little and/or inaccurate attributional feedback (why they succeeded or failed)	Provide credible attributional feedback
Emphasize end products	Emphasize progress
	Include student self-assessment

know what will be assessed and how it will be scored, and if they believe that the assessment will be fair, they are likely to be more motivated to learn.

Motivation also increases when the assessment tasks are relevant to the students' backgrounds and goals, challenging but possible, and structured to give students individualized feedback about their performance. What good is a high score on an easy test? Authentic assessments provide more active learning, which increases motivation. Giving students multiple assessments, rather than a single assessment, lessens fear and anxiety. When students are less apprehensive, risk taking, exploration, creativity, and questioning are enhanced.

Finally, the student–teacher relationship is influenced by the nature of assessment. When teachers construct assessments carefully and provide feedback to students, the relationship is strengthened. Conversely, if students have the impression that the assessment is sloppy, not matched with course objectives, designed to trick them (like some true/false questions we have all answered!), and provides little feedback, the relationship is weakened. How quickly do you return papers or tests to students? What types of comments do you write on papers or projects? Assessment affects the way students perceive the teacher and gives them an indication of how much the teacher cares about them and what they learn.

Positive Consequences for Teachers

Like students, teachers are affected by the nature of the assessments they give their students. Just as students learn depending on the assessment, teachers tend to teach to the test. Thus, if the assessment calls for memorization of facts, the teacher tends to teach lots of facts; if the assessment requires reasoning, then the teacher structures exercises and experiences that get students to think. The question, then, is how well your assessments promote and encourage the teaching you want and what you want your students to learn.

There is often a trade-off between instructional time and the time needed for assessment. If your assessments require considerable time for preparation, administration, and scoring, then there is less time for instruction.

Alignment

One of the most important influences of high-stakes testing is much greater emphasis on the "alignment" of standards, tests, curriculum, and instruction (National Research Council, 2001). **Alignment** is the degree of agreement among these different components. There is usually a concerted effort to align the state standards with the local curriculum. It makes sense, obviously, that what is taught is about the same as what is tested (instructional validity). But "degree of agreement" and "about the same" are a matter of professional judgment. Although such judgments can be made reliably, the process is far from standardized because there are different types or levels of alignment.

With high-stakes accountability tests with state standards, at least four different questions can be asked (American Educational Research Association [AERA], 2003, p. 3):

- Does the test's content match the content (topics and skills) in the standards?
- Do the tests and standards cover a comparable "range" or breadth of knowledge, and is there an appropriate "balance" of knowledge across the standards?
- Does the level of cognitive demand or challenge called for in the standards match that required for students to do well on the assessment?
- Does the test avoid adding material that is irrelevant to the standard supposedly being assessed?

The first two questions are concerned primarily with whether test items correspond to a standard and whether the number of items in different areas matches with the emphasis of different areas in the standards. Cognitive demand is a judgment about the nature of the mental skill required to answer the test item. For instance, does the item require knowledge or deep understanding? Is it primarily a function of recall or application? The cognitive level is determined by the standard; then the item is matched to that level. Of course, what is simple understanding to one teacher might be deep understanding to another teacher. That's the nature of professional judgment, so some level of agreement among your colleagues is desirable.

For the purpose of aligning your instruction and classroom assessments with state standards, it is critical to examine the standards and determine the nature of the cognitive skill demanded. It is also good to examine sample test items, if they are available, but the standard is the most important source of information. Once the cognitive skills embodied in the standard are identified, you can begin the process of judging alignment with your curriculum, instruction, and classroom assessments. The type of judgment you make is represented in Figure 3.12. This continuum shows that the more easily made judgment (*primitive*) is not nearly sufficient to inform you about what to teach, how much to teach, and how to assess each area. This is because the alignment is based on a cursory review of the standards and assessments as a whole. *Rough* alignment adds a systematic way of simply checking for the presence of each standard and matching assessment. *Good* alignment includes judgments about depth of knowledge and understanding. It also incorporates the item formats of state tests. Ratings would be more sophisticated and show the alignment by degree, rather than making a yes/no judgment.

The *refined* approach includes matching the cognitive demand (*depth*) with the standards, whether the *range* of what is covered in the standards is consistent with your instruction and assessment, and whether the degree of emphasis of different areas (*balance*) is appropriate. And, of course, you also need to have your classroom assessments align with your learning targets, theories of learning and motivation, instructional tasks given to students, assignments, questions asked, and criteria for scoring student work. Yes, this is a *lot* of alignment!

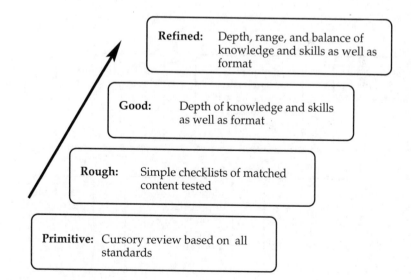

FIGURE 3.12 Types of Alignment Judgments

If you teach in a grade level and subject area that is assessed with a state accountability test, you will need to align, at a minimum, your coverage of content and classroom assessments with the state standards. Some districts have developed pacing guides that all teachers follow. These guides outline what is taught and for how long. It is also common for teachers to key classroom tests to the state standards. But doing so at the wrong cognitive level will not help students nearly as much as making sure that your teaching and assessments demand the right cognitive skills. Simply covering content as directed and matching classroom test items to content areas is comparatively superficial and often results in superficial coverage of many areas.

Figure 3.13 shows a series of steps that you can use to approach alignment in a systematic way. Because of the pervasiveness of state accountability tests, the first step is to understand the state standards and then combine them with local learning targets. It is helpful to use simple ratings at each step so that the alignment is clear and in a format that can be shared with others. The goal is to plan and implement instruction and classroom assessment that will document the attainment of important targets, including state standards, and provide feedback to promote instructional correctives needed for students to meet state standards.

One kind of alignment that teachers are increasingly asked to do is to make their classroom assessments like the high-stakes tests. For most states, this means using multiple-choice items for classroom assessments. There are two important issues with this. First, it is difficult to develop multiple-choice test items that measure advanced cognitive skills (more about this in Chapter 8). Second, there may be an ethical issue if your classroom assessments are practically the same as those on the state accountability tests. There is nothing wrong with using the same item format for both classroom and high-stakes tests; actually this is desirable. You want

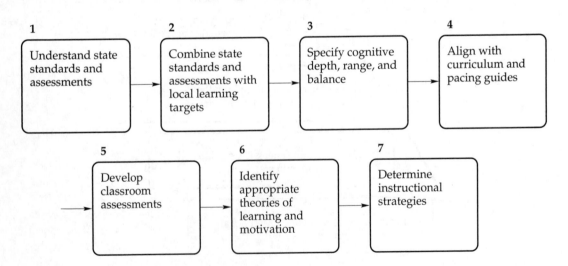

FIGURE 3.13   Steps in Achieving Alignment

students to be familiar with the format. But it is not appropriate to use classroom test items that essentially mimic items that are used in the high-stakes tests. This is closer to teaching the test, rather than teaching *to* the test. Also, remember that your ultimate goal is increasing student learning, not achieving high test scores. These two outcomes do not necessarily go hand in hand. It would be unethical to drill students to get high scores while simultaneously decreasing their learning, especially when many of your learning targets may not correspond to state standards.

Practicality and Efficiency

High-quality assessments are practical and efficient. It is important to balance these aspects of assessment with previously mentioned criteria. As I have already pointed out, time is a limited commodity for teachers. It may be best to use extensive performance assessments; but if these assessments take away too much from instruction, it may be better to think about less time-consuming assessments. Essentially, ask yourself this question: Is the information obtained worth the resources and time required to obtain it? Other factors to consider include your familiarity with the method of assessment, the time required of students to complete the assessments, the complexity of administering the assessments, the ease of scoring, the ease of interpretation, and cost. We'll consider each briefly.

Teacher Familiarity with the Method

Teachers need to know about the assessment methods they select. This includes knowledge of the strengths and limitations of the method, how to administer the assessment, how to score and properly interpret student responses, and the appropriateness of the method for given learning targets. Teachers who use assessment methods with which they are not familiar risk time and resources for questionable results.

Time Required

Other things being equal, it is desirable to use the shortest assessment possible that provides credible results. In other words, gather only as much information as you need for the decision or other use of the results. The time required should include how long it takes to construct the assessment, how much time is needed for students to provide answers, and how long it takes to score the results. The time needed for each of these aspects of assessment is different for each method of assessment. Multiple-choice tests take a long time to prepare but a relatively short time for students to complete and for teachers to score. Thus, if you plan to use this format over and over for different groups of students, it is efficient to put in considerable time preparing the assessment as long as you can use many of the same test items each semester or year (keep objective tests secure so you don't have to construct an entirely new test each time). Essay tests, on the other hand, take less time to prepare but take a long time to score. Performance assessments are probably most time intensive (in preparation, student response time, and scoring). For all types of assessments, reuse questions and tasks whenever possible.

Another consideration in deciding about time for assessment is reliability. The reliability of a test or other assessment is directly related to its length—the longer the test, the greater is its reliability. In general, assessments that take 30 or 40 minutes provide reliable results for a single score on a short unit. If separate scores are needed for subskills, more time may be needed. A general rule of thumb is that 6 to 10 objective items are needed to provide a reliable assessment of a concept or specific skill.

Complexity of Administration

Practical and efficient assessments are easy to administer. This means that the directions and procedures for administration are clear. Assessments that require long, complicated directions and setup, like some performance assessments, are less efficient and may, because of student misunderstanding, have adverse effects on reliability and validity.

Ease of Scoring

It is obvious that some methods of assessment, such as objective tests, are much easier to score than other methods, such as essays, papers, and oral presentations. Like other traits, scoring needs to match your method and purpose. In general, use the easiest method of scoring appropriate to the method and purpose of the assessment. Objective tests are easiest to score and contribute less scoring error to reliability. Scoring performance assessments, essays, papers, and the like is more difficult because more time is needed to ensure reliability. For these assessments, it is more practical to use rating scales and checklists rather than writing extended individualized evaluations.

Ease of Interpretation

Objective tests that report a single score are usually easiest to interpret, and individualized written comments are more difficult to interpret. Many subjectively evaluated products are given a score or grade to enhance ease of interpretation. It is necessary to provide sufficient information so that whatever interpretation is made is accurate. Often grades or scores are applied too quickly without enough thought and detailed feedback to students. This can be partially remedied by sharing a key with students and others that provides meaning to different scores or grades. Interpretation is easier if you are able to plan, before the assessment, how to use the results.

Cost

Because most classroom assessments are inexpensive, cost is relatively unimportant. It would certainly be unwise to use a more unreliable or invalid assessment just because it costs less. Some performance assessments are exceptions because the cost of materials can be an important factor. Like other practical aspects, it is best to use the most economical assessment, other things being equal. But economy should be thought of in the long run, and unreliable, less-expensive tests may eventually cost more in further assessment.

Summary

High-quality classroom assessments provide reliable, valid, fair, and useful measures of student performance. Quality is enhanced when the assessments meet these important criteria:

- It is best to match the method of assessment to learning targets. Knowledge and simple understanding targets are matched best with selected-response and brief constructed-response items, deep understanding and reasoning targets with essays, and affective targets with observation and student self-reports. Performance assessments are best for measuring deep understanding skills and products.
- Validity is the degree to which a score-based inference is appropriate, reasonable, and useful. Inferences are valid or invalid—not tests.
- Different types of evidence are used to establish the validity of classroom tests, the most important of which is content-related evidence.
- Whether face validity, a test blueprint, or instructional validity, the teacher's professional judgment is needed to ensure that there is adequate content-related evidence.
- Construct-related evidence is provided by theoretical, logical, and statistical analyses.
- Reliability is used to estimate the error in testing. It measures the degree of consistency when several items measure the same thing and stability when the same measures are given across time.
- Different sources of error should be taken into consideration when interpreting test results.
- Sources of evidence for obtaining reliable scores include stability, equivalence, internal consistency, scorer or rater consistency, and decision consistency.
- Reliability is improved with increases in the spread of scores, number of items, number and heterogeneity of students, and with items that are clear and have medium difficulties.
- Assessment is fair if it is unbiased and provides students with a reasonable opportunity to demonstrate what they have learned.
- Fairness is enhanced by student knowledge of learning targets before instruction, the opportunity to learn, the attainment of prerequisite knowledge and

skills, unbiased assessment tasks and procedures, teachers who avoid stereo-types, and accommodating special needs and English language learners.

- High-quality assessments are aligned with standards, learning targets, and instruction.
- Positive consequences for both teachers and students enhance the overall quality of assessment, particularly the effect of the assessments on student motivation and study habits. Assessments need to take into consideration the teacher's familiarity with the method, the time required, the complexity of administration, the ease of scoring and interpretation, and the cost to deter-mine the assessment's practicality and efficiency.

Self-Instructional Review Exercises

1. Should teachers be concerned about relatively technical features of assessments such as validity and reliability? Why or why not?

2. Match the description with the type of assessment.

   _____ **(1)** Based on verbal instructions

   _____ **(2)** Made up of questionnaires and surveys

   _____ **(3)** Selection or supply type

   _____ **(4)** Constructs unique response to demonstrate skill

   _____ **(5)** Either restricted- or extended-constructed response

   _____ **(6)** Used constantly by teachers informally

   a. Selected response

   b. Essay

   c. Performance

   d. Oral question

   e. Observation

   f. Self-assessment

3. For each of the following situations or questions, indicate which assessment method provides the best match (selected response, S; essay, E; performance, P; oral question, OR; observation, OB; and self-report, SR).

   a. Mrs. Keen needs to check students to see if they are able to draw graphs correctly like the example just demonstrated in class.
   b. Mr. Garcia wants to see if his students are comprehending the story before mov-ing to the next set of instructional activities.
   c. Ms. Powell wants to find out how many spelling words her students know.
   d. Ms. Tanner wants to see how well her students can compare and contrast the Vietnam War with World War II.
   e. Mr. Johnson's objective is to enhance his students' self-efficacy and attitudes toward school.
   f. Mr. Greene wants to know if his sailing clinic students can identify different parts of a sailboat.

4. Which of the following statements is correct, and why?

   a. Validity is impossible without strong reliability.
   b. A test can be reliable without validity.
   c. A valid test is reliable.

5. Mr. Nelson asks the other math teachers in his high school to review his midterm to see if the test items represent his learning targets. Which type of evidence for validity is being used?

   a. content-related
   b. criterion-related
   c. instructional
   d. construct-related

6. The students in the following lists are rank ordered, based on their performance on two tests of the same content (highest score at the top, next highest score second, etc.). Do the results suggest a reliable assessment? Why or why not?

Test A	Test B
Germaine	Ryann
Cynthia	Robert
Ryann	Steve
Steve	Germaine
Robert	Cynthia

7. Which aspect of fairness is illustrated in each of the following assessment situations?

   a. Students complained because they were not told what to study for the test.
   b. Students studied the wrong way for the test (e.g., they memorized content).
   c. The teacher was unable to cover the last unit that was on the test.
   d. The story students read, the one they would be tested on, was about life in the northeast during winter. Students who had been to that part of the country in winter showed better comprehension scores than students who had rarely even seen snow.
   e. Students complained that most of what was taught was not on the test.

8. Is the following test item biased? Why or why not?

   Ramon has decided to develop a family budget. He has $2,000 to work with and decides to put $1,000 into the mortgage, $300 into food, $200 into transportation, $300 into entertainment, $150 into utilities, and $50 into savings. What percent of Ramon's budget is being spent in each of the categories?

9. Why is it important for teachers to consider practicality and efficiency in selecting their assessments, as well as more technical aspects such as validity and reliability?

Answers to Self-Instructional Review Exercises

1. Yes, but not in the way psychometricians do with published, standardized tests. Validity and reliability are essential to fairness, proper interpretation of assessments, and teacher decision making. Both validity and reliability are best estimated by teacher judgment and logical analysis and not statistically, unless the statistics are easily provided.

2. (1) d, (2) f, (3) a, (4) c, (5) b, (6) e.

3. a. OB, b. OR, c. S, d. E, e. SR, f. S.

4. a. Yes; if the score is not consistent or stable, the inference will likewise not be consistent or stable and hence inaccurate and invalid. b. Yes; a measure of the circumference of your big toe is very reliable but not very valid for measuring your ability to read. c. No; tests are not valid or invalid, only inferences are.

5. a.

6. Not very reliable. Germaine scored highest on Test A but near the bottom on Test B; Robert scored at the bottom on Test A but near the top on Test B. A reliable assessment would result in nearly the same rank ordering for both tests.

7. a. Student knowledge of assessment. b. Student knowledge of assessment. c. Opportunity to learn. d. Biased content. e. Alignment.

8. Probably not. For bias to exist, it needs to be fairly obvious. In this example, a minority group name is used, but it would be unlikely to elicit negative affect from Hispanic members of the class. There is no content that is clearly biased.

9. Because the time you have is limited, and priorities need to be set so that you balance instruction with assessment.

Suggestions for Action Research

1. Interview a teacher and ask about the types of assessments he or she uses. See if there is a match between the assessment methods and targets consistent with Figure 3.2. Also ask about validity and reliability. How does the teacher define these concepts, and how are they determined informally, if at all, by the teacher? How does the teacher account for error in testing? Finally, ask about additional criteria for making assessments fair and unbiased. Does the teacher make it clear to students what they will be tested on? Do all students have the same opportunity to do well?

2. Prepare a table of specifications for a test of this chapter. Include all the major target areas. Compare your table with those of other students to see how similar you are with respect to what you believe is most important to assess. Also include examples of test items.

3. Ask a group of high, middle, or elementary school students, depending on your interest in teaching, about what they see as fair, high-quality assessment. Ask them to generate some qualities that they believe contribute to good assessments, and then ask them specifically about each of the criteria in the chapter. Also, ask them how different kinds of assessments affect them; for example, do they study differently for essay and multiple-choice tests?

Endnote

1. There are three common types of internal consistency estimates: split-half, Kuder-Richardson, and Coefficient Alpha. In the split-half method, the test items are divided into "equal" halves and each half is scored as a separate test. The two tests are then correlated. The Kuder-Richardson formulas (KR20 and KR21) are used for tests in which each item is scored dichotomously (e.g., right or wrong). You can think of KR approaches as the average of correlating the totals from all possible halves. This is the type of reliability that is calculated for teachers on most scoring software. The Coefficient Alpha is used when a scale has more than two possible responses, such as attitude surveys.

Formative Assessment I: Gathering Evidence

In this chapter and the next, we will examine formative assessment. Many claim it is the most important set of assessment activities for teachers to use, and many experts believe is an activity that can literally revolutionize your teaching. Popham (2008) uses the term *transformative assessment* to emphasize how full implementation

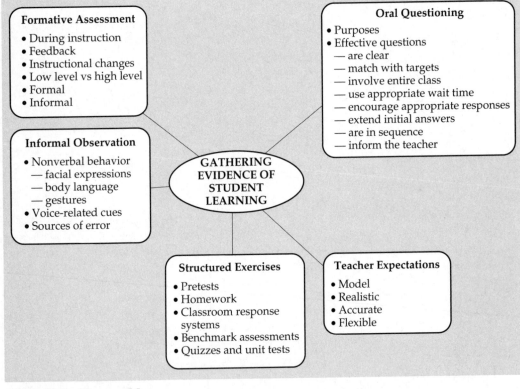

Formative Assessment

- During instruction
- Feedback
- Instructional changes
- Low level vs high level
- Formal
- Informal

Informal Observation

- Nonverbal behavior
  — facial expressions
  — body language
  — gestures
- Voice-related cues
- Sources of error

Oral Questioning

- Purposes
- Effective questions
  — are clear
  — match with targets
  — involve entire class
  — use appropriate wait time
  — encourage appropriate responses
  — extend initial answers
  — are in sequence
  — inform the teacher

GATHERING EVIDENCE OF STUDENT LEARNING

Structured Exercises

- Pretests
- Homework
- Classroom response systems
- Benchmark assessments
- Quizzes and unit tests

Teacher Expectations

- Model
- Realistic
- Accurate
- Flexible

CHAPTER 4   Concept Map

of formative assessment can "fundamentally transform [your] instructional approach" (p. viii). Research shows that formative assessment has a positive and substantial impact on student learning (Black & Wiliam, 1998, 2004; Brookhart, 2005, 2007). Because formative assessment is a ubiquitous buzzword in education, we need to take a close look at what it means and how it is different from other kinds of assessment. Then we will turn to how evidence of student understanding is gathered when the goal is to use assessment formatively.

What Is Formative Assessment?

Formative assessment is a package deal. It's not only a type of assessment with respect to how and when evidence of student learning is gathered, but it also consists of a number of components that work together to effect student motivation and achievement. A good starting definition is the following:

> Formative assessment involves the gathering of evidence of student learning, providing feedback to students, and adjusting instructional strategies to enhance achievement.

There is emphasis on the function that is served with formative assessment—the idea that evidence of student learning is "fed back" into students' and teachers' decision making about what and how to learn. In other words, assessment *forms* instruction (Wiliam & D. Leahy, 2007). It is a purposeful process in which the teacher is consciously and continuously absorbing evidence of student learning in relation to identified learning targets, and then using the information for teacher decision making, to give feedback to students, and to make instructional adjustments (Wiliam, 2010). The intent is to close the "gap" between what students need to know and their current level of knowledge by establishing a path to facilitate student learning (Furtak, 2009).

The goal of formative assessment is the *improvement of student motivation and learning*. To reach this goal, teachers must employ a circular, continuing process involving their evaluations of student work and behavior, feedback to students, and instructional adjustments, or what is sometimes called "correctives" (Figure 4.1). After teachers gather evidence of students' knowledge, understandings, and skills, that evidence is interpreted (evaluation), and appropriate specific feedback is provided. This feedback, which either supports and extends proper understandings, or targets deficiencies, is followed by instructional adjustments that will build on understandings to broaden and expand their learning or correct misconceptions (Guskey, 2010; Shepard, 2004). It is important that correctives contain new strategies and approaches and include a message that *making errors or being wrong is a part of learning*. It doesn't do too much good to simply repeat what was already an unsuccessful activity. Rather, correctives need to be qualitatively different from the initial teaching. Following student involvement with the correctives, additional evaluations of student learning are conducted, and the cycle is repeated.

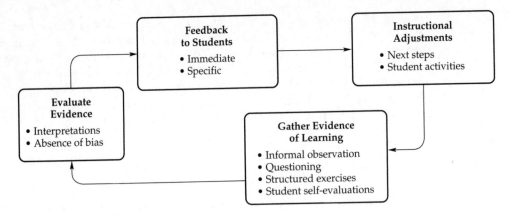

FIGURE 4.1   Formative Assessment Cycle

When students' judgments about what more is needed are used, the process is particularly helpful in motivating students (Brookhart, 2007; Harlen, 2003). Formative assessment techniques are judged by the extent to which they are embedded within instruction and promote learning. *Assessment without the use of instructional changes is not formative.*

Teachers have always had to determine how well students are doing. Formative assessment formalizes an approach to that role by providing a more organized structure in which their decisions about next steps (instructional adjustments) are based on carefully gathered and interpreted evidence. This process is consistent with cognitive theories that emphasize the importance of actively constructing meaning with what is learned. As students relate new ideas and knowledge to existing understandings, formative assessment helps them see the connections and clarify meaning in small, successive steps. As pointed out by Matese (2005), it is important for teachers to know how to create assessment opportunities to informally gather evidence of student learning.

Figure 4.1 lays out the four essential characteristics of formative assessment. In practice, more complexity is added, and variations of formative assessment may be used. It is as if there are different versions of formative assessment. Some versions may provide feedback on a "minute-by-minute" basis as instruction progresses, whereas other types may give feedback a day or two after a test.

Table 4.1 summarizes 11 possible characteristics of formative assessment and shows how each can be defined and put into practice. What is called formative assessment can differ with respect to which characteristics are emphasized. Some formative assessment might only include evidence of student learning and providing feedback, whereas other versions contain all 11 characteristics. For example, teachers may provide meaningful feedback with little emphasis on student self-evaluation or may provide feedback without instructional adjustments, but both could be called formative assessment.

These differences are reflected in the continuum that ranges from *low-level* to *high-level* (McMillan, 2010). *Low-level* formative assessment is rudimentary or

TABLE 4.1 Formative Assessment Characteristics[1]

Characteristic	*Low-Level* **Formative**	⟵ ⟶	*High-Level* **Formative**
Evidence of student learning	Mostly objective, standardized	Some standardized and some anecdotal	Varied assessment, including objective, constructed response, and anecdotal
Structure	Mostly formal, planned, anticipated	Informal, spontaneous, "at the moment"	Both formal and informal
Participants involved	Teachers	Students	Both teachers and students
Feedback	Mostly delayed (e.g., give a quiz and give students feedback the next day) and general	Some delayed and some immediate and specific	Immediate and specific
When done	Mostly after instruction and assessment (e.g., after a unit)	Some after and during instruction	Mostly during instruction
Instructional adjustments	Mostly prescriptive, planned (e.g., pacing according to an instructional plan)	Some prescriptive, some flexible, unplanned	Mostly flexible, unplanned
Choice of task	Mostly teacher determined	Some student determined	Teacher and student determined
Teacher–student interaction	Most interactions based primarily on formal roles	Some interactions based on formal roles	Extensive, informal, trusting, and honest interactions
Role of student self-evaluation	None	Tangential	Integral
Motivation	Extrinsic (e.g., passing a competency test)	Both intrinsic and extrinsic	Mostly intrinsic
Attributions for success	External factors (teacher; luck)	Internal stable factors (e.g., ability)	Internal, unstable factors (e.g., moderate student effort)

[1]Adapted from McMillan (2010).

primitive. The process could be as simple as students taking a test and receiving simple feedback. *High-level* formative assessment fully integrates ongoing gathering of evidence, feedback, and instructional adjustments and also includes additional characteristics that are often cited as important components. For example, within a supportive and trusting environment, high-level formative assessment may be implemented so that both teachers and students are invested in improved

TABLE 4.2   Characteristics of Informal and Formal Formative Assessment

	Informal	Formal
Nature of evidence	• Observation • Questioning	• Homework • Quizzes and tests • In-class assignments • Structured activities • Benchmark tests
Gathering of evidence	• Spontaneous • Ongoing • Close monitoring	• Planned • Follows instruction
Feedback	• Immediate	• Delayed
Instructional adjustments	• Immediate	• Delayed

achievement, or there may be an emphasis on developing student self-assessment, intrinsic mastery goal orientation, and independent learning.

Another way to conceptualize formative assessment is to think of two kinds—informal and formal (Ruiz-Primo & Furtak, 2007). *Informal* formative assessment is conducted in the context of day-to-day instruction. It occurs as learning takes place, continuously woven into instruction through teacher observation, questioning, and timely feedback. A distinguishing characteristic is that it is ongoing, constant. *Formal* formative assessment is a planned evaluation activity, such as a test, paper, or structured exercise, and results in delayed feedback and instructional correctives. Differences between informal and formal formative assessment are summarized in Table 4.2. We will focus first on informal formative assessment.

Gathering Informal Formative Assessment Evidence

A key element in the process of instruction is continuous monitoring by teachers to ascertain their students' reactions to instruction and students' progress toward understanding the content or accomplishing the skill. Carlson, Humphrey, and Reinhardt (2003) describe the process as *continuous assessment*. How is the flow of activities? How are students responding to the activities? Are they interested and attentive? Should I speed up or slow down? Should I give more examples? Here is where good assessment is essential to effective teaching and where assessment drives instruction. You need to know what to look for in your students while you deliver instruction, how to interpret what you see and hear, how to respond to the students, and then how to adjust your teaching. Strickland and Strickland (1998) point out that effective teachers are "always searching for patterns, supporting students as they take risks and move forward, and watching in order to better facilitate student learning . . . and try to understand how each student is progressing" (p. 31).

Informal formative assessment can occur at any time during the school day as a result of teacher–student and student–student interaction. It can involve individual students, small groups, or the entire class. Evidence is gathered constantly by the teacher during instruction and as students learn. The evidence can be verbal or nonverbal, and it has a spontaneous, "at-the-moment," or "real-time" character. With informal formative assessment, it is critical for the teacher to use diverse learning opportunities with a variety of tasks to provide evidence of student understanding, to closely monitor student behavior, and to provide immediate, specific feedback. The emphasis is on eliciting information from students that demonstrate their understanding, interpreting this information immediately, and providing feedback quickly (Ruiz-Primo & Furtak, 2007).

The mainstays of informal formative assessment are observations and questioning.

Informal Formative Assessment Observation

No assessment activity is more pervasive for teachers than the informal observation of student behavior. These observations are made to determine such factors as:

- The nature of student participation in class discussion
- The interpersonal skills used in cooperative groups
- The correctness of student responses to questions
- The verbal skills demonstrated in expressing thoughts
- Whether more examples are needed
- Which students to call on
- The interest level of the students
- The degree of understanding demonstrated in student answers

This list could go on and on. Informal observation is unstructured in the sense that there is no set format or procedure, but it is not random (Nilsen, 2008). For example, effective teachers learn to observe key students in each class who show their reactions more clearly than others. Some of these students are vocal and stand out, and others are quiet leaders.

We first consider the observation of nonverbal behavior, and then we will look at vocal cues such as pauses and tone of voice.

Assessing Nonverbal Behavior.   Teachers rely greatly on students' body language, facial expressions, and eye contact to accurately observe and interpret student behavior. These actions are called *nonverbal* because the message is communicated by something about the student other than the content of what he or she says. These nonverbal cues are often more important than what is said, largely because they are usually unintentional and uncontrollable (Mottet & Richmond, 2000). According to Mehrabian (1981), as much as 90% of the emotions conveyed in a message is communicated by nonverbal factors. Some of this is through general appearance and behavior such as body language, gestures, and facial expressions, and some is communicated by vocal cues that accompany what is said, such as tone of voice, inflection, pauses, and emphasis.

Nonverbal behaviors help you to assess both meaning and emotion. For instance, we rely on facial and bodily expressions to determine the intent of the message. Nonverbal cues punctuate verbal messages in much the same way that exclamation points, question marks, boldface, and italics focus the meaning of written language. Knapp and Hill (2010) suggest that this punctuation occurs in the following ways:

- *Confirming or Repeating.* When nonverbal behavior is consistent with what is said verbally, the message is confirmed or repeated. For instance, when Sally gave the correct answer to a question, her eyes lit up (facial expression), she sat up straight in her chair and her hand was stretched up toward the ceiling (body motion), and her answer was animated and loud (voice quality). She indicated nonverbally as well as verbally that she knew the answer.
- *Denying or Confusing.* Nonverbal and verbal messages are often contradictory, suggesting denial or confusion. For example, Ms. Thomas has just asked her class if they are prepared to begin their small-group work. The students say yes, but at the same time look down with confused expressions on their faces. The real message is that they are not ready, despite what they have said.
- *Strengthening or Emphasizing.* Nonverbal behavior can punctuate what is said by adding emotional color, feelings, and intensity. These emotions strengthen or emphasize the verbal message. Suppose Mr. Terrell suggested to Teresa that she take the lead in the next school play. Teresa responds by saying, "No, I wouldn't want to do that," while she shakes her head, avoids eye contact, and becomes rigid. Teresa doesn't just mean no, she means NO! If she really wanted to take the lead, her nonverbal behavior would deny her verbal response.
- *Controlling or Regulating.* Nonverbal behavior can be used to control others and regulate the nature of the interaction. In a cooperative learning group, you may observe that when Tom goes to ask David for some help, David controls the conversation by looking away.

Not only are nonverbal cues the richest source of information on affect, but they are also the most stable and consistent. Because most nonverbal behavior is not consciously controlled, the messages are relatively free of distortion and deception. It is not difficult, when you consciously attend to appropriate nonverbal behavior, to determine mood, mental state, attitude, self-assurance, responsiveness, confidence, interest, anger, fear, and other affective and emotional dispositions. This is especially helpful when the nonverbal message conflicts with the verbal one. That is, *how* students say something, through their nonverbal behavior, is as important, if not more so, than *what* they say. Think about a student who answers a question but does so with a slow, low voice, looking away. Even if the answer is correct, these nonverbal cues may tell you something important about

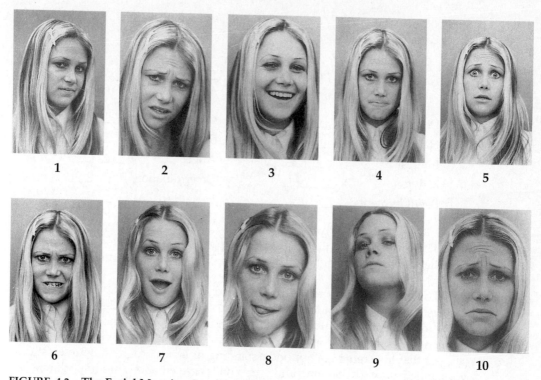

FIGURE 4.2   The Facial Meaning Sensitivity Test

Source: From *Successful Nonverbal Communication: Principles and Applications,* third edition by D. G. Leathers. Copyright © 1997. Published by Allyn & Bacon. Reprinted by permission of Nancy J. Leather.

the student's level of confidence. Your interpretation would be different for a student who looked directly at you, spoke with authority, and whose face displayed excitement. In this section we look at how specific nonverbal behaviors communicate different meanings and emotions and how teachers respond to these cues.

Facial Expressions.   The face is the most important source of nonverbal information because it is the primary outlet for emotions and it rarely distorts meaning (Hill, 2007). The face projects a great variety of messages, in part because of the complex and flexible set of muscles. To know what to look for it is best to focus on three areas: the brows and forehead; the eyes, lids, and nose; and the lower face. The upper portion of the face is more likely to indicate feelings of concern and anger (e.g., the brows are lowered and drawn together in anger). The lower area, particularly the mouth, will communicate happiness and amusement. Smiles, frowns, twisted lips, a raised chin, a clenched mouth, and other expressions are also fairly clear in what they communicate.

Let's see how you do with a short test of facial meaning (The Facial Meaning Sensitivity Test, Leathers & Eaves, 2008). Figure 4.2 shows ten photographs of different facial expressions. Match the following states with the pictures *before* looking at the correct answers:

Facial Meaning	Photograph # (from Figure 4.2)	Facial Meaning	Photograph # (from Figure 4.2)
Disgust	_____	Contempt	_____
Happiness	_____	Surprise	_____
Interest	_____	Anger	_____
Sadness	_____	Determination	_____
Bewilderment	_____	Fear	_____

The correct choices are disgust = 1, happiness = 3, interest = 8, sadness = 10, bewilderment = 2, contempt = 9, surprise = 7, anger = 6, determination = 4, and fear = 5.

For the purposes of teaching, you need to be especially careful to attend to facial expressions of bewilderment and interest. Teachers use these emotions extensively to gauge student understanding and motivation. Emotions similar to bewilderment are confusion, doubt, frustration, and puzzlement. Obviously these cues suggest that the student is not understanding or is not progressing. Interest conveys anticipation, excitement, and attention. These emotions are important as an indication of attention.

The most informative aspect of the face is the eyes and the nature of eye contact. Eye contact indicates a readiness to communicate, and continued direct eye contact signifies confidence and competence. Students who use positive eye contact, who look directly at you and watch your movements, are probably attentive and interested. Longer and more frequent eye contact suggests trust and respect.

Averted eyes often suggest an unwillingness to respond, a lack of confidence, or a general sense of apathy. For example, if a student looks down before responding, looks away from teachers when interacting with them, keeps eyes downcast, or looks at the ceiling, a reasonable interpretation is that the student may lack confidence, knowledge, or skills and may have other negative emotions. When most of the students in a class start looking around the room, at each other, and out the window, they have lost interest and are not involved. This may mean that students do not understand well enough, or it may mean they are bored (in some cultures the lack of eye contact may indicate respect for an authority figure or older person, and not a lack of self-confidence or other negative feeling).

The pupils of the eyes convey the intensity of emotion shown more generally in the face. They tend to enlarge as we become more interested in something, more emotionally aroused, and happier with positive anticipation. Pupils contract as we become less interested and have more negative emotions such as sadness, sorrow, and indifference.

Body Language and Signals.   Like facial expressions and voice, body language, movement, and posture communicate messages. The meaning associated with different bodily cues is best understood by considering five categories of nonverbal behavior, each of which is based on a different function or purpose: emblems, illustrators, affect displays, regulators, and adapters (Ekman & Friesen, 1969).

An *emblem* is a body cue that has a direct one- or two-word verbal translation. Emblems are used to consciously communicate a particular message, such as holding up your hand with your palm facing the other person (which means "wait"), putting your finger to your puckered lips ("quiet"), and waving toward yourself ("come over"). Most of these emblems are substitutes for words.

In observing emblems, be aware of possible cross-cultural differences. For example, nodding your head in the United States means that you agree, but in Japan it acknowledges only that you have received the other person's message.

An *illustrator* is used to increase clarity and awareness and to augment what is being said. It reinforces the strength of the emotional message. For example, holding your fingers close together augments "small," and pointing to an object clarifies what you intend to communicate about. If a student's fist is clenched, it may indicate anger in association with what the student has verbalized.

The third type of bodily communication is the *affect display.* These cues show emotion through the position and posture of the body and certain gestures. If the student has a rigid, tense, slumped body with arms and legs crossed, the affect is negative and defensive. Students with open, relaxed bodies who lean toward the teacher and do not fidget or tap something communicate positive affect, attention, and confidence. Suppose you notice that a student is slumped in her chair and has one hand to her mouth and the other arm clenched to her body. How would you interpret this body language? It is likely that the student is not very confident about the lesson or assignment and generally has negative emotions that will probably interfere with learning.

Regulators are used to indicate the initiation, length, and termination of verbal messages. Students use these cues to inform the teacher about whether they want to initiate a response, are finished with a comment or thought, or want to continue speaking. An obvious initiation regulator is to raise the hand or index finger. Other initiation regulators include eye contact, head nodding, smiles, and raised eyebrows. When students do not want to make a comment, they may use such "turn-denying" behaviors as staring at something (especially looking down at the desk) and slumping in the chair. Students who want to continue speaking may lean toward you, use gestures to punctuate their thoughts, and display an enthusiastic, expectant face.

Regulators are vital for teachers as they observe students' signs about whether they understand something or are ready to move on. These are given in response to teacher questions and consist of response cards, clickers, stickers, and other methods of receiving quick and often confidential feedback from students (more on these in the next section).

The final category to describe different functions is the *adapter.* Adapters are a rich source of information about attitudes, levels of confidence, and anxiety. They include behaviors such as picking at oneself, chewing nails, and fidgeting (these

Teacher's Corner

Beth Carter

National Board Certified Elementary and Middle School Teacher

It has taken me a few years of teaching to really understand how important nonverbal messages are from my students. I look for facial expressions, such as smiling, active engagement with their eyes, or confused facial expressions. I have learned that body language is another crucial aspect, especially when working in a small group. A few things I look for are if the student's arms are crossed or if he/she has pulled away from the group. If I see these things, I know I need to ask some questions to understand the confusion, then clarify with the child. Something I have noticed recently is the use of avoidance behaviors, such as asking to go to the bathroom or to sharpen a pencil and even losing work so he/she does not have to participate.

indicate nervousness, anxiety, and concern). Covering the face with one's hands indicates that a message is undesirable, painful, or unpleasant.

Gestures.   Gestures are hand and arm movements that individuals use to communicate either supplementing verbal messages or acting as the sole means through which meaning is conveyed. Gestures clarify, contradict, or replace verbal messages and play an important role in child development and learning. For example, young children often point to answers or use some kind of gesture to indicate understanding. Students often use gestures as part of an explanation of something or as an answer. Gesturing allows students to express learning in a simple and direct way, often demonstrating understanding that is not apparent through language.

By paying attention to gestures, teachers are able to confirm whether students have a complete or partial understanding of something. Understanding is partial when there is discord between gestures and speech. It is more complete when gestures and speech are in concurrence. Some research suggests that gesture–speech mismatches indicate a readiness for learning (Roth, 2001).

Assessing Voice-Related Cues.   Voice-related cues include tone of voice, loudness, intensity, pauses, silences, voice level, inflection, word spacing, emphases, and other aspects of voice that add color to the content of what is said. The potential of vocal cues to provide information about a student's level of understanding, confidence, and emotional state is exceeded only by facial expressions.

TABLE 4.3   Vocal Cues and Messages

Vocal Cue	Message
Loudness	*Loud*—competent, enthusiastic, forceful, self-assured, excited *Quiet*—anxious, unsure, shy, indifferent
Pitch (musical note voice produces)	*High*—excited, explosively angry, emotional *Low*—calm, sad, stunned, quietly angry, indifferent *Variety*—dynamic, extroverted
Rate	*Fast*—interested, self-assured, angry, happy, proud, confident, excited, impulsive, emotional *Slow*—uninterested, unsure, unexcited, unemotional
Quality (combination of attributes)	*Flat*—sluggish, cold, withdrawn *Nasal*—unattractive, lethargic, foolish

A summary of research on the relationship between vocal cues and messages is presented in Table 4.3 (Leathers & Eaves, 2008). Although this research has not been conducted with teacher/student dyads or groups, the findings do have important implications. For example, on the basis of vocal cues you would expect students who are confident in their knowledge or skill to be relatively loud rather than quiet, to speak in a high pitch, to have a rather rapid speaking rate, and to speak fluently with few pauses, "ahs," sentence changes, throat clearings, word repetitions, and incomplete sentences. Students who are unsure of their knowledge or ability to perform a skill are likely to speak quietly, in a low pitch with little variety, and to speak slowly with many pauses and frequent throat clearings. The student who lacks confidence will speak nonfluently, the voice will be flat, more like a monotone rather than showing variety in pitch and rate. Research has also determined that persons who demonstrate little variation in pitch and rate tend to be viewed as introverts, lacking assertiveness and dynamism. Voices that are clear, articulate, and confident are viewed as positive.

You will need to be careful not to infer lack of knowledge, confidence, anxiety, or motivation *solely* on the basis of vocal cues. Like nonverbal behavior, voice is one of many pieces of evidence that you need to consider to make an accurate assessment.

The challenge is being able to observe these nonverbal and verbal cues, make appropriate interpretations, and then take corrective action when needed. To help you with this I have prepared a table that combines different types of nonverbal behaviors and vocal cues in relation to particular messages students send (Table 4.4).

I also asked some teachers to summarize the nonverbal behavior and vocal cues they attend to, how they interpret what they see and hear, and the action they take following their observation and interpretation. Examples of the teachers' responses include the following:

Nonverbal Behavior	Interpretation	Action
Students start to look around the room and at each other.	Some students are not understanding; some may be bored.	Refocus students; review previous lesson; reteach lesson; regroup students.
Room quiets; students are writing in their notebooks.	Students are motivated and on task.	Keep going—it may not last long!
Students squint and adjust the focus of their eyes.	Indicates a lack of understanding, frustration, or boredom.	Rephrase the question or ask the students what it is that they do not understand.

TABLE 4.4   Messages Students Convey through Nonverbal Behavior and Vocal Cues

Message	Facial Expressions	Body Language	Vocal Cues
Confident	Relaxed, direct eye contact; pupils enlarged	Erect posture; arms and legs open; chin up; hands waving; forward position in seat	Fluent; few pauses; variety in tone; loud
Nervous	Tense; brows lowered; pupils contracted	Rigid; tense; tapping; picking	Pauses; "ah" sounds; repetition; shaky; soft; fast; quiet
Angry	Brows lowered and drawn together; teeth clenched; eyes narrow	Fidgety; hands clenched; head down	Loud or quiet; animated
Defensive	Downcast eyes; pupils contracted; eyes squinted	Arms and legs crossed; leaning away; leaning head on hands	Loud; animated
Bored	Looking around; relaxed; pupils contracted	Slumped posture; hands to face	Soft; monotone; flat
Frustrated	Brows together; eyes downcast; squinting	Tense; tapping; picking; placing fingers or hands on each side of head	Pauses; low pitch
Happy	Smiling, smirking; relaxed; brows natural; pupils enlarged	Relaxed; head nodding; leaning forward	Animated; loud; fast
Interested	Direct eye contact; brows uplifted	Leaning forward; relaxed; opening arms and legs; nodding; raising hand or finger	Higher pitch; fast
Not Understanding	Frowning; biting lower lip; squinting eyes; looking away	Leaning back; arms crossed; head tilted back; hand on forehead; fidgeting; scratching chin; leaning head on hands	Slow; pauses; "ah," "um," "well" expressions; low pitch; monotone; quiet; soft

Beginning of Year Observations.   During the first few days of the year, teachers use informal observation extensively to learn about their students. Although this data gathering is not used immediately for instruction and as a consequence may be *low-level* formative assessment, these observations give teachers insights into student characteristics that should be taken into account in planning instruction. The emphasis is more on general traits that will influence instruction than specific student understanding. At the elementary level, teachers are concerned about both academic and social characteristics. At the secondary level, teachers tend to focus on academic preparation, ability, and student interest in the subject.

During the first few days of school, teachers are constantly looking for any clues about the nature of their students. These observations are made from spontaneous student behavior. The typical four steps involved are collecting information, interpreting the information, synthesizing the information, and naming the characteristic of the student the observation describes (Gordon, 1987).

During the first step, the teacher observes student appearance and behavior. What type of clothes does the student wear? Is the student clean? Does the student talk with other students? What nonverbal cues are present? What kind of vocabulary does the student use? How well does the student speak? How does the student's face look? Is the student courteous? Does the student volunteer to answer questions? It is not so much a matter of looking for certain types of appearance or behavior as it is a careful mental recording of student actions, reactions, and interactions with other students. Stiggins (2008b) uses the term **personal communication** to describe forms of teacher–student interactions that provide preinstructional information as well as information throughout the year. Like a good physician, with experience effective teachers know what to attend to.

The second step is interpreting what has been observed. At this point, teachers make judgments about what the appearance or behavior means. For example, a teacher may form the following tentative explanations:

> "Tom is always late to school and unprepared. I wonder if there is a situation at home that I need to know about."

> "Anne is eager to answer almost every question with a smile. She is listening and motivated to learn and participate."

> "Tim doesn't participate much and rarely looks directly at me when I speak to him. This may mean he has low self-esteem."

> "Jane does not interact much with the other students. Perhaps she is not well liked by them."

In each case, an interpretation is made from the observation. It is this interpretation that provides meaning.

Naturally, different teachers can observe the same behavior and come up with different interpretations. In this sense, informal observations are *subjective*. That is, meaning is derived only by professional judgment of what is observed. Of course, it is possible for an observation to be *biased*, or heavily influenced by what the teacher wants to see or wants to believe. Your own perspectives, preferences, and attitudes influence how you interpret your observations. Because each of us views the world differently, differences in interpretation can be expected. It is important to understand how your background may influence your interpretations, and it is best to obtain corroborating interpretations provided by different sources of information (e.g., another teacher or more structured assessment).

In the third step, interpretations are synthesized into meaningful traits or characterizations of the students. This involves inductive thinking whereby several separate interpretations are pulled together to form a tentative conclusion about the trait or characteristic (e.g., "Tom is motivated," "Erin is from a dysfunctional home," "Jose is way behind on social skills"). At this point it is important to be aware of the need to have a sufficient number of interpretations so that the synthesis provides an accurate description. It is also helpful to use others' interpretations to validate your own.

The fourth step is naming the trait or characteristic. This step is idiosyncratic in that your definitions of terms, such as *motivated, behind, uncooperative, easily distracted, talkative, able,* and so on, are not necessarily the same as others' definitions. Thus, how you characterize a student or class has meaning according to your definition of the trait. Furthermore, the more general name of the trait is likely to be remembered and influence subsequent interactions. That is, you are less likely to remember the specific behaviors and more likely to recall that the student was self-confident, lazy, shy, capable, and the like.

Sources of Error in Informal Observation.   In a busy classroom, it's difficult to make continuous informal observations that are accurate, whether of individual students or of groups. Some of the more common errors that teachers make in their informal observations and interpretations are presented in Table 4.5. To make accurate, reliable observations, it is best to first learn what to look for and listen to. Next, you need to be aware of the types of errors that are possible and consciously monitor yourself so that these errors are not made. Finally, it is helpful if you are able to use a few simple procedures:

- Ask yourself, is the verbal message consistent with the nonverbal behavior? Is this behavior normal or unusual?
- Plan time to do informal observation while not actively teaching a lesson to the entire class (e.g., during seat work, small-group work, and individual interactions).
- Keep a list of possible errors from Table 4.5 in a place that is easily referred to, such as in your desk. Make a habit of referring to the list frequently.
- When possible during the school day, write down informal observations, your interpretations, and the action you took. Be sure to keep the interpretations separate from the observations. The brief, written descriptions of behavior are essentially **anecdotal observations** or *notes*. These notes will provide accurate records of what transpired and will help make observations more accurate. In addition, anecdotal records can be used to document personal

TABLE 4.5   Sources of Error in Informal Observation

1. Leniency or generosity	Teachers, as observers, tend to be lenient or generous.
2. Primacy effects	Teachers' initial impressions have a distorting effect on later observations.
3. Recency effect	Teachers' interpretations are unduly influenced by his or her most recent observation.
4. Logical generalization errors	Teachers make assumptions that some nonverbal behavior generalizes to other areas (e.g., lack of confidence in math means lack of confidence in English).
5. Failure to acknowledge self	Teachers fail to take into account his or her influence on the students.
6. Unrepresentative sampling	Teachers erroneously interpret behaviors that do not accurately reflect the student or do not occur frequently enough to provide a reliable measure.
7. Observer bias	Teachers' preconceived biases and stereotypes distort the meaning of what is observed.
8. Failure to consider student perspective	Teachers fail to obtain student interpretations that would clarify the teacher's impressions.
9. Student reactions to being observed	Some students get nervous or uneasy when observed by teachers (e.g., students would behave differently if the teacher were not present).
10. Lack of consideration for the rapid speed of relevant action	Teachers may miss critical behaviors because of the speed of what occurs in the classroom.
11. Lack of consideration for the simultaneity of relevant action	Teachers may fail to account for more than one message being sent at the same time.
12. Student faking	Teachers may fail to realize that students are faking (e.g., eye contact and nodding does not always indicate engagement); as students become more sophisticated they develop strategies to make themselves appear to be on task.

Source: From M. C. Wittrock (Editor), Merlin C. Wittrock (Editor), American Educational Research Association (Corporate Author). *Handbook of Research on Teaching,* third edition. Copyright © 1985 Gale, a part of Cengage Learning, Inc. Reproduced by permission. www.cengage.com/permissions.

insights and student reactions that otherwise are easily forgotten or distorted (see Hill, Ruptic, & Norwick, 1998, and Nilsen, 2008, for a more extensive discussion of anecdotal notes).

- At the end of the day, set aside a few minutes to record, briefly, important informal observations. Refer to your notes each week to look for patterns and trouble spots that need attention.
- If you are unsure about what a nonverbal behavior may mean, and the implications are serious, check them out with the student during an individual conference. For example, if you are picking up from nonverbal behavior that

a student does not understand a procedure, even though the student's answers are correct on worksheets, ask the student directly about how he or she felt about the procedure and inquire about his or her confidence. You may discover that the student was concerned with other things at the time, and this affect was being displayed.

- Consciously think about informal observations of behavior in relation to student understanding and performance of learning targets. Those that directly relate to the targets are most important.
- Don't be fooled by students who appear to be on task and interested but aren't.

Remember, do not base an interpretation solely on the basis of a single nonverbal behavior or vocal cue. Observe and interpret multiple nonverbal behaviors to confirm your conclusions (Mottet & Richmond, 2000).

Informal Oral Questioning

Effective teaching requires constant monitoring of student understanding. Along with observations, teachers rely heavily on how students answer questions during instruction to know if students understand what is presented or can perform targeted skills. Good questioning is flexible because it can be used with individuals or groups of students and can be customized based on specific student answers (Green & Johnson, 2010). A technique such as the "traffic light" approach can be used effectively to gauge student understanding. With the traffic light technique, students are taught how to use green, red, and yellow stickers, cards, or self-adhesive spots to indicate their self-perceived level of understanding. Red indicates, "Please stop, I don't understand," yellow, "I'm not sure," and green, "Got it." Questions also serve several purposes as they actively engage students in the lesson to promote students' thinking and comprehension, to review important content, and to control students for classroom management.

Questioning typically occurs in four formats: whole class teacher-led reviews of content, discussions, recitations, and interactions with individual students and small groups of students. The review may be a fast-paced drill that is designed to cover specific knowledge. Discussions are used to promote student questioning and exchange ideas and opinions to clarify issues, promote thinking, generate ideas, or solve a problem. In a recitation, the teacher asks questions as part of the presentation of material to engage students in what they are learning. Teachers question students individually and in small groups to obtain information that is specific to the students. This allows teachers to individualize assessment and target suggested next steps.

Questions can efficiently grab students' attention and engage them in the lesson. Questions can challenge beliefs and get them to think about the topic under discussion by creating a sense of cognitive dissonance, imbalance, or disequilibrium. McTighe and Wiggins (2005) describe "essential" questions as those that provoke and engage students in inquiry and argument about plausible responses.

Second, questions can promote student reasoning and comprehension by helping them think through and verbalize their ideas. By actively thinking through answers to questions, student understanding is enhanced. Learning is also enhanced by listening to the answers of other students because these answers may represent a way of expressing ideas that makes more sense to the student than the way the teacher explains things.

Questions signal to students important content to be learned and provide an opportunity for students to assess their own level of understanding in these areas. The types of questions asked also indicate how the students should prepare to demonstrate their understanding. For instance, asking questions that compare and contrast (e.g., How were presidents Carter and Clinton similar?) will cue students that they need to learn about how these presidents were similar and different, not just characteristics of each one. If you ask simple recall questions (e.g., What three major legislative initiatives occurred during the Clinton presidency?), you will tell your students that they need to memorize the names of these initiatives.

Questions are also used to control student behavior and manage the class. Questions asked at random of different students—and that require brief, correct answers—maintain student attention. Teachers often ask a specific question of a student who is not paying attention to stop inappropriate behavior. Conversely, questions can be used to reinforce good behavior. Questions are also used to refocus students and to remind them of the classroom rules and procedures. Through the use of good questions, students will keep actively involved in learning, preventing opportunities for student misbehavior.

Most important for formative assessment, questioning is used to obtain information about student understanding and progress. This is accomplished if the questions are effective and elicit information that will help you understand the depth of knowledge of your students and what follow-up will help them learn. The elements of good questions and questioning skills for this purpose are presented next as 10 characteristics.

Characteristics of Effective Questioning to Assess Student Progress

Your goal is to ask questions during instruction that will provide you with accurate information about what students know, understand, and can do. With this goal in mind, the following suggestions and strategies will help you:

   1. State Questions Clearly and Succinctly So That the Intent of the Question Is Understood.   Students understand the question if they know how they are to respond. Questions are vague to students if there are too many possible responses or if the question is too general. With such a question, students wonder, "What does he mean?" Because they are unsure of what is intended, they are less willing to answer the question, and you are less likely to find out what they know. This occurs for a single vague question and for run-on questions (those in which two or more questions are asked together). For example, if a fourth-grade teacher wants to determine current student understanding of noun–verb agreement in sentences, an inappropriately vague question might be:

> What is wrong with the sentences on the board?

It would be better to ask:

> Read each of the three sentences on the board. In which sentence or sentences is there agreement between the noun and the verb? In which one or ones is there disagreement? How would you correct the sentence(s) in which the verb and noun do not agree?

Other questions that are too vague:

> What did you think about this demonstration?
> What about the early explorers of America?
> Can you tell me something about what you learned?
> What do you know about the solar system?

As emphasized by Green and Johnson (2010), design brief, succinct questions that are directly related to their understanding of the task. Here are some examples:

> What cause of the Vietnam War do you believe was most misunderstood by the media?
> What was the primary reason for Columbus to come to the Americas?
> Why did the leading character in this story decide to leave his home?

   2. **Match Questions with Learning Targets.**   The questions you ask should reflect your learning targets, the degree of emphasis of different topics that will be assessed more formally in a unit test, and the difficulty of learning targets. Ask more questions and spend more time questioning with difficult learning targets. This will give you sufficient information to make sure students understand. Try to ask questions in rough proportion to how you will eventually test for student learning. We have all been in classes where much class time was spent discussing something that was covered only lightly on the test. Try to avoid this.

   Matching questions to learning targets requires that the questions be phrased to elicit student responses that are required in the learning target. For this purpose, most oral questions will correspond to either knowledge or understanding targets. Knowledge targets focus on remembering and understanding. Questions that assess knowledge targets often begin with *what, who, where,* and *when.* For example, "What is the definition of *exacerbate*?" "When did Columbus discover America?" "Who is Martin Luther King?" These are examples of knowledge questions that generally require factual recall or rote memorization of dates, names, places, and definitions.

Other knowledge questions assess student understanding and comprehension. Students are required to show that they grasp the meaning of something by answering questions that require more than rote memory, for example, "What is the major theme of this article?" "What is an example of a metaphor?" "Explain what is meant by the phrase 'opposites attract.'" and "How do you find the area of a parallelogram?" These types of questions are effective when you want to assess more than one student in whole group instruction because each student uses his or her own words for the answer. If there is only one way to state the correct answer, only one student can answer it correctly.

More time is needed to respond to reasoning questions. These questions are generally *divergent* in that more than one answer can be correct or satisfactory. In a reasoning question, the teacher asks students to mentally manipulate what they know to analyze, synthesize, problem solve, create, and evaluate. Reasoning questions will include words or intents such as *distinguish, contrast, generalize, judge, solve, compare, interpret, relate,* and *predict,* such as "Relate the causes of the Civil War to the causes of World War I. How are they the same and how are they different?" "What was the implication of the story for how we live our lives today?" "What would happen if these two liquids were mixed?" As you might imagine, reasoning questions are excellent for promoting student thinking and discussion.

An effective approach to engaging students in reasoning is to have a one-on-one conversation with the student in which questions can be specific to that student. Asking students to "think out loud" when responding or when solving a problem can reveal their ability to employ appropriate thinking strategies and steps (Stiggins, 2008b).

3. Involve the Entire Class.   You will want to ask questions to a range of different types of students in your class, rather than allowing a few students to answer most questions. Balance is needed between students who volunteer and those who don't, high- and low-ability students, males and females, and students near and far from you. It is easy to call on the same students most of the time, so it's best to be aware of who has and who has not participated. If you are judging the progress of the class as a whole, it is especially important to obtain information from different students, although normally if your better students are confused or having difficulty, chances are good that this is true for the rest of the class as well. If slower students respond correctly, then most students are ready to move on.

Involvement will be enhanced if everyone's responses are supported. One technique for engaging most students is to address the question to the class as a whole, allow students time to think about a response, and then call on specific students. This encourages all the students to be responsible for an answer, not just a single student if you call the name first and will result in a better understanding of overall student progress.

4. Allow Sufficient Wait Time for Student Responses.   A more accurate assessment of what students know will occur if students have sufficient time to think about and then respond to each question. Students need this time to process their thoughts and formulate their answers. Research shows that some teachers have difficulty waiting more than a second or two before cuing a response, calling on another student, or rephrasing a question. It has been shown that when teachers can wait three to five seconds, the quality and quantity of student responses are enhanced. It follows from these findings that longer wait time will result in better assessment, but only if the questions are such that students will be engaged in thinking. A longer wait time for a simple recall question is not nearly as effective as a question that engages students to deepen their understanding. This point is illustrated nicely by the following teacher comments (Black & Wiliam, 2004, p. 26).

> Not until you analyze your own questioning do you realize how poor it can be. I found myself using questions to fill time and asking questions which required little thought from the students . . . it is important to ask questions which get them thinking about the topic and will allow them to make the next step in the learning process. Simply directing them to the "correct answer" is not useful.

It may be difficult for you to wait more than a couple of seconds because the silence may seem much longer. It's helpful to tell students directly that such wait time is not only expected, but required, so that immediate responses do not take opportunities away from students who need a little more time. This will help alleviate your own insecurity about having so much silence during a lesson.

5. Give Appropriate Responses to Student Answers.   Your responses to student answers will be very important for gathering valid information about student progress because your style and approach—the climate and pattern of interaction that is established—will affect how and if students are likely to answer your questions. Each student's response should be acknowledged with some kind of meaningful, honest feedback. Feedback is part of ongoing assessment because it lets students know, and confirms for you, how much progress has been made. In the course of a class recitation or discussion, this feedback is usually a short, simple phrase indicating correctness, such as answering, for example, "right," "correct," "no," or maybe by doing something as simple as nodding your head. We will consider more about feedback in the next chapter.

6. Avoid Questions Answered by a "Yes" or "No."   There are two reasons to avoid yes/no questions or other questions that involve a choice between stated alternatives. First, if there are two alternatives, such as those available when answering a yes/no or true/false question, students can guess the correct answer 50% of the time. After a while, students tend to key into teacher behaviors or the way such a question is phrased to guess correctly. In any event, you will need to ask a lot of such questions to assess student progress accurately.

Second, these types of questions do not reveal much about a student's understanding of the content. They are not very diagnostic in nature. If you want to use such questions, do so sparingly and as a warm-up to questions that are better able to assess student learning. Adding a simple *why* after an answer to a yes/no question will increase its diagnostic power considerably. It is better to use these types of questions with students individually rather than in groups.

7. Use Probes to Extend Initial Answers.   Probes are specific follow-up questions. Use them to better understand how students arrived at an answer, their reasoning, and the logic of their response. Examples of probes include phrases such as

- Why did you think that was the correct answer?
- How did you arrive at that conclusion?
- Explain why you think you are correct.
- Explain how you arrived at that solution.
- Give another example.
- Could you argue that that is not the best solution?
- Tell me more about your conclusion.
- How did you come up with that answer?
- How would you explain the solution to someone else?

Essentially you are asking students to extend their understanding, to think about what they have learned. When students are asked to explain their answers, their learning improves (Black & Wiliam, 1998). Also, a benefit of this technique is that it shows students that thinking about what they are learning is as important as giving the right answer.

8. Avoid Tugging, Guessing, and Leading Questions.   Asking these types of questions makes it difficult to obtain an accurate picture of student knowledge and reasoning. Tugging questions ask a student to answer more without indicating what the student should focus on. They are usually vague questions or statements that follow what the teacher judges to be an incomplete answer. For example, "Well? . . ." "And? . . ." and "So? . . ." are tugging questions. It is better to use a specific probe. For example, if the question is "Why were cities built near water?" and a student answered, "So the people could come and go more easily," a tugging question would be "And what else?" A better probe would be "How did coming and going affect the travel of products and food?"

Guessing questions obviously elicit guessed answers from students, for example, "How many small computer businesses are there in this country?" This type of question is useful in getting students' attention and getting students to think about a problem or area, but it is not helpful in assessing progress.

Leading questions, like rhetorical questions, are more for the teacher to pace a lesson than for obtaining information about student knowledge. Therefore, these types of questions ("That's right, isn't it?" or "Let's go on to the next chapter, okay?") should be avoided.

9. Avoid Asking Students What They Think They Know.   It is not usually helpful to ask students directly if they know or understand something. The question might be, "Do you know how to divide fractions?" or "Is everyone with me?" Students may be reluctant to answer such questions in class because of possible embarrassment, and if they do answer, the tendency is to say they know and understand when the reality is that they don't. If your relationship with your students is good, asking them if they understand or know something may work well.

TABLE 4.6   Do's and Don'ts of Effective Questioning for Formative Assessment

Do	Don't
State questions clearly and succinctly.	Ask yes/no questions.
Match questions with learning targets.	Ask tugging questions.
Involve the entire class (all students).	Ask guessing questions.
Allow sufficient wait time for students to respond.	Ask leading questions.
Give appropriate responses to student answers.	Ask students what they know.
Extend initial answers with probes.	
Sequence questions appropriately.	
Ask questions of all students, not just those you know will answer correctly.	

10. Ask Questions in an Appropriate Sequence.   Asking questions in a planned sequence will enhance the information you receive to assess student understanding. Good sequences generally begin with knowledge questions to determine if students know enough about the content to consider reasoning questions. Consider the following situation. After having her students read an article about the United States military involvement in Haiti in 1994, Mrs. Headly asks the question, "Should the United States stay in Haiti and enforce the local laws until a new government is formed?" Students give some brief opinions, but it's clear that this reasoning question is premature. She then asks some knowledge questions to determine whether students understand enough from the article to ask other reasoning questions, such as "What was the condition of Haiti before the U.S. involvement?" "Historically, what has happened in Haiti the last two times a new government has taken control?" "How did the people of Haiti receive the American soldiers?" Such questions also serve as a review for students to remind them about important aspects of the article. Once students show that they understand the conditions and history, then divergent questions that require reasoning would be appropriate.

Table 4.6 summarizes the do's and don'ts of using effective questioning to assess student understanding.

Formal Formative Assessment

Formal formative assessment is a planned activity, usually for the entire class, that has a specific sequence of activities. Student knowledge and understanding is assessed, and the results are used by teachers to give feedback and plan instruction. It is set up in advance and administered as planned, with some amount of time between the gathering of data and interpretation that allows teachers to reflect and determine the next most appropriate instructional activities. Typically, there would be hours, days, or even weeks between the assessment and feedback to students with instructional adjustments. For example, it could be a unit test covering several weeks' instruction that is used to see what students did not understand, with further small-group instruction focused in specific areas in subsequent weeks. We will consider six different types of formal formative assessments that can be used to gather information about student understanding: preinstructional structured exercises, pretests, homework, classroom response systems, benchmark assessments, and quizzes and unit tests.

Preinstructional Structured Exercises

A good approach to evaluating current student knowledge and skills before beginning formal instructional, is to design informal, structured exercises that will provide you with an opportunity to observe students in the context of specific performance situations. These exercises are not like a formal pretest, but they are more structured than informal observation.

One approach is to design a class activity in which all the students participate. This could be a writing assignment, an oral presentation, or group work. For example, asking students to write about their summer vacation, in class, can help to identify language arts skills. Students can interview each other about their summer vacations and make short presentations to the class. Games can be used to observe students' math skills. Students can be asked to read aloud. A common technique is to ask students to write information about themselves on cards, such as names of family members, hobbies, and interests. Any one of these demonstrations of knowledge or skills would not be sufficient for instructional planning, but as you build a portrait of your students from many such observations—and combine this information with previous test scores, student records, and comments from other teachers—by the end of the first week of school you will have a pretty accurate idea of the strengths and weaknesses of your students.

It is best to keep structured exercises *nonthreatening*. This is important because you want to minimize student anxiety. Obviously, it is best not to grade the exercise. In addition, you will want to arrange the conditions to be as comfortable as possible. Having a student read orally to a small group or only to you is probably less threatening than reading to the entire class. If students are able to work at their own pace, without strict time constraints, they are more likely to feel less threatened. Avoid comparisons of students.

Pretests

Some teachers ask students to complete a formal pretest of the content that will be covered. The pretest would supposedly indicate what students know and don't know or what they can or cannot do. For several reasons, however, it is doubtful that the information from a pretest will be very helpful in planning instruction. First, at least in the fall, students have returned from vacation and have probably not thought too much about world history, algebra, or other school subjects. Their actual or true knowledge may not be reflected on a surprise test. Second, it is hard to motivate students to do their best on such tests. What do they have to gain by trying hard to answer the questions? This is especially true for older students. Third, to be helpful diagnostically, the pretest would need to be fairly long and detailed. Finally, presenting students with a pretest may not be the best way to start a class. Asking students what they know about something they will learn may be intimidating and create anxiety about the class (on the other hand, a pretest can communicate to students that the teacher is serious about learning). For these reasons, formal pretests are not used very often. The validity of the information is questionable, and the effect on the classroom environment and teacher–student relationships may be negative.

If a pretest is to be used successfully, it needs to be short and targeted to specific knowledge and skills. Students need to be motivated to do their best work, and the teacher needs to make clear to students that the purpose of a pretest is to help them learn more and help the teacher plan more effective instruction. The results may suggest the need for further diagnostic assessment.

Homework

The primary purpose of homework for most teachers is to provide extra practice in applying knowledge and skills. Homework is also used to extend, expand, and elaborate student learning. A third purpose is to check on student learning, which acts primarily as way for teachers to determine whether students, individually and as a group, are demonstrating correct performance. In this sense homework can be used diagnostically to determine which specific areas of knowledge and skill need further instruction. The information can be used to give further assignments, group students, and provide individualized help.

There are well-known limitations with homework, most important differential input and assistance from parents, siblings, and friends, and research suggests that the learning benefits to students on average are minimal (Cooper, Lindsay, Nye, & Greathouse, 1998). Because of this, homework that provides good diagnostic information should require students to complete, in their own writing, answers to constructed-response questions and assignments that show, where appropriate, work that led to their answers (e.g., with math problems). By reviewing students' work in small steps you will be able to provide greater specificity in the feedback you provide as well as with the instructional correctives to help students. Simply giving correct answers and having students check their work, without any prescriptive information, is not very helpful. Students need to know why they do not understand or have not correctly applied a skill. This increases their sense of self-determination and intrinsic motivation. Directions to students about the help they can receive need to be clear. Younger students should receive short assignments to avoid stress. There are also interesting issues about how homework is included in grading, which will be discussed in Chapter 13.

In-Class Assignments

Through the use of a variety of in-class student assignments, teachers are able to obtain feedback about student learning from multiple perspectives, increasing the validity of their inferences about what students know, understand, and can do. With seat work and other individualized activities, teachers can circulate, monitor student performance, and provide immediate, specific feedback. Although the use of "drill and kill" worksheets is discouraged, more direct models of teaching, which are becoming more popular, often use seat work to give students practice. Seat work can be used to provide formative information as long as there is close monitoring, frequent feedback, and opportunities for students to self-assess according to rubrics and criteria that have been provided. To use seat work as formative assessment the teacher must be actively involved. It is not a time simply to allow students to be on their own. At the very least, students should be required to come to the teacher to have their work checked and to have meaningful feedback.

Quizzes and Unit Tests

Teachers use quizzes and unit tests for both formative and summative purposes. From a formative standpoint the quiz is a structured procedure to check on student learning of specific skills, standards, or objectives that are part of more general goals for major units of instruction. Often objective in nature, the purpose is to provide the teacher, quickly, with an indication of current knowledge and skills. This information is then used immediately to individualize instruction, form small groups, and provide instructional correctives that will address learning deficits and move students as appropriate to the next level of learning.

The influence of standard-based, high-stakes assessment on quizzes has been dramatic. Some teachers are now required to use multiple-choice items for most of their assessments, and textbook and test publishers provide multiple-choice item test banks that allow teachers to select items for "diagnosing" student knowledge and understanding. This relatively new development in assessment will become more and more popular because it is relatively easy to draw on large banks of items electronically and give students online quizzes.

For example, Educational Testing Service (ETS) has what is called the National Formative Assessment Item Bank that includes more than 50,000 standards-based multiple-choice and constructed-response questions. The item bank can be used to generate tests and quizzes that are aligned with state standards. Teachers can select items or can have tests formed automatically. Students can take the tests or quizzes online, and there are various report options. ETS also has an instructional improvement model that combines standards, instruction, and both formative and summative assessment (Instructional Data Management System). Pearson has the Progressive Assessment Series for grades 3–8 and Stanford Learning First, a formative instructional assessment system for grades 3–8 customized to state standards. What remains to be seen is whether such services can actually provide formative information in an efficient and targeted way. Research suggests that the most helpful diagnostic information is from constructed-response assessments (McMillan & Workman, 1999).

Classroom Response Systems

A relatively new type of structured activity, often referred to as a *classroom response system*, uses technology for determining student understanding by having students respond to questions on some sort of keyboard or remote transmitter (e.g., clicker, iPods, or cell phones). The instructor presents material to students then poses a question. Students respond to the question electronically, which allows the instructor to immediately gauge student understanding. Often teachers will ask students to discuss the results in small groups and retest. With most systems, the teacher can tabulate and graph student responses, which can be immediately displayed to students (e.g., how many students selected each alternative in a multiple-choice question). The results can be stored for further analysis. Some systems are integrated with course management systems, such as Blackboard.

Although classroom response systems have been used extensively in higher education for years, especially in lecture classes, the technology is also available to classroom teachers at all levels. Short quizzes, as well as individual questions, can also be used. In addition to providing teachers with whole-class responses, such systems claim that they enhance student engagement and increase participation. And no doubt many of the available systems, when used effectively, accomplish this. Table 4.7 provides a summary of popular classroom response systems. As with all technology, these will change with time, and new ones will be developed.

TABLE 4.7   Examples of Classroom Response Systems

Name of System	Type of Transmitter	Description
TurningPoint	Infrared, radio, or wireless transmitters	Very popular; allows extensive integration with PowerPoint and other software
InterWrite	Infrared or radio transmitter	Allows self-testing with several questions; allows students to indicate their level of confidence in their answers
eInstruction		Basic, inexpensive system
H-ITT	Infrared transmitter	Inexpensive system; also has grading software
TI-Navigator	Radio transmitters	Calculators connect to teacher's PC; great for math
Qwizdom		Provides for more one-to-one communication

Source: Based on "A Teaching with Technology White Paper," Office of Technology for Education, Pittsburg, PA: Carnegie Mellon University.

Benchmark Assessments

High-stakes accountability demands have led to widespread implementation of periodic testing during the school year (e.g. every 9 weeks) to determine student progress toward meeting standards that will be assessed on the end-of-the-year high-stakes tests. These assessments are called **benchmark tests**. They are also called *interim* or *quarterly* tests. What is pertinent to this chapter is that many in the commercial testing industry, as well as others, contend that these tests are also formative. For example, the Regional Educational Laboratory Mid-Atlantic states that "a benchmark assessment is a formative assessment" (Brown & Coughlin, 2007, p. 2). However, this claim and the nature of the testing clearly illustrates *low-level* formative assessment. There is often little feedback to students and little use of the data to influence subsequent instruction, especially when compared to assessments prepared and administered by teachers for their classes (Goertz, Olah, & Riggan, 2009; Marsh, Pane, & Hamilton, 2006).

The primary purpose of benchmark tests is summative, to document what students have learned over a 9-week period. To use the results in a formative manner is not straightforward for several reasons. First, the amount of material covered by these tests, which typically have 40–50 multiple-choice test items, is considerable. This does not allow for diagnostic testing that would suggest specific deficiencies. There is insufficient detail to suggest specific instructional correctives. Feedback to students is spotty at best. Often there is no feedback to students. Finally, when these tests are prepared by the school districts, which is often the case, the technical quality of the items may be low. The result is that many teachers find them restrictive, burdensome, and unnecessary, especially if nothing new is found. For students, such testing tends to interrupt instruction and contributes to what many believe is a serious overtesting of students. This is consistent with the more generalized finding that it is difficult to use the results from summative tests formatively (Perie, Marion, & Gong, 2009).

On the positive side, benchmark tests are designed to give teachers immediate results, usually broken out by student and item. For secondary teachers, this creates a mountain of data. Some teachers have reported using benchmark test results to identify student strengths and weaknesses, to set subsequent instructional priorities, and to differentiate instruction (Abrams, McMillan & Wetzel 2010). There have also been reports of increased collaboration among teachers (Wayman & Cho, 2009). Some research suggests that positive formative uses of benchmark tests depend on a supportive culture that expects use of test data, having high-quality test items, and conditions in which teachers can discuss together the meaning of results (Abrams & McMillan, 2010). If you are asked to use benchmark testing, consider results diagnostically, but confirm deficiencies in understanding with other evidence and discuss results with others to identify trends and reasons for poor performance. Often students are not motivated to do their best work for these tests, with obvious implications for interpretation.

Benchmark testing may have some formative value, but be wary. It is insufficient to simply administer a test after several weeks of learning, give teachers results, and call the test formative. There is a need to structure the benchmark testing process so that instruction is actually affected and student learning improved. Because the level of resources school districts invest in what they may think is "formative" is significant (a half billion dollars spent in the United States in 2007 [*Education Week*, September 17, 2008]), especially when the tests are purchased from commercial testing companies, there needs to be careful consideration of the factors that need to be addressed so that the "return on investment" is high.

Teacher Expectations

An important aspect of gathering information about students, whether from formative or summative sources of information, is that the teacher will probably form some kind of expectation about what the students can achieve. Teacher expectations are beliefs about what students are capable of knowing or doing.

Initial expectations are based on information about students before teachers meet them and during initial interactions, including attributes such as socioeconomic status, previous test scores, appearance, race/ethnicity, name, language skills, and gender. These expectations influence subsequent interactions and whether pretests and structured exercises are administered to establish or confirm initial expectations. This information leads to the formation of confirmed expectations, which in turn influence student–teacher relationships and differential treatment. These interactions influence student expectations, which affect student performance. The performance of students then feeds back to further confirm initial and subsequent expectations. This cycle is illustrated in Figure 4.3.

In their worst form, teacher expectations can be self-fulfilling and detrimental. Students become what is expected of them. According to Good and Brophy (2008), the process looks like this:

1. Early in the year, the teacher forms expectations.
2. The teacher interacts differently with the students, consistent with these expectations.
3. This treatment informs students about what they may achieve or what behavior is appropriate for them.
4. If the teacher's treatment is consistent over time and students do not resist, it will affect the self-concept and classroom conduct of the students.
5. Subsequent student behavior reinforces the teacher's initial expectations.
6. Eventually, student achievement is affected: High-expectation students will achieve at their potential; low-expectation students will achieve less than their potential.

It is best for teachers to obtain as much information as possible about their students so that their expectations are accurate. Classroom observation and classroom performance of students are what teachers use most to form initial expectations. Standardized tests and other external sources of information are helpful

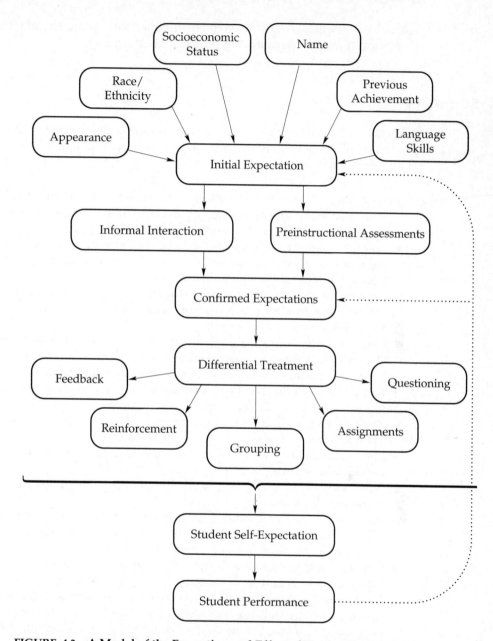

FIGURE 4.3   A Model of the Formation and Effect of Teacher Expectations

because they are independent of what are sometimes a teacher's unconsciously biased perceptions. If anything, teachers tend to dismiss low test scores in their evaluations of students. This is a safe approach; if you are going to err, err toward more positive expectations. It is better, however, to have realistic expectations of students. This will allow you to target instruction more accurately, and it will help to provide appropriate evaluations of student performance.

Summary

This chapter focused on what you can do to improve instruction by gathering appropriate information from students as they learn. Key points in the chapter include the following:

- Assessing student progress consists of a teacher monitoring students and their academic performances to inform instructional decision making and the nature of feedback given to students.
- Formative assessment provides ongoing feedback from students to teachers and from teachers to students; summative assessment measures student learning at the end of a unit of instruction.
- Benchmark assessments are used to monitor student achievement, at regular intervals during the school year, on standards used for end-of-year, high-stakes tests.
- Informal observation includes the teacher "reading" nonverbal behavior such as facial expressions, eye contact, body language, and vocal cues. These behaviors indicate student emotions, dispositions, and attitudes.
- Emotion is communicated best through facial expression. Eye contact is key to assessing attentiveness, confidence, and interest.
- Body language includes gestures, emblems, illustrators, affect displays, regulators, adapters, body movement, and posture.
- Voice-related cues such as pitch, loudness, rate, and pauses indicate confidence and emotions.
- Pretests should be short and should not interfere with establishing a positive classroom climate.
- Informal observation consists of observing student behavior, interpreting it, synthesizing, and naming the trait or characteristic. Nonthreatening, informal exercises are used to assess specific skills.
- Errors in informal observation are often associated with when the observations are made, sampling of student behavior, and teacher bias.
- Teachers use oral questioning to involve students, promote thinking, review, control students, and assess student progress. Effective questions are clear, matched with learning targets, involve the entire class, and allow sufficient wait time. Avoid yes/no, tugging, guessing, and leading questions, and keep questions in the proper sequence.
- Homework, in-class assignments, and quizzes can be used effectively for formative assessment as long as they are sufficiently specific, targeted, and diagnostic.
- Benchmark assessments, given every 9 weeks, may be helpful in identifying areas for remediation.

- Classroom Response Systems allow teachers to gather student self-reports of learning.
- Teacher expectations are teacher beliefs about what students are capable of achieving.
- Expectations are formed from many sources of information before instruction. These expectations should be realistic and avoid negative self-fulfilling prophecies.

Self-Instructional Review Exercises

1. To sharpen your interpretation of facial expressions, match the pictures below to the 10 emotions listed in the chapter from Figure 4.2.

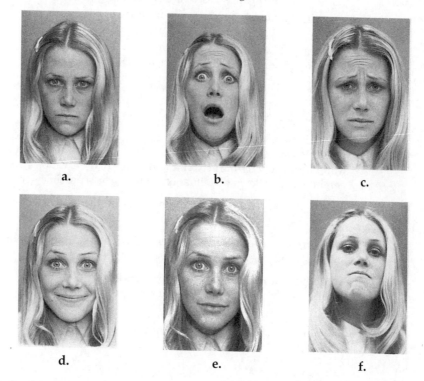

a.   b.   c.

d.   e.   f.

Source: Leathers, D. G. (1997). *Successful nonverbal communication: Principles and applications* (3rd ed.). New York: Macmillan, pp. 38–39. Reprinted by permission of Nancy Leathers.

2. Identify each of the following examples of body language as an emblem (E), illustrator (I), affect display (AD), regulator (R), or adapter (A).

   a. Student leans toward you and raises both hands immediately after you ask a question.
   b. Student points to the pencil sharpener as if to ask, "May I sharpen my pencil?"

    c. It seems that Johnny is always chewing on the end of his pencil.

    d. You notice that Ken is picking at his cuticles.

    e. Mary is sitting upright in her chair, arms on desk, chin up, with an expectant expression on her face.

    f. Sam uses his hands to show how large the fish was.

3. Match the messages most likely to be conveyed with the descriptions provided. Each message may be used once, not at all, or more than once.

_____ (1) Pauses when speaking; eyes downcast	**A.** Confident
_____ (2) Eyebrows uplifted; speaks fast; raises hand	**B.** Nervous
_____ (3) Looks around room; slumped in chair with head resting in one hand	**C.** Angry
	D. Defensive
_____ (4) Direct eye contact; speaks clearly with few pauses; uses variety in tone	**E.** Bored
	F. Frustrated
_____ (5) Enlarged pupils; chin up; arms open	**G.** Happy
_____ (6) Taps pencil; rigid body; pupils contracted	**H.** Interested
_____ (7) Loud; eyebrows lowered; hands make fists	
_____ (8) Arms and legs crossed; leans away	

4. Mr. Bush had observed Trent carefully over the past few days because he was concerned that Trent would revert to his old pattern of cheating by looking at others' papers. What observation error is Mr. Bush most susceptible to, and why?

5. Mrs. Greene saw Renee staring out the window, obviously not concentrating on her work. Because Renee is a good student and this is not very typical of her, Mrs. Greene ignores the behavior. What type of observation error was Mrs. Greene careful *not* to make in this situation? What error is possible in her interpretation?

6. Why is it important to match the type of question you ask students in class with your learning targets?

7. How would a teacher preface a question to make sure students took sufficient time to think about the answer before responding?

8. What type of question—convergent or divergent—would be best to determine whether students knew how to find the area of a rectangle?

9. What are the do's and don'ts for effective use of homework, in-class assignments, and quizzes to be effective formative assessments?

Answers to Self-Instructional Review Exercises

1. a. anger, b. fear, c. sadness, d. happiness, e. interest, f. determination.

2. a. R, b. E, c. A, d. A, e. AD, f. I.

3. (1) F, (2) H, (3) E, (4) A, (5) A, (6) B, (7) C, (8) D.

4. Mr. Bush is using previous behavior to motivate his informal observations, so his initial impressions may distort what he finds (primacy effect). He may also have a preconceived idea about what Trent would do (observer bias).

5. At least Mrs. Greene did not commit the error of unrepresentative sampling, because this was not a common occurrence. However, her interpretation that Renee was not thinking about her lesson may not be accurate. If this type of behavior became frequent and extensive, Mrs. Greene would want to ask Renee to get her perspective.

6. Matching questions with targets (a) helps to clarify to students what is important, (b) allows you to check student understanding of targets, (c) reinforces learning, and (d) balances emphasis given to each target.

7. The easiest way is the most direct—simply tell the students to wait a certain number of seconds before answering (e.g., 15 or 30 seconds). You can also ask them to write their answer, then think about it, before responding orally.

8. Convergent; only one or two possible ways are correct.

9.

	Do	**Don't**
Homework	Make it clear how much help, from whom, is permitted. Use constructed-response exercises. Have students show their work. Give instructional correctives with feedback. Give younger students shorter assignments.	Allow any kind of help. Use primarily selected-response items. Give only correct answers. Use homework for motivation, without feedback or correctives. Simply check for correct answers.
In-class assignments	Monitor student engagement and performance. Give private correctives. Give frequent, immediate, specific, and individualized feedback. Use observation, checklists, and individual accountability for cooperative group learning. Use checkpoint quizzes.	Sit at a desk while students complete assignments. Give general feedback to all students. Wait until all students have completed the work to give feedback. Use only group achievement accountability for cooperative learning.
Quizzes	Keep short. Use frequently. Use results to provide individualized instructional correctives. Use primarily constructed-response items. Be wary of quizzes from test item banks.	Use long quizzes. Use infrequently. Surprise students. Fail to connect results with instructional correctives. Use mostly selected-response items. Rely solely on items prepared by others.

Suggestions for Action Research

1. While in a classroom, informally observe students' nonverbal behavior. It would be best if another observer could also observe in the class so that you could compare notes. Take a sheet of paper and draw a line down the middle. On the left-hand side, record a description of the nonverbal behavior—such as a facial expression, body language, or vocal cue—and on the right side, summarize your interpretation of each one. It would be interesting to check these out with the teacher for accuracy.

2. Ask a teacher about the kinds of questions he or she asks and what kinds of student responses are typical. Compare the teacher's comments to the suggestions for effective questioning presented in Table 4.6. If possible, observe the teacher and record examples of effective and ineffective questioning.

3. Using Figure 4.3 as a general guide, draw a diagram that illustrates a teacher expectation that has applied to you or one that you have observed. Label each part of the diagram so you can identify each step of the expectation process.

Formative Assessment II: Feedback and Instructional Adjustments

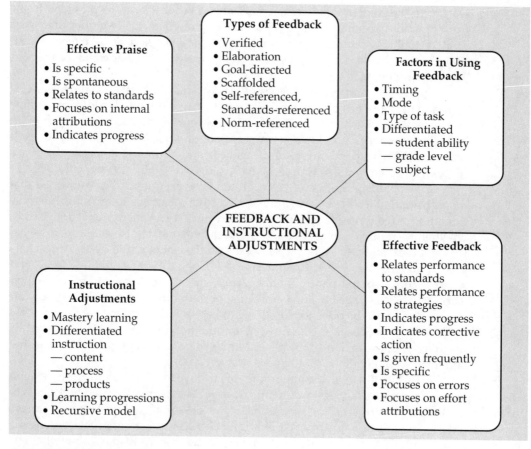

Types of Feedback
- Verified
- Elaboration
- Goal-directed
- Scaffolded
- Self-referenced, Standards-referenced
- Norm-referenced

Effective Praise
- Is specific
- Is spontaneous
- Relates to standards
- Focuses on internal attributions
- Indicates progress

Factors in Using Feedback
- Timing
- Mode
- Type of task
- Differentiated
  — student ability
  — grade level
  — subject

FEEDBACK AND INSTRUCTIONAL ADJUSTMENTS

Instructional Adjustments
- Mastery learning
- Differentiated instruction
  — content
  — process
  — products
- Learning progressions
- Recursive model

Effective Feedback
- Relates performance to standards
- Relates performance to strategies
- Indicates progress
- Indicates corrective action
- Is given frequently
- Is specific
- Focuses on errors
- Focuses on effort attributions

CHAPTER 5   Concept Map

In the previous chapter we learned about gathering information for formative assessment, both informal, real-time data gathering and information that is collected from more formal assessments, such as quizzes and structured exercises. This chapter completes our discussion of formative assessment by considering two components that make formative assessment effective—providing feedback and implementing instructional adjustments. We will first consider feedback—a dimension of teaching that is more complex than what may appear at first to be a simple process.

Providing Effective Feedback

One way teachers use assessment information is to know how to respond to students after they demonstrate their knowledge, reasoning, skill, or performance. The teacher's response is called **feedback**—the transfer of information from the teacher to the student following an assessment. Feedback can be provided in the form of grades on unit tests and report cards, though normally grades offer very limited feedback. Our discussion will focus on the characteristics of effective feedback that is provided both during and after instruction. In Chapter 13 feedback as grades is discussed in greater detail.

The nature, purpose, and types of feedback teachers give to students based on academic work has been extensively researched, with initial studies of positive reinforcement published nearly 100 years ago. More recently, several reviews of literature on feedback provide a strong case about what works and what doesn't when teachers respond to student answers and products in particular ways (Brookhart, 2008; Hattie & Timplerly, 2007; Kluger & DeNisi, 1996; Shute, 2008).

Research literature, as well as commonsense experience, has confirmed that the right kind of feedback is essential for effective teaching and learning. A simple definition of feedback is confirming the correctness of an answer or action, that is, whether it is right or wrong. This is what we do with most tests—tell students what they got right and what they missed; it is also the extent of the feedback teachers give to students' answers to oral questions—"Good," "That's right," "Close," and so on. Feedback of this nature is only part of what students need to improve their learning. They also need to know how their performance compares to learning targets and what can be done to close the gap between their performance and these targets. When feedback is presented as information that can guide the student's meaningful construction of additional knowledge and understanding, learning and intrinsic motivation are enhanced (Mayer, 2002).

To further illustrate the importance of effective feedback, allow me to tell you another short story about my daughter, Ryann. As a gymnast, Ryann had a goal to earn a score of 10 on each of her routines. After she completed a routine, the judges gave her a score of, say, 8.5 or 9.2. This is analogous to a teacher giving a student a score or grade. But simply *knowing* the score didn't help Ryann know what she needed to do to *improve* her score. When the judge immediately indicated, specifically, why certain points were deducted, then she knew what to work on. Furthermore, if the judge or coach told Ryann how she could correct the skill, she had the corrective procedures needed. Similarly, a student who receives a 70% on a test knows that he or she has not done well, but unless otherwise indicated, this information alone does not tell the student what to do next. Or suppose you just started to learn golf. You miss the ball. Your skill level is obviously low. But knowing that is not enough. You need to get feedback about *why* you missed it. Is it because of your stance, your hand grip, the position of your head, your backswing, or some other aspect of your swing? When the teacher tells you precisely what you did wrong, what you need to correct, how you can correct it, and how you can advance, effective feedback has been provided.

Because teaching is complex, depending on the nature of students, the context, and the subject being taught, effective feedback is also no simple matter. There are many choices about what kind of feedback to give, how much to give, and when to give it, depending on the learning targets and student characteristics. As Brookhart (2008) says, "In the final analysis, feedback is always adaptive. It always depends on something else" (p. 112). Effective feedback, then, is more than keeping in mind a few important principles, such as "keep feedback specific and individualized," or "keep it positive and brief." Rather, good feedback depends on appropriate teacher decision making and responses to students contingent on several important variables. That is, effective feedback is differentiated—what works for one student may not be effective for another student. An initial consideration is based on the type of feedback that is most appropriate to improve student learning and motivation.

Types of Feedback

There are many different types of feedback. Some of these are summarized in Table 5.1, which shows feedback based on complexity, as either simple (verified feedback) or more complex (elaborated feedback). Interestingly, the research on whether increased complexity is better for learning than simple feedback is mixed (Schute, 2008). The inconclusive findings suggest that other factors in the nature of feedback may be more important than complexity. In addition to these, five other types of feedback are important for formative assessment—goal-directed, scaffolded, self-referenced, standards-referenced, and norm-referenced.

Goal-Directed

Feedback that is goal directed provides information about learners' progress toward achieving a specific learning target. It is important that the targets are challenging yet attainable and that the learner has an expectation that they can achieve the goal. Goals that are too high will promote more failure and discouragement, whereas goals that are too low will not result in increased efficacy.

TABLE 5.1   Types of Feedback Based on Complexity

Feedback Type	Description
Verification	Informs students of the correctness of their answers
Correct response	Acknowledges student's correct answer with no additional information
Try again	Acknowledges student's incorrect answer and allows attempts to relearn in the same way
Error flagging	Highlights errors in response without giving the correct answer or suggestions for improvement
Elaboration	Includes explanation about why an answer was correct or incorrect; may allow for additional time to relearn
Attribute isolation	Presents central attributes of what is being learned
Response contingent	Describes why an incorrect answer is wrong and why a correct answer is right
Hints	Prompts or cues guiding the student in the right direction to learn the correct answer
Bugs	Misconceptions are explained with error analysis and diagnosis
Informative tutoring	Includes verification feedback, error flagging, and strategic hints on how to proceed without providing the correct answer

Source: Based on Shute, 2008, p. 160.

Moderately difficult, attainable targets also result in greater student motivation and engagement. This is especially true if the feedback is directed toward greater mastery and understanding, rather than simply obtaining a right answer. It has been well established that individuals with a *mastery* or *learning goal orientation* will be more motivated than individuals with a *performance orientation,* demonstrating greater persistence despite failure, and choosing more challenging tasks. A performance orientation, in contrast, results in a tendency to disengage with failure, show less interest in challenging tasks, and shows selection of tasks that are easy. Providing feedback that stresses mastery or learning helps to develop a mastery goal orientation. That is, the nature of the feedback can influence goal orientation in a way that can have a significant positive effect on learning and motivation.

Scaffolded

Scaffolding is an approach to instruction in which the teacher provides support to enhance learning by breaking a task down into smaller parts and interacting with students to help them learn each part sequentially to reach a learning target (like what my daughter experienced in gymnastics). Typically, teachers give tips, strategies, new materials, and cues to students as "supports" that allow students to gradually develop autonomous learning strategies. Supports are removed as students progress in their learning and understanding.

Although there are many levels and types of instructional scaffolding, the elements of scaffolding that are important for feedback include the emphasis on manageable, sequential steps and the goal of gradually shifting responsibility for learning from the teacher to the student. Feedback is focused on skills that are just beyond the student's capabilities and efforts, with guidance to pursue additional learning. This principle is based on Lev Vygotsky's *zone of proximal development*, in which teachers identify and focus on skills that are within student capabilities and also challenge to move them to higher learning (Horowitz, Darling-Hammond, Bransford, Comer, Rosebrock, Austin, & Rvst, 2005). Teachers guide student attention by giving them ideas and directions to enhance performance without giving correct answers.

Self-Referenced

This type of feedback compares student work or expectations with previous performance. Showing students how they progressed from what they did previously helps them see the improvement they made. The focus is on how work builds on or is better than previous performance (e.g., "Pat, your writing today shows a better understanding of noun–verb agreement than what you handed in last week"). This encourages students to believe that they are capable of subsequent learning and helps students define what needs to be done next; for example,

> "Maria, your division has improved by showing each step you used in your work. Now you need to be more careful about subtraction."

When students complete a learning task, they often think about why they were successful or unsuccessful. These messages are called attributions, and it is important for teachers to help students internalize the appropriate reasons. Motivation will be enhanced if students believe they were successful because of the effort they put forth (Pintrich & Schunk, 2002). Effort attributions are helpful because they help establish a positive self-efficacy that communicates an ability to do the work successfully. Hence, teachers can point out how students' specific effort was responsible for being correct. Effort attributions are especially important for low-performing students. Too often these students develop external attributions that when they are successful, it is for some reason that is not under their control (e.g., luck or teacher help), rather than an internal attribution such as effort. These attributions should emphasize a moderate amount of effort. Too much effort may suggest less emphasis on ability attributions.

Teacher's Corner

Carole Fokey

National Board Certified Elementary and Middle School Biology Teacher

The feedback I give to students based on their work or performance needs to be immediate, consistent, and fair. The feedback I give is constructive as well as probing. I will ask, "Why did you put that?" or "What were you thinking, when you wrote that response?" This allows for misconceptions to be addressed and it serves to help shape future instructional decisions. The feedback serves to alert the students to areas of improvement but also serves to show the effectiveness of instruction or instructional activities used.

Standards-Referenced

Standards define expected learning. Comparing student performance to identified standards of performance and exemplars is generally the most important and effective type of feedback to move students to higher learning. This type of feedback is goal directed, with an emphasis on helping students understand how their current performance relates to criteria that demonstrates targeted learning. The emphasis is on showing students how their work compares with the criteria and standards, rather than to their previous work or how others performed (e.g., "Alicia, your writing has demonstrated successful noun–verb agreement, but further work is needed on the use of adjectives to describe character intent.").

As previously emphasized, it is important for students to know the standards they will be judged against before a learning assessment. This makes it much easier for you to show students how their performance compares to the standard and for students to self-assess their work. You can write standards on the board, have exemplars of student work available, and reinforce the meaning of scores and grades to make this process more efficient. Word your feedback to refer to the standards. For example, "Jon, your paper did not include an introductory paragraph, as shown here in our exemplar" or "Your answer is partially correct but, as I said in my question, I am looking for an example of a sentence with both adjectives and adverbs."

Norm-Referenced

Norm-referenced feedback compares a student's performance to what other students have achieved. This could be a comparison to other students in a specific class or to students in other or previous classes (e.g., "Jon, your work is simply not up to the rest of the class."). Generally norm-referenced feedback is discouraged, especially for struggling or less-able students. This is because such feedback suggests attributions to ability that may be interpreted to mean that a student is unable to learn. Limited norm-referenced feedback may be helpful in motivating higher-ability students (e.g., "Your performance is not yet up to the level of others who, in the past, have been accepted at highly selective colleges.").

Factors to Consider in Determining the Nature of the Feedback

Feedback can differ on a number of dimensions. In keeping with our emphasis on how feedback needs to be tailored to the context, these few factors are important in determining the nature of the feedback that is provided.

Amount

Generally, feedback that is specific and descriptive is better than making general comments. A specific, descriptive statement specifies in exact terms the nature of the performance, for example, "Your speech was delivered too quickly. It will help you to pronounce each word more slowly and to pause between each sentence." Or, "I really liked the way you read your story this morning. You pronounced the words very clearly and spoke enthusiastically." How often have you received feedback like "good work," "nice job," "excellent," "awkward," "OK," and "try harder"? What do vague messages like these convey? There is only verification of correctness, with little or nothing that helps students understand in greater detail the particular aspects of their work or behavior that are appropriate or that need improvement.

There are limits, however, to specificity. It is possible to provide so much specific, narrow feedback that it is overwhelming or difficult to understand. Helpful feedback is not too general and not too specific. It is something in between that can help the student move forward. For example, if you return a paper with comments about every paragraph or most sentences, the student may not be able to internalize the more important points. Not only does it take the teacher a long time to give this kind of feedback, but also it is not as effective as selecting key paragraphs or sentences and making specific comments. Also, you don't want to do the students' work for them.

It is not practical to provide specific feedback to every student. You will need to make some choices about what to focus on, and it is best to determine where the most error is or what changes will be most helpful to the student. For example, it is relatively easy to comment on misspellings and grammatical errors on student papers, but are these the most important aspects of the paper the student needs feedback about?

Timing

It is generally recommended that feedback should be given during or immediately following student performance or given with as small a delay as possible. By giving immediate feedback to students, they are able to use the information while they have time to act on it to improve their learning. If there is a significant delay, the feedback will not be as meaningful. Giving feedback during a performance is especially effective. When Ryann did her gymnastics, her coach gave her feedback on her performance as she did her routine, not just after she finished ("straighten your legs, point your toes, lift your chin, smile").

You provide more frequent, immediate feedback when you:

- Develop or select activities with built-in opportunities for feedback.
- Circulate to monitor individual work, making comments to students.
- Use examples of ongoing student work to show all students' mistakes and corrections.
- Use techniques during recitations to monitor the progress of all students.

It should be noted, however, that there is evidence that some kinds of delayed feedback are as or more effective than immediate feedback (Shute, 2008). Immediate feedback is clearly more effective than delayed feedback in learning simple cognitive tasks and for less-able or struggling students, whereas delayed feedback may be more effective for more complex tasks and higher-ability students. In any event, it is generally better to return student work promptly. Feedback given weeks later is typically not very helpful.

Teacher's Corner
Tami Slater
National Board Certified Elementary Reading Specialist

Feedback is important to give to students during any unit of study. I try to give feedback on an every other day basis. Feedback can come in the form of one-to-one conferences, small-group conversations, or comments written on papers. A simple percentage or letter grade does not help the student learn from their mistakes or revise their work to make it better. When giving feedback, I give them one positive comment about their work or performance. Then I give them feedback in one area for improvement. Feedback is given on both their product and their effort. I also always ask them to do some self-evaluating and ask them for their interpretation of their product and performance.

Mode

There are three modes of delivering feedback—oral, written, and demonstration. Oral feedback is needed when the teacher is circulating and monitoring student seat work, sees opportunities for effective feedback, and then provides it. Oral feedback is more effective for younger students and for students who have difficulty reading. Written feedback is most effective when there is a need to provide specific comments for each student on completed papers, projects, and tests. Written feedback also provides comments that students can save and use at a later time. Demonstrations of correct procedures are helpful with whole classes, when many students are struggling to learn, and for psychomotor learning targets.

Audience

Feedback is either given to individuals or groups, both small and large. Most feedback is individualized, but when the same message or information is helpful to many students, group feedback is appropriate and more efficient. Often teachers will observe many students struggling with a seat work task and will interrupt their efforts with an explanation or feedback for the entire group. It would be inappropriate to stop student seat work and give group feedback if only two or three students needed help.

Type of Task

Feedback typically focuses on either *what* was learned or *how* it was learned. In giving feedback about what was learned, the focus is on knowledge and understanding, on content that needs to be mastered. The emphasis is on what was successfully understood, what still needs work, and actions to improve knowledge and understanding.

An emphasis on how performance improved can also focus on the skills, strategies, and procedures students used as they were learning. Here the emphasis is on procedural targets, how well they are applying specific thinking strategies or steps. Feedback is directed toward important skills and strategies, noting which were used well and which need further work, and explaining how students can improve these skills and strategies; for example, "Gerald, your answer to the problem is correct. I can see that you used the right three steps in solving the problem."

For relatively simple learning tasks (e.g., simple recall and recognition, knowledge, as determined by the student's capabilities) it is generally best to use immediate feedback. When learning a complex task, though, delayed feedback is more effective. For difficult new tasks, it is better to give immediate feedback, at least initially. When the task is a thinking skill or strategy, delayed and elaboration feedback are most effective. Elaboration feedback provides cues to the student to identify the correct answer, rather than verifying the right answer.

Differentiated Formative Feedback

It has been stressed that effective feedback is differentiated, that it depends on matching the type and nature of the feedback with contextual variables. We'll now consider three of these variables—learner level of ability, grade level, and subject.

Learner Level of Ability

Higher-ability students benefit more from delayed, more general feedback, especially for complex learning tasks. Some research suggests that low-ability students may need more immediate, specific feedback and might benefit more from receiving both verification and elaboration feedback and knowing they are on track, rather than something like, "Try again," without knowing the correct response. Norm-referenced comparisons should be avoided; instead, scaffolded feedback should be emphasized. With struggling students, it is also helpful to check to make sure they understand the feedback. Because they are performing poorly, they may not want to ask clarification or explanation questions about the feedback.

Lower-ability students need to know specifically how their performance relates to effort. This encourages a hopeful and positive approach to further learning. They need self-referenced feedback that stresses the importance of their effort in making progress. However, lower-ability students may need instruction in self-referenced feedback first, which is important to not be demoralized by what is judged to be continual failure.

Finally, feedback must be honest for lower-ability students without unjustified praise, but there is also a need to avoid a self-fulfilling prophecy in which poor work is continually expected and produced. For low-ability students who are reluctant to learn, feedback needs to be sensitive to their tendency to think that any kind of feedback is "critical" and affirms their self-perception of being inadequate, inferior, or even stupid. According to Brookhart (2008), it is important to deal with the negative feelings about feedback first, then to provide scaffolded feedback so that students are able to understand and use it. It is best to select one or two suggestions. It is also important to avoid constant "negative" feedback (e.g., this is wrong, this is wrong, and this is wrong!). Although teachers should never lie to students about their performance, too much negativity only reinforces their poor self-efficacy. It is best to use self-referenced feedback for these students and to set goals that provide initial success before moving on to more difficult goals.

Higher-ability students benefit more by being challenged as well as by questioning that takes them to higher learning. To the extent that higher-ability students have a larger base of knowledge from which to draw, feedback that enables them to examine errors in thinking is best. Higher-ability students are often more receptive to feedback, especially in messages that not only improve their understanding but also extend it to further learning. These students are more receptive to critical comments because they see these as needed to improve, as an integral aspect of learning. They need elaboration feedback that challenges them to learn

Teacher's Corner

Arleen Rinehart

National Board Certified Secondary English and Special Education Teacher

I try to give students constructive feedback, telling them one or two things that they did well and how they did meet the objectives. However, I will always (even if a student receives an A) offer suggestions for improvement. I usually write rhetorical questions that begin with, "What about. . . ." or "Perhaps," "Did you consider" or "What if" in the margins beside student responses. I hope that students will use my questions to see other perspectives and/or to make their arguments stronger or to clarify their ideas. I also give this type of feedback when I am assessing students informally.

more and feedback that emphasizes processes such as cognitive skills and strategies. Higher-ability students may also be more receptive and skilled at self-referenced feedback.

Grade Level

At the elementary level, where teachers are primarily responsible for one class, it is much easier to give immediate feedback, to scaffold, to check student understanding of feedback, and to use elaborative feedback compared to the secondary level. Elementary teachers have more opportunities to work individually with students to guide their thinking and efforts. Elementary-level instruction tends to be more teacher directed than student directed, with more control over feedback resting with the teacher.

With older students feedback is often delayed and more planned. Limited class time and high numbers of students limits what can occur immediately, especially individually. Oral feedback is more group oriented. Secondary teachers can depend more on student initiative and responsibility for letting teachers know their confidence that they understand and their self-evaluations. This is demonstrated by students using colors, cards, or electronic devices to indicate their level of understanding and is often the best way for teachers to identify current understanding (e.g., rather than giving a quiz). Older students, including those in higher elementary grades, are also more adept at using scoring rubrics and criteria and using self-assessment.

Subject

To what extent would or should feedback vary, according to the subject matter that is taught? We know that feedback is not a single process for every context, and there are differences for different subjects. Math and science have relatively clear paths of progression for learning and understanding. Typically a predetermined sequence of knowledge is taught and learned, promoted by external standards-based accountability tests. This suggests that most formative assessment is planned and structured, resulting in delayed, predetermined feedback based on student performance on tests (the exception is science projects). Scaffolded feedback is relatively easy with math and science, as is an emphasis on fairly structured patterns of thinking, skills, and strategies in these subjects. Demonstrations as a way to give feedback are highly effective in science.

In contrast, English and humanities tend to be taught and assessed in a more meandering, less-planned manner, with an emphasis in English on ideas, imagination, and creativity. Questioning and feedback are used to enhance students' thinking skills and deep understanding, initiated by impromptu, varied, and unpredictable student comments and questions. In these classrooms, much feedback is immediate, designed to fit the nature of what is happening in a specific classroom at a specific time. Even two classes with the same learning targets can stimulate different types of feedback, based on what occurs in each class. Although it is more difficult to scaffold feedback in English, social studies classes, with an emphasis on content knowledge, lend themselves to scaffolded feedback. The emphasis on content also encourages a verification type of delayed feedback.

Feedback will clearly be different according to subject, although research is only beginning to show the nature of these differences. It is important to understand that many of the principles of feedback are the same in different subjects. Regardless of the subject, teachers make decisions about when to give feedback, what it will look like, and how it will help students learn more. Grade level, student ability, and the type of task may be more important than subject. Overall, the nature of the learning target is critical.

Anticipating Feedback

As you may be thinking, the variables affecting feedback can make giving it a very challenging task, given the context of classroom learning. Effective teachers are able to anticipate the nature of the feedback they provide (Furtak, 2009). Through their understanding of the subject, student knowledge, and typical barriers to learning, they are able to informally plan out feedback. Although seemingly cumbersome, this teaching task is far more effective than waiting for each opportunity for feedback during the class. Having even a few feedback phrases will be helpful.

To anticipate the nature of the feedback to provide, using three steps will be helpful (Furtak, 2009):

1. Understand the learning target.
2. Know probable student errors.
3. Establish feedback ideas.

TABLE 5.2 Example of Steps in Anticipating Feedback

Learning Target	Students will understand that density is an independent property of shape or size of a material.
Probable Student Errors	Students believe that density changes when the size and/or shape of the material is changed.
Feedback Ideas	Ask students to explain their thinking to focus on either shape or size or both.
	Ask students to think about the fundamental idea of density.
	Tell students that density is independent of size and shape.
	Show students what happens to different pieces of soap in water, and use the demonstration to help them understand that size is not a factor in density.
	Have students cut different shapes of the same material, measure mass and volume, then calculate density.

Use of these steps is illustrated in Table 5.2 for a unit on density. The learning target is stated in terms of what students will know. Probable student errors consist of probable alternative explanations and conceptions. In the third step, feedback ideas are summarized. With this information it is much easier and efficient for the teacher to identify thinking errors and provide feedback that will move students toward achievement of the learning target.

Skill in anticipating and responding to student misconceptions is a key attribute of effective teaching, one that develops with experience and in-depth knowledge of the subject being taught. You may also be able to identify sources of information that suggest possible misconceptions and can use these clues to arm yourself with what to look for. An interesting aspect of misconceptions is that they are often found in multiple-choice items. Good distracters focus on misconceptions, so that when students select a particular distracter, the teacher has knowledge of how student thinking is inaccurate. Once the error is identified appropriate feedback and instructional adjustments can be provided. This is often done when teachers grade multiple-choice quizzes and tests. In addition to knowing if students are correct in their answers, an analysis of the wrong choices is key to how teachers take the next steps toward greater student understanding.

Table 5.3 shows key do's and don'ts for effective feedback.

What About Giving Praise?

Most teachers use praise ubiquitously in the classroom. It can be thought of as a type of feedback to the student, but it is also used frequently to control student behavior and for classroom management. In general, research shows that teachers

TABLE 5.3 Key Dos and Don'ts for Effective Feedback

Do	Don't
Use challenging yet attainable goals	Use goals that are too high or too low
Emphasize mastery goal orientation	Emphasize performance goal orientation
Ensure that feedback is clear and easily understood	Use feedback that is unclear and/or difficult to understand
Compare student performance to standards, criteria, cognitive strategies, and previous performance	Compare student performance to the performance of other students or emphasize the person rather than the task
Use a moderate amount of specific, individualized, and descriptive feedback	Use general or vague feedback
Give feedback as soon as possible, not more than a day later, especially for simple cognitive tasks, tests, and other assignments	Give delayed feedback, except for slightly delayed feedback for cognitively complex tasks, especially for high achievers
Use both verification and elaboration feedback	Use only verification feedback
Match feedback to student ability	Use the same feedback for all students
Focus on key errors	Ignore key errors
Emphasize effort attributions	Emphasize external attributions
Give feedback as students learn	Give feedback only after performance
Anticipate probable feedback messages	Rely on unplanned or unanticipated feedback

Case Study
for Reflection

Ms. Watson, a tenth-grade algebra teacher at Eastbrook High School, recently attended a professional development workshop. The presenter addressed the characteristics of appropriate feedback for high school students. He said that it should, among other things, be given frequently and immediately. Ms. Watson argued that her students were old enough to wait for feedback from the teacher. She said that high school student tests could be quite lengthy and that sometimes it could take her a couple of weeks to get them all graded and returned to the students. She assured the presenter that her tenth-grade students never complained about her assessment practices.

QUESTIONS FOR CONSIDERATION

1. What advice could you give Ms. Watson to convince her that this assessment practice is not in the best interest of her students?
2. Do younger, elementary students need more feedback than older students?

use too much praise and use it inappropriately as positive reinforcement (Good & Brophy, 2008).

Like effective feedback, praise can be helpful to students if it draws attention to student progress and performance in relation to standards. It is also a good type of message to accompany other types of feedback. This is especially true when the praise focuses on student effort and other internal attributions so that students know that their efforts are recognized, appreciated, and connected to their performance.

Praise is most effective when it is delivered as a spontaneous but accurate message, giving the teacher's genuine reaction to student performance, and when it includes a specific description of the skill or behavior that is commended. You should praise students simply and directly, in natural language, without gushy or dramatic words. A straightforward, declarative sentence is best. For example, say: "Good; you did a wonderful job of drawing the vase; your lines are clear and the perspective is correct," not "Incredible!" or "Wow!" Try to be specific about what you are praising, and include your recognition of the student's effort. For example, say, "This is an excellent job of paraphrasing the story. It is well organized, and you have captured each of the major elements of the story. I like the way you kept at this assignment and worked hard to provide the detail you did." Call attention to progress and evidence of new skills. For instance, say, "I notice that you have learned to move sentences around with the blocking feature on your computer. Keep learning new ways to improve your computer and writing skills."

Try to use as many different phrases as you can when praising. If you say the same thing over and over, it may be perceived as insincere with little serious attention to the performance. This is especially true if the phrase is a vague generality such as "good" or "nice job." It is also best to keep your verbal praise consistent with your nonverbal behavior. Students quickly and accurately pick up teachers' nonverbal messages. So if the performance really is good, and progress is demonstrated, say your praise with a smile, using a voice tone and inflection that communicates warmth and sincerity.

Additional useful guidelines for effective praise are given in Table 5.3.

Instructional Adjustments

An essential component of formative assessment is to provide students with instructional adjustments (or what may be called *instructional correctives*) that will help students reach learning targets. These adjustments need to help students understand what is needed to close the gap between current performance and what is specified by the learning target.

Corrective action is pragmatic and possible. It gives students specific actions in which they can engage to improve, and typically these actions use instruction that is different from what was initially used for student learning. (If it didn't work the first time, why use it again?) For example:

> "You have made seven errors in the use of commas in your paper. Please refer to Chapter 3 in your text and generate three sentences that follow the rules for using commas."

> "Your understanding of how to use adverbs can be enhanced if you work through a special computer program that is now available."

When an entire class is effectively monitored, the teacher can decide to slow down, speed up, review material, or try new instructional approaches for the entire class, small groups of students, or individual students. The professional judgment of the teacher is used continuously as students learn to adapt instruction to meet student needs.

Students who have mastered the learning target can still benefit from feedback that tells them what actions are required to extend and deepen their understanding. This feedback is not "corrective" in the sense that there is a deficit to be addressed, but such feedback keeps students on task and furthers their learning.

Two major approaches to providing instructional correctives are closely related to formative assessment—mastery learning and differentiated instruction. We will look briefly at each of these, and one additional strategy, beginning with mastery learning. Mastery learning was the first major theory on individualizing teaching to students based on assessment.

Mastery Learning

As noted by Guskey (2007, 2010) a major change in education occurred with the work of Benjamin S. Bloom, who, in the 1960s, introduced a concept he initially called *learning for mastery learning,* which was shortened to *mastery learning* in the 1970s. The goal of mastery learning was to change the prevailing view of education in which teaching was essentially the same for all students, resulting in variation in student achievement. In mastery learning, instruction would vary to result in similar achievement. This would be accomplished by initial assessment, feedback, corrective instruction based on the results of this assessment, and "second-chance" opportunities for student performance (additional assessment).

The purpose of the initial assessment in mastery learning was to show what students had accomplished and what was not yet learned. With this knowledge, additional instruction was designed to close the gap between what was learned and what needed to be learned. Each assessment was paired with additional instructional opportunities (e.g., additional sources of information, use of different textbooks, or videos, as well as additional practice). Following this additional instruction, students were reassessed to verify "mastery" of the material. Thus, each student could theoretically have a detailed prescription of what needed to be done following the initial assessment. As students show mastery, enrichment activities can be provided.

With his ideas and research, Bloom maintained that all children could learn (a precursor to "no child left behind"), given appropriate assessments and instructional correctives. At the time, this was a very different approach to teaching, and it serves as an important foundation to formative assessment. Assessment for Bloom was required to diagnose what students knew and could do, provide students with meaningful feedback, and prescribe to each student individually tailored instruction until reaching mastery, resulting in higher overall student achievement.

Bloom also emphasized that effective corrective instruction needed to be different from the initial teaching approach. An alternative approach to teaching and learning was essential. These correctives needed to be based on individual students' current understandings, with sensitivity to different learning styles, learning modalities, preferences, interests, and types of intelligence.

Differentiated Instruction

Differentiated instruction is essentially an updating of mastery learning, incorporating new research and a more comprehensive approach to teaching. It has emerged as a way of providing students alternative approaches to learning and has integrated assessment as a main tenant.

Differentiated instruction is a theory of teaching and learning in which learner needs, as determined by assessments, are used in planning and executing lessons tailored to small groups of students. Student needs include interests, abilities, prior achievement, and other factors that define readiness to learn and receptivity to engagement. The teacher designs learning environment options to match student needs and interests. Often three different options are provided, based on students who are behind, in the middle, or advanced. Instruction is not individualized to such an extent that each student has a separate lesson plan. Rather, groups of students are given different instructional paths with the goal of having all students at an appropriate level of challenge. The idea is that learning is maximized when students are challenged to move slightly beyond what they are able to do on their own.

Teachers are encouraged to differentiate three key elements of instruction—content, process, and products. Content refers to what parts of subject matter are emphasized. Using pretests and other assessments, teachers determine where students need to begin to study a topic or unit. Process is concerned with how students learn and what learning strategies are used. Here teachers match student learning styles and strategies with how material is presented. Differentiation based on products means how students demonstrate what they know and understand. The intent is to use whatever assessment techniques provide the best opportunity for success, including the use of student choice of assessments. In addition, teachers are urged to use a variety of assessment strategies for all students.

Differentiated instruction takes into account different ways of learning for students who bring a variety of talents, interests, and readiness to the classroom. It is organized yet flexible, changing as needed to maximize learning of all students. A toolbox of techniques and approaches is needed by the teacher to adequately differentiate instruction. Based on assessments of important student values, interests, learning styles, and previous achievement, the teacher provides the best-matched instruction to enhance student motivation and learning. Assessment is an ongoing, diagnostic aspect of differentiated instruction.

Learning Progressions

For most instruction there is a trajectory or sequence of how knowledge and understanding develops, a series of sequential steps that students take in moving from an initial level of proficiency to a more sophisticated understanding (Alonzo & Gearhart, 2006; Heritage, 2007; Heritage & Anderson, 2009). Essentially, these progressions lay out how students go from point A to point B. By being aware of the steps that need to be taken, teachers are able to focus their formative assessment on these steps to inform them about further instruction. They are able to plan potential feedback and instructional correctives that are based on the progression (Heritage, 2008).

Learning progressions are relatively new and hold great promise as supplements to standards-based education. Here are two recent definitions:

> (1) descriptions of successively more sophisticated ways of thinking about an idea that follow one another as students learn; they lay out in words and examples what it means to move toward more expert understanding. (Wilson & Bertenthal, 2005, p. 3)

> (2) a carefully sequenced set of building blocks that students must master en route to a more distant curricular aim. The building blocks consist of sub skills and bodies of enabling knowledge. (Popham, 2007, p. 2)

Learning progressions provide a road map for knowing what information needs to be gathered about student understanding and corresponding instructional adjustments that are needed. This makes it possible for teachers to match learning activities to the progression and to know criteria for evaluating successful performance with each step. Once a teacher confirms that a student is at a specific point in the learning progression, appropriate instruction can be implemented. The goal is to promote more sophisticated ways of reasoning and thinking within a content domain. Learning progressions are a relatively new approach to instruction that uses formative assessment, and it holds promise for novel ways to plan and execute instructional correctives.

An important contribution of learning progressions is that it provides more detailed information than a standard about how learning should progress. Standards are endpoints, but typically they do not help teachers know how to get there. By instituting intermediate or substandards along a continuum of progress, teachers have a much improved curriculum guide to help them focus formative assessment on these important steps.

Part of a learning progression for attainment in history is illustrated in Figure 5.1. Note the increasing complexity and depth of understanding that develops as students move from level 1 to level 2. It is readily apparent how to match

Level 1 ⟹ **Level 2** ⟹ **Level 3** ⟹ **Level 4** ⟹ **Level 5**

Recognize distinction between present and past events; emerging sense of chronology of events; recall episodes from the past; find answers from simple questions about the past.

Developing sense of chronology; place events in order, showing differences between the present and past; recognition of reasons for previous events and behavior; use simple observation to answer questions about the past.

Understand that the past can be divided into different periods of time, recognizing similarities and differences; understand main events of the past; beginning to give reasons for main events and changes; use sources of information.

Recall factual knowledge and understanding of previous events; describe characteristic features of previous periods; give reasons for and results of main events and changes; beginning to combine information from different sources.

Show increasing depth of factual knowledge and understanding; begin to make links between different periods; show how aspects of the past have been interpreted in different ways; beginning to evaluate sources of information.

FIGURE 5.1   Learning Progression for History

Source: From *The National Curriculum for England.* Copyright © 1999 by Crown. Copyright © 1999 by Qualifications and Curriculum Authority. http://www.nc.uk.net.

instruction to these steps. Teachers attend to key words and concepts, such as from "recognizing" to "understanding" to "increasing depth." These outcomes suggest particular ways of doing assignments, giving feedback, and using instructional correctives matched to each level.

A Model of Instructional Adjustments for Formative Assessment

Mastery learning and differentiated instruction theories and practices are integrated in Figure 5.2 to show how instructional adjustments are used with formative assessment. Based on an initial assessment, the teacher considers what content and process targets need attention and provides appropriate feedback to students. Then, based on further assessments of student needs, different instructional approaches are selected and implemented. After the instruction, more formative assessment is used to repeat the process of matching learning tasks, activities, assignments, and assessments to student needs.

Whether based on mastery learning, differentiated instruction, or other theories and approaches to teaching, the important point is that instructional correctives are used to complete the formative assessment process. This results in assessment that is truly integrated with instruction and shows that both are needed to maximize student learning.

A final important point about instructional adjustments is that they are not always determined by the teacher. The process of identifying next steps is sometimes most effective if the student is involved in deciding what these steps should look like (Harlen, 2003). Teachers can give students alternative approaches or ask them directly how they think they can obtain a better understanding. Students are not treated as passive recipients of feedback and suggestions for further learning. Rather, students become partners with teachers. This is also effective in improving students' self-efficacy and feelings of internal control of their learning.

Summary

- Effective feedback relates performance to standards, progress, and corrective procedures. It is given frequently and immediately, and it focuses specifically and descriptively on key errors.
- Feedback should be differentiated based on learner level of ability, grade level, and subject.
- Effective praise is sincere, spontaneous, natural, accurate, varied, and straightforward. It focuses on progress, internal attributions, specific behaviors, and corrective actions.
- Instructional adjustments, through the use of mastery learning, learning progressions, and differentiated instruction, provide students specific activities, different from the original instruction, to aid them in closing their knowledge gap and achieving the learning target.

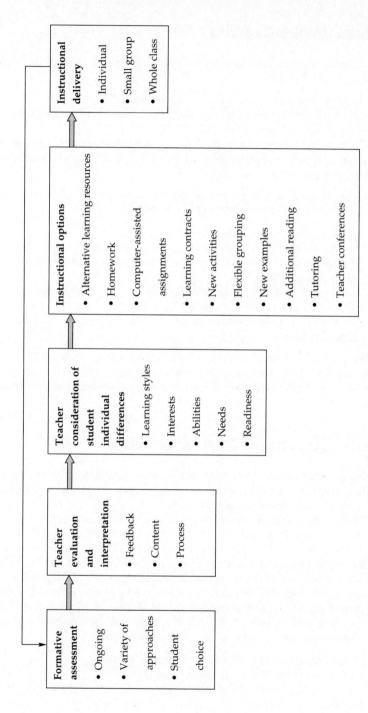

FIGURE 5.2 Recursive Model for Instructional Adjustments

Source: Adapted from Tomlinson (1999) and Guskey (2007).

Self-Instructional Review Exercises

1. Evaluate each of the following forms of feedback on the basis of the eight characteristics in the chapter.

   a. "Lanette, that was a great job you did yesterday!"
   b. "Jeff, your writing is improving. Your *b*s are much better because you are making a straighter line and not a loop."
   c. "Robert, you have a good report. Your grammar is excellent, although you have some problems with sentence structure. The conclusion is incomplete. Work harder on providing more detail."

2. Indicate whether each of the following is characteristic of effective praise (EP) or ineffective praise (IP). If ineffective, indicate why.

   a. "Sally, you did the best in the class!"
   b. "Jon, I can see by your work that you are really good in math!"
   c. "This shows that you did the report well because you worked hard and because you are a good writer."
   d. "Good work. This time you doubled the length and width before adding them to find the perimeter of the rectangle."
   e. "You typed thirty-five words a minute with seven mistakes. This was among the best in the class."

3. From your experience, consider a high-achieving and low-ability-level student related to a specific learning target. How might instructional adjustments differ for these two students? What are your goals in offering differentiated instruction?

Answers to Self-Instructional Review Exercises

1. a. Poor in almost all respects. Feedback is not specific or descriptive, it is not related to standards, nor does it focus on key errors. It is not given immediately, and no corrective actions are suggested.
    b. This is pretty good feedback as praise. It is specific, descriptive, and focuses on improvement. However, it might be better to include areas to improve as well.
    c. This feedback seems okay at first; you may well have received something like this many times. But when you look closely at what is said, the feedback is weak. The teacher does not indicate how Robert can improve nor does the teacher identify Robert's specific mistakes or problems in sentence structure, conclusion, or providing detail. The teacher has indicated there is "improvement," but this is not clear indication of progress. The teacher also does not say how Robert can improve his difficulties, only that he has them.

2. a. IP; too general, compares performance only to others.
    b. IP; too general, and attributes success only to ability.
    c. IP; although general, still attributes success to both effort and ability (internal factors).
    d. EP; specific, shows progress.

    e. Both EP and IP; on the one hand the praise is specific, but on the other hand success is indicated by comparison to others.

3. Answers to this question will vary based on the learning target, content, process and products, and student needs. Your goal for the high-achieving students should be to develop adjustments that extend and deepen their understanding. On the other hand, instructional adjustments for low-ability-level students serve to help them understand how to progress from their current state of knowledge to the learning target.

Suggestions for Action Research

1. Ask a group of students about the kind of feedback they get from teachers. Ask questions about how the feedback affects them.

2. Observe how teachers in two of three different classrooms use praise. What kind of praise is given by each teacher? What is the effect of the praise on the students? How could the praise you observe be improved?

3. Ask some teachers about the feedback they provide students. Ask if it is verification or elaboration feedback. Compare answers to the checklist for giving effective feedback.

4. Identify a standard in your grade level and subject and prepare a learning progression that would take students from their initial understanding at the beginning of the year to the standard. Trade your progression with others in the same subject and grade level and compare answers.

Planning and Implementing Classroom Summative Assessments

As described in Chapter 1, summative assessments are used primarily to document student performance; it is assessment *of* learning, completed after instruction. Summative assessments are used to monitor and record student proficiency, to give students grades, to report to parents, for selection into special

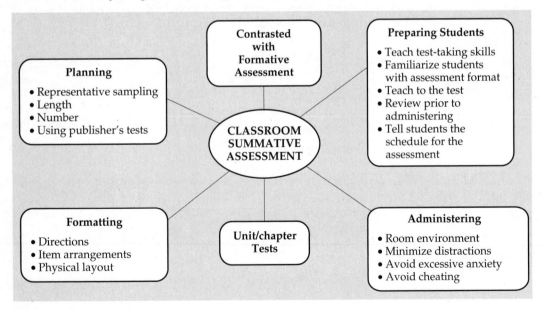

Planning
- Representative sampling
- Length
- Number
- Using publisher's tests

Contrasted with Formative Assessment

Preparing Students
- Teach test-taking skills
- Familiarize students with assessment format
- Teach to the test
- Review prior to administering
- Tell students the schedule for the assessment

CLASSROOM SUMMATIVE ASSESSMENT

Formatting
- Directions
- Item arrangements
- Physical layout

Unit/chapter Tests

Administering
- Room environment
- Minimize distractions
- Avoid excessive anxiety
- Avoid cheating

CHAPTER 6   Concept Map

programs, for conferring of honors, and for establishing a record of performance used by colleges for admissions and hiring by employers. Examples include chapter and unit tests, semester tests, final papers, reports, and presentations. They are also used by teachers to plan instruction. Actually, some formative assessment during instruction could be thought of as a "mini" summative assessment in the sense that there is evidence of student proficiency in relation to learning targets. The difference between what is typically called summative and formative assessment is in when it occurs and the primary use of the evidence.

Because summative classroom assessments are typically aligned closely to standards and learning targets, there has been considerable attention on the formative for instructional planning. These could be called *formative postassessments* (Ainsworth & Viegut, 2006). They occur at the end of an instructional segment to document student proficiency and provide diagnostic information that can be used to plan subsequent instruction. Often, these are tests that are developed by teams of teachers to provide a common check of student achievement.

Summative assessment is contrasted with formative assessment in Table 6.1. Keep in mind that the differences in characteristics are typical and not complete. For example, some formative assessment may not provide immediate feedback to students, and some summative assessments are used effectively for instructional adjustments.

TABLE 6.1 Characteristics of Formative and Summative Assessment

Characteristic	Formative	Summative
Purpose	To provide feedback and instructional correctives during instruction	To document student proficiency and plan instruction
When Conducted	During instruction	After instruction
Teacher Role	To diagnose immediately, provide feedback, and make suggestions for further learning	To plan, administer, and record performance and to use for subsequent instruction
Student Involvement	Encouraged	Discouraged
Student Motivation	Intrinsic, mastery oriented	Extrinsic, performance oriented
Learning emphasized	Comprehension, application, deep understanding, and reasoning	Knowledge, comprehension, and application
Level of Specificity	Highly specific, individual oriented	General, group oriented
Structure	Flexible, adaptable, changing, informal	Rigid, structured, formal

Source: Adapted from McMillan, 2008.

Planning Summative Assessment

As you think about how to construct the summative assessment, a number of preliminary steps will be helpful. The first step is to review what you think you want to do in light of the criteria for ensuring high-quality assessments that were presented in Chapter 3:

- Do I have clear and appropriate learning targets?
- What method of assessment will match best with the targets?
- Will I have good evidence that the inferences from the assessments will be valid?
- How can I construct an assessment that will minimize error?
- Will my assessment be fair and unbiased? Have students had the opportunity to learn what is being assessed?
- Will the assessment be practical and efficient?
- Will my assessment be aligned with instruction?
- Are consequences of the assessment positive?

Additional considerations include how you will obtain a representative sample of what has been learned, the length and number of assessments, whether you should use tests provided by publishers, how students should be prepared for the assessment, when the assessment should be scheduled, and when you should construct the assessment.

Representative Sampling

Most assessments *sample* what students have learned. It is rare, except for quizzes over short lessons, that you will assess everything that is included in your learning targets. There simply is not enough time to assess each fact or skill. Rather, you will select a sample of what students should know and then assume that the way they respond to assessments of this sample is typical of how they would respond to additional assessments of the entire unit.

As pointed out in Chapter 3, an important step in representative sampling is preparing a test blueprint or outline. This set of specifications is helpful because it indicates what students are responsible for learning. When assessment items are based on this outline, there is a greater likelihood that the sampling will be reasonable. You will literally be able to look at the blueprint to see how the sampling came out. Without a test blueprint or some type of outline of content, there is a tendency to oversample areas that you particularly like and to overload the assessment with a disproportionately large number of questions about simple facts (mainly because these questions are much easier to write).

Another consideration when preparing a representative sample is to construct or select the appropriate number of items for the assessment. Suppose you are preparing a test for a 6-week social studies unit on early civilizations, and you want to assess how much knowledge the students retained. How many items will be needed? Thirty? Sixty? Eighty? In the absence of any hard-and-fast rules, a couple of rules of thumb will help determine how many items are sufficient. First, a minimum of 10 items is needed to assess each knowledge learning target that encompasses the unit. Thus, if one learning target is that "students will identify the location of 25 ancient cities on a map," preparing a test that asks them to identify 10 of the 25 would be reasonable. Which 10, you may be thinking? You can select randomly if all the cities are equally difficult to locate. Normally, however, your sampling will be purposeful so that a good cross section of difficulty is selected (in this case, different types of cities).

With more specific learning targets, as few as five items can provide a good assessment. For example, you can get a pretty good idea if a student knows how to multiply three-digit numbers by requiring students to supply answers to five problems.

Number and Length of Assessments

Knowing how many items or questions are needed, you then decide how many separate assessments will be given and the length of each one. This decision will depend on several factors, including the age of the students, the length of classes, and the types of questions. One rule of thumb, though, is that the time allocated for assessment is sufficient for all students to answer all the questions. We generally do not want to use *speeded* tests in school when it is important to obtain a fair assessment of what students know and can do. This is because **speeded tests**, which require students to answer as quickly as possible to obtain a high score, increase the probability that other factors, such as anxiety and test-taking skills, will influence the result.

There is an obvious relationship between the number and length of assessments. Many short assessments can provide the same, if not better, information than a single long assessment. It will help you to focus on length first without regard to the number of assessments. This will indicate what is needed to obtain a representative sample. Then you can decide whether what is needed is best given in one large block of time, three smaller tests, weekly assessments, or whatever other combination is best. If you wait until the end of a unit to begin constructing your assessment, you may find that there is insufficient time to administer the test so that other high-quality criteria are met.

The age of students and the length of their classes are other important considerations. Kindergarten and first-grade students have relatively short attention spans, so summative assessments usually last only 5 to 10 minutes. Attention spans and stamina increase with age, but it is still best to use many short assessments rather than one or two long ones for elementary students. Thus, in later elementary grades, summative assessments typically should last between 15 and 30 minutes.

Ironically, when students are old enough to have longer attention spans, they are in middle or high schools where the length of the class usually determines the maximum length of the assessment. Consequently, most teachers plan unit and other summative assessments to last one class period, or approximately 45 minutes in many schools. In this situation, you need to provide time for directions and student questions, so you have to be careful not to end up with a speeded test. With block scheduling and other innovations, more time is available for assessment.

Another important influence on the length of time it takes students to complete an assessment is the type of item used. Obviously, essay items require much more time to complete than objective items. It also takes students longer to complete short-answer items than multiple-choice or true/false questions. The nature of the subject is also important. For example, in a test of simple knowledge in a content area, students can generally answer as many as two to four items per minute. For more difficult items, one per minute is a general rule of thumb. In math, students may need as long as 2 or 3 minutes for each item. Experience will be your best guide. Initially, try some assessments that are short so you can get an idea of how long it takes students to complete each item. Using practice questions will also give you an idea about the number of items that would be reasonable in a unit test. The best practice is to give your students too much time rather than too little time to complete the assessment.

Use of Assessments Provided by Textbook and Test Publishers

You will receive ready-made tests from textbook and instructional packages that can be used for summative assessments. These tests are prepared by the publisher for chapters and units. Some of these tests are adequate and may be useful if you remember a few key points. First, you can't assume that just because a test is provided that the results will be reliable or valid. You need to review the test carefully to make sure that fundamental principles of good assessment are followed. Second, a decision to use *any* type of assessment—whether provided in instructor's materials, by other teachers, or by yourself—is always made *after* you have identified the learning targets that you will assess. The prepared test may be technically sound, but if there is not a good match between what it tests and what you need tested, it should not be used in its entirety. Also, because these tests are often prepared by someone other than the textbook author(s), some sections may be stressed much more than others. Third, check the test carefully to make sure the language and terminology are appropriate for your students. The author of the test may use language that is not consistent with the text or the way you have taught the material. The vocabulary and sentence complexity may not be at the right level for your students. Fourth, the number of items for each target needs to be sufficient to provide a reliable measure.

As pointed out in Chapter 4, test publishers are now heavily in the business of preparing assessments for teachers. These assessments can be either formative or summative. The companies can literally customize a test for you once you have identified the state standard or target. Of course there is a charge for this service.

There is no guarantee that the test items will be of high quality, or whether they necessarily match well with your instruction. However, test company items are probably of higher quality than items prepared by textbook publishers. The best advice I can give you, if there are resources to access banks from test publishers, is to do so with caution.

The obvious advantage of using these "prepared" tests is that they can save you a great deal of time, especially when the test is provided in a format that can be simply copied. Feel free, however, to use only part of the test and to modify individual questions. Often the best use of prepared items is to get ideas that provide a good starting point for you to prepare your own test.

Preparing Students for Summative Assessments

Your objective in summative assessment is to obtain a fair and accurate indication of student learning. This means that you need to take some simple, yet often neglected, steps to prepare your students so that they will be able to demonstrate what they know, understand, and can do (see Figure 6.1).

The first step is to make sure that all your students have adequate test-taking skills, such as paying attention to directions, reading each item in its entirety before answering it, planning and outlining responses to essay questions, and pacing themselves while answering the questions. (As one teacher told me, "When I first gave math tests students would include the item number with the problem; for example, if item 2 was 3 + 4, they would answer 9—incorrect answer but they knew how to add!") Students should be directed to answer all questions (guessing is rarely penalized in classroom tests, though you don't want to encourage mindless guessing). If there is a separate sheet for recording responses, teach students to check the accuracy of their answers.

A second step is to make sure students are familiar with the format and type of question and response that will be needed on the test. This is accomplished by giving students practice test items. If time is available, it is very instructive to have students practice writing test items themselves. This is good for review sessions. Familiarity with the type of question lessens test anxiety. Of course, you don't want to teach the test—that is, use examples in class that are identical to the test items— or give students practice on the test items before they take the test. It's fine to teach

---

FIGURE 6.1   Preparing Students for Summative Assessments

- Teach test-taking skills.
- Familiarize students with test length, format, and types of questions.
- Teach to the test (do not teach *the* test).
- Review before the test.
- Tell students when the test is scheduled.

to the test, in the sense that you want to instruct students about what they will eventually be tested on. It's also helpful to students if they know the length of the test and how much the test will count in their grade.

It is likely that you will be asked or required to use test item formats that match the ones in state accountability tests. This typically comes down to two formats—multiple-choice and writing in response to prompts. But it is easy to over-stress multiple-choice formats. Remember, your primary objective is to increase student learning. This will rarely be achieved if only one type of test item is used. *Use the type of item that is best for maximizing student engagement and learning.* Students need to demonstrate their knowledge and understanding in different ways, and constructed-response items are often the best kind of assessment for detecting errors.

A review of the unit or chapter learning targets is both fair and helpful. There are several purposes for the review: to reacquaint students with material taught early in the unit, to allow students an opportunity to ask questions for clarification, to reemphasize the important knowledge and skills that students should focus on, and to provide an opportunity for students to check their understanding of what will be tested.

Finally, you will want to tell students, as soon as possible after beginning the unit, when the test is scheduled. This gives students an adequate period of time to prepare for the test. The lack of time to prepare and review for the test contributes to student anxiety and lessens the validity of the results.

Scheduling the Summative Assessment

To give students the best opportunity to show what they have learned you need to be careful when scheduling the test. Try to avoid giving a test on days that make it difficult for students to perform to their capability (e.g., prom day, right after spring vacation, after a pep rally). Also, try to schedule the test when you know you will be present and not when the class has a substitute.

You may also want to construct an instructional/assessment map (see Figure 6.2). This kind of map includes major topics in sequence, then shows when summative assessments will be included.

When Summative Assessments Should Be Constructed

Summative assessments need to be planned well in advance of the scheduled testing date. A good procedure is to construct a general outline of the test before instruction, based on your learning targets and a table of specifications. At least identify the nature of the evidence needed to provide a fair indication of student learning. This does not include the development or selection of specific items, but it provides enough information to guide you in instruction. As the unit proceeds, you can make decisions about the format of the test and begin to construct individual items. The final form of the test should be determined no later than the review session. But don't try to finalize the test too soon. You will find that as you

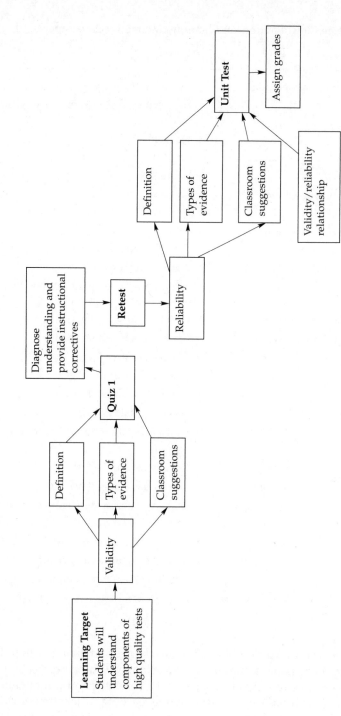

FIGURE 6.2   Instruction/Assessment Map

TABLE 6.2   Key Considerations in Planning Summative Assessments

Consideration	Key Elements
What will result in high-quality assessments?	• Appropriate learning targets • Assessment methods matched with learning targets • Reliability • Validity • Fairness
Will the sampling of content be appropriate? Will the number and length be appropriate?	• Test blueprint • Use a sufficient number of items • Avoid speeded tests; give too much rather than too little time • Age of students • Many short assessments or few long assessments
Should textbook/publisher/testing company assessments be used?	• Check quality of items • Check match to instruction • Check cognitive levels assessed • Use with caution • Combine with teacher-made items
How should students be prepared?	• Teach test-taking skills • Familiarize students with examples of item formats • Review before the test
When should the assessments be scheduled?	• Avoid distracting days • Construct instructional/assessment map • Announce test date in advance
When should assessments be constructed?	• Well in advance of testing date • Identify needed evidence before teaching • Finalize just before administering

teach, your learning targets will most likely change somewhat or that the emphasis you place on certain topics is not as you planned. These expected instructional variations should be reflected in the test. Consequently, you want to allow the test and instruction to influence each other while teaching the content or skills.

Table 6.2 summarizes key considerations in planning for summative assessments.

Putting Summative Assessments Together

Once you have developed test items, they need to be put together in the form of a test. The following guidelines, which include suggestions for directions, arranging items, and the physical layout of the test, should be followed.

Preparing Test Directions

According to Miller, Linn, and Gronlund (2009), test directions should include the following:

1. Purpose
2. Time allowed for completing the test
3. Basis for responding
4. Procedures for recording answers
5. What to do about guessing
6. How constructed-response items will be scored

The purpose of the test should be made clear to students well in advance of the testing date. This is usually done when the test is announced. Students need to know why they are taking the test and how the results will be used.

Students need to know *exactly* how much time they will have to complete the test, even if the test is not speeded. It is helpful to indicate to students how they should distribute their time among various parts of the test. It is best to allow plenty of time for students so that they do not feel rushed. As indicated earlier, students can be expected to complete at least one multiple-choice and two binary-choice items per minute, but the actual time will depend on the difficulty of the items and student preparation. Your judgments about how many items to include will improve with experience. In the beginning, err on the side of allowing too much time.

The basis for responding simply refers to what students are to do to answer the question, that is, how to respond. This should be a simple and direct statement (e.g., "Select the correct answer," or "Select the best answer"). The procedure for responding indicates how students show their answers, whether they circle the answer, write the answer next to the item, write the word in the blank, and so on. If computations are to be shown, tell the students where they should write them.

In a test on which all the items are of the selection type, students may ask about whether there is a penalty for guessing. In classroom tests it is very rare to find a correction for guessing. The best practice is to be very clear to students that they should try to answer each item (e.g., "Your score is the total number of correct answers, so answer every item").

The final suggestion for directions concerns the scoring criteria for constructed-response items. For these items it is important to clearly indicate the basis on which you will grade the students' answers *before* they study for the test. We will explore this in Chapter 8.

Arranging Items

Arranging items by level of difficulty (e.g., easy items first, then difficult ones) has little effect on the results. If you think your students gain confidence by answering the easiest items first, it's fine to order the items by increasing difficulty. The most important consideration in arranging items is item type. *Keep all the items that use the same format together.* Keep all the multiple-choice items in one section, all the matching items in another, and so on. This reduces the number of times students need to shift their response mode. It also minimizes directions and makes scoring easier. Generally it is best to order items, in sections determined by type, based on how quickly students can answer. Items answered more quickly, such as completion and binary-choice, would generally come first, followed by multiple-choice and short-answer items. If possible, it is best to group the items according to learning targets and keep assessments of the same target or content together.

Physical Layout

Assessment items need to be formatted so that they are easy to read and answer. A few commonsense suggestions help to achieve this goal. First, all the information needed to answer an item should be on the same page. Avoid having part of an item on one page and the rest of the item on another page. Second, do not crowd too many items onto a page. Although we all need to be careful about wasting paper, a test that is crowded is likely to contain more errors than one that has reasonable spacing and white space. This means that multiple-choice options should not be listed horizontally on the same line. Rather, it is best if the options are listed vertically below the item.

Finally, the format of the test should enhance scoring accuracy and efficiency. For older students, it is best to use a separate answer sheet that can be designed for scoring ease or use online tests. This can be accomplished by simply repeating the directions and listing the items by number. Students circle or write in their answers or select the answer online. If you have students answer on the same piece of paper that contains the questions, leave blanks to the left of each binary-choice, multiple-choice, or matching item and blanks on the right-hand side of the page for completion items. For younger students, it is best to minimize transfer of answers by having them circle or underline the correct answer or write the answer in the space provided in the item or answer on the same screen if online.

Administering Summative Assessments

When administering summative tests, several procedures are desirable. First, the environment during testing needs to be conducive to student performance. This means that there is sufficient light, the temperature is appropriate, and efforts are made to ensure quiet with no interruptions. Put a sign on your door—Testing,

Do Not Disturb. Special arrangements will need to be made for students with disabilities (see Chapter 12). In essence, the physical environment should not interfere with students' demonstrating what they know, understand, and can do.

Second, students should not be overly anxious about taking the test or completing the assessment. Although some anxiety is good, too much inhibits students so that their performance will not reflect their actual level of attainment. Your challenge is to find the correct balance between too much and too little anxiety. Anxiety is increased when successful student performance depends on comparisons with other students in the class, when there is insufficient time to complete the test or assessment, when attaching negative contingencies if students do not do well, when the stakes are raised, and when the purpose is to audit learning.

Third, you want to arrange an assessment to both discourage and prevent cheating. Research summarized by Cizek (1999, 2003) indicates that many, if not most, students cheat or know that others cheat. This includes looking at other students' test answers, using crib notes or a cheat sheet, plagiarism, getting others to do the students' work, obtaining copies of a test or correct answers, collusion, and using prohibited materials (Cizek, 2003). Of special note is plagiarism. With the Internet, students have access to prepared text on just about any topic. In addition to the issue of simply using such text, students may claim that they did not understand what constitutes plagiarism.

Cheating can be prevented by making sure there are clear guidelines for students regarding cheating and the importance of providing honest answers for improving student learning, by formatting tests and answer sheets to make it difficult to cheat, by careful and continuous close monitoring of students when completing the test, by using special seating arrangements, and by using more than one form of the test (e.g., different item order; Miller, Linn, & Gronlund, 2009). If plagiarism is possible, special precautions should be made, including providing examples to students and explaining how the information could be presented so that it is not plagiarized. It is also good to let students know how you can use the Internet to detect term papers that have been purchased or otherwise obtained from the Internet.

Unit/Chapter Tests

The advantage of using unit and chapter summative tests to plan instruction is that these tests can be constructed to focus on essential understandings and other targets that are clear prerequisites for further instruction. Results need to be analyzed with other sources of data to provide evidence for validity. The technical aspects of these tests, especially reliability and fairness, may not be stellar, which only increases the need for other sources of data. Sometimes the results will indicate that the test was not fair because of a mismatch between planned and actual instruction. Achievement of the best students may indicate an instructional problem if their responses are incorrect. Even so, the results can be used for whole class, small group, and/or individual student remediation.

Whole-class analysis is used to understand how the students, as a group, are performing. The results for the whole class can be reviewed to search for overall patterns of understanding and misunderstanding. Once trends and patterns are identified for the whole class, the teacher can "zoom in" on homogeneous subgroups. Subgroup analysis helps teachers answer the following questions (DiRanna, Osmundson, Topps, Barakos, Gearhart, Cerwin, Carnahan, & Strang, 2008):

How did each group of students perform?
Are there differences between different groups?
Are students within the group showing similarity of responses?
Are there differences between high-, medium-, and low-achieving groups?
Do students who tend to be more global in their learning style achieve different from students who have an analytic learning style?
Are there any differences between students based on race/ethnicity, gender, and socioeconomic status?

Individual student performance allows teachers to group students for further instruction and, when needed, to provide individualized remediation. It's also helpful to compare individual performance of students expected to do best to students expected to perform poorly. This is a check on validity, providing evidence of a match between achievement leading up to the test and performance on the test. Often "target students," those identified before testing who will receive focused analysis, will help the teacher design differentiated further instruction.

Summary

This chapter has summarized characteristics of classroom summative tests. It included discussion of how summative assessments are different from formative assessments, how to plan summative assessments, what summative tests should look like, and how they should be implemented. Major points include the following:

- Summative is assessment *of* learning; formative is assessment is *for* learning. Summative assessment documents student performance.
- Classroom summative assessments are taken after an instructional unit.
- Summative assessments tend to discourage student involvement, promote extrinsic motivation, and emphasize testing of knowledge.
- Well-planned summative assessment consists of representative sampling of learning targets, the appropriate number and length, and skeptical use of items provided by test publishers.
- Students should be prepared for taking summative tests by having adequate test-taking skills, knowledge of the format and types of questions, and an adequate review of material.
- When administering summative tests, it is best to establish an appropriate physical environment and amount of student anxiety and to prevent cheating.

Self-Instructional Review Exercises

1. Indicate which of the following characteristics of assessments would be summative (S) and which would be formative (F):

   a. To certify student learning
   b. Structured
   c. Mastery oriented
   d. After instruction
   e. Student feedback
   f. Individualized

2. Under what circumstances would it be reasonable to use summative assessments for instructional planning?

3. Match the descriptions in column A with the criteria for constructing summative assessments in column B. Each criterion may be used once, more than once, or not at all.

   Column A

   _____ **(1)** Revision of a test provided in instructional materials
   _____ **(2)** Use of test blueprint
   _____ **(3)** Teaching test-taking skills
   _____ **(4)** Using an adequate number of items for each area
   _____ **(5)** Providing time for student questions
   _____ **(6)** Chapter review

   Column B

   a. Representative sampling
   b. Length of assessment
   c. Number of assessments
   d. Use of publisher's test
   e. Preparing students
   f. Scheduling assessments

4. Indicate whether each of the following practices is desirable (D) or undesirable (U) in putting summative tests together.

   a. Plan on students completing at least four multiple-choice questions per minute.
   b. Tell students to work as quickly as possible.
   c. Arrange items so that the most difficult are first.
   d. Keep items with the same format together.
   e. Be sure to keep white space on pages to a minimum.

Answers to Self-Instructional Review Exercises

1. (a) S; (b) S; (c) F; (d) S; (e) F; (f.) F.

2. It would be appropriate to use summative assessments if the scores were disaggregated to show specific strengths and weaknesses, were clearly related to subsequent learning, and were confirmed by other sources of information.

3. (1) d; (2) a; (3) e; (4) a; (5) b; (6) e.

4. (a) U; (b) U; (c) U; (d) D; (e) U.

Suggestions for Action Research

1. Identify test items that are available from instructional packages that could be used for a unit or chapter test. Review the items for representativeness. Are there about the right number of items? Is there a table of specifications? If possible, compare the items to a test prepared by a classroom teacher.

2. Ask five other students in your class about summative assessments they have taken recently in a course. See if suggestions for planning and administering the tests meet those identified in the chapter.

3. Ask several teachers about how they prepare and administer their summative assessments. Compare their answers to suggestions contained in the chapter.

4. Conduct a review of research on the differences between formative and summative assessment. Compare what you find with what is presented in Table 6.1.

Selected-Response Assessment: Multiple-Choice, Binary-Choice, and Matching

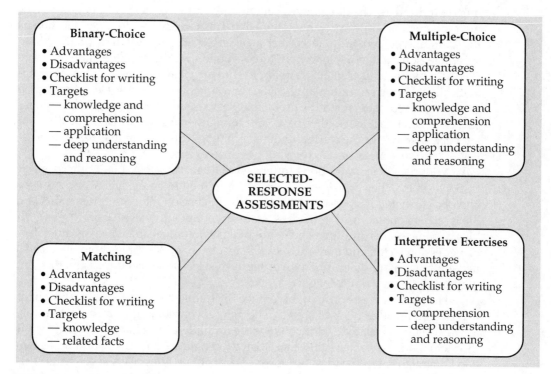

CHAPTER 7   Concept Map

With learning targets established, your attention is directed toward the kind of assessment that will provide the best evidence of student performance. In this chapter and the next, we will consider what have traditionally been called *paper-and-pencil* tests. These are assessments that have been used for decades for measuring student achievement. As pointed out in Chapter 3, there are two major kinds of paper-and-pencil items: selected response and constructed response. This chapter is concerned with selected-response assessments, familiar formats to all of us that direct students to select a correct answer from two or more possible answers that are provided. Although we have all taken selected-response tests, familiarity does not mean that these items are not challenging to construct! The principles, guidelines, and examples that are presented will help you write high-quality selected-response items. We'll begin with the ubiquitous multiple-choice format.

Multiple-Choice Items

Multiple-choice items are used widely in schools, even though they may *not* be the best method for assessing recall knowledge (see Figure 3.3). Multiple-choice items have a **stem**, in the form of a question or incomplete statement, and three or more **alternatives**. The alternatives contain one correct or best answer and two or more **distractors**. For measuring knowledge, it is usually best to use a question as the stem and to provide one correct answer. A direct question is preferred for several reasons: It is easier to write, it forces you to state the complete problem more clearly in the stem, its format is familiar to students, it avoids the problem of grammatically tailoring each alternative to the stem, and questions place less demand on reading skills to understand the problem. Questions are clearly better for younger students. Items that assess the "best" answer allow for greater discrimination and are very effective for measuring understanding. In this type of item, each alternative may have some correct aspect, but one answer is better than the others.

Multiple-choice questions offer several advantages. Like other select-response items, they can provide a broad sampling of knowledge. Scoring is easy and objective, and it's good to give students practice on the type of items they are likely to encounter on high-stakes state accountability tests. Compared with binary-choice items, multiple-choice are typically more reliable. There is much less of a guessing factor, and they are free from response set. Multiple-choice items also usually have more diagnostic power because selection of certain distractors can pinpoint an error in knowledge.

However, there are also disadvantages. Multiple-choice questions take longer to answer than other types of objective items, and consequently they do not sample as well. Also, it is relatively difficult to write multiple-choice items, especially good distractors. Many teachers find that it isn't too hard to come up with one or two good distractors, but the third or fourth ones are often giveaways to students. This increases the probability that students will guess the right answer. Students learn that the way to study for multiple-choice items is to read and reread the material to focus on recognition. Much less energy is spent to recall information. Thus, like

FIGURE 7.1   Checklist for Writing Multiple-Choice Items

✓ Is the stem stated as clearly, directly, and simply as possible?
✓ Is the problem self-contained in the stem?
✓ Is the stem stated positively?
✓ Is there only one correct answer?
✓ Are all the alternatives parallel with respect to grammatical structure, length, and complexity?
✓ Are irrelevant clues avoided?
✓ Are the options short?
✓ Are complex options avoided?
✓ Are options placed in logical order?
✓ Are the distractors plausible to students who do not know the correct answer?
✓ Are correct answers spread equally among all the choices?

other selected-response items, the type of mental preparation prompted by knowledge of multiple-choice items is not consistent with more contemporary theories of learning and information processing.

Suggestions for writing multiple-choice items are summarized in the following points and in Figure 7.1 in the form of questions. When you need to write the items, begin with the stem, then the correct response, and finally the distractors.

1. Write the Stem as a Clearly Described Question or Task.   You want the stem to be meaningful by itself. It should clearly and succinctly communicate what is expected. If the stem makes sense only by reading the responses, it is poorly constructed. It is best, then, to put as much information as possible in the stem and not the responses, as long as the stem does not become too wordy. The general rule is this: Use complete stems and short responses. This reduces the time students need to read the items and reduces redundant wording. Of course, you do not want to include words in the stem that are not needed; the stem is longer than the alternatives but is still as succinct as possible. In the end, a good indicator of an effective stem is if students have a tentative answer in mind quickly, before reading the options.

Examples

 Poor: Validity refers to
  a. the consistency of test scores.
  b. the inference made on the basis of test scores.
  c. measurement error as determined by standard deviation.
  d. the stability of test scores.

 Improved: The inference made on the basis of test scores refers to
  a. reliability.
  b. stability.
  c. validity.
  d. measurement error.

Poor: What is the length of the table?

    a. 1 foot
    b. 3 feet
    c. 15 inches
    d. 24 inches

Improved: What is the length of the table in feet?

    a. 1
    b. 2
    c. 3
    d. 4

2. Avoid the Use of Negatives in the Stem.   Using words such as *not* and *except* will confuse students, create anxiety, and lead to frustration. Often students simply overlook the negative. It also takes longer to respond to such items. So try to word the stem positively. In cases in which knowing what not to do is important, as in knowing rules of the road for driving, the negative stem is fine as long as the negative word is emphasized by boldface or underlining.

Examples

Poor: Which of the following is not a mammal?

    a. Bird
    b. Dog
    c. Horse
    d. Whale
    e. Cat

Improved: Which of the following is a mammal?

    a. Bird
    b. Frog
    c. Whale
    d. Fish
    e. Lizard

3. Write the Correct Response with No Irrelevant Clues.   There should not be any difference between the correct answer and distractors that would clue the student to respond on some basis other than the knowledge being tested. Common mistakes include making the correct response longer, more elaborate or detailed, more general, or more technical. Qualifiers such as *usually, some,* and *generally* are clues to the correct answer.

4. Write the Distractors to Be Plausible Yet Wrong.   The distractors are useless if they are so obviously wrong that students do not even consider them as possible answers. The intent of a multiple-choice item is to have students *discriminate* among what they see as possible answers. Distractors should appear to be plausible to poorly prepared students. Distractors are intended to appeal to the uniformed and should not result in tricking students. A good approach to determining good distracters is to identify common misunderstandings or errors by students and then write distractors that appeal to students who have the misunderstandings. Other ways to write good distractors include the use of words that have verbal associations with the stem, important words (e.g., *enduring, major, noteworthy*), length and complexity that matches the stem, and the use of qualifiers such as *generally* and *usually*. Poor distractors contain content that is plainly wrong, grammatical inconsistencies, or qualifiers such as *always* and *never,* or they state the opposite of the correct answer.

The number of distractors depends on several factors. Most multiple-choice items have two, three, or four distractors. Other things being equal, an item with two or three distractors is best. More questions are possible with only two distractors, which may provide better coverage. Questions for young children often have only two distractors. One thing is sure: Don't add obviously wrong distractors just to get to three or four. Once you have had some experience with writing distractors, you can do an **item analysis** to determine whether the distractors are being used with equal frequency. If a particular distractor is rarely selected, then it should be modified to be more plausible. (Item analysis is also done to see if the item *discriminates* between high and low performers on the test, i.e., whether most high performers answered it correctly and most low performers missed it, and to determine item difficulty.)

Examples

> *Poor:*   Which of the following is the largest city in the United States?
> > **a.** Michigan
> > **b.** London
> > **c.** New York
> > **d.** Berlin
>
> *Improved:*   Which of the following is the largest city in the United States?
> > **a.** Los Angeles
> > **b.** Chicago
> > **c.** New York
> > **d.** Miami
>
> *Poor:*   The first step in writing is to
> > **a.** always rewrite.
> > **b.** outline.
> > **c.** be grammatically correct.

5. Avoid Using "All of the Above," "None of the Above," or Other Special Distractors.   These phrases are undesirable for a number of reasons. "All of the above" is the right answer if all the options are correct, and some students may select the first item that is correct without reading the others. Only when students need to know what *not* to do would "none of the above" be appropriate. Be sure to avoid options such as "A and C but not D" or other combinations. Items with this type of response tend to measure reasoning ability as much as knowledge, and, especially for measuring knowledge, the items take far too long to answer.

6. Use Each Alternative as the Correct Answer about the Same Number of Times. If you have four possible choices, about 25 percent of the items should have the same letter as the correct response (20 percent if there are five choices). This avoids a pattern that can increase the chance that students will guess the correct answer. Perhaps you have heard the old admonition from test-wise students, "when in doubt, pick C." There is some truth to this for test writers who are not careful to use all the responses equally as the correct one.

Assessing Knowledge and Comprehension

Knowledge and comprehension targets are important in all subjects. Declarative knowledge of terminology and facts is effectively assessed with multiple-choice items, as is procedural knowledge. Here are some examples of good items for measuring terminology:

Examples

Which of the following best defines *reliability*?
  a. Consistency of scores
  b. Accuracy of scores
  c. Fairness of the assessment
  d. Test specifications

What one word best defines *reliability*?
  a. Consistency
  b. Accuracy
  c. Fairness
  d. Blueprint

What word is defined by the following: "The reasonableness of the inferences made from test scores"?
  a. Reliability
  b. Validity
  c. Fairness
  d. Bias

Knowledge of facts builds an important foundation for other kinds of learning, such as application, deep understanding, and reasoning. We normally think about facts as the four Ws—what, where, when, and who. The following items illustrate the assessment of specific facts:

Who was the first president of the United States?
  a. Thomas Jefferson
  b. John Adams
  c. George Washington
  d. Benjamin Franklin

What was the name of the general in the Civil War who later became president?

    a. Andrew Jackson
    b. Abraham Lincoln
    c. William Tecumseh Sherman
    d. Ulysses Grant

Multiple-choice items are also useful for measuring knowledge of principles, for example:

Which of the following is the best description of the principle of supply and demand?

    a. As supplies go up, prices go up.
    b. As supplies go down, prices go down.
    c. As prices go up, supplies go up.
    d. As supplies go up, prices go down.

Comprehension is demonstrated when students understand the essential meaning of a concept, principle, or procedure. They show this by identifying explanations and examples, by converting and translating, and by interpreting and predicting.

Test items that assess knowledge can be changed easily to assess comprehension. For instance, simply change the words used to describe or define something so that it is not verbatim from the instructional materials. Higher levels of comprehension require more work. Suppose that as a student you have learned that "photosynthesis is the process by which plants use light to make glucose." The following examples show how to measure this as comprehension.

In plants, sugar is made by energy from the sun from which of the following?

    a. Respiration
    b. Photosynthesis
    c. Energizing
    d. Growing

Which of the following is most consistent with the process of photosynthesis?

    a. Plants that get light do not need to make glucose.
    b. Plants that get less light make less glucose.
    c. Glucose is produced from plants before photosynthesis.
    d. Energy is stored in plants as glucose.

Assessing Application

Understanding is demonstrated through application when students are able to *use* what they know to solve problems in a *new* situation. This is a more sophisticated type of understanding than comprehension, and it includes the ability to interpret new information with what is known and to apply rules, principles, and strategies to new problems and situations. Obviously this is a very important type of learning target, because we want students to apply what they learn in school to new situations outside school. Knowing something well enough to apply it successfully to new situations is called learning for *transfer*. The goal is to have sufficient understanding to transfer what is known to different situations.

Perhaps the best example of learning for application is mathematics. At one level, students can memorize the steps for solving certain kinds of math problems—that is, what to do first, second, and so forth. They may even show some comprehension by being able to explain the steps in their own words. But if they cannot apply the steps to new problems and get the right answer, we conclude that they really don't *understand* the process. That's why we give math tests with new problems. Likewise, much of what we do in language arts instruction is focused on understanding at the application level. Students learn rules for grammar, sentence structure, to write drafts before final copy, and reading skills. We conclude that they actually understand how to read and write by demonstrating their skill with new material.

Your goal in assessing application is to construct items that contain new data or information that the student must work with to obtain the answer and to create new problems or applications in which students must extend what they know in a novel way. The extent of newness determines, to some extent, item difficulty and degree of understanding demonstrated. Items that contain completely new or unfamiliar material are generally more difficult than items in which there are only small differences between what was learned and the content of the question. This is why students may be able to solve new mathematics computational problems well but have trouble applying the same procedures to word problems that put the question in a new context.

The key feature of application items, then, is presenting situations that the students have not previously encountered. There are several strategies for constructing such items. One approach is to present a fictional problem that can be solved by applying appropriate procedural knowledge. For example, if students have learned about electricity and resistance, the following objective questions would test at the application level.

Examples

Application

1. Shaunda has decided to make two magnets by wrapping wire around a nail and attaching the wires to a battery so that the electric current can create a magnetic force. One magnet (A) uses thin wire, and one magnet (B) uses thick wire. Which magnet will be the strongest?

   a. A
   b. B
   c. A and B will be the same
   d. Cannot be determined from the information provided

2. A researcher investigated whether a new type of fertilizer would result in greater growth of corn plants. What is the independent variable?

   a. Growth of corn plants
   b. The researcher
   c. Type of fertilizer
   d. Amount of sunlight

3. William is given a $2.00 allowance each week. He wants to save enough money to go to the movie, which costs $4.00, and buy some candy and a soft drink at the movie. The candy will cost $1.50 and the drink will cost $2.50. How many weeks will William have to wait before he can go to the movie and buy the candy and soft drink?

   a. 2
   b. 3
   c. 4
   d. 5

Assessing Deep Understanding and Reasoning

Before we consider several methods that do a good job of assessing deep understanding and reasoning skills, two points should be emphasized. First, remember that each of the assessment methods we discuss in this book can be used to measure any learning target. Reasoning can be measured by selected-response items, and knowledge can be evaluated in student essays or performance products. However, some methods are better than others for assessing particular types of targets. Second, normally when we assess reasoning, we are also measuring how much students understand. This is clearly illustrated in the scoring criteria for many essay items, in which students are graded for demonstrating an understanding of certain concepts or principles. But there is an important trade-off. Items that assess reasoning and deep understanding well cannot begin to sample the *amount* of knowledge and simple understanding that can be tested with simple items.

Single multiple-choice items can be used to assess reasoning in two ways. One way is to focus on a particular skill, to determine whether students are able to recognize and use that skill. A second use is to assess the extent to which students can use their knowledge and skills in performing a problem-solving, decision-making, or other reasoning task. The first use is illustrated with the following examples:

Examples

(Distinguishing fact from opinion) Which of the following statements about our solar system is a fact rather than an opinion?

   a. The moon is made of attractive white soil.
   b. Stars can be grouped into important clusters.

    c. A star is formed from a white dwarf.

    d. Optical telescopes provide the best way to study the stars.

(Identifying assumptions) When Patrick Henry said "give me liberty or give me death," his assumption was that:

    a. everyone would agree with him.

    b. Thomas Jefferson would be impressed by the speech.

    c. if he couldn't have freedom he might as well die.

    d. his words would be taught to students for years.

(Recognizing bias) Peter told the group that "the ill-prepared, ridiculous senator has no business being involved in this important debate." Which words make Peter's statement biased?

    a. Important, senator

    b. Important, business

    c. Ill-prepared, ridiculous

    d. Debate, involved

(Comparison) One way in which insects are different from centipedes is that:

    a. they are different colors.

    b. one is an arthropod.

    c. centipedes have more legs.

    d. insects have two body parts.

(Analysis) Reginald decided to go sailing with a friend. He took supplies with him so he could eat, repair anything that might be broken, and find where on the lake he could sail. Which of the following supplies would best meet his needs?

    a. Bread, hammer, map

    b. Milk, bread, screwdriver

    c. Map, hammer, pliers, screwdriver

    d. Screwdriver, hammer, pliers

(Synthesis) What is the main idea in the following paragraph?

Julie picked a pretty blue boat for her first sail. It took her about an hour to understand all the parts of the boat and another hour to get the sail on. Her first sail was on a beautiful summer day. She tried to go fast but couldn't. After several lessons she was able to make her boat go fast.

    a. Sailing is fun

    b. Julie's first sail

    c. Sailing is difficult

    d. Going fast on a sailboat

    The next few examples show how multiple-choice items can be used to assess the students' ability to perform a reasoning task.

Examples

(Hypothesizing) If there were a significant increase in the number of hawks in a given area,

>   a. the number of plants would increase.
>   b. the number of mice would increase.
>   c. there would be fewer hawk nests.
>   d. the number of mice would decrease.

(Problem solving) Farmers want to be able to make more money for the crops they grow, but too many farmers are growing too many crops. What can the farmers do to make more money?

>   a. Try to convince the public to pay higher prices
>   b. Agree to produce fewer crops
>   c. Reduce the number of farmers
>   d. Work on legislation to turn farmland into parks

(Critical thinking) Peter is deciding which car to buy. He is impressed with the sales representative for the Ford, and he likes the color of the Buick. The Ford is smaller and gets more miles to the gallon. The Buick takes larger tires and has a smaller trunk. More people can ride in the Ford. Which car should Peter purchase if he wants to do everything he can to ensure that his favorite lake does not become polluted?

>   a. Ford
>   b. Buick
>   c. Either car
>   d. Can't decide from the information provided

(Predicting) Suppose that the midwest United States, which grows most of the country's corn, suffered a drought for several years and produced much less corn than usual. What would happen to the price of corn?

>   a. The price would rise.
>   b. The price would fall.
>   c. The price would stay the same.
>   d. People would eat less corn.

Binary-Choice Items

When students select an answer from only two response categories, they are completing a **binary-choice item**. This type of item may also be called *alternative* *response, alternate response,* or *alternate choice.* The most popular binary-choice item is the true/false question; other types of options can be right/wrong, correct/incorrect, yes/no, fact/opinion, agree/disagree, and so on. In each case, the student selects one of two options.

Binary-choice items are constructed from propositional statements about knowledge. A *proposition* is a declarative sentence that makes a claim about content or relationships among content. Simple recall propositions include the following:

> Lansing is the capital of Michigan.
> Peru is in the southern hemisphere.
> The area of a square is found by squaring the length of one side.

These propositions provide the basis for good test items because they capture an important thought or idea. Once the proposition is constructed, it is relatively easy to keep it as is, rephrase and keep the same meaning, or change one aspect of the statement and then use it for a binary-choice test item. As such, the items provide a simple and direct measure of one's knowledge of facts, definitions, and the like, as long as there is no exception or qualification to the statement. That is, one of the two choices must be *absolutely* true or false, correct or incorrect, and so on. Some subjects, such as science and history, lend themselves to this type of absolute proposition better than others.

Using binary-choice items has several advantages. First, the format of such questions is similar to what is asked in class, so students are familiar with the thinking process involved in making binary choices. Second, short binary items provide for an extensive sampling of knowledge because students are able to answer many items in a short time (two to five items per minute). Third, these items can be written in short, easy-to-understand sentences. Compared to multiple-choice items, binary-choice questions are relatively easy to construct, and scoring is objective and quick.

The major disadvantage of binary-choice items is that they are susceptible to guessing, particularly if the items are poorly constructed, and often test-wise students can find clues to the correct answer. Thus, a combination of some knowledge, guessing, and poorly constructed items that give clues to the correct answer will allow some students to score well, even though their level of knowledge is weak.

Assessing Knowledge and Comprehension

Writing good binary-choice items begins with propositions about major knowledge targets. In converting the propositions to test items, you will need to keep the items short, simple, direct, and easy to understand. This is best accomplished by avoiding ambiguity and clues to the correct answer. The following suggestions, summarized in Figure 7.2, will help accomplish this.

FIGURE 7.2   Checklist for Writing Binary-Choice Items

✓ Does the item contain a single proposition or idea?
✓ Is the type of answer logically consistent with the statement?
✓ Are the statements succinct?
✓ Is the item stated positively?
✓ Is the length of both statements in an item about the same?
✓ Do the correct responses have a pattern?
✓ Are unequivocal terms used?
✓ Does the item try to trick students?
✓ Is trivial knowledge being tested?
✓ Are about half the items answered correctly with same response?

1. Write the Item So That the Answer Options Are Consistent with the Logic in the Sentence.   The way the item is written will suggest a certain logic for what type of response is most appropriate. For example, if you want to test spelling knowledge, it doesn't make much sense to use true/false questions; it would be better to use correct/incorrect as options.

2. Include a Single Fact or Idea in the Item.   For assessing recall knowledge, avoid two or more facts, ideas, or propositions in a single item. This is because one idea or fact may be true and the other false, which introduces ambiguity and error.

Examples

> *Poor:* T F   California is susceptible to earthquakes because of the collision between oceanic and continental plates.
>
> *Improved:* T F   Earthquakes in California are caused by the collision between oceanic and continental plates.

3. Avoid Long Sentences.   Try to keep the sentences as concise as possible. This allows you to include more test items and reduces ambiguity. Longer sentences tend to favor students who have stronger reading comprehension skills.

Examples

> *Poor:* T F   A cup with hot water that has a spoon in it will cool more quickly than a similar cup with the same amount of hot water that does not have a spoon in it.
>
> *Improved:* T F   Hot water in a cup will cool more quickly if a spoon is placed in the cup.

4. Avoid Insignificant or Trivial Facts and Words.   It is relatively easy to write "tough" binary-choice items that measure trivial knowledge. Avoid this by beginning with what you believe are the most significant learning targets.

Examples

> *Poor:*   Charles Darwin was twenty-two years old when he began his voyage of the world.

> *Poor:*   An elephant spends about fifteen hours a day eating and foraging.

5. Avoid Negative Statements.   Statements that include the words *not* or *no* are confusing to students and make items and answers more difficult to understand. Careful reading and sound logic become prerequisites for answering correctly. If the knowledge can be tested only with a negatively worded statement, be sure to highlight the negative word with boldface type, underlining, or all caps.

Examples

> *Poor:*   United States senators are not elected to six-year terms.

> *Improved:*   United States senators are elected to six-year terms.

6. Avoid Clues to the Answer.   Test-wise students will look for specific words that suggest that the item is false. When adjectives and adverbs such as *never, all, every, always,* and *absolutely* are used, the answer is usually false. Also, avoid any kind of pattern in the items that provides clues to the answer, such as all true items being longer, alternating true and false answers, tending to use one type of answer more than the other, or all the items being either true or false. It is best to write questions so that about 50% of the answers are true.

7. Do Not Try to Trick Students.   Items that are written to "trick" students by including a word that changes the meaning of an idea or by inserting some trivial fact should be avoided. Trick items undermine your credibility, frustrate students, and provide less valid measures of knowledge.

8. Avoid Using Vague Adjectives and Adverbs.   Adjectives and adverbs such as *frequent, sometimes, occasionally, typically,* and *usually* are interpreted differently by each student. It is best to avoid these types of words because the meaning of the statement is not equivocal.

Assessing Deep Understanding and Reasoning

Binary-choice items can be used to assess reasoning skills in several different ways. Students can be asked to indicate whether a statement is a fact or an opinion:

Examples

If the statement is a fact, circle F; if it is an opinion, circle O.

> F   O   Literature is ancient Rome's most important legacy.
> F   O   The word *Mississippi* has eleven letters.
> F   O   The best way to wash a car is with a sponge.

Additional reasoning skills can be assessed using the same approach by developing some statements that are examples of the skill and some statements that are not examples. This can be done with many of the critical thinking skills (e.g., identifying stereotypes, biased statements, emotional language, relevant data, and verifiable data).

Examples

If the statement is an example of a stereotype, circle S; if it is not a stereotype, circle N.

    S N Mexican Americans are good musicians.
    S N Women live longer than men.

If emotional language is used in the statement, circle E; if no emotional language is used, circle N.

    E N Health insurance reform is needed so that poor people with serious injuries will be able to lead productive lives.
    E N Health insurance is going to cost a lot of money.

Logic can be assessed by asking if one statement follows logically from another:

Examples

If the second part of the sentence explains why the first part is true, circle T for true; if it does not explain why the first part is true, circle F for false.

    T F Food is essential *because* it tastes good.
    T F Plants are essential *because* they provide oxygen.
    T F Reggie is tall *because* he has blue eyes.

Assessing Application

Assessing application with binary-choice items is essentially the same process as is used with multiple-choice items. Knowledge needs to be used to answer questions that present novel situations. For example, the following questions would test what students have learned about electricity and resistance at the application level.

Examples

1. T F Other things being equal, an electric stove with greater resistance will be hotter than a stove with less resistance.
2. T F Jon is building a new electric motor. His decision to use thicker wire results in less resistance.

Matching Items

Matching items effectively and efficiently measure the extent to which students know related facts, associations, and relationships. Some examples of such associations include terms with definitions, persons with descriptions, dates with events, and symbols with names.

The major advantage of matching is that the teacher can efficiently obtain a good sampling of a large amount of knowledge. Matching is easily and objectively scored. Constructing good matching items is not as difficult as preparing multiple-choice items. However, poor matching items are constructed when there is insufficient material to include in the item and irrelevant information is added that is unrelated to the major topic that has been targeted for assessment.

In a matching item, the items on the left are called the *premises*. In the right-hand column are the *responses*. The student's task is to match the correct response with each of the premises. As long as the suggestions listed next are followed, matching items are excellent for measuring knowledge that includes associations.

1. Make Sure Directions Are Clear to Students.   Even though matching items are familiar to students, it is helpful to indicate in writing (or orally for young students) the basis for the matching and where and how student responses should be recorded. Generally, letters are used for each response in the right-hand column, and students are asked to write the selected letter next to each premise. Younger students can be asked to draw lines to connect the premises to the responses. It is important in the directions to indicate that *each response may be used once, more than once, or not at all.* This lessens the probability that, through a process of elimination, guessing will be a factor in the results.

2. Include Homogeneous Premises and Responses.   Avoid putting information from different lessons in the same matching item. You wouldn't want to include recent scientists, early U.S. presidents, and sports figures in the same item. Even though what is homogeneous varies from one person to another, this principle is the one most violated. For example, it makes good sense to use matching to test student knowledge of important dates during the Civil War. It would not be a good idea to contain both dates and men's names as responses. Testing homogeneous material with matching is effective for fairly fine discriminations among facts. For example, matching dates with events in one of the Civil War battles provides greater discrimination than matching dates with major battles.

3. Use Four to Eight Premises.   You do not want to have too long a list of premises. A relatively short list will probably be more homogeneous and will be perceived by students as more fair.

4. Keep Responses Short and Logically Ordered.   Usually the responses include a list of one- or two-word names, dates, or other terms. Definitions, events, and descriptions are in the premise column. Students will be more accurate in their answers if the responses are in logical order. Thus, if responses are dates, they should be rank ordered by year; words or names should be alphabetized. Like premises, keep the number of responses to eight, ten at the most. Longer lists waste students' time and contribute to error by including reasoning abilities as part of what is needed to answer the item correctly.

5. Avoid Grammatical Clues to Correct Answers.   As with completion items, you need to be careful that none of your matches are likely because of grammatical clues, such as verb tense agreement.

6. Put Premises and Responses on the Same Page.   You don't want students to have to flip back and forth between two pages to answer the items. This is distracting and only contributes to error.

7. Use More Responses Than Premises.   Using more responses than premises provides greater coverage of information and is a better indicator of knowledge by reducing guessing of some correct answers that occurs if the same number of premises and responses are used and each response is used only once.

Example

The following is an example of a good matching set. Notice the complete directions, responses on the right in logical order, and homogeneous content (achievements of early presidents).

Directions: Match the achievements in column A with the names of presidents in column B. Write the letter of the president who had the achievement on the line next to each number. Each name in column B may be used once, more than once, or not at all.

Column A

_____ 1 Second president
_____ 2 President when there were no severe external threats to the country
_____ 3 Declined to run for a third term
_____ 4 Wrote the Declaration of Independence
_____ 5 Last of the presidents from Virginia

Column B

A. John Adams
B. John Quincy Adams
C. Andrew Jackson
D. Thomas Jefferson
E. James Madison
F. James Monroe
G. George Washington

Suggestions for writing matching items are summarized in Figure 7.3.

FIGURE 7.3   **Checklist for Writing Matching Items**

✓ Is it clear how and where students place their answers?
✓ Is it clear that each response may be used once, more than once, or not at all?
✓ Is the information included homogeneous?
✓ Are there more responses than premises?
✓ Are the responses logically ordered?
✓ Are grammatical clues avoided?
✓ Is there only one feasible answer for each premise?
✓ Is the set of premises or responses too long?
✓ Are premises and responses on the same page?

Interpretive Exercises

The interpretive exercise consists of some information or data, followed by several questions. The information or data are typically in the form of maps, paragraphs, charts, figures, a story, a table of data, or pictures. The form of the question makes it possible to assess interpretation, analysis, application, critical thinking, and other reasoning skills, as well as comprehension.

Interpretive exercises have four major advantages over other types of items. First, because there are several questions about the same information, it is possible to measure more reasoning skills in greater depth. Second, because information is provided, it is possible to separate the assessment of the reasoning skills from content knowledge of the subject. If content is not provided in the question, as is the case with most multiple-choice items, then a failure to provide a good answer could be attributed to either the student's lack of knowledge or lack of reasoning skill. In the interpretive exercise, students have all or most of the information needed as part of the question, so successful performance provides a more direct measure of reasoning skill. Clearly, the intent of the exercise is to assess how students use the information provided to answer questions. If students know ahead of time that the information will be provided, then they can concentrate their study on application and other uses of the information.

A third advantage of the interpretive exercise is that it is relatively easy-to-use material that students will encounter in everyday living, such as maps, newspaper articles, and graphs. Consistent with constructivist learning theory, this connects the material better with the student, increasing meaningfulness and relevance. Finally, because interpretive exercises provide a standard structure for all students, the results tend to be more reliable. Students are unable to select a reasoning skill they are most proficient with, as they can do with essay questions. They must use the one called for in each question.

Interpretive exercises have three limitations. First, they are time consuming and difficult to write. Not only do you need to locate or develop the information or data that will be new for the students and at the right difficulty level, which could

FIGURE 7.4   Checklist for Writing Interpretive Exercises

✓ Are reasoning targets clearly defined before writing the exercise?
✓ Is introductory material brief?
✓ Is introductory material new to the students?
✓ Are there several questions for each exercise?
✓ Does the exercise test deep understanding and reasoning (and not just simple understanding)?

take considerable time, but you also need to construct the questions. The information you first identify may need to be modified, and most teachers are not accustomed to writing several questions for a single passage or example.

A second limitation is that you are unable to assess how students organize their thoughts and ideas or to know whether students can produce their own answers without being cued. Third, many interpretive exercises rely heavily on reading comprehension. This puts poor readers at a distinct disadvantage. It takes them longer to read the material for understanding, let alone reason with it. This disadvantage holds for other types of items that require extensive reading as well, but it is especially troublesome for interpretive exercises.

Whether you develop your own interpretive exercises or use ones that have already been prepared, the following suggestions will help ensure high quality (see Figure 7.4 for a checklist summary).

1. Identify the Comprehension and Reasoning Skills to Be Assessed before Selection or Development of the Interpretive Exercise. The sequence you use is important because you want the exercise to fit your learning targets, not have learning targets determined by the interpretive exercise. This is especially important given the number of different conceptualizations of thinking and reasoning skills. What may be called "critical thinking" or "analysis" in a teacher's manual may not coincide with what you think the target is. You need to have a clear idea of the skill to be assessed and then select or develop the material that best fits your definition.

2. Keep Introductory Material as Brief as Possible. Keeping the introductory material brief minimizes the influence of general reading ability. There should be just enough material so that the students can answer the questions.

3. Select Similar but New Introductory Material. Deep understanding and reasoning skills are best measured with material that is mostly new to the students. If the material is the same as that covered in class, you will measure rote memory or simple understanding rather than reasoning. The goal is to find or develop examples that are similar to what students have already studied. The material should vary slightly in form or content, but it should not be completely new. A good strategy to use to accomplish this is to take passages, examples, and data students have been exposed to and alter them sufficiently so that correct answers cannot be given by memory.

4. Construct Several Test Items for Each Exercise. Asking more than one question for each exercise obtains a better sample of their understanding and the proficiency of students' reasoning skills. It would be particularly inefficient to have a very long introductory passage and a single question.

5. Construct Items to Require Understanding and Reasoning. You do not want to use questions that can be answered without even reading the introductory material. This happens when students' general knowledge is such that they can determine the correct answer from the question alone.

Assessing Comprehension

The most common type of interpretive exercise with selected responses is in the area of reading comprehension. A reading passage is presented, followed by several questions that test the student's comprehension.

Interpretive exercises are illustrated in the following four examples. Note that many different formats can be used for the items. The reasoning skills that are assessed in Examples 2, 3, and 4 are indicated in parentheses next to each example number.

Example 1.

Hummingbirds

The hummingbird is amazing! Their wings flap so fast that they are a blur, flapping as much as 80 times a second. The flapping wings also make a soft buzzing sound, which is why it is called a humming bird. The fast flapping wings are used to go straight up or down, sideways, backward, or upside down.

The hummingbird eats the sugary juice of flowers, which is called nectar. It hovers in the air while it is eating with its long, thin bill. Much energy is needed by the hummingbird, so that it eats about every 10 minutes and travels to about 1,500 different flowers each day.

1. Which of the following best describes nectar?

   a. Food that comes from insects
   b. Sweet food from flowers
   c. Food found in flower petals
   d. Food that is found in small pools of water

2. What is the main idea in the second paragraph?

   a. Hummingbird wings flap very fast.
   b. Hummingbirds have narrow bills to suck out nectar.
   c. Hummingbirds are small.
   d. Hummingbirds go up or down.

3. Why do hummingbirds need to eat all the time?

    a. To obtain nectar
    b. To provide energy needed to fly
    c. To fly up or down
    d. To eat sugar

4. T   F   Nectar is a sweet kind of food.

Assessing Deep Understanding and Reasoning

Interpretive items are especially good at assessing reasoning and critical thinking skills.

Example 2.   (drawing inferences, analyzing perspectives)

Two citizens spoke at the city council meeting. Here are their statements. Use the information to help you answer the questions.

> **CITIZEN A:** The Bower House should be restored and used as a museum. A museum would help the people of the community learn about their heritage and would attract tourists to Grenville. We should not sell the property to the Opti Company. Grenville has grown too quickly, and a factory would bring even more people into the area. In addition, a factory's industrial waste would threaten the quality of our water.

> **CITIZEN B:** Grenville needs the Opti factory. The factory would provide needed jobs. The tax money it would bring into the community would help improve our streets, schools, and other city services. A museum, on the other hand, would hurt our local economy. Taxes would have to be raised to pay for the restoration of the Bower House. A museum would not create enough jobs to solve our unemployment problem.

Write the letter A next to each statement that Citizen A would most likely agree with. Write the letter B next to each statement that Citizen B would most likely agree with.

    _____ **(10)** Jobs are the foundation of a community.
    _____ **(11)** Pollution problems will multiply.
    _____ **(12)** We are in danger of losing the history of our community.
    _____ **(13)** Hanging on to the past hurts the future.

Example 3.   (recognizing the relevance of information)

Sally lost her pencil on her way to school. It was red and given to her by her grandmother. She wanted the teacher to ask the class if anyone found the pencil.

Circle *yes* if the information in the sentence will help the class find the pencil.

Circle *no* if the information in the sentence will not help the class find the pencil.

yes   no   **1.** The pencil was new.
yes   no   **2.** Sally rides the bus to school.
yes   no   **3.** The pencil is red.
yes   no   **4.** The pencil was a present from Sally's grandmother.
yes   no   **5.** The pencil had a new eraser.
yes   no   **6.** The teacher knows Sally's grandmother.

Example 4. (analysis, inference, error analysis)

Based on Figure 7.5, circle T if the statement is true and F if the statement is false.

T   F   In 1990, more female than male students graduated from high school.
T   F   From 1980 to 1990, the percentage of female students graduating from high school increased gradually.
T   F   Overall, the best year for graduating students was 1987.
T   F   From 1980 to 1990, more female than male students graduated from high school.

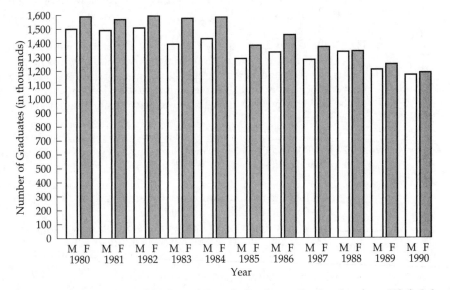

FIGURE 7.5   Number of Male and Female Students Graduating from High School in the United States

Source: U.S. Department of Education, Office of Educational Research and Improvement. (1994). *Digest of education statistics*, p. 188.

Summary

This chapter has examined the nature of selected-response assessments, including multiple-choice, binary-choice, matching, and interpretive exercises. It was shown how these formats can be used for different types of learning targets. Suggestions for writing each type, with examples, were summarized. Major points include the following:

- Multiple-choice items consist of a stem, correct answer, and distractors.
- It is best to format the stem in a multiple-choice item as a question.
- Multiple-choice items can be used for efficient assessment of a large domain of knowledge, generally provide reliable scores, and are easily and objectively scored.
- Multiple-choice items are difficult to write, especially for deep understanding and reasoning targets.
- The use of negatives in multiple-choice item stems should be avoided.
- For multiple-choice items, it is better to have longer stems than alternatives.
- Multiple-choice items are effective if they are clearly and directly stated with one correct answer, include plausible distractors, and do not provide clues to the correct answer.
- Multiple-choice items can be used to assess specific reasoning skills or to use reasoning in problem solving.
- Binary-choice items, such as true/false items, are effective if they are clearly, succinctly, and positively stated as single propositions or statements.
- Matching items are effective for assessing simple understanding of related facts or concepts as long as responses are short, premises and responses are homogeneous, lists are logically ordered, no grammatical clues are given, and no more than ten premises are in one matching item.
- Selected-response interpretive exercises include information and/or data, followed by several questions.
- Interpretive exercises are effective for assessing comprehension, application, and reasoning skills and can reflect real-life situations, contexts, and issues.
- Interpretive exercises are effective if learning targets are clearly defined, if introductory material is new to students, and if they are not too long.

Self-Instructional Review Exercises

1. Match the suggestions or descriptions from column A with the type(s) of objective items in column B. Each type of item may be used once, more than once, or not at all; each suggestion or description may have more than one correct match.

Column A	Column B
_____ (1) Generally more time consuming to construct	**a.** Matching
_____ (2) Effectively measures relations	**b.** Binary choice
_____ (3) Conveniently constructed from instructional materials	**c.** Multiple choice
_____ (4) Responses ordered logically	
_____ (5) Correct answers spread equally among all possible choices	
_____ (6) Verbatim language from textbooks is avoided	
_____ (7) Uses clear, concise statements	

2. Using the checklist for writing matching items, evaluate each of the following items and revise them so that they will be improved.

(1) Match the states with the characteristics.

_____ Florida	**a.** St. Augustine
_____ New York	**b.** Bordered by Missouri and Minnesota
_____ Michigan	**c.** Alamo
_____ Colorado	**d.** Jamestown
_____ Iowa	**e.** Outer Banks
_____ Texas	**f.** Lincoln
_____ Utah	**g.** Largest city
_____ Illinois	**h.** Great Lake State
_____ Virginia	**i.** Great Salt Lake
_____ North Carolina	**j.** Denver

(2) T F   Students do not construct their own answers to every type of item except multiple choice.

(3) Circle the best answer.
Michigan is a(n) (a) Great Lake State, (b) state in which the Rocky Mountains are located, (c) example of a state that is west of the Mississippi, (d) none of the above.

(4) Circle the correct answer.

Biodegradable substances are

a. nonrenewable resources.
b. materials that can be broken down into substances that are simpler and do not result in environmental pollution.
c. becoming less popular.
d. like fossil fuels.

Answers to Self-Instructional Review Exercises

1. 1. c, 2. a, 3. b, 4. a, c, 5. c, 6. a, b, c, 7. a, b, c.

2. (1) There are probably too many items in one list. Additional responses should be included as distractors. Better to have states listed on the right. Directions are inad-

equate. Format is difficult to score. Premises are not homogeneous and are on the wrong side. Do not mix cities with historical figures, geographic descriptions, and state mottos.

Revision: On the line next to each number in column A, write the letter of the state from column B that matches the geographic descriptions. Each state may be used once, more than once, or not at all.

Column A	*Column B*
_____ **(1)** Is bordered by three Great Lakes	**a.** New York
_____ **(2)** Contains part of the Rocky Mountains	**b.** Virginia
_____ **(3)** Has an upper and lower peninsula	**c.** Ohio
_____ **(4)** Is bordered by the Ohio and Mississippi	**d.** Michigan
rivers	
_____ **(5)** Contains the Blue Ridge Mountains	**e.** Texas
	f. Colorado
	g. Illinois
	h. Maryland
	i. North Carolina

(2) The negatives in this item make it very hard to understand. State more directly the proposition to be tested. Directions need to be included.

Revision: If the statement is true, circle T; if it is false, circle F.
T   F   Students construct answers to multiple-choice items.

(3) The directions should indicate "correct" answer, not "best" answer. The alternatives should be listed vertically under the stem. The stem should be long, the alternatives short. Option (c) does not fit grammatically and is not concise. "None of the above" should be avoided. It would be better to use a question.

Revision: Circle the correct answer.
Which of the following is a characteristic of Michigan?

a. It is surrounded by the Great Lakes.
b. It contains the Rocky Mountains.
c. It is a single peninsula.
d. It borders the Atlantic Ocean.

(4) The correct answer, b, is obvious because of the complexity of the sentence in relation to the others. Fossil fuels are also biodegradable, so more than one correct answer is possible. The stem is short and the correct alternative long. It is more clearly stated as a question.

Revision: Circle the correct answer.
What type of material is broken down by decomposers into simpler substances that do not pollute the environment?

a. Nonrenewable
b. Biodegradable
c. Fossil fuel
d. Decomposition

Suggestions for Action Research

1. Collect some examples of selected-response test items. Analyze the items and the format of the test in relation to the suggestions provided in the chapter. Show how you would improve the items and format of the test.

2. With another student, make up a knowledge test of each of the three types of selected-response items of the content of this chapter that could be taken in 1 hour. Begin with a table of specifications or outline and indicate the learning targets. Give the test to four other students for their critique, and then revise the test as needed. Show the original test and the revised one to your supervisor or teacher for his or her critique and further suggestions. Keep a journal of your progress in making up the test. What was difficult? How much time did it take? What would have made the process more efficient?

Constructed-Response Assessment: Completion, Short-Answer, and Essay Items

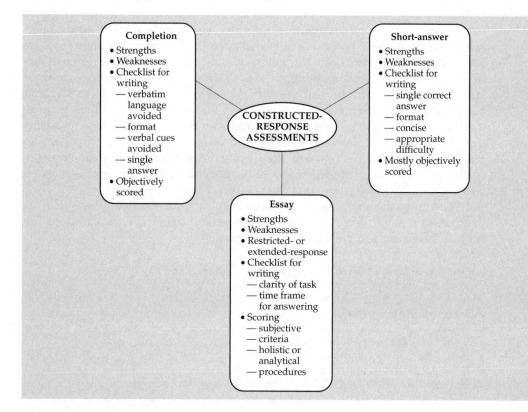

CHAPTER 8   Concept Map

Constructed-response assessment (also called *supply-type*) has been, and continues to be, a mainstay tool of teachers. When students are able to recall answers to direct questions, without cues to the correct answer as are evident in selected-response items, teachers are able to clearly determine if students have a thorough understanding, can apply knowledge to solve problems, and can reason. Teachers use constructed responses continually in a formative manner to detect errors in thinking.

We will consider three paper-and-pencil types of constructed-response items in this chapter—completion, short answer, and essay—then examine more complex constructed-response assessments—performance and portfolio—in the following two chapters. Completion and short-answer items are often considered "objective" because the scoring of the items is quick and straightforward. This distinguishes these formats from essays, which require more subjective judgments in scoring.

Completion Items

The most common and effective way to assess knowledge is simply to ask a question and require the students to answer it from memory. Items for which the student responds to an incomplete statement are *completion items*.

The completion item offers the least freedom of student response, calling for one answer at the end of a sentence. Responses may be in the form of words, numbers, or symbols. If properly constructed, completion items are excellent for measuring how well students can recall facts because of these strengths: (a) they are easy to construct, (b) their short response time allows a good sampling of different facts, (c) guessing contributes little to error, (d) scorer reliability is high, (e) they can be scored more quickly than short-answer or essay items, and (f) they provide more valid results than a test with an equal number of selected-response items (e.g., multiple choice). There are only two limitations of using completion items to measure knowledge. The first is in the scoring. It takes a little more time to score completion items than selected-response items. Second, if the sentence is not well written, more than one answer may be possible.

The following suggestions for constructing completion items use examples that measure either declarative or procedural knowledge. The suggestions are summarized in the form of a checklist in Figure 8.1.

Figure 8.1   Checklist for Writing Completion Items

✓ Is verbatim language from instructional materials avoided?
✓ Is knowledge being assessed?
✓ Is a single, brief answer required?
✓ Is the blank at the end of the sentence?
✓ Is the length of each blank the same?
✓ Is the precision of a numerical answer specified?
✓ Is it worded to avoid verbal clues to the right answer?

1. Paraphrase Sentences from Textbooks and Other Instructional Materials. It is tempting to lift a sentence verbatim from materials the students have studied, and replace a word or two with blanks. However, statements in textbooks, when taken out of context, are often too vague or general to be good completion items. Also, you don't want to encourage students to memorize phraseology in the text. Consistent with constructivistic principles, you want students to connect what they learn with what they already know, even when it is recall. Thus, you want to paraphrase or restate facts in words that are different from those the students have read.

Examples

The textbook statement is "James Buchanan, elected president in 1856, personally opposed slavery."

> *Poor:* James Buchanan, elected president in 1856, personally opposed _____.

> *Improved:* The name of the president who was elected in 1856, and who thought slavery was not proper, was _____.

2. Word the Sentence So That Only One Brief Answer Is Correct.   The single greatest error in writing completion items is to use sentences that can be legitimately completed with more than one response. This occurs if the sentence is too vague or open-ended.

Examples

> *Poor:* Columbus first landed on "America" _____.

> *Improved:* Columbus first landed on "America" in _____.

> *Better:* Columbus first landed on "America" in the year _____.

In the first example, students could logically provide correct answers having nothing to do with the year. In the improved version an answer like "a boat" would be correct.

3. Place One or Two Blanks at the End of the Sentence.   If blanks are placed at the beginning or in the middle of the sentence, it may be more difficult for students to understand what response is called for. It is easier and more direct to first read the sentence and then determine what will complete it correctly. (That's why it's called a *completion* item!)

Examples

> *Poor:* In 1945, _____ decided to have the atomic bomb dropped on Japan.

> *Improved:* The name of the president who decided to have the atomic bomb dropped on Japan in 1945 was _____.

You also will not want to use several blanks in a single sentence. This will confuse students and measure reasoning skills as much, if not more, than knowledge.

Example

> *Poor:* The name of the _____ who decided to have the _____ _____ dropped on _____ in 1945 was _____.

4. If Answered in Numerical Units, Specify the Unit Required. For completion items that require numerical answers, the specific units or the degree of precision should be indicated.

Examples

> *Poor:* The distance between the moon and the earth is _____.

> *Improved:* The distance between the moon and the earth is _____ miles.

5. Do Not Include Clues to the Correct Answer. Test-wise students will look for clues in the way sentences are worded and the length of blanks that may indicate a correct answer. The most common wording errors are using single or plural verbs and wording the sentence so that the blank is preceded by "a" or "an." These clues can be eliminated by avoiding verb agreement with the answer, by using "a(an)," and by making all blanks the same length.

Examples

> *Poor:* The two legislative branches of the United States federal government are the _____ and the _____ _____ _____.

> *Improved:* The two legislative branches of the United States federal government are the _____ and the _____.

Short-Answer Items

Short-answer items, in which the student supplies an answer consisting of one word, a few words, or a sentence or two, are generally preferred to completion items for assessing knowledge targets. First, this type of item is similar to how teachers phrase questions and direct student behavior during instruction. This means that the item is more natural for students. Students are familiar with answering questions and providing responses to commands that require knowledge (e.g., "Write the definition of each of the words on the board"). Second, it is easier for teachers to write these items to more accurately measure knowledge.

Assessing Knowledge and Comprehension. Short-answer items are usually stated in the form of a question (e.g., "Which state is surrounded by three large bodies of fresh water?"). They can also be stated in general directions (e.g., "Define each of the following terms"), and they can require responses to visual stimulus materials (e.g., "Name each of the countries identified with arrows A–D").

FIGURE 8.2   Checklist for Writing Short-Answer Items

✓ Is only one answer correct?
✓ Are questions from textbooks avoided?
✓ Is it clear to students that the answer is brief?
✓ Is the precision of a numerical answer specified?
✓ Is the item written as succinctly as possible?
✓ Is the space designated for answers consistent with the length required?
✓ Are words used in the item too difficult for any students?

Like completion items, short-answer items are good for measuring knowledge because students can respond to many items quickly, a good sample of knowledge is obtained, guessing is avoided, scoring is fairly objective, and results are generally more valid than those obtained from selected-response formats. The main disadvantage of short-answer items is that scoring takes longer and is more subjective than completion or selected-response items. The following suggestions, summarized in Figure 8.2, will help you write good short-answer items.

1. State the Item So That Only One Answer Is Correct.   Be sure that the question or directions are stated so that what is required in the answer is clear to students. If more than one answer is correct, the item is vague and the result is invalid. If you are expecting a one-word answer, use a single short blank.

Examples

> *Poor:* Where is the Eiffel Tower located?
> *Improved:* In what country is the Eiffel Tower located? *or* Name the country in which the Eiffel Tower is located.

Obviously, in the first item students could give several responses—Europe, Paris, France—each of which would be technically correct.

2. State the Item So That the Required Answer Is Brief.   Remember that short-answer items of knowledge have answers that are *short!* Keep student responses to a word or two, or a short sentence, or two or three if necessary, by properly wording the item, offering clear directions, and providing space or blanks that indicate the length of the response. In the directions, state clearly that students should not repeat the question in their answer.

Examples

> *Poor:* What does the term *reptile* mean? _____
>
> _____
>
> *Improved:* Name three characteristics of reptiles.
>
> 1. _____

2. _____

3. _____

Examples

> List three ways the recession of the 1980s was like the depression of the 1920s.
>
> How does a pine tree differ from an oak tree?
>
> Name one difference between vertebrate and invertebrate animals.

3. Do Not Use Questions Verbatim from Textbooks or Other Instructional Materials.   Most textbooks include review questions and questions for study. You don't want to use these same questions on tests because it encourages rote memorization of answers.

4. Designate Units Required for the Answer.   Students need to know the specific units and the degree of precision that should be used in their answer. This will avoid the time students may take to try to figure out what is wanted—such as asking a question for clarification during the test—and it will mitigate scoring difficulties.

Examples

> *Poor:* When was President John F. Kennedy killed?
> *Improved:* In what year was President John F. Kennedy killed?

5. State the Item Succinctly with Words Students Understand.   It is best to state questions or sentences as concisely as possible and to avoid using words or phrases that may be difficult for some students to understand.

Examples

> *Poor:* What was the name of the extraordinary president of the United States who earlier had used his extensive military skills in a protracted war with exemplary soldiers from another country?
> *Improved:* What United States general defeated the British and later became president?

Assessing Deep Understanding and Reasoning

Short-answer items can assess deep understanding as long as the response that is required is brief. Students are required to use their knowledge, not simply recall it. Here are examples of short-answer items that assess deep understanding:

Examples

> What are two different points of view about whether it is best to have nationalized medicine?

What is the implication on the environment of using more nuclear power to provide electricity?

How would the validity of an assessment be judged if the teacher used multiple-choice items rather than essay items to test student knowledge?

Short-answer items have a limited capacity to assess reasoning skills, although reasoning to come up with an answer that shows the ability to apply a thinking skill can be readily assessed.

Short-answer items can assess reasoning skills when students are required to supply a brief response to a question or a situation that can be understood only by the use of the targeted thinking skills. Reasoning tasks, such as decision making and critical thinking, are not assessed very well with short-answer items.

(Deductive Reasoning): Coach Greene substitutes his basketball players by height, so that the first substitute is the tallest player on the bench, the next substitute is the next tallest, and so forth. Reginald is taller than Sam, and Juan is taller than Reginald. Which of these three players should Coach Greene play first?

(Credibility of a Source): The principal needs to decide if the new block schedule allows teachers to go into topics in greater detail. He can ask a parent, a teacher, or a principal from another school. Whom should he ask to get the most objective answer?

(Analysis/Prediction): People want health insurance, but they don't want to be forced to buy it from a company in their community. The law says that a person must buy health insurance from a company in his or her community. What action by the people is most likely?

Teacher's Corner

Arleen Reinhardt

National Board Certified High School English Teacher

I use short-answer questions when I want students to give me quick and accurate responses that might apply information or analyze content. For example, I might ask students to apply the content of their reading to the stages of plot structure. Thus, students would have to know the definition of the stages of plot to do so. If my objective is for students to analyze and synthesize information—to use critical thinking skills—I will use essay questions. In this way I am requiring students to show their thinking skills. Students cannot simply memorize information but must compare/contrast, show cause/effect relationships, interpret, or discuss; and all ideas must be substantiated with details from the content studied.

(Analysis/Prediction): Explain how a plant, a mouse, a snake, and a human can be part of a food chain.

An effective approach for fostering deep understanding is to ask students to justify and explain their answers. This is best accomplished by providing opportunities for them to examine different responses and evaluate these responses according to scoring criteria and/or a rubric. Students can be asked to determine which criteria are met, and they can examine inadequate responses and explain why. By critiquing responses and making suggestions for improvements, understanding is richer and more complete (Parke, Lane, Silver, & Magone, 2003).

Deep understanding is effectively assessed with constructed-response interpretive exercises. An example of an interpretive item that assesses deep understanding in mathematics is illustrated in Figure 8.3. The target is student understanding of the concept "average." Students know in advance that they will need to explain their answer. The scoring criteria are summarized in Figure 8.4, and examples of responses are shown in Figures 8.5 and 8.6. Can you match the answers with the scoring criteria?[1] (See Endnote 1 to check your evaluation.)

Essay Items

Essays can tap complex thinking by requiring students to organize and integrate information, interpret information, give arguments, give explanations, evaluate the merit of ideas, and conduct other types of reasoning. Although more objective formats are clearly superior for measuring knowledge, the essay is an excellent way to measure deep understanding and mastery of complex information. Research on student learning habits shows that when students know they will face an essay test they tend to study by looking for themes, patterns, relationships, and how information can be organized and sequenced. In contrast, when studying for objective tests students tend to fragment information and memorize each piece.

Essay items that assess knowledge and simple understanding require relatively brief answers. These may be called *short essay* or *restricted-response essay* to distinguish them from short-answer items, even though the length of the answer does not necessarily indicate the type of target being measured. We will focus here on both *restricted-response* and *extended-response* essay items. The extended-response format is the best one for assessing deep understanding and reasoning targets.

Examples: Restricted-Response Essay Questions

Why are hurricanes more likely to strike Florida than California?
Why are tomatoes better for your health than potato chips?
What is the effect on inflation of raising the prime interest rate?

Examples: Extended-Response Essay Questions

Explain how the fertilizer farmers use to grow crops may pollute our lakes and streams.

Anita has four 20-point projects for science class. Anita's scores on the first three projects are shown below.

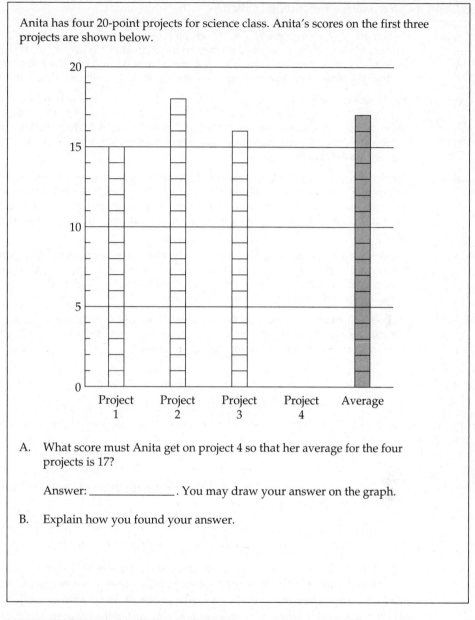

A. What score must Anita get on project 4 so that her average for the four projects is 17?

Answer: _____ . You may draw your answer on the graph.

B. Explain how you found your answer.

FIGURE 8.3   Example of Interpretive Item

Source: Reprinted from page 96 in *Using Assessment to Improve Middle-Grades Mathematics Teaching and Learning: Suggested Activities using QUASAR Tasks, Scoring Criteria, and Students' Work* by C. S. Parke, S. Lane, E. A. Silver, & M. E. Magone. Copyright © 2003 by the National Council of Teachers of Mathematics. Reprinted by permission of the publisher.

FIGURE 8.4 Bar Average Task Scoring Criteria

Level 4   Explanation, work, or drawing on the graph shows a correct and complete understanding of the concept of average in the context of the problem. The strategy used to obtain the correct answer is appropriate and is implemented completely and correctly. (Various solution strategies are provided in the task description.)

Level 3   Explanation, work, or drawing on the graph shows a good understanding of the concept of average in the context of the problem; however, the implementations of the strategy contain a minor error or omission. For example, in finding the total of the first three scores, the student may make a calculation error, which leads to an incorrect answer for the fourth score.

Level 2   Explanation, work, or drawing on the graph shows some understanding of the concept of average in the context of the problem, but the use of a strategy to obtain the answer is somewhat incomplete, unclear, or incorrect. For instance, the work may show a correct answer but provide only a general explanation that states that the scores were added to find an answer that worked.

Level 1   A beginning understanding of the concept of average in the context of the problem is revealed. The strategy used to obtain the answer is unclear or incorrect, or no strategy is apparent. The answer may be correct, but no explanation is provided, or possibly, the average of the nearest three scores is found.

Level 0   No understanding of the concept of average in the context of the problem is evident. Calculations are meaningless, and no explanation is provided, or the explanations are meaningless, and no explanation is provided or the explanation simply restates the problem.

Source: Reprinted from page 97 in *Using Assessment to Improve Middle-Grades Mathematics Teaching and Learning: Suggested Activities using QUASAR Tasks, Scoring Criteria, and Students' Work* by C. S. Parke, S. Lane, E. A. Silver, & M. E. Magone. Copyright © 2003 by the National Council of Teachers of Mathematics. Reprinted by permission of the publisher.

> Describe the major events that led to the beginning of the Civil War, showing how the events are related.

> Give an example, new to me and not one from class, of how the law of supply and demand would make prices of some products increase.

The major advantage of using essay questions is that deep understanding, complex thinking, and reasoning skills can be assessed. Essays motivate better study habits and provide students with flexibility in how they wish to respond. Written responses allow you to evaluate the ability of students to communicate their reasoning. Compared to developing selected-response items that measure reasoning, essay items are less time-consuming to construct. However, constructing a *good* essay question may take considerable time.

The major disadvantages of essay items are related to scoring student responses. Reading and scoring answers is very time consuming, especially if done conscientiously so that meaningful feedback is given to students. From a practical

Anita has four 20-point projects for science class. Anita's scores on the first three projects are shown below.

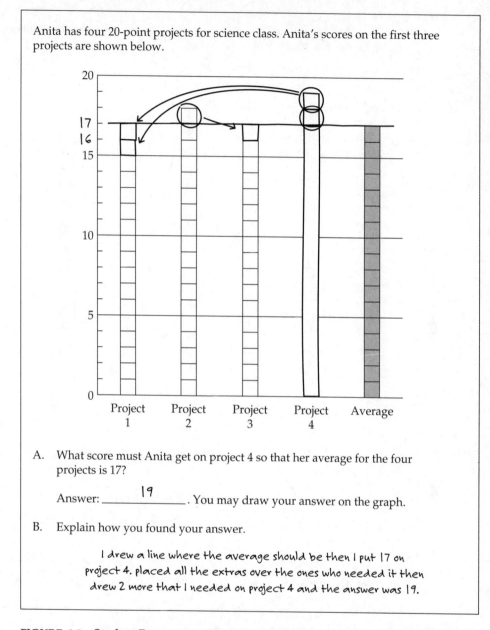

A. What score must Anita get on project 4 so that her average for the four projects is 17?

Answer: _____19_____ . You may draw your answer on the graph.

B. Explain how you found your answer.

> I drew a line where the average should be then I put 17 on project 4. placed all the extras over the ones who needed it then drew 2 more that I needed on project 4 and the answer was 19.

FIGURE 8.5   Student Response to Bar Average Task

Source: Reprinted from page 99 in *Using Assessment to Improve Middle-Grades Mathematics Teaching and Learning: Suggested Activities using QUASAR Tasks, Scoring Criteria, and Students' Work* by C. S. Parke, S. Lane, E. A. Silver, & M. E. Magone. Copyright © 2003 by the National Council of Teachers of Mathematics. Reprinted by permission of the publisher.

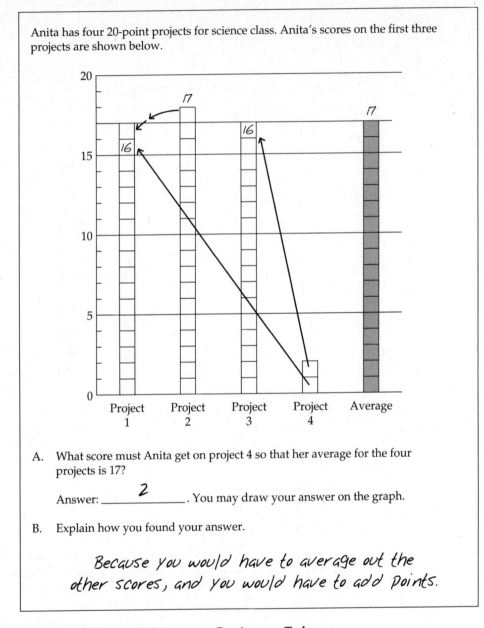

Anita has four 20-point projects for science class. Anita's scores on the first three projects are shown below.

A. What score must Anita get on project 4 so that her average for the four projects is 17?

Answer: _____2_____ . You may draw your answer on the graph.

B. Explain how you found your answer.

Because you would have to average out the other scores, and you would have to add points.

FIGURE 8.6   Student B Response to Bar Average Task

standpoint, most teachers find that they can give only a few essay items. Scoring essays is also notoriously unreliable.

In most classrooms, only a single individual, the teacher, judges the answers, and variations in mood, halo effects, expectations, the order in which students are evaluated, and other factors, affect the professional judgments that are made. This is not meant to imply that it is inappropriate to use subjective judgments in scoring. You *want* to be able to make judgments; that's one reason for using the essay format. When done appropriately, these judgments are professional, not intuitive. We will review guidelines for ensuring high-quality scoring shortly.

A final shortcoming of essay items is that they do not provide for very good sampling of content knowledge. The essay cannot sample well because relatively few questions are asked. Sampling is also limited to the reasoning skills that are assessed. For example, a single extended-response essay item that asks students to make a decision based on information provided may give you a good indication of one or two reasoning skills, but several shorter items could sample different types of skills.

Constructing Essay Items   Essay items are strengthened by adhering to the following suggestions, summarized in Figure 8.7. In the next section we will review important principles for scoring student answers.

1. Construct the Item to Elicit Skills Identified in the Learning Target.   Once the reasoning skill is identified, the wording in the question needs to be such that the specific skill(s) will need to be used to answer the question. This is easier with restricted-response items that focus on a single reasoning skill. With extended-response items, the scoring criteria can be matched to the skills assessed. A good way to begin writing the item to match the target is to start with a standard stem, then modify it as needed for the subject and level of student ability. Some examples of such items are illustrated in Figure 8.8.

2. Write the Item So That Students Clearly Understand the Specific Task.   After reading an essay item, students ask, "What does the teacher want in my answer?" If the assessment task is described ambiguously, so that students interpret what is called for in the answer differently, many responses will be off target. Such responses lead to flawed interpretations by teachers. When students misinterpret the task, you don't know if they have the targeted skill or not, leading to invalid conclusions.

To clearly set forth the nature of the task, try to make the essay question as specific as possible. Don't be hesitant about stating the desired response explicitly.

FIGURE 8.7   Checklist for Writing Essay Items

✓ Is the targeted reasoning skill measured?
✓ Is the task clearly specified?
✓ Is there enough time to answer the questions?
✓ Are choices among several questions avoided?

FIGURE 8.8   Sample Item Stems for Assessing Reasoning Skills

Skill	Stem
Comparing	Describe the similarities and differences between . . . Compare the following two methods for . . .
Relating Cause and Effect	What are major causes of . . . ? What would be the most likely effects of . . . ?
Justifying	Which of the following alternatives do you favor and why? Explain why you agree or disagree with the following statement.
Summarizing	State the main points included in . . . Briefly summarize the contents of . . .
Generalizing	Formulate several valid generalizations from the following data. State a set of principles that can explain the following events.
Inferring	In light of the facts presented, what is most likely to happen when . . . ? How would Senator X be likely to react to the following issue?
Classifying	Group the following items according to . . . What do the following items have in common?
Creating	List as many ways as you can think of for . . . Make up a story describing what would happen if . . .
Applying	Using the principle of . . . as a guide, describe how you would solve the following problem. Describe a situation that illustrates the principle of . . .
Analyzing	Describe the reasoning errors in the following paragraph. List and describe the main characteristics of . . .
Synthesizing	Describe a plan for proving that . . . Write a well-organized report that shows . . .
Evaluating	Describe the strengths and weaknesses of . . . Using the given criteria, write an evaluation of . . .

Source: Linn, R. L., & Miller, M. D. (2005). *Measurement and assessment in teaching,* 9th edition, p. 235. Adapted by permission of Pearson Education, Inc., Upper Saddle River, New Jersey.

Examples

Poor: Why do Haitian farmers have trouble making a living?

Improved: Describe how the weather, soil, and poverty in Haiti contribute to the plight of farmers. Indicate which of these three factors contributes most to the difficulties farmers experience, and give reasons for your selection.

Poor: How was World War I different from World War II?

Improved: How were the social and political factors leading up to World War I in Germany different from those leading up to World War II? Focus your answer on the 10-year period that preceded the beginning of each war.

You can see that each of the "poorly" worded items gives students too much freedom to write about any of a number of aspects of either Haiti or differences between the wars.

Another way to clarify to students the nature of the task is to indicate the criteria for scoring their answer in the question. This can be labeled a *scoring plan, scoring criteria,* or *attributes to be scored.* It essentially tells the students what you will be looking for when grading their answers. This is particularly important if the organization of the response or writing skills are included as criteria.

Examples of Scoring Criteria

(For Scoring Writing Skills)

- Organization
- Clarity
- Appropriateness to audience
- Mechanics

(For Scoring an Argument)

- Distinguishing between facts and opinions
- Judging credibility of a source
- Identifying relevant material
- Recognizing inconsistencies
- Using logic

(For Scoring Decision Making)

- Identifying goals or purpose
- Identifying obstacles
- Identifying and evaluating alternatives
- Justifying the choice of one alternative

3. Indicate Approximately How Much Time Students Should Spend on Each Essay Item.   You should have some idea of how much time students will need to answer each item. For restricted-response questions, the amount of time needed is relatively short and easy to estimate. For extended-response items, the estimate is more difficult. You can get some idea by writing draft answers, and as you gain more experience, the responses of previous students to similar questions will be helpful. Take into consideration the writing abilities of your students, and be sure that even your slowest writers can complete their answers satisfactorily in the time available. (You want to assess reasoning, not writing speed!) If you are unsure about the time needed, err by providing more time than is needed rather than less time.

4. Avoid Giving Students Options as to Which Essay Questions They Will Answer. Many teachers offer students a choice of questions to answer. For example, if there are seven questions, the teacher may tell students to answer their choice of three. Students love such questions because they can answer the items they are best prepared for. They will especially like this approach if they know before taking the test that they will have a choice. Then they can restrict their study to part of the material, rather than to all of it (you can avoid this by telling students *you* will select the items they will write on).

Giving students a choice of questions, however, means that each student may be taking a different test. Differences in the difficulty of each question are probably unknown. This makes scoring more problematic, and your inferences of student ability less valid. It is true that you can't measure every important target, and giving students a choice does provide them an opportunity to do their best work. However, this advantage is outweighed by difficulties in scoring and making sound inferences.

Scoring Essays.   Scoring essay question responses is difficult because each student writes a unique answer and because many distractions affect scoring reliability. Obviously scoring is subjective, so it is important to practice a few procedures to ensure that the professional judgments are accurate.

The following guidelines will help (see Figure 8.9).

1. Outline What Constitutes a Good or Acceptable Answer as a Scoring Key. This should be completed before administering or scoring student responses. If done before the test is finalized, an outline provides you with an opportunity to revise the stem or question on the basis of what you learn by delineating the response. It's important to have the points specified before reading student answers so that you are not unduly influenced by the initial papers you read. These papers can set the standard for what follows. The scoring key provides a common basis for evaluating each answer. An outline lessens the influence of other extraneous factors, such as vocabulary or neatness.

FIGURE 8.9   Checklist for Scoring Essays

✓ Is the answer outlined before testing students?
✓ Is the scoring method—holistic or analytic—appropriate?
✓ Is the role of writing mechanics clarified?
✓ Are items scored one at a time?
✓ Is the order in which the papers are graded changed?
✓ Is the identity of the student anonymous?

2. Select an Appropriate Scoring Method.   Essays are scored in two ways: holistically or analytically. In **holistic** scoring, the teacher makes an overall judgment about the answer, giving it a single score or grade. The score can be based on a general impression or on attending to several specific scoring criteria to come up with a single score for each essay. This is often accomplished by placing essays in designated piles that represent different degrees of quality. The holistic method is most appropriate for extended-response essays (in which the responses are not limited and are generally long). Figure 8.10 shows an example of a holistic scoring guide for an extended-response essay item.

Analytic scoring is achieved by giving each of the identified criteria separate points. Thus, there would be several scores for each essay, and probably a total score that results from adding all the component scores. Analytic scoring is preferred for restricted-response questions (for which there is a limit to the amount of response the student provides). The advantage of analytic scoring is that it provides students with more specific feedback (though this should not replace individualized teacher comments). However, analytic scoring can be very time consuming, and sometimes adding scored parts does not do justice to the overall student response. To avoid excessive attention to specific factors, keep the number of features to be scored analytically to three or four. The holistic scoring guide used in Figure 8.10 is transformed into an analytic guide in Figure 8.11.

3. Clarify the Role of Writing Mechanics.   Suppose you are a biology teacher and you use essay questions. Does it matter if students spell poorly or use bad sen-

---

FIGURE 8.10   Example of Essay Holistic Scoring Guide

Item: Compare and contrast the first and second Iraq wars. Show how they were similar and how they were different along geographic, political, and natural resource dimensions.

Level of Performance	Description
Exceptional (5)	Thorough and detailed understanding of both wars; provides justifications for all points; complete listing of similarities and differences for all dimensions; provides additional insights
Excellent (4)	Complete understanding of both wars; justifications for most points; lists similarities and differences for all dimensions
Very Good (3)	Mostly complete understanding of both wars; justifications for some points; lists most similarities and differences for two dimensions
Acceptable (2)	Incomplete understanding of one or both wars; justifications provided for some points though incomplete; similarities and differences listed with some attention to dimensions
Poor (1)	Incomplete understanding of both wars; justifications inadequate or not present; similarities and differences not correct

FIGURE 8.11   Example of Essay Analytic Scoring Guide

Item: Compare and contrast the first and second Iraq wars. Show how they were similar and how they were different along geographic, political, and natural resource dimensions.

Facet	Inadequate	Adequate	Very Good	Excellent	Points
	1	*2*	*3*	*4*	
Understands both wars	Clearly does not understand	Demonstrates minimal understanding	Demonstrates complete understanding of most aspects	Demonstrates complete understanding of all aspects	
Similarities	Does not address	Shows one correct similarity	Shows two correct similarities	Shows at least three correct similarities	
Differences	Does not address	Shows one correct difference	Shows two correct differences	Shows at least three correct differences	
Inclusion of dimensions	Fails to include any dimensions	Includes one correct dimension	Includes two correct dimensions	Includes at least three correct dimensions	
TOTAL POINTS					

tence structure? Such writing mechanics can certainly influence your overall impression of an answer, so it is important to decide early about whether, and to what extent, these factors are included as scoring criteria. Regardless of how you decide to incorporate writing mechanics, it is generally best to give students a separate score for these skills (as long as it was one of your targets) and not add this score into the total.

4. **Use a Systematic Process in Scoring Many Essays the Same Time During Period.**   When faced with a pile of papers to grade, it's tempting to simply start with the first paper, grade all the questions for that student, and then go on to the next student. To lessen the influence of order and your own fatigue, however, it is best to score one item at a time for all students, and to change the order of the papers for each question. Reliability will increase if you read all responses to question 1 in one order, all responses to question 2 in a different order, and so on. This avoids the tendency to allow the answer a student gives to the first question to influence subsequent evaluations of the remaining questions. It is also best to score all answers to each item in one sitting, if possible. This helps you to be consistent in applying criteria to the answers.

5. If Possible, Keep the Identity of the Student Anonymous.   It is best not to know whose answer you are grading. This avoids the tendency to be influenced by impressions of the student from class discussion or other tests. This source of error, which is probably the most serious one that influences results, is difficult to control because most teachers get to know the writing of their students. You can have students put their names on the back of the papers, but the best guard is to be consciously aware of the potential bias to keep it minimized.

Summary

This chapter focused on paper-and-pencil constructed-response assessments, namely, completion, short answer, and essay. The following points summarize the chapter:

- Completion items require a constructed response at the end of a sentence.
- Completion items are good for assessing facts. They are easy to construct with objective scoring. Verbatim language from learning materials should be avoided.
- Short-answer items, typically written as questions that are new for students, are best for assessing knowledge and comprehension and can also be used to assess understanding and reasoning.
- Assessment of deep understanding with short-answer questions show how students can use their knowledge.
- The scoring of short-answer items should be fairly objective, with single correct answers.
- Short-answer interpretive exercises, with graphs, data, and other information, are excellent for assessing deep understanding.
- Essay items are used primarily for assessing deep understanding, complex thinking, and reasoning skills.
- Essay items allow students to show their understanding reasoning skills by constructing an answer.
- Extended-response essays are best for assessing complex reasoning skills such as decision making and problem solving, and restricted-response items are better for assessing specific thinking skills, comprehension, and application.
- The major disadvantage of essays is in the scoring, which is time consuming and fraught with many potential sources of error.
- Good essays clearly define the task to students, specifically in terms of the skills that will be assessed. Students should know about how much time to spend on each essay item, and the option to choose items should be avoided.
- The scoring of essays is enhanced when an outline of an acceptable answer is made before testing students; when the correct method of scoring is used (holistic or analytical); when the scoring is done by question, not by student; when the order of papers is changed; and when students are anonymous.

Self-Instructional Review Exercises

   1. Indicate whether each of the following would be best measured by a short-answer item (SA), an interpretive exercise (I), or an essay question (E).

   a. Discerning the meaning of a series of pictures
   b. Asking students about the validity of an argument used in a debate tournament
   c. Analyzing a passage to identify irrelevant information and opinions
   d. Being able to construct a logical argument
   e. Knowing the sequence of steps involved in problem solving
   f. Giving examples of the principle of tropism
   g. Being able to distinguish critical thinking from decision making
   h. Determining whether Michelangelo would be regarded as a great artist if he lived today and, if so, why
   i. Identifying several valid generalizations from the data presented

   2. Evaluate the following interpretive exercise. Is it clear? How could the format improve? What cognitive skills are assessed? *Directions.* Based on the food web presented in Figure 8.12, answer these questions:

   1. What must the perch eat to get energy generated from the sun?

Food Web

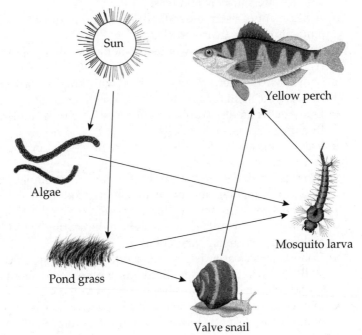

FIGURE 8.12   Food Web

Source: Virginia Department of Education Released Test Items. Retrieved November 2005
www.pen.k12.va.us/VDOE/Assessment/Release2004/5SciCorr1WEB.pdf.

2. What happens to the food for perch if some chemicals spilled into the water and kill the pond grass?
3. What happens to the valve snail population if the pond grass is fertilized?
4. What happens to the valve snail and mosquito larva populations if all the yellow perch are caught by fishermen?

3. Evaluate the following essay question. What learning targets does it appear to assess? How could it be improved?

Do you think freedom of the press should extend to the irresponsible sensationalism of Hearst during the era of the Spanish-American War? Justify your answer.

Answers to Self-Instructional Review Items

1. a. I; b. I or E; c. I; d. E; e. SA; f. E; g. SA; h. E; i. I.

2. The general format of the question is appropriate, and it is good to have several questions about the material presented. Introductory information is kept to a minimum. Presumably students have been studying food chains or webs; this one should be new. Clearly the questions cannot be answered correctly unless the student can understand the food web. The format of the questions could be improved so that students check or circle correct answers rather than taking time to write their answers (e.g., What must the perch do to get energy generated from the sun? a. live in warmer areas, b. eat pond grass, c. swim on the surface of the water, d. eat mosquito larva and valve snail). This would reduce the time students need to answer the questions and the time needed for scoring. The reasoning target assessed by the question is primarily inference and deductive reasoning. Application and understanding targets are also assessed. The assessment could be improved by asking additional "what-if" questions, especially about things that indirectly affect the food web (e.g., What if there is cloudy weather? What would happen to the amount of algae if fishermen were allowed to catch more perch?).

3. This essay question assesses evaluation and critical thinking skills. A decision must be made with reasonable justification. It also assesses constructing support and deductive reasoning. The item could be improved by indicating how much time students should take in answering it, by indicating scoring criteria, and by providing more specific information about what is expected. Including the word *irresponsible* gives students a clear tip to what the teacher is looking for. Phrases such as *justify your answer* give students some direction but are vague. What level of detail is expected? How many reasons are adequate? What is meant by *justify*? There should also be an indication of the total points for the item.

Suggestions for Action Research

1. Write an essay question with criteria for analytic or holistic scoring and examples of responses that would be graded A, B, and C. Give the question, scoring criteria, and

examples of responses with grades deleted to four other students for them to grade. Compare their judgments with the grades you assigned.

2. Examine two or three textbooks written for the area in which you wish to teach, either teacher's editions or the ones students use, and identify examples of constructed-response test items. Critique two completion, short-answer, and essay items.

3. Ask a teacher how he or she uses short-answer and essay items. Obtain examples of each and evaluate them according to the checklists presented in the chapter.

4. Observe some students as they take a constructed-response test that assesses deep understanding. How long does it take them to formulate an answer? How much time does it take to write an answer? If possible, examine their responses. How would you evaluate their work?

Endnote

1. Student A's answer was at level 4; student B's answer was at level 2 (incorrect answer though some understanding of leveling is demonstrated by the drawing on the graph; an error is made in using data from other projects to obtain an answer).

Constructed-Response Assessment: Performance Assessment

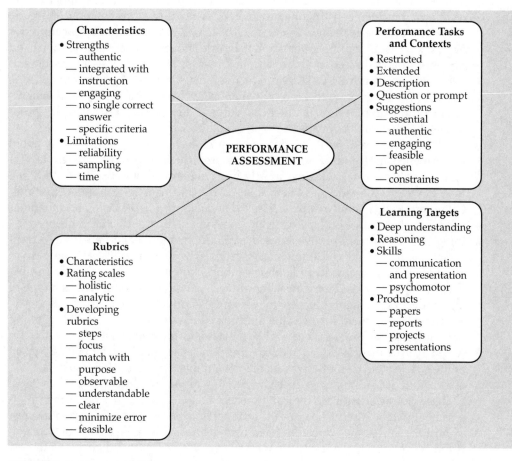

Characteristics
- Strengths
  — authentic
  — integrated with instruction
  — engaging
  — no single correct answer
  — specific criteria
- Limitations
  — reliability
  — sampling
  — time

Performance Tasks and Contexts
- Restricted
- Extended
- Description
- Question or prompt
- Suggestions
  — essential
  — authentic
  — engaging
  — feasible
  — open
  — constraints

PERFORMANCE ASSESSMENT

Learning Targets
- Deep understanding
- Reasoning
- Skills
  — communication and presentation
  — psychomotor
- Products
  — papers
  — reports
  — projects
  — presentations

Rubrics
- Characteristics
- Rating scales
  — holistic
  — analytic
- Developing rubrics
  — steps
  — focus
  — match with purpose
  — observable
  — understandable
  — clear
  — minimize error
  — feasible

CHAPTER 9   Concept Map

In Chapters 7 and 8, we examined what are often called conventional *paper-and-pencil* methods of assessment. These techniques have been used effectively for many years to assess knowledge and understanding targets and, to a lesser extent, to assess reasoning and skill targets. We now turn to assessments that engage students in activities and tasks that require application of knowledge and skills to result in products. This kind of "alternative" assessment is consistent with current theories of learning and motivation, but has actually been emphasized less in schools that allow standards-based multiple-choice testing to dominate in the classroom.

What Is Performance Assessment?

Simply put, a **performance assessment** is one in which the teacher observes and makes a judgment about the student's demonstration of a skill or competency in creating a product, constructing a response, or making a presentation. There are two parts to a performance assessment—a task and a systematic procedure for evaluation (using scoring criteria and rubrics). The term *performance* is shorthand for performance-based or *performance-and-product*. The emphasis is on the students' ability to perform tasks by producing their own work with their knowledge and skills. In some cases this is a presentation, such as singing, playing the piano, or performing gymnastics. In other cases, this ability is expressed through a product, such as a completed paper, project, or solution.

Over the past two decades, educators have taken what is best about performance-and-product assessment and used these principles to assess targets that previously were measured mostly by conventional objective tests. In doing this, however, the field has been deluged by confusing terms and definitions. Other terms, such as *alternative assessment* and *authentic assessment,* are sometimes used interchangeably with performance assessment, but they actually mean something different. An **alternative assessment** is any method that differs from conventional paper-and-pencil tests, most particularly objective tests. Examples of alternative assessments include observations, exhibitions, oral presentations, experiments, portfolios, interviews, and projects. Some think of essays as a type of alternative assessment because they require students to construct responses. **Authentic assessment** involves the direct examination of a student's ability to use knowledge to perform a task that is like what is encountered in real life or in the real world. Authenticity is judged in the nature of the task completed and in the context of the task (e.g., in the options available, constraints, and access to resources).

Figure 9.1 summarizes the characteristics of performance assessments. Most of these characteristics are typically present to some extent in a performance assessment. But be careful. Because the term *performance assessment* is so popular, test publishers and some educators have come to use it as a label for constructed-response, interpretive exercises, and essay items. It's as though there is an ideal for what a performance assessment should look like, and many variations in practice.

FIGURE 9.1   **Characteristics of Performance Assessments**

- Students perform, create, construct, produce, or do something.
- Deep understanding and/or reasoning skills are needed and assessed.
- Involves sustained work, often days and weeks.
- Calls on students to explain, justify, and defend.
- Involves engaging ideas of importance and substance.
- Relies on trained assessor's judgments for scoring.
- Multiple criteria and standards are prespecified and public.
- There is usually no single "correct" answer.
- If authentic, the performance is grounded in real-world contexts and constraints.

Strengths and Limitations of Performance Assessments

The major benefits of performance assessments are tied closely to instruction. This explains much of the appeal of the approach. Learning occurs while students complete the assessment. Teachers interact with students as they do the task, providing feedback and prompts that help students learn through multiple opportunities to demonstrate what they have learned. Opportunities are provided for teachers to assess the reasoning processes students use in their work. Because the assessments are usually tied to real-world challenges and situations, students are better prepared for such thinking and performance once out of school. Students justify their thinking and learn that often no single answer is correct. In this way, the assessments influence the instruction to be more meaningful and practical. Students value the task more because they view it as rich rather than superficial, engaging rather than uninteresting, and active rather than passive.

As pointed out in Chapter 1, much instruction is now based on constructivistic principles of learning, with an emphasis on applied reasoning skills and integrated subject matter. Performance assessments are better suited to measure these kinds of targets than are selected-response tests. Students are more engaged in active learning as a part of the assessment because that is what they need to perform successfully. Because the emphasis is on what students *do,* skills are more directly assessed, and there are more opportunities to observe the process students use to arrive at answers or responses. Students who traditionally do not perform well on paper-and-pencil tests have an opportunity to demonstrate their learning in a different way.

Another advantage of performance assessments is that teachers identify multiple, specific criteria for judging success. Teachers share these criteria with students before the assessment so that the students can use them as they learn. In this way, students learn how to evaluate their own performance through self-assessment. They learn how to ask questions and, in many assessments, how to work effectively with others.

Performance assessment is simply applying the teaching/learning methods used successfully for years in the adult world. Musicians, artists, athletes, architects, and doctors all learn by getting feedback on what they do, and the important goal is not what they know but how what they know is demonstrated in practice.

Thus, an important advantage of performance assessment is that this same approach can be applied to learning all content areas. It helps instruction target more important outcomes.

Finally, performance assessment motivates educators to explore the purposes and processes of schooling. Because of the nature of the assessments, teachers revisit their learning goals, instructional practices, and standards. They explore how students will use their classroom time differently and whether there are adequate resources for all students.

The limitations of using performance assessment lie in three areas: reliability, sampling, and time. Unfortunately, performance assessments are subject to considerable measurement error, which lowers reliability. Like essay items, the major source of measurement error with performance assessments lies in the scoring. Because scoring requires professional judgment, there will be variations and error due to bias and other factors, similar to what affects evaluating essay answers. Although procedures exist that can minimize scoring error—such as carefully constructed criteria, tasks, and scoring rubrics; systematic scoring procedures; and using more than one rater—rating reliability is likely to be lower than what is achieved with other types of assessment. Inconsistent student performance also contributes to error. That is, student performance at one time may differ noticeably from what the student would demonstrate at another time (this might occur, for example, if on the day of the performance the student is ill).

Because it takes a lot of time for students to do performance assessments, you will have relatively few samples of student achievement and ability. Furthermore, we know that performance on one task may not provide a very good estimate of student proficiency on other tasks. This means that if you intend to use the results of performance assessment to form conclusions about capability in a larger domain of learning targets, you need to accumulate information from multiple tasks. It also helps to select tasks that can optimize generalization to the learning targets. Suppose the learning target is concerned with skills associated with making a PowerPoint presentation. If the task is relatively restricted (e.g., using only a few PowerPoint features with a short presentation, making a 2-minute speech), generalization is more confined than when the task encompasses more of the skills (e.g., PowerPoint is longer and contains many features, making a 15-minute speech). Your choice is to use many restricted tasks of limited generalizability or few tasks that have greater generalizability.

The third major limitation of performance assessment concerns time. First, it is very time consuming to construct good tasks, develop scoring criteria and rubrics, administer the task, observe students, and then apply the rubrics to student performance. For performances that cannot be scored later, adequate time needs to be taken with each student as he or she performs the task. Second, it is difficult, in a timely fashion, to interact with all students and give them meaningful feedback *as they learn* and make decisions. Finally, it is difficult to estimate the amount of time students will need to complete performance assessments, especially if the task is a new one and if students are unaccustomed to the format and/or expectations.

The strengths and weaknesses of performance assessments are summarized in Table 9.1. The weaknesses are usually outweighed by the strengths, but that is

TABLE 9.1   **Strengths and Weaknesses of Performance Assessments**

Strengths	Weaknesses
Integrates assessment with instruction.	Reliability may be difficult to establish.
Learning occurs during assessment.	Measurement error due to subjective nature of the scoring may be significant.
Provides opportunities for formative assessment.	
Tends to be more authentic than other types of assessments.	Inconsistent student performance across time may result in inaccurate conclusions.
More engaging; active involvement of students.	Few samples of student achievement.
Provides additional way for students to show what they know and can do.	Requires considerable teacher time to prepare and student time to complete.
Emphasis on reasoning skills.	Difficult to plan for amount of time needed.
Forces teachers to establish specific criteria to identify successful performance.	Limited ability to generalize to a larger domain of knowledge.
Encourages student self-assessment.	
Emphasis on application of knowledge.	
Encourages reexamination of instructional goals and the purpose of schooling.	

Teacher's Corner

Patricia Harris

National Board Certified Elementary Art Teacher

As I develop a lesson, I first create a sample of the lesson artwork so that I can analyze the experience of what the student will need to know and encounter and what the potential learning and product results will be. Specifically, in developing my fifth-grade animation art unit, I created a scoring criteria and rubric based on my experience in analyzing the lesson as well as adjustments that I have made in reflecting on my past teaching of this unit.

I established a point scale for varying levels of accomplishment and weighted the different criteria according to what was most valuable to the students' success. I also created a bonus points category, awarding special independently created "aha moments" to further encourage students to be independent thinkers and innovators. The students work collaboratively throughout this unit and use the rubric as a guide during the creation of their animation movies as well as a collective assessment tool to gauge their success when they view their and fellow students' animation movies.

only the case if the teacher's approach is thoughtful, reflective, and rigorous. Performance assessment is complex and demanding. Time, energy, and resources must be invested to meet goals identified in the strengths listed.

Learning Targets for Performance Assessments

Performance assessments are primarily used for four types of learning targets—deep understanding, reasoning, skills, and products. Deep understanding and reasoning involve in-depth, complex thinking about what is known and application of knowledge and skills in novel and more sophisticated ways. Skills include student proficiency in reasoning, communication, and psychomotor tasks. Products are completed works, such as term papers, projects, and other assignments in which students use their knowledge and skills.

Deep Understanding

The essence of performance assessment includes the development of students' deep understanding of something. The idea is to involve students meaningfully in hands-on activities for extended periods of time so that their understanding is rich and more extensive than what can be attained by more conventional instruction and traditional paper-and-pencil assessments. Deep understanding in performance assessments focuses on the *use* of knowledge and skills. Student responses are constructed in unique ways to demonstrate depth of thought and subtleties of meaning in novel situations. Students are asked to demonstrate what they understand through the application of knowledge and skills.

Reasoning

Like deep understanding, reasoning is essential with performance assessment. Students will use reasoning skills as they demonstrate skills and construct products. Typically, students are given a problem to solve or are asked to make a decision or other outcome, such as a letter to the editor or school newsletter, based on information that is provided. They use cognitive processes such as analysis, synthesis, critical thinking, inference, prediction, generalizing, and hypothesis testing.

Skills

In addition to reasoning skills, students are required to demonstrate communication, presentation, and psychomotor skills. These targets are ideally suited to performance assessment. We'll consider each one.

Communication and Presentation Skills.   Learning targets focused on communication skills involve student performance of reading, writing, speaking, and listening. For reading, targets can be divided into process—what students do before, during, and after reading—and product—what students get from the reading. Reading targets for elementary students progress from targets such as phonemic awareness skills (e.g., decoding, phonological awareness, blending), to skills needed for comprehension and understanding (such as discrimination, contextual cues, inference, blending, sequencing, and identifying main ideas). For effective performance assessment, each of these areas needs to be delineated as a specific target. For instance, a word identification target may include naming and matching uppercase and lowercase letters, recognizing words by sight, recognizing sounds and symbols for consonants at the beginnings and ends of words, and sounding out three-letter words. For older students, reading targets focus on comprehension products and strategies and on reading efficiency, including stating main ideas; identifying the setting, characters, and events in stories; drawing inferences from context; and reading speed. More advanced reading skills include sensitivity to word meanings related to origins, nuances, or figurative meanings; identifying contradictions; and identifying possible multiple inferences. All reading targets should include the ability to perform a specific skill for novel reading materials. A variety of formats should also be represented.

Writing skill targets are also determined by a student's grade level. The emphasis for young students is on their ability to construct letters and copy words and simple sentences legibly. For writing complete essays or papers, elaborate delineations of skills have been developed. Typically, important dimensions of writing are used as categories, as illustrated in the following writing targets:

Purpose	Clarity of purpose; awareness of audience and task; clarity of ideas
Organization	Unity and coherence
Details	Appropriateness of details to purpose and support for main point(s) of writer's response
Voice/tone	Personal investment and expression
Usage, Mechanics, and Grammar	Correct usage (tense formation, agreement, word choice), mechanics (spelling, capitalization, punctuation), grammar, and sentence construction

Other dimensions can be used when the writing skill being measured is more specific, such as writing a persuasive letter, a research paper, or an editorial. Writing targets, like those in reading, should include the ability to perform the skill in a variety of situations or contexts. That is, if students have been taught persuasive writing by developing letters to editors, the student may write a persuasive advertisement or speech to demonstrate that he or she has obtained the skill.

Oral communication skill targets can be generalized to many situations or focused on a specific type of presentation, such as giving a speech, singing a song, speaking a foreign language, or competing in a debate. When the emphasis is on general oral communication skills, the targets typically center on the following three general categories (Airasian & Russell, 2008):

Physical expression	Eye contact, posture, facial expressions, gestures, and body movement
Vocal expression	Articulation, clarity, vocal variation, loudness, pace, and rate
Verbal expression	Repetition, organization, summarizations, reasoning, completeness of ideas and thoughts, selection of appropriate words to convey precise meanings

A more specific set of oral communication skill targets is illustrated in the following guidelines for high school students:[1]

A. Speaking clearly, expressively, and audibly
   1. Using voice expressively
   2. Speaking articulately and pronouncing words correctly
   3. Using appropriate vocal volume

B. Presenting ideas with appropriate introduction, development, and conclusion
   1. Presenting ideas in an effective order
   2. Providing a clear focus on the central idea
   3. Providing signal words, internal summaries, and transitions

C. Developing ideas using appropriate support materials
   1. Being clear and using reasoning processes
   2. Clarifying, illustrating, exemplifying, and documenting ideas

D. Using nonverbal cues
   1. Using eye contact
   2. Using appropriate facial expressions, gestures, and body movement

E. Selecting language to a specific purpose
   1. Using language and conventions appropriate for the audience

For specific purposes, the skills are more targeted. For example, if a presentation involves a demonstration of how to use a microscope, the target could include such criteria as clarity of explanations, understanding of appropriate steps, appropriateness of examples when adjustments are necessary, dependency on notes, and whether attention is maintained, as well as more general features such as posture, enunciation, and eye contact.

Psychomotor Skills. There are two steps in identifying psychomotor skill learning targets. The first step is to describe clearly the physical actions that are required. These may be developmentally appropriate skills or skills that are needed

TABLE 9.2   Examples of Psychomotor Skills

Fine Motor	Gross Motor	Complex	Visual	Verbal and Auditory
Cutting paper with scissors	Walking	Perform a golf swing	Copying	Identify and discriminate sounds
Drawing a line	Jumping	Operate a computer	Finding letters	Imitate sounds
Tracing	Balancing	Drive a car	Finding embedded figures	Pronounce carefully
Eye–hand coordination	Throwing	Dissect a frog	Identifying shapes	Articulate
Penmanship	Skipping	Perform back walkover on balance beam	Discriminating on the basis of attributes such as size, shape, and color	Blend vowels
Coloring	Pull-ups	Operate a microscope		Use proper lip and tongue placement to produce sounds
Drawing shapes	Hopping	Sail a boat		
Connecting dots	Kicking	Operate a drill press		
Pointing				
Buttoning				
Zippering				

for specific tasks. I have divided the psychomotor area into five categories in Table 9.2 to help you describe the behavior: fine motor skills (such as holding a pencil, focusing a microscope, and using scissors), gross motor actions (such as jumping and lifting), more complex athletic skills (such as shooting a basketball or playing golf), some visual skills, and verbal/auditory skills for young children.

The second step is to identify the level at which the skill is to be performed. One effective way to do this is to use an existing classification of the psychomotor domain. This system is hierarchical. At the most basic level is *perception,* the ability to use sight, smell, hearing, and touch to be aware of a stimulus. The second level is *set,* which is a state of readiness to take action. The next level is *guided response,* which involves imitating a behavior or following directions. The fourth level is reached when an action becomes habitual and is done correctly with confidence. This is called *mechanism. Complex overt response* is the fifth level and involves correct actions comprising complex skills. The sixth level is *adaptation,* through which students can make adjustments to suit their needs. The final and highest level is *origination,* which refers to creating new actions to solve a problem. You can use the levels to determine the nature of the target for the skills identified from step 1. For instance, suppose you are interested in assessing your students' abilities to write capital letters correctly. At one level students need to be able to identify the letter, perhaps by locating an example of it on the wall (the perception level). Then they need to be physically prepared to write correctly (the set level—pencil sharpened, paper in the correct position), followed by being able to copy letters from the board (guided response). Then they can demonstrate their skill when drafting paragraphs (mechanism) and alter the shapes to accommodate different widths between lines (adaptation).

Products

Performance assessment products are completed works. For years, students have done papers, reports, and projects. What makes these products different when used for performance assessment is that they are more engaging and more authentic and are scored more systematically with public criteria and standards. For example, rather than having sixth graders report on a foreign country by summarizing the history, politics, and economics of the country, students write promotional materials for the country that would help others decide if it would be an interesting place to visit. In chemistry, students are asked to identify an unknown substance. Why not have them identify the substances from a local landfill, river, or body of water? In music, students can demonstrate their proficiency and knowledge by creating and playing a new song. Table 9.3 presents some other examples, varying in authenticity.

As a learning target, each product needs to be clearly described in some detail so that there is no misunderstanding about what students are required to do. It is not sufficient to simply say, for example, "Write a report on one of the planets and present it to the class." Students need to know about the specific elements of the product (e.g., length, types of information needed, nature of the audience, context, materials that can be used, what can be shown to the audience) and how they will be evaluated. One effective way to do this is to show examples of completed

TABLE 9.3   Performance Products and Skills Varying in Authenticity

Relatively Unauthentic	Somewhat Authentic	Authentic
Indicate which parts of a garden design are accurate.	Design a garden.	Create a garden.
Write a paper on zoning.	Write a proposal to change fictitious zoning laws.	Write a proposal to present to city council to change zoning laws.
Answer a series of questions about what materials are needed for a trip.	Defend the selection of supplies needed for a hypothetical trip.	Plan a trip with your family, indicating needed supplies.
Explain what you would teach to students learning to play basketball.	Show how to perform basketball skills in practice.	Play a basketball game.
Listen to a tape and interpret a foreign language.	Hold a conversation with a teacher in a foreign language.	Hold a conversation with a person from a foreign country in his or her native language.

projects to students. These are not meant to be copied, but they can be used to communicate standards and expectations. In other words, show examples of the target to the students. If the examples can demonstrate different levels of proficiency, so much the better. A good way to generate products is to think about what people in different occupations do. What does a city planner do? What would an expert witness produce for a trial? How does a mapmaker create a map that is easy to understand? What kinds of stories does a newspaper columnist write? How would an advertising agent represent state parks to attract tourists?

Constructing Performance Tasks

Once learning targets have been identified and you have decided that a performance assessment is the method you want to use, three steps remain to constructing the complete performance task. The first is to identify the performance task in which students will be engaged; the second is to develop descriptions of the task and the context in which the performance is to be conducted; the third is to write the specific question, prompt, or problem the students will receive (Figure 9.2).

The performance task is what students are required to do in the performance assessment, either individually or in groups. The tasks can vary by subject and by level of complexity. Some performance tasks are specific to a content area, and others integrate several subjects and skills. With regard to level of complexity, it is useful to distinguish two types: restricted and extended.

Restricted- and Extended-Type Performance Tasks

Restricted-type tasks target a narrowly defined skill and require relatively brief responses. The task is structured and specific. These tasks may look similar to short essay questions and interpretive exercises that have open-ended items. The difference is in the relative emphasis on characteristics listed in Figure 9.1. Often the performance task is structured to elicit student explanations of their answer. Students may be asked to defend an answer; indicate why a different answer is not correct; tell how they did something; draw a diagram; construct a visual map, graph, or flowchart; or show some other aspect of their reasoning. In contrast, short essay questions and interpretive exercises are designed to infer reasoning from correct answers. Although restricted-type tasks require relatively little time

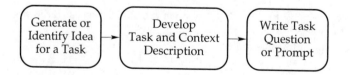

FIGURE 9.2   Steps in Constructing Performance Tasks

for administration and scoring in comparison with extended-type tasks (providing greater reliability and sampling), it is likely that fewer of the important characteristics of authentic performance assessments are included. Many publishers provide performance assessments in a standardized format, and most of them contain restricted-type tasks. Further examples of restricted-type performance tasks are listed in Table 9.4.

Extended-type tasks are more complex, elaborate, and time consuming. Extended-type tasks often include collaborative work with small groups of students. The assignment usually requires that students use a variety of sources of information (e.g., observations, library, interviews). Judgments will need to be made about which information is most relevant. Products are typically developed over several days or even weeks, with opportunities for revision. This allows students to apply a variety of skills and makes it easier to integrate different content areas and reasoning skills.

TABLE 9.4   Examples of Restricted- and Extended-Type Performance Assessment Tasks

Restricted-Type	Extended-Type
Construct a bar graph from data provided.	Construct a PowerPoint presentation.
Talk in French about what is on a menu.	Design a playhouse and estimate the cost of materials and labor.
Read an article from a newspaper and answer questions.	Plan a trip to another country; include the budget and itinerary.
Review a zoning map of a city and indicate changes that would encourage more commercial development.	Conduct a historical reenactment (e.g., Boston Tea Party, the Lincoln–Douglas debates).
Flip a coin 10 times. Predict what the next 10 flips would be. Explain why.	Diagnose and repair a car problem.
Listen to Fox News and explain whether you believe the stories are biased.	Design an advertising campaign for a new or existing product.
Construct a poster that explains the parts of flowers.	Publish a newspaper.
Sing a song.	Design a park.
Type at least 35 words a minute with five or fewer mistakes.	Create a commercial.
Using scissors, cut outlined figures from a page.	Write and perform a song.
Recite a poem.	Prepare a plan for dealing with waste materials.
Write a paper about the importance of protecting forests from being converted to farmland.	Design and carry out a study to determine which grocery store has the lowest prices.
Write examples of good and poor multiple-choice questions.	Plan and install a new car radio stereo system.

It is not too difficult to come up with ideas for what would be an engaging extended-type task. As previously indicated, one effective approach is to think about what people do in different occupations. Another way to generate ideas is to check curriculum guides and teacher's editions of textbooks because most will have activities and assignments that tap student application and reasoning skills. Perhaps the best way to generate ideas is by brainstorming with others, especially members of the community. They can be particularly helpful in thinking about authentic tasks that involve reasoning and communication skills. Some ideas that could be transformed into extended-type tasks are included in Table 9.4. Once you have a general idea for the task, you need to develop it into a more detailed set of specifications.

Performance Task Descriptions and Contexts

The performance task needs to be specified so that it meets the criteria for good performance assessment and is clear to students. This is accomplished by preparing a *task description.* The purpose of the task description is to provide a blueprint or listing of specifications to ensure that essential criteria are met, that the task is reasonable, and that it will elicit desired student performance. The task description is not the same as the actual format and wording of the question or prompt that is given to students; it is more like a lesson plan. The task description should include the following:

> Content and skill targets to be assessed
> Description of student activities
> > Group or individual
> > Help allowed
> Resources needed
> Teacher role
> Administrative process
> Scoring procedures

It is essential to clearly describe the specific targets to be assessed to make certain that the activities and scoring are well matched to ensure both valid and practical assessments. Think about what students will actually do to respond to the question or solve the problem by specifying the context in which they will work:

> Will they consult other experts, use library resources, do experiments?
> Are they allowed to work together, or is it an individual assignment?
> What types of help from others are allowed?
> Is there sufficient time to complete the activities?

Once the activities are described, the resources needed to accomplish them can be identified.

Are needed materials and resources available for all students?

What needs to be obtained before the assessment?

It will be helpful to describe your role in the exercise.

Will you consult your students or give them ideas?

Are you comfortable with and adequately prepared for what you will do?

What administrative procedures are required?

Finally, identify scoring procedures.

Will scoring match the learning targets?

Is adequate time available for scoring?

Do you have the expertise needed to do the scoring?

Is it practical?

One effective way to begin to design the task is to think about what has been done instructionally (Smith, Smith, & De Lisi, 2001). The assessment task should be structured to mirror the nature of classroom instruction so that what you are asking students to do is something that they are already at least somewhat familiar with.

Once the task description is completed and you are satisfied that the assessment will be valid and practical, you are ready to prepare the specific performance task question or prompt.

Performance Task Question or Prompt

The actual question, problem, or prompt that you give to students will be based on the task description. It needs to be stated so that it clearly identifies what the final outcome or product is, outlines what students are allowed and encouraged to do, and explains the criteria that will be used to judge the product. A good question or prompt also provides a context that helps students understand the meaningfulness and relevance of the task.

Because considerable time is required to construct good performance tasks, you will want to use or adapt ones that have already been developed. Several professional organizations have organized networks and other resources for developing performance tasks. Many subject-oriented professional organizations, such as the National Council of Teachers of Mathematics, have good resources for identifying performance tasks, and the Internet can be used to tap into a vast array of examples.

Whether you develop your own tasks or use intact or modified existing ones, you will want to evaluate the task on the basis of the following suggestions (summarized in Figure 9.3) and characteristics summarized in Figure 9.4, which shows how they are defined and contrasted with what occurs with more traditional assessment.

FIGURE 9.3   Checklist for Writing Performance Tasks

✓ Are essential content and skill targets integrated?
✓ Are multiple targets included?
✓ Is the task authentic?
✓ Is the task teachable?
✓ Are multiple solutions and paths possible?
✓ Is the nature of the task clear?
✓ Is the task challenging and stimulating?
✓ Are criteria for scoring included?
✓ Are constraints for completing the task included?

Source: "Performance Task Prompt" adapted from R. J. Marzano, D. Pickering, & J. McTighe (1993), *Assessing Student Outcomes: Performance Assessment using the Dimensions of Learning Model*. Alexandria, VA: Association for Supervision and Curriculum Development, p. 51. McREL. Copyright © 1993. Reprinted by permission of McREL.

FIGURE 9.4   Criteria for Performance Tasks

Essential	• The task fits into the core of the curriculum. • It represents a "big idea."	vs. Tangential
Authentic	• The task uses processes appropriate to the discipline. • Students value the outcome of the task.	vs. Contrived
Rich	• The task leads to other problems. • It raises other questions. • It has many possibilities.	vs. Superficial
Engaging	• The task is thought provoking. • It fosters persistence.	vs. Uninteresting
Active	• The student is the worker and decision maker. • Students interact with other students. • Students are constructing meaning and deepening understanding.	vs. Passive
Feasible	• The task can be done within school and homework time. • It is developmentally appropriate for students. • It is safe.	vs. Infeasible
Equitable	• The task develops thinking in a variety of styles. • It contributes to positive attitudes.	vs. Inequitable
Open	• The task has more than one right answer. • It has multiple avenues of approach, making it accessible to all students.	vs. Closed

Source: Reprinted from page 38 in *Mathematics Assessment: Myths, Models, Good Questions, and Practical Suggestions* by Jean Kerr Stenmark. Copyright © 1991 by the National Council of Teachers of Mathematics. Reprinted by permission of the publisher.

1. The Performance Task Should Integrate the Most Essential Aspects of the Content Being Assessed with the Most Essential Skills.   Performance assessment is ideal for focusing student attention and learning on the "big ideas" of a subject, the major concepts, principles, and processes that are important to a discipline. If the task encourages learning of peripheral or tangential topics or specific details, it is not well suited to the goal of performance assessment. Tasks should be broad in scope. Similarly, reasoning and other skills essential to the task should represent essential processes. The task should be written to integrate content with skills. For example, it would be better to debate important content or contemporary issues rather than something relatively unimportant. A good test for whether the task meets these criteria is to decide if what is assessed could be done as well with more objective, less time-consuming measures.

Examples

> *Poor:* Estimate the answers to the following three addition problems. Explain in your own words the strategy used to give your answer.
>
> *Improved:* Sam and Tyron were planning a trip to a nearby state. They wanted to visit as many different major cities as possible. Using the map, estimate the number of major cities they will be able to visit on a single tank of gas (fourteen gallons) if their car gets twenty-five miles to the gallon.

2. The Task Should Be Authentic.   This suggestion lies at the heart of authentic performance assessment. Authentic tasks are student centered, relevant to real-world and real-life contexts (Groeber, 2007), though research has shown that many have a broader view of what constitutes authenticity (Frey, Schmitt, & Bowen, 2009). Grant Wiggins has developed a set of six standards for judging the degree of authenticity in an assessment task (Wiggins, 1998). He suggests that a task is authentic if it:

A. *Is realistic.* The task replicates the ways in which a person's knowledge and abilities are "tested" in real-world situations.

B. *Requires judgment and innovation.* The student has to use knowledge and skills wisely and effectively to solve unstructured problems, and the solution involves more than following a set routine or procedure or plugging in knowledge.

C. *Asks the student to "do" the subject.* The student has to carry out exploration and work within the discipline of the subject area, rather than restating what is already known or what was taught.

D. *Replicates or simulates the contexts in which adults are "tested" in the workplace, in civic life, and in personal life.* Contexts involve specific situations that have particular constraints, purposes, and audiences. Students need to experience what it is like to do tasks in workplace and other real-life contexts.

E. *Assesses the student's ability to efficiently and effectively use a repertoire of knowledge and skill to negotiate a complex task.* Students should be required to integrate all knowledge and skills needed, rather than to demonstrate competence of isolated knowledge and skills.

F. *Allows appropriate opportunities to rehearse, practice, consult resources, and get feedback on and refine performances and products.* Rather than rely on secure tests as an audit of performance, learning should be focused through cycles of performance-feedback-revision-performance, on the production of known high-quality products and standards, and learning in context. (pp. 22, 24)

A similar set of standards has been developed by Fred Newmann (Newmann, 1997). In his view, authentic tasks require the following:

Construction of meaning (use of reasoning and higher-order thinking skills to produce meaning or knowledge)
1. Organization of information
2. Consideration of alternatives

Disciplined inquiry (thinking like "experts" searching for in-depth understanding)
3. Disciplinary content
4. Disciplinary process
5. Elaborated written communication

Value beyond school (aesthetic, utilitarian, or personal value apart from documenting the competence of the learner)
6. Problem connected to the world
7. Audience beyond the school

Newmann summarizes these standards by saying that authentic tasks "demand construction of knowledge through disciplined inquiry and result in discourse, products, and performance that have value or meaning beyond success in school" (p. 366).

Examples

Poor: Compare and contrast different kinds of literature.

Improved:[2] You have volunteered to help your local library with its literacy program. Once a week after school, you help people learn how to read. To encourage your students to learn, you tell them about the different kinds of literature you have read, including poems, biographies, mysteries, tall tales, fables, and historical novels. Select three types of literature and compare them, using general characteristics of literature and the specific characteristics of each genre that you think will help your students see the similarities and differences among the types of literature. Create a table or chart to visually depict the comparison.

Notice also how the improved version integrates content and language arts with two skills, comparison and communication.

3. Structure the Task to Assess Multiple Learning Targets. As pointed out in the first suggestion, it is best if the task assesses both content and skill targets.

Within each of these areas there may be different types of targets. For instance, assessing content may include both knowledge and understanding and, as in the preceding example, both reasoning and communication skills. It is also common to include different types of communication and reasoning skills in the same task (e.g., students provide both a written and an oral report or need to think critically and synthesize to arrive at an answer).

4. Structure the Task So That You Can Help Students Succeed.   Good performance assessment involves the interaction of instruction with assessment. The task needs to be something that students learn from, which is most likely when there are opportunities for you to increase student proficiency by asking questions, providing resources, and giving feedback. In this kind of active teaching, you are intervening as students learn, rather than simply providing information. Part of teachability is being certain that students have the needed prerequisite knowledge and skills to succeed.

5. Think through What Students Will Do to Be Sure That the Task Is Feasible.   Imagine what you would do if given the task. What resources would you need? How much time would you need? What steps would you take? It should be realistic for students to implement the task. This depends both on your own expertise and willingness and on the costs and availability of equipment, materials, and other resources so that every student has the same opportunity to be successful.

6. The Task Should Allow for Multiple Solutions.   If a performance task is properly structured, more than one correct response is not only possible but desirable. The task should not encourage drill or practice for which there is a single solution. The possibility of multiple solutions encourages students to personalize the process and makes it easier for you to demand that students justify and explain their assumptions, planning, predictions, and other responses. Different students may take different paths in responding to the task.

7. The Task Should Be Clear.   An unambiguous set of directions that explicitly indicates the nature of the task is essential. If the directions are too vague, students may not focus on the learning targets or may waste time trying to figure out what they should be doing. A task such as "Give an oral report on a foreign country" is too general. Students need to know the reason for the task, and the directions should provide sufficient detail so that students know how to proceed. Do they work alone or with others? What resources are available? How much time do they have? What is the role of the teacher? Here is an example of a clearly defined task (Marzano, Pickering, & McTighe, 1993):

> We will be reading George Orwell's *1984*, which could be described as a work of projective investigation. We will also be studying what was happening in the world around the time this book was written, the decade of the 1940s.
>
> First, working in small groups, your task is to select specific events, ideas, or trends from the 1940s and show how Orwell projected them into the future. You'll be given a chart on which you can graphically depict these connections.

Teacher's Corner

Elizabeth O'Brien

National Board Certified Teacher

In my geometry classes, when studying volume I have students bring in products from home that come in double containers. For example, toothpaste comes in a tube and then is packaged in a box, and most pills come in a bottle and then are packaged in a box. Students are asked to find the volume of the outer package using the formulas we have studied, and then find the volume of the inner package by displacement. When they find the difference between the volumes we discuss how companies could save money on packaging and why they might use the double package method. To conclude the unit, students are asked to write a letter to the manufacturer of the product describing their findings and what and why they think changes should be made.

Overall, students enjoy this project. It allows them to use geometry for something they see as useful. They also love taking a side and using their data to argue for or against a change. The letters allow me to see a depth of understanding a typical problem does not allow for.

Second, each person is to select a field of study that interests you (economics, science and technology, health care, fashion, sports, literature, the arts, politics, sociology) and select current events, ideas, and trends in that field, with an emphasis on areas where there is some controversy or disagreement.

Finally, using your knowledge of the field, construct a scenario for the future that makes sense and is a plausible extension of the present. Present your scenario in any way you wish (written prose or poetry, art form, oral or video presentation, etc.). In your presentation, clearly communicate your predictions and how they plausibly extend the present. (p. 61)

8. The Task Should Be Challenging and Stimulating to Students. One of the things you hope for is that students will be motivated to use their skills and knowledge to be involved and engaged, sometimes for days or weeks. You also want students to monitor themselves and think about their progress. This is more likely to occur when the task is something students can get excited about or can see some relevance for, and when the task is not too easy or too difficult. Persistence is fostered if the task is interesting and thought provoking. This is easier if you know your students' strengths and limitations and are familiar with what kinds of topics would motivate them. One approach is to blend what is familiar with novelty. Tasks that are authentic are not necessarily stimulating and challenging.

9. Include Explicitly Stated Scoring Criteria as Part of the Task. By now you are familiar with this admonition. Specifying criteria helps students understand what they need to do and communicates learning priorities and your expectations. Students need to know about the criteria *before* beginning work on the task. Sometimes criteria are individually tailored to each task; others are more generic for several different kinds of tasks. What is shared with students as part of the task, however, may not be the same instrument or scale you use when evaluating their work. For example, for the task in suggestion 7, the following criteria could be shared with students (Marzano, Pickering, & McTighe, 1993):

You will be assessed on and provided rubrics for the following:

A. Your understanding of the extent to which the present can inform the future
B. Your depth of understanding of major events, ideas, and trends from a field of study
C. Your ability to accurately identify what is already known or agreed upon about the future event
D. Your ability to construct a scenario for some future event or hypothetical past event for which a scenario is not readily available or accepted
E. Your ability to express ideas clearly
F. Your ability to communicate effectively in a variety of ways (p. 61)

The identification of criteria, and how you translate those criteria into a scale for evaluation, is discussed in the next section. From a practical perspective, the development of the task and scoring criteria is iterative: One influences the other as both are developed.

10. Include Constraints for Completing the Task. One of the hallmarks of authentic thinking and decision making is that such performance is done under constraints that are defined by context, rules, and regulations that are similar to conditions outside the classroom. According to Borich and Tombari (2004), these constraints include

Time. How much time should a learner or group of learners have to plan, revise, and finish the task?

Reference material. What resources (dictionaries, textbooks, class notes, CD-ROMs) will learners be able to consult while they are completing the assessment task?

Other people. Will your learners be able to ask for help from peers, teachers, and experts as they take a test or complete a project?

Equipment. Will your learners have access to computers, calculators, spell checkers, or other aids or materials as they complete the assignment?

Scoring criteria. Will you inform your learners about the explicit standards that you use to evaluate the product or performance? (p. 220).

The intent of considering such constraints is to define in a more realistic way the nature of the situation in which the performance or product is demonstrated.

Performance Criteria

After students have completed the task, you must evaluate their performance. Because responses are constructed by students, this is always a matter of reviewing their work and making a professional judgment about the performance or product. Rather than relying on unstated rules for making these judgments, performance assessments include *performance criteria,* what you call on or use to determine student proficiency. Performance criteria serve as the basis for evaluating the quality of student work (Stiggins, Arter, Chappuis, & Chappuis, 2007).

Performance criteria (or *scoring criteria* or simply *criteria*) are what you look for in student responses to evaluate their progress toward meeting the learning target. In other words, performance criteria are the dimensions or traits in products or performance that are used to illustrate and define understanding, reasoning, and proficiency. Explicitly defined performance criteria help to make what is a subjective process clear, consistent, and defensible (Arter & McTighe, 2001).

Determining defensible criteria begins with identification of the most important dimensions or traits of the performance. This is a summary of the essential qualities of student proficiency. These dimensions should reflect your instructional goals as well as teachable and observable aspects of the performance. Ask yourself this question: "What distinguishes an adequate from an inadequate demonstration of the target?"

One of the best ways to identify criteria is to work backward from examples of student work (Moskal, 2003). These examples (or *exemplars*) are analyzed to determine what traits or that the dimensions distinguish them are used as the basis for concluding that one student's work meets a specific standard or target. The dimensions become criteria. For example, for evaluating a speech, dimensions could include content, organization, and delivery. Delivery may be composed of additional criteria, such as posture, gestures, facial expressions, and eye contact. For a singing performance, you could include pitch, rhythm, diction, and tone quality as criteria, then determine additional criteria for each of these four. As you might imagine, you can go into great detail describing dimensions. But to be practical, you need to balance specificity with what is manageable.

The following is an example of reasonable criteria for a specific learning target.

Learning target: Students will be able to write a persuasive paper to encourage the reader to accept a specific course of action or point of view.

Criteria: Appropriateness of language for the audience.
Plausibility and relevance of supporting arguments.
Level of detail presented.
Evidence of creative, innovative thinking.
Clarity of expression.
Organization of ideas.

Rubrics

The second essential part of evaluating performance assessments is to have well-developed, clear rubrics. A **rubric** is a scoring guide that includes a scale that spans different levels of competency. This scale is used with the criteria to establish a two-dimensional table, with criteria on one side and the scale on the other. Within the table are descriptions of how teachers differentiate between different scale points for each criteria. That is, a rubric uses descriptions of different levels of quality on each of the criteria.

The rubric organizes and gives more detail to the criteria. They are worded in ways that communicate to students how their teacher evaluates the essence of what is being assessed. Wiggins (1998) uses the following questions to help understand the function of rubrics:

By what criteria should performance be judged?
What should we look for to judge performance success?
What does the range in the quality of the performance look like?
How should the different levels of quality be described and distinguished from one another?

For example, if a teacher is evaluating the logic of an argument, one of the criteria could be the trustworthiness and relevance of supporting facts. Different levels of quality for those criteria could be expressed as follows:

No supporting facts
Facts presented have weak trustworthiness and relevance
Facts presented have acceptable trustworthiness or relevance
Facts presented are clearly trustworthy and relevant

The goal of having rubrics, then, is to communicate standards-based judgments of teachers so that both teachers and students are clear about what is used in making the judgments. In this way, students are informed about specific strengths and deficiencies. An example of an excellent rubric is shown in Figure 9.5.

With this general understanding of rubrics, we will now discuss rating scales in more detail, followed by suggestions for developing rubrics.

Rating Scales

A rating scale is used to indicate the degree to which a particular dimension is present. It provides a way to record and communicate qualitatively different levels of performance. Several types of rating scales are available; we will consider three: numerical, qualitative, and numerical/quantitative combined.

The numerical scale uses numbers on a continuum to indicate different levels of proficiency in terms of frequency or quality. The number of points on the scale

FIGURE 9.5   Exemplary Example of a Rubric: Assessing a High School Senior Essay on Substance Abuse

9–8   The upper-range responses satisfy the following criteria:

    a. *Summary.* The summary should identify the main idea [of the reading].

    b. *Focus of agreement.* Agreement or disagreement may be complete or partial but writer must make clear what he/she is agreeing/disagreeing with. Specifically, 9–8 papers must address author's thesis, not substance abuse in general.

    c. *Support for agreement/disagreement.* Support should provide an analysis of argument and/or relevant and concrete examples.

    d. *Style and coherence.* These papers demonstrate clear style, overall organization, and consecutiveness of thought. They contain few repeated errors in usage, grammar, or mechanics.

    [The four phrases in italics represent the dimensions being scored. Two of the criteria are underlined.]

7   This grade is used for papers that fulfill basic requirements for the 9–8 grade but have less development, support, or analysis.

6–5   Middle range papers omit or are deficient in one of these four criteria:

    a. *Summary.* Summary is absent or incomplete, listing only author's thesis.

    b. *Focus of agreement/disagreement.* What the writer is agreeing/disagreeing with is not clear or is unrelated to author's proposals. Example: writer doesn't use enough phrasing like "on the one hand . . . on the other hand . . ." [an indicator].

    c. *Support.* Writer only counterasserts; examples are highly generalized or not distinguishable from examples in the article. Analysis may be specious, irrelevant, or thin.

    d. *Style and coherence.* These papers are loosely organized or contain noticeable errors in usage, grammar, or mechanics.

4   This grade is used for papers that are slightly weaker than the 6–5 papers. Also, a student who writes his/her own parallel essay in a competent style should receive a 4.

3–2   These papers are deficient in *two* or more of the criteria. Typically they weakly paraphrase the article *or* they have serious organization/coherence problems. Papers with serious, repeated errors in usage, grammar, or mechanics must be placed in this range. [This whole paragraph, like all the previous ones, is a descriptor for this point on the scale.]

Source: Adapted from Wiggins, G. P. (1998). *Educative assessment: Designing assessments to inform and improve student performance.* San Francisco: Jossey-Bass, p. 155. Reprinted by permission of John Wiley & Sons, Inc.

can vary, from as few as 2 to 10 or more. The number of points is determined on the basis of the decision that will be made. If you are going to use the scale to indicate low, medium, and high, then three points are sufficient. More points on the scale permit greater discrimination, provide more diagnostic information, and permit more specific feedback to students.

Here are some examples of numerical scales:

Complete Understanding   5 4 3 2 1   No Understanding
of the Problem   of the Problem

Little or No Organization   1 2 3 4 5 6 7   Clear and Complete Organization

Emergent Reader   1 2 3   Fluent Reader

A qualitative scale uses verbal descriptions to indicate student performance. There are two types of qualitative descriptors. One type indicates the different gradations of the dimension. The simplest form is the checklist. This lists different dimensions and provides a way to check each dimension. An example of a checklist is illustrated in Figure 9.6 for the PowerPoint presentation criteria. More complex scales summarize different levels of the dimensions, for example:

minimal, partial, complete

never, seldom, occasionally, frequently, always   ·

consistently, sporadically, rarely

Complete Understanding	*Nearly Complete Understanding*	*Some Understanding*	*Limited Understanding*
Uses capital letters appropriately most or all of the time	*Uses capital letters appropriately some of the time*	*Rarely uses capital letters appropriately*	
Always speaks clearly	*Speaks clearly most of the time*	*Speaks clearly some of the time*	*Rarely speaks clearly*

FIGURE 9.6   Checklist for Evaluating a PowerPoint Presentation

Yes   No

_____ _____ **1.** The topic has been extensively and accurately researched.

_____ _____ **2.** A storyboard, consisting of logically and sequentially numbered slides, has been developed.

_____ _____ **3.** The introduction is interesting and engages the audience.

_____ _____ **4.** The fonts are easy to read and point size varies appropriately for headings and text.

_____ _____ **5.** The use of italics, bold, and underline contributes to the readability of the text.

_____ _____ **6.** The background and colors enhance the text.

_____ _____ **7.** The graphics, animation, and sounds enhance the overall presentation.

_____ _____ **8.** Graphics are of proper size.

_____ _____ **9.** The text is free of spelling, punctuation, capitalization, and grammatical errors.

A second type of qualitative scale includes gradations of the criteria and some indication of how the performance compares to established standards. This is the most frequently used type of rating scale for performance assessments. Descriptors such as the following are used:

novice, emergent, proficient, advanced
novice, intermediate, advanced, superior
inadequate, needs improvement, good, excellent
excellent, proficient, needs improvement
absent, developing, adequate, fully developed
limited, partial, thorough
emerging, developing, achieving
not there yet, shows growth, proficient
excellent, good, fair, poor

Developing Rubrics

Rubrics are best developed by combining several different procedures (Gallavan, 2009; Schwartz & Kenney, 2008). It is helpful to begin by clarifying how the discipline defines different levels of performance. This will give you an idea of the nature and number of gradations that should be used. It is also helpful to obtain samples of how others have described and scored performance in the area to be assessed.

Another approach is to gather performance samples and determine the characteristics of the works that distinguish effective from ineffective ones. The samples could be from students as well as so-called experts in the area. You could start by putting a group of student samples into three qualitatively different piles to indicate three levels of performance. Then examine the samples to see what distinguishes them. The identified characteristics provide the basis for the dimensions of the rating scale. At this point, you can review your initial thinking about the scale with others to see whether they agree with you. With feedback from others, you can write the first draft of the descriptors at each point of the rating scale.

Use the first draft of the rubric with additional samples of student work to verify that it works as intended. Revise as needed, and try it again with more samples of student work until you are satisfied that it provides a valid, reliable, and fair way to judge student performance. Don't forget to use student feedback as part of the process. As you might realize, this entire process is repeated to improve the rubric.

An important decision is whether the rubric scale will be *holistic* or *analytic*. A **holistic scale** is one in which each category of the scale contains several criteria, yielding a single score that gives an overall impression or rating. Advantages of using a holistic scale are its simplicity and the ability to provide a reasonable summary rating. All the traits are efficiently combined, the work is scored quickly, and only one score results. For example, in gymnastics, a single holistic score between 1 and 10 is awarded, in which separate judgments for various dimensions (flexibility, balance, position, etc.) are combined. The disadvantage of a holistic score is that it reveals little about what needs to be improved. Thus, for feedback purposes, holistic scores provide little specific information about what the student did well and what needs further improvement.

When the purpose of the assessment is summative, at the end of a unit or course, a holistic scale is appropriate. But even when used summatively, holistic scales can vary greatly in the specificity of what is used in the judgments. For example, the following holistic scale for reading is rather skimpy; very little is indicated about what went into the judgment.

> Level 4: Sophisticated understanding of text indicated
> with constructed meaning.
> Level 3: Solid understanding of text indicated with some
> constructed meaning.
> Level 2: Partial understanding of text indicated with tenuous
> constructed meaning.
> Level 1: Superficial understanding of text with little or no
> constructed meaning.

Popham (2007) refers to this type of holistic rubric as *hypergeneral*. Such rubrics are so general and limited that there is little indication of the criteria that should be used to make judgments about student achievement. This does not provide much instructional guidance or student awareness of criteria. Contrast this scale with the one in Figure 9.7, which is also concerned with reading. It is obvious that this more developed and specific rubric provides a more detailed explanation of how the reading was judged and why each level was assigned. Even with this more specific scale, however, how do you judge a student who showed multiple connections between the text and the reader's ideas/experiences but had interpretations that were not directly supported by appropriate text references? This kind of problem, in which the traits being assessed do not all conform within a single category, is almost certain to exist with holistic scales for some students.

Another example of a holistic scale is illustrated in Figure 9.8 for graphing data. Note how several criteria are included in each of the three levels.

An **analytic scale** (or *analytic-trait scale)* is one in which each criterion receives a separate score. If analytic scoring were used in gymnastics, each criterion such as flexibility, balance, and position would be scored separately. This kind of scale provides much better diagnostic information and feedback for the learner and is more useful for formative evaluation during instruction. Students are able to see their strengths and weaknesses more clearly. They are able to connect their preparation and effort with each evaluation. However, analytic scales take longer to create and score.

In general, to the extent possible based on practical constraints, it is best to use analytic rating scales. Like other good assessment techniques, once established, good analytic scales will serve you well for many years. For that reason, and the instructional advantages, it makes good sense to invest time in developing them. An analytic scale is illustrated in Figure 9.9. This scale transforms the holistic scale in Figure 9.8 about graphing data into an analytic one. In this example four criteria are evaluated separately—title, labels, accuracy, and neatness. The rubric

Figure 9.7 Example of Holistic Rating Scale and Rubric

Reading Rubric

Rating Scale	Evaluative Criteria
4	Reader displays a sophisticated understanding of the text. There is substantial evidence of constructed meaning from the text. Meaningful and sophisticated interpretations are supported with text references. There is evidence of connections between the text and the reader's ideas / experiences. Reader takes a critical stance (e.g., analyzes the author's style of writing, questions the text, provides alternative interpretations, views the text from different perspectives).
3	Reader displays a solid understanding of the text. There is adequate evidence of constructed meaning. Some but not many connections are made between the text and the reader's ideas / experiences. Interpretations are generally supported by appropriate text references. There is some evidence of a critical stance toward the text.
2	Reader displays only partial understanding of the text. There is incomplete evidence of constructed meaning. While some connections are made between the text and the reader's ideas / expressions, these connections are superficial and not well developed. Interpretations are not displayed and / or not supported by appropriate text references. Reader shows little or no evidence of critical stance toward the text.
1	Reader displays a poor, superficial understanding of the text. There is very limited evidence of constructed meaning. There is no evidence of connections between the text and the reader's ideas / experiences. There are no interpretations or evidence of a critical stance.

Source: Adapted from page 23 in *Assessing Learning in the Classroom* by J. McTighe & S. Ferrara. Copyright © 1993. Reprinted by permission of National Education Association.

also shows the weight that each criteria will have in determining the overall score. Actually, an analytic scale can be as simple as a numerical scale that follows each criterion, such as the following, which could be used to evaluate creative writing:

Criterion	Outstanding		Competent		Marginal
Creative ideas	5	4	3	2	1
Logical organization	5	4	3	2	1
Relevance of detail	5	4	3	2	1
Variety in words and sentences	5	4	3	2	1
Vivid images	5	4	3	2	1

However, such scales still do not indicate much about why ideas were "competent" and not "outstanding" or why vivid images were rated "marginal." Analytic scales use language that is as descriptive as possible about the nature of the criterion that differentiates it from one level to the next. It will be much more helpful, for example, for students to know "that eye contact with the audience was direct and sustained for most of the presentation," rather than receiving feedback such as

Figure 9.8 Holistic Rubric for Graphic Display of Data

3	All data are accurately represented on the graph. All parts of the graph (units of measurement, rows) are correctly labeled. The graph contains a title that clearly tells what the data show. The graph is very neat and easy to read.
2	Data are accurately represented on the graph *or* the graph contains minor errors. All parts of the graph are correctly labeled *or* the graph contains minor inaccuracies. The graph contains a title that generally tells what the data show. The graph is generally neat and readable.
1	The data are inaccurately represented, contain major errors, or are missing. Only some parts of the graph are correctly labeled, or labels are missing. The title does not reflect what the data show, or the title is missing. The graph is sloppy and difficult to read.

Source: McTighe, J., & Wiggins, G. (2004). *Understanding by design: Professional development workbook.* Alexandria, VA: Association for Supervision and Curriculum Development. Reprinted by permission.

FIGURE 9.9 Example of Analytic Scale Rubric for Graphic Display of Data[1]

Criteria	Score			Weight
	1	2	3	
Title	Missing or does not reflect data	Title included though only a general indication of data	Title included that clearly tells what the data show	10%
Labels	Labels missing or only for some parts of the graph	Labels included though some are incorrect	Labels accurately included for all parts of the graph	20%
Accuracy	Data are not included, inaccurate, or contain major errors	Data are included, though with minor errors	Data accurately included for all parts of the graph	50%
Neatness	Graph is sloppy and difficult to read	Graph is generally neat and readable	Graph is very neat and easy to read	20%

[1]Adapted from McTighe & Wiggins (2004).

"excellent" or "completely." The difference between holistic and analytic scales is illustrated in Figure 9.10.

The following suggestions, summarized in Figure 9.11, will provide further help as you develop rubrics.

1. Be Sure the Criteria Focus on Important Aspects of the Performance. There are many ways to distinguish between different examples of student work. You want to use those criteria that are essential in relation to the learning targets

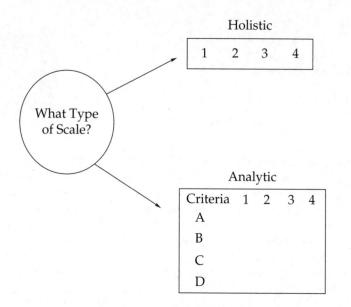

FIGURE 9.10   Differences Between Holistic and Analytic Scales

Source: Adapted and redrawn from *Scoring Rubrics in the Classroom: Using Performance Criteria for Assessing and Improving Student Performance* by J. Arter & J. McTighe. Copyright © 2001. Sage Publications.

FIGURE 9.11   Checklist for Writing and Implementing Rubrics

✓ Do criteria focus on important aspects of the performance?
✓ Is the type of rating matched with purpose?
✓ Are the traits directly observable?
✓ Are the criteria understandable?
✓ Are the traits clearly defined?
✓ Is scoring error minimized?
✓ Is the scoring system feasible?

you are assessing. Because it is not feasible to include every possible way in which performances may differ, you need to identify those that are most important. For example, if you are making judgments about writing and use mechanics as one of the criteria, it would not be practical to include every grammatical rule in characterizing the descriptions. Rather, you need to select the few most important aspects, such as tense formation, agreement, and punctuation.

2. Match the Type of Rating with the Purpose of the Assessment. If your purpose is more global and you need an overall judgment, a holistic scale should be used. If the major reason for the assessment is to provide feedback about different aspects of the performance, an analytical approach would be best.

3. Descriptions of the Criteria Should Be Directly Observable. Try to keep the descriptions focused on behaviors or aspects of products or skills that you can

Teacher's Corner

Arleen Reinhart

National Board Certified High School English Teacher

I generate my scoring criteria and rubrics by first considering the skills that the students have attained from previous assignments. I expect students to continue using these learned and practiced skills. I also expect students to show evidence of the new skills learned. I don't want students to believe that skills are to be used to do well only on one assessment and that they are not important again until the exam. I want to see growth in their skill level. Thus, I consider both past skills that are crucial to development, as well as the skills that students should have acquired based on their recent instruction. As a result, instruction and my objectives drive the scoring criteria. Students are always given a copy of the scoring criteria or rubric prior to submission of the work. It is only fair that they know the skills on which they will be judged.

observe directly. You want to use clearly visible, overt behaviors for which relatively little inference is required (e.g., behaviors such as loudness, eye contact, and enunciation are easily and reliably observed). It is best to avoid high-inference criteria that are judged on the basis of behavior, such as attitudes, interests, and effort, because the behaviors are easily faked and are more susceptible to rater error and bias. This means that when the target is affective, the focus needs to be on behaviors that can be directly observed. Avoid the use of adverbs that communicate standards, such as *adequately, correctly,* and *poorly.* These evaluative words should be kept separate from what is observed.

Examples

> *Poor:* Demonstrates a positive attitude toward learning keyboarding skills.

> *Improved:* Voluntarily gives to the teacher or other students two reasons why it is important to learn keyboarding skills.

4. Criteria Should Be Written So That Students, Parents, and Others Understand Them.   Recall that the criteria should be shared with students before instruction. The purpose of this procedure is to encourage students to incorporate the descriptions as standards in doing their work. Obviously, if the descriptions are unclear, students cannot apply them to their work, and the meaningfulness of your feedback is lessened. Consequently, pay attention to wording and phrases; write so that students easily comprehend the criteria. A helpful approach to ensure understanding is simple but often overlooked—ask the students! It is also helpful to provide examples of student work that illustrate different descriptions.

5. Characteristics and Traits Used in the Scale Should Be Clearly and Specifically Defined.   You need to have sufficient detail in your descriptions so that the criteria are not vague. If a few general terms are used, observed behaviors are open to different interpretations. The wording needs to be clear and unambiguous.

Examples (wood shop assignment to build a letter holder)

Poor: Construction is sound.

Improved: Pieces fit firmly together; sanded to a smooth surface; glue does not show; varnish is even.

Note the clarity and specificity of the analytic scale illustrated in Figure 9.12. This is an example of an excellent rubric, in this case for writing a persuasive essay.

6. Take Appropriate Steps to Minimize Scoring Error.   The goal of any scoring system is to be objective and consistent. Because performance assessment involves professional judgment, some types of errors in particular should be avoided to achieve objectivity and consistency. The most common errors are associated with the *personal bias* and *halo effects* of the person who is making the judgment. Personal bias results in three kinds of errors. **Generosity error** occurs when the teacher tends to give higher scores; **severity error** results when teachers use the low end of the scale and underrate students' performances. A third type of personal bias is **central tendency error,** in which students are rated in the middle.

The **halo effect** occurs when the teacher's general impression of the student affects scores given on individual traits or performances. If the teacher has an overall favorable impression, he or she may tend to give ratings that are higher than what is warranted; a negative impression results in the opposite. The halo effect is mitigated if the identity of the student is concealed (though this is not possible with most performance assessments), by using clearly and sufficiently described criteria, and by periodically asking others to review your judgments. Halo effects can also occur if the nature of a response to one dimension, or the general appearance of the student, affects your subsequent judgments of other dimensions. That is, if the student does extremely well on the first dimension, there may be a tendency to rate the next dimensions higher, and students who look and act nice may be rated higher. Perhaps the best way to avoid the halo effect is to be aware of its potential for affecting your judgment and monitoring yourself so that it doesn't occur. Other sources of scoring error, such as order effects and rater exhaustion, should also be avoided.

To be consistent in the way you apply the criteria, rescore some of the first products scored after finishing all the students, and score one criterion for all students at the same time. This helps avoid order and halo effects that occur because of performance on previous dimensions. Scoring each product several times, each time on a different criterion, allows you to keep the overall purpose of the rubric in mind.

7. The Scoring System Needs to Be Feasible.   There are several reasons to limit the number and complexity of criteria that are judged. First, you need to be

FIGURE 9.12   Example of a Persuasive Essay Rubric (Grades 3 & 4)

	4	3	2	1
Ideas and content	The paper clearly states an opinion and gives 3 clear, detailed reasons in support of it.	An opinion is given. One reason may be unclear or lack detail.	An opinion is given. The reasons given tend to be weak or inaccurate. May get off topic.	The opinion and support for it is buried, confused and/or unclear.
Organization	The paper has a beginning with an interesting lead, a middle, and an ending. It is in an order that makes sense. Paragraphs are indented and have topic and closing sentences and main ideas.	The paper has a beginning, middle and end. The order makes sense. Paragraphs are indented; some have topic and closing sentences.	The paper has an attempt at a beginning and or ending. Some ideas may seem out of order. Some problems with paragraphs.	There is no real beginning or ending. The ideas seem loosely strung together. No paragraph formatting.
Voice and tone	The writing shows what the writer thinks and feels. It sounds like the writer cares about the topic.	The writing seems sincere but not enthusiastic. The writer's voice fades in and out.	The paper could have been written by anyone. It shows very little about what the writer thought and felt.	The writing is bland and sounds like the writer doesn't like the topic. No thoughts or feelings.
Word choice	Descriptive words are used ("helpful" instead of "good' or "destructive" instead of "bad").	The words are mostly ordinary, with a few attempts at descriptive words.	The words are ordinary but generally correct.	The same words are used over and over. Some words are used incorrectly.
Sentence fluency	The sentences are complete, clear, and begin in different ways.	The sentences are usually correct.	There are many incomplete sentences and run-ons.	The story is hard to read because of incomplete and run-on sentences.
Conventions	Spelling, punctuation, capitalization, and grammar are correct. Only minor edits are needed.	Spelling, punctuation and caps are usually correct. Some problems with grammar.	There are enough errors to make the writing hard to read and understand.	The writing is almost impossible to read because of errors.

Source: Andrade, H. L., Du, Y., & Wang, X. (2008). Putting rubrics to the test: The effect of a model, criteria generation, and rubric referenced self-assessment on elementary school students' writing. *Educational Measurement: Issues and Practice, 27*(2), 12.

Case Study
for Reflection

Here is how a high school teacher recently described the use of student suggestions in the development of a rubric for grading an action-research essay (Strickland & Strickland, 1998):

"So, we did the assessment brainstorming, and put all of the students' suggestions on the blackboard. Then, I asked them to lump the individual points into larger categories, and we arrived at these four: style, structure, quality of argument, and presentation. And then, I told them that they had 100 points to distribute among the four categories. We argued about that for a while, and eventually reached consensus (more or less) on this arrangement: 20, 20, 50, and 10, respectively. It's always interesting listening to the students' arguments about how to do this: The reasoning here was that the essay was content driven, according to the kids, so most of the marks should be for content. I didn't really agree with that: I wanted the reflection, and therefore possibly the structure, to be worth more, but I lost. The whole exercise was quite democratic, especially for a school setting, and I didn't want to impose my values on their opinions. As well, this was not the first time that we had done this kind of negotiated assessment thing during the semester, and so the students knew how to play the game." (p. 86)

QUESTIONS FOR CONSIDERATION

1. From this example, what would you say are the advantages and disadvantages of using student suggestions to develop a scoring rubric?
2. Did the issue of grading seem to interfere in any way with the establishment of the criteria?
3. How does the teacher modify the suggestions to incorporate more criteria that he or she believes are important and should be included?

practical with respect to the amount of time it takes to develop the scoring criteria and do the scoring. Generally, five to eight different criteria for a single product are sufficient and manageable. Second, students will be able to focus only on a limited number of aspects of the performance. Third, if holistic descriptions are too complex, it is difficult and time consuming to keep all the facets in mind. Finally, it may be difficult to summarize and synthesize too many separate dimensions into a brief report or evaluation.

One last suggestion will be helpful as you design rubrics. Because performance assessment is well established, there are numerous examples of rubrics for every subject and grade level. Along with many books and guides (see Corwin Press), the Internet can be used to access all kinds of rubrics. Just type in your area and grade level (e.g., intermediate mathematics rubrics), and much will be displayed. Like all material on the Internet, the quality of these examples will vary, so be a critical consumer.

Summary

This chapter introduced performance assessment as a method to measure skill and product learning targets, as well as knowledge and reasoning targets. Important points made in the chapter include the following:

- In contrast to paper-and-pencil tests, performance assessment requires students to construct an original response to a task that is scored with teacher judgment.
- Authentic assessment involves a performance task that approximates what students are likely to have to do in real-world settings.
- Performance assessment integrates instruction with evaluation of student achievement and is based on constructivist learning theory. Multiple criteria for judging successful performance are developed.
- Major limitations of performance assessments include the resources and time needed to conduct them, bias and unreliability in scoring, and a lack of generalization.
- Performance assessment is used most frequently with deep understanding, reasoning, skill, and product learning targets.
- Communication skill targets include reading, writing, and speaking.
- Psychomotor skill targets consist of physical actions (fine motor, gross motor, complex athletic, and visual, and verbal/auditory) and the level to which the action is demonstrated (perception, set, guided response, mechanism, complex overt response, adaptation, and origination).
- Product targets are completed student works, such as papers, written reports, and projects.
- Presentation targets include oral presentations and reports.
- The performance task defines what students are required to do.
- Restricted-type tasks target a narrowly defined skill and have a brief response.
- Extended-type tasks target complex tasks and have extensive responses. These may take several days or even weeks to complete.
- The task description needs to clearly indicate the target, student activities, resources needed, teacher role, administrative procedures, and scoring procedures.
- Effective tasks have multiple targets that integrate essential content and skills, are grounded in real-world contexts, rely on teacher help, are feasible, allow for multiple solutions, are clear, are challenging and stimulating, and include scoring criteria.
- Scoring criteria and rubrics are used to evaluate student performances.
- Criteria are narrative descriptions of the dimensions used to evaluate the students.
- Rating scales are used to indicate different levels of performance.
- Holistic rubrics contain several dimensions together; analytic rubrics provide a separate score for each dimension.
- Complete scoring rubrics include both descriptions and evaluative labels for different levels of the dimension.

- Scoring criteria are based on clear definitions of different levels of proficiency and samples of student work.
- High-quality scoring criteria focus on important aspects of the performance, match the type of rating (holistic or analytical) with the purpose of the assessment, are directly observable, are understandable, are clearly and specifically defined, minimize error, and are feasible.

Self-Instructional Review Exercises

1. How does authentic assessment differ from performance assessment?

2. Explain how each of the following words is important in describing the nature of performance assessment: *explain, reasoning, observable, criteria, standards, engaging,* and *prespecified*.

3. Identify each of the following as an advantage (A) or disadvantage (D) of performance assessment.

    a. Resource intensive
    b. Integrates instruction with assessment
    c. Student self-assessment
    d. Scoring
    e. Reasoning skills
    f. Active learning
    g. Use of criteria
    h. Length

4. Identify each of the following skills as fine motor (FM), gross motor (GM), or complex (C), and use the hierarchy described on page 227 to identify the level of the skill.

    a. Making up new dives
    b. Tracing a picture of a lion just as the teacher did
    c. Making cursive capital letters easily
    d. Changing running stride to accommodate an uneven surface

5. Classify each of the following as a restricted (R) or extended (E) performance task.

    a. Tie shoes
    b. Prepare a plan for a new city park
    c. Construct a building from toothpicks
    d. Interpret a weather map
    e. Enact the Boston Tea Party
    f. Read a tide table

6. Evaluate the following performance task description. What is missing?

    You have been asked to organize a camping trip in North Dakota. There are seven campers. Indicate what you believe you will need for a three-day trip, and provide reasons for your answer. Also include a detailed itinerary of where you will go while camping. You may use any library resources that you believe are helpful, and you may interview others who have had camping experience. As your teacher, I will answer questions about how you gather information, but I will not evaluate your answer until you have something to turn in.

7. Create a scoring rubric for the task presented in question 6. Show how each of the elements of writing and implementing scoring criteria presented in Figure 9.11 is followed in your answer. Include reasoning skills in your rubric.

Answers to Self-Instructional Review Exercises

1. Authentic assessment refers to the nature of the task that approximates what is done in the real world. Performance assessment involves the construction of responses by students—it may or may not be authentic.

2. Students are required to *explain* their responses as well as to produce them; *reasoning* targets are usually assessed, students use *reasoning* skills to demonstrate their proficiency; student performance is judged by what is directly *observable*; *criteria* are used to judge the adequacy of the performance on the basis of *prespecified standards* that relate a description of the performance to a statement of worth; good performance tasks are those that are *engaging* for students.

3. a. D; b. A; c. A; d. D; e. A; f. A; g. A; h. D.

4. a. C, origination; b. FM, guided response; c. FM, mechanism; d. GM, adaptation.

5. a. R; b. E; c. E; d. R; e. E; f. R.

6. As a performance prompt, this isn't too bad, but as a performance task description it could be improved considerably. There is no indication of the targets, whether this is an individual or group project, the administrative process, and most important, no indication of the scoring criteria. It is a fairly authentic task and integrates different subjects. It does say something about the role of the teacher and resources, but more detail on both of these aspects could be provided.

7. There will be individual answers to this question, so you'll need to review each other's work by applying the questions in Figure 9.11. I would begin with an analysis of the essential understandings and skills needed to plan the trip. This would comprise the dimensions that are evaluated (e.g., the ability to use maps, the ability to understand the impact of terrain and time of year on what will be needed, the extent to which plans follow from assumptions, the logic and soundness of reasons stated). I would then employ a scale to indicate the extent to which each of these dimensions is present (e.g., inadequate, adequate, more than adequate, or absent; developing, proficient, advanced). For example, for the extent to which plans follow from assumptions, you might note the following:

Absent	There is no indication of assumptions or how plans are based on assumptions.
Developing	Assumptions are not clearly stated but implied; plans are not explicitly related to assumptions but are implied.
Proficient	Some assumptions are clearly stated and plans are explicitly related to the assumptions.
Advanced	A comprehensive and well-thought-out list of assumptions is used; assumptions are explicitly related to plans.

Suggestions for Action Research

1. Identify a teacher who is using performance assessments and observe students during the assessment. Are they actively involved and on task? Do they seem motivated, even eager to get feedback on their performance? How "authentic" is the task? Can there be more than one correct answer? Is instruction integrated with the assessment? If possible, interview some students and ask them how they react to performance assessments. What do they like and dislike about them? How do they compare to more traditional types of assessment? How could they be more effective?

2. Devise a performance assessment for some aspect of this chapter. Include the performance task and scoring rubric, using the criteria in Figure 9.4. Critique the assessments through class discussion.

3. Try out some scoring rubrics with teachers. You will need to formulate learning targets and the performance task. Construct exemplars of student work that illustrate different scores. Ask the teachers to give you some feedback about the scoring rubric. Is it reasonable? Does it allow for meaningful differentiation between important dimensions of the task? Is it practical? Would students understand the rubric? How could the scoring rubric be improved?

4. In a small group with other students, do some research on three examples of performance tasks in your field. Do they appear to meet the criteria in Figure 9.4? How could they be improved? Be prepared to present your findings to the class for discussion.

Endnotes

1. From "District 214's speech assessment rating guide." (n.d.) Township High School District 214, Arlington Heights, IL.
2. A comparison task from Marzano, Pickering, & McTighe, 1993, p. 50. *Assessing student outcomes: Performance assessment using the dimensions of learning model.* Alexandria, VA: ACSD.

Constructed-Response Assessment: Portfolios

Portfolio assessment is a type of constructed-response approach that is an excellent strategy for integrating assessment with instruction, particularly when student self-reflection is an important learning outcome. It is becoming increasingly clear that this method of collecting and evaluating student work over time

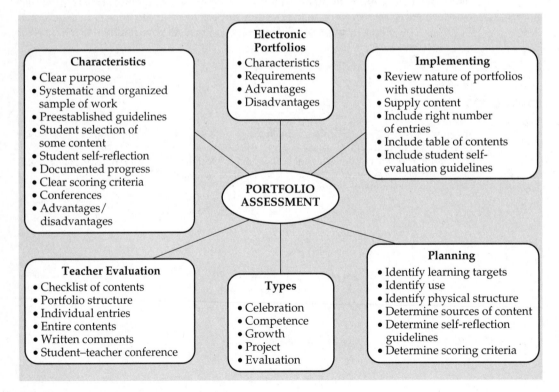

CHAPTER 10   Concept Map

has significant advantages over more conventional approaches to assessment. Portfolios are much more than large student folders containing examples of student work. Using them requires some changes in how students are involved in assessment. In this chapter, we review essential characteristics of effective portfolios, show how they can be integrated with instruction, and illustrate, with examples, how portfolios are designed and implemented.

What Are Portfolios?

In many professions, *portfolio* is a familiar term. Portfolios have constituted the primary method of evaluation in fields such as art, architecture, modeling, photography, and journalism. These professions have realized the value of documenting proficiency, skill, style, and talent with examples of actual work. In education, a **portfolio** can be defined as a purposeful, systematic process of collecting and evaluating student products to document progress toward the attainment of learning targets or show evidence that a learning target has been achieved. Portfolios include specific and predetermined guidelines for the selection of materials and criteria for scoring and evidence of student self-reflection on what has been accomplished.

Defined in this way, then, a portfolio has several essential characteristics (Figure 10.1). First, a portfolio is *purposeful*. There is a clear reason why certain works would be included and how the portfolio is to be used. Second, rather than reflecting a haphazard collection of examples, the portfolio represents a *systematic* and *well-organized* collection of materials that make up a *sample*, not a comprehensive or exhaustive collection, of student work. Third, *preestablished guidelines* are set up so that it is clear what materials should be included. Fourth, students are engaged in the process by *selecting some of the materials* and by continually evaluating and *reflecting* on their work. Fifth, based on clear and well-specified *scoring criteria, progress* is documented with the evaluations. Finally, *conferences* are held

---

FIGURE 10.1   Characteristics of Portfolio Assessment

- Clearly defined purpose and learning targets
- Systematic and organized collection of student products
- Preestablished guidelines for what will be included
- Student selection of some of what is included
- Student self-reflection and self-evaluation
- Progress documented with specific products and/or evaluations
- Clear and appropriate criteria for evaluating student products
- Portfolio conferences between students and teachers

Source: Adapted with permission from Arter, J., & Spandel, V. (1992). Using portfolios of student work in instruction and assessment. *Educational Measurement: Issues and Practice, 11,* 36–44.

between teacher and student to review progress, identify areas that need further improvement, and facilitate student reflection.

Although the precise nature of what is called portfolio assessment will be unique to a particular setting, five types have developed (Stiggins, Arter, Chappuis & Chappuis, 2006). Each type is distinguished primarily by the purpose it serves. The *celebration* or *showcase* portfolio includes a student selection of his or her best work, what they are most proud of. Because the student chooses the work, each profile of accomplishment is unique, and individual profiles emerge. This encourages self-reflection and self-evaluation, but makes scoring more difficult and time consuming because of the unique structure and content of each portfolio. The *competence* or *achievement* portfolio is structured to provide evidence that a targeted level of performance has been achieved. For this kind of portfolio, the criteria for determination of mastery or competence needs to be clearly defined. The *growth* portfolio reveals change in student proficiency over time. Selections of student work are collected at different times to show how skills have improved. The same evaluative criteria should be used throughout the period of time that the portfolio is used. The focal point of *project* portfolios is on a single example or illustration of the competence of the student. Typically there is documentation of reaching each important target that the project is intended to show. In this sense, it is similar to a competence portfolio. The *evaluation* portfolio is more standardized. The focus is more to asssess student learning than to enhance instruction, although student self-reflection may be included. Most of the examples are selected by teachers or are predetermined. Table 10.1 shows examples of each of these types of portfolios.

Burke (1999) lists the following as more specific types of portfolios.

- Writing—dated writing samples to show progress
- Process Folios—first and second drafts of assignments along with final product to show growth
- Literacy—combination of reading, writing, speaking, and listening pieces
- Best-Work—student and teacher selections of the student's best work
- Unit—one unit of study
- Integrated—a thematic study that brings in different disciplines
- Yearlong—key artifacts from entire year to show growth
- Career—important artifacts collected to showcase employability
- Standards—evidence to document meeting standards
- Working—collection of all student work before selections are made

Regardless of the specific type or label, portfolios have advantages and disadvantages that determine whether you will find them useful in your own teaching. Portfolios combine the strengths of performance assessments with the ability to provide a continuous record of progress and improvement. The advantages that result serve as compelling reasons to use portfolios if needed resources are provided. Like any method of assessment, there are limitations and trade-offs, so the choice depends on your overall goals and philosophy of instruction and learning.

TABLE 10.1   Different Types of Portfolios

Type	Description	Examples
Celebration	Shows student's best work	Highest scored test Highest graded paper Best project
Competence	Shows levels of achievement reached in relation to learning targets	Mastery of each competency needed to do electrical work Recent writing samples keyed to different criteria
Growth	Shows improvement of student competence over time	Different writing samples that show performance before and after instruction Drawings from the first part of the semester to the last week of the semester
Project	Illustrates competence on completion of a single task	History unit final presentation Small-group project on identifying chemicals in a water sample
Evaluation	Common set of examples of student work	Writing assignments graded with criteria Examples of art that demonstrate balance and perspective

Advantages

Perhaps the most important advantage of using portfolios is that students are actively involved in self-evaluation and self-reflection (Borich & Tombari, 2004; Hebert, 1998; Wolf, 1989). Students become part of the assessment process. They reflect on their performance and accomplishments, critique themselves, and evaluate their progress. This leads to setting goals for further learning. Students learn that self-evaluation is an important part of self-improvement; portfolios encourage and support critical thinking through student self-reflection (Kingore, 2008). Students also apply decision-making skills in selecting certain works to be included and providing justifications for inclusion. In this sense, portfolios are open and always accessible to the student. This is quite different from teachers maintaining a private record of student accomplishments.

Closely related to self-assessment is the notion that portfolios involve *collaborative assessment*. Students learn that assessment is most effective when it is done with others. In addition to self-reflections, students learn from peer reviews and teacher feedback. They may evaluate the work of others and interact with teachers to come to a better understanding of the quality of their performance.

Another important advantage of portfolios is that they promote an ongoing process wherein students demonstrate performance, evaluate, and revise to learn and produce quality work. Assessment is continuous and integrally related to learning. Rather than being only summative, systematic formative evaluation is conducted. This is different from the type of informal feedback teachers give to students, as summarized in Chapter 5. With portfolios, well-developed criteria are used to continually evaluate student progress.

Because most portfolios contain samples of student work over time, they focus on self-improvement rather than comparison with others. The samples clearly document how students have progressed. This reinforces the idea that what is most important is how each student, as an individual, improves. This helps to focus the assessment on what is done correctly and on strengths, rather than on

Teacher's Corner

Ann Marie Seeley

National Board Certified High School English Teacher

Portfolio assessment works only when students understand where they are, where they need to go and are provided with instruction to support the journey. Oftentimes, teacher see storing a student's writing in a folder as "portfolio assessment." They create a check sheet for each item that should be in the folder and grade based on completion. True portfolio assessment is personal, and it has to have an element of choice by the person being assessed. In order for students to choose the best pieces to represent their growth as writers, they need to know what constitutes success. Personal goal setting based on clear criteria for success is important to the portfolio process as is frequent reflection on those goals. At the beginning of the year, students begin their portfolios with a writing sample. That sample is scored based on the rubric we will use throughout the year, but it is not graded. After students see the score, they are asked to write a reflection about their areas of strength and areas for improvement. This reflection becomes part of the portfolio. As students move through instruction and learn how to improve their writing, they revisit the samples in their portfolio and reflect on their growth. Finally, students are asked to select several pieces of writing that show their growth as writers. Students are allowed to revise those pieces and/or add outside writing—such as poems, short stories, other academic writing, etc.—in order to demonstrate their growth. Their final piece of the portfolio is a personal reflection. While this reflection might take the form of an essay, it might also be done orally (through a podcast, perhaps). Portfolio assessment takes time and dedication on the part of the teacher, but when implemented correctly, it can truly show individual student growth.

weaknesses or what is wrong. When each student has a unique set of materials in his or her portfolio, assessment and learning are individualized. Thus, portfolios easily accommodate individual differences among students, even though the overall learning targets are the same and can show unique capabilities and accomplishments. As we will see, however, this is also a disadvantage when it comes to scoring.

Motivation is enhanced as students see the link between their efforts and accomplishments and as they exert greater control over their learning. They become more engaged in learning because both instruction and assessment shift from being completely externally controlled by the teacher to a mix of external and internal control. A sixth-grade teacher relates this kind of impact on students (Martin-Kniep, 1998): "With this portfolio, I saw better work than I had in the past. Students were more excited than they had ever been in my class. They were thrilled about what they had accomplished" (p. 60). As pointed out by Borich and Tombari (2004), this enables teachers to focus on students' persistence, effort, and willingness to change.

A hallmark of portfolios is that they contain examples of student products. This emphasis on products is helpful in several ways. First, products reinforce the importance of performance assessment to students and parents. Products provide excellent evidence to help teachers diagnose learning difficulties, meet with students, and provide individualized feedback. The concrete examples provided by the products are very helpful in explaining student progress to parents. It is much easier to clarify reasons for your evaluations when you have a set of examples in a parent conference.

Finally, portfolios are flexible. They can be adapted to different ages, types of products, abilities, interests, and learning styles. There is no single set of procedures, products, or grading criteria that must be used. You have the opportunity to customize your portfolio requirements to your needs and capabilities, to different learning targets, to available resources, and, most important, to differences among the students.

Disadvantages

There are some limitations to using portfolios that must be considered. Like other performance assessments, scoring is the major drawback. Not only is scoring time consuming, but research on the reliability of scoring portfolios has shown that it is also difficult to obtain high inter-rater reliability. Inconsistent scoring results from criteria that are too general and can be interpreted differently, from such detailed criteria that raters are overwhelmed, or from the inadequate training of raters. Usually, criteria are too general, and raters have not received much training.

A second disadvantage is that portfolio assessment takes considerable time and resources to do correctly. Many hours are needed to design the portfolios and scoring criteria, and many more hours will be spent reviewing, scoring, and conferencing with students and parents. Additional time may be needed to obtain the training to feel confident and to implement the portfolios properly. You need to

FIGURE 10.2   Advantages and Disadvantages of Portfolio Assessment

Advantages	Disadvantages
• Promotes student self-assessment • Promotes collaborative assessment • Enhances student motivation • Systematic assessment is ongoing • Focus is on improvement, not comparisons with others • Focus is on students' strengths—what they can do • Assessment process is individualized • Allows demonstration of unique accomplishments • Provides concrete examples for parent conferences • Products can be used for individualized teacher diagnosis • Flexibility and adaptability	• Scoring difficulties may lead to low reliability • Teacher training needed • Time-consuming to develop criteria, score, and meet with students • Students may not make good selections of which materials to include • Sampling of student products may lead to weak generalization • Parents may find portfolios difficult to understand

decide if this amount of time is worth the effort. Let me emphasize that time and resources are needed to do portfolio assessment *correctly*. It's not the same as producing a folder of student work. Portfolio assessment, when done correctly, is very demanding; it requires time, expertise, and commitment.

A final disadvantage to consider is the potential for limited generalizability. With portfolios, you generalize from the examples and demonstrated performance according to the criteria to broader learning targets. In doing this, we need to be careful that the generalization is justified and that what is in the portfolio provides each student with a fair opportunity to demonstrate his or her level of competency on the general learning target. For example, if you are making judgments about the ability of a student to communicate by writing and the only types of writing in the portfolio are creative and expository, then the validity of the conclusion about writing more generally is weak. Figure 10.2 summarizes the advantages and disadvantages of portfolio assessment.

Planning for Portfolio Assessment

The process of planning and implementing portfolio assessment is illustrated in Figure 10.3. In this section of the chapter, we examine the planning phase of the process, which is represented in the first four steps. These steps are completed before implementation. Suggestions for planning are presented in the form of a checklist in Figure 10.4.

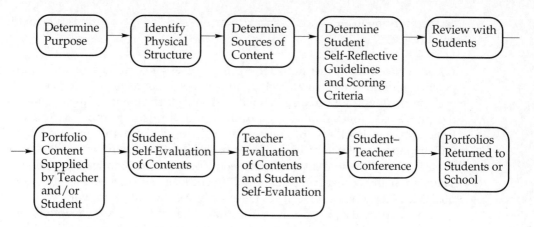

FIGURE 10.3   Steps for Planning and Implementing Portfolio Assessment

FIGURE 10.4   Checklist for Planning Portfolio Assessment

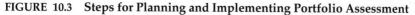

✓ Are learning targets clear?
✓ Are uses of the portfolio clear?
✓ Is the physical structure for holding materials adequate and easily accessed?
✓ Are procedures for selecting the content clear?
✓ Does the nature of the content match the purpose?
✓ Are student self-reflective guidelines and questions clear?
✓ Are scoring criteria established?

Purpose

Designing a portfolio begins with a clear idea about the purpose of the assessment. This involves both the specific learning targets and the use of the portfolio (Seitz & Bartholomew, 2008).

Learning Targets.   As suggested by the title of this chapter, portfolios may be used to assess understanding but are ideal for assessing product, skill, and reasoning targets. This is especially true for multidimensional skills such as writing, reading, and problem solving that are continually improved and demonstrated through products. With extensive self-reflection, critical thinking is an important target. Students also develop metacognitive and decision-making skills. As with other performance assessments, portfolios generally are not very efficient for assessing knowledge targets.

It is important to distinguish between learning targets for individual work samples and for the contents of the portfolio as a whole. The targets that reflect all contents tend to be broader and more general, such as "development as a reader," "adapts writing to audience," "speaks clearly," and "adapts writing style to differ-ent purposes."

Uses.   I have already mentioned five primary uses for portfolios: celebration, com-petence, growth, project, and evaluation. You need to indicate the degree to which each one is important because this will influence the contents of the portfolio and the criteria used for evaluation. For example, if the primary purpose is to document typical student work and progress, the portfolio will be highly individualized. It will tend to be a relatively loosely organized collection of samples selected by both the teacher and the student, accompanied by both student and teacher evaluations. There are many entries, representing different levels of performance, because the goal is to show what is typical, not necessarily the student's best work.

If the primary purpose is to illustrate what students are capable of doing, then the orientation is more toward a celebration type of portfolio. Only the stu-dent's best work is included. The emphasis is on student selection, self-reflection, and self-assessment, rather than on standardization for evaluation. This approach uses the portfolio to showcase what each individual has achieved. Teachers often display the results in a book or folder. There may or may not be much indication of progress, but the emphasis is clearly on what has been accomplished rather than on improvement.

In a growth portfolio, improvement over time is shown by comparing early products or efforts with later ones. A good example could be a persuasive letter to the editor. At the beginning of the semester students write such a letter. Later in the semester, after learning about what is needed to be persuasive, another letter is writ-ten. Growth is demonstrated by comparing the two products using the same criteria.

If the portfolios are used primarily for evaluation, there will be greater stan-dardization about what to include and how the portfolios are reviewed. Most samples are selected by the teacher, and scoring is emphasized.

Some portfolios are used to show parents and others what students have achieved. If this is the primary purpose, more attention needs to be given to what will make sense to parents, with somewhat less attention to student self-reflection. In contrast, if portfolios are used primarily diagnostically and with students to help them progress, then more time is spent with student–teacher conferences dur-ing the school day. If the purpose is to help students self-reflect or peer review, then structure and support for these activities needs to be provided.

Most teachers implement portfolios for multiple purposes. Because your time and energy are limited, try to identify a *primary* purpose and design the port-folio based on that purpose. Wiggins (1998) points out that portfolio assessment is often implemented without sufficient attention to purpose and corresponding implications. He indicates, for example, that portfolios can primarily serve as instruction or assessment tools, focus on documentation or evaluation, be con-trolled by the teacher or student, and contain a sample of best work or show change over time. The specific nature of portfolio assessment differs depending on the importance of these various purposes. As a consequence, determining primary purpose, with clarity, is critical.

Identify Physical Structure

Once your purpose has been clarified, you need to think about some practical aspects of the portfolio. What will it look like? Most portfolios are contained in envelopes or folders. How large do the folders need to be? Where are they stored so that students can have easy access to them? Do you have boxes to put them in? Commonly used containers include cardboard boxes, file folders, file cabinets, cereal boxes, and accordion files. Putting folders on shelves where they are visible and accessible tells students they are important and should be used continuously. Your choices for these physical demands will influence to some extent what will be put in the portfolios. In addition, you will need to think about the actual arrangement of the documents in the portfolio. Is it done chronologically, by subject area, or by type of document? What materials will be needed to separate the documents? Later in the chapter we will review electronic structures.

Determine Sources of Content

The content of a portfolio consists of work samples and student and teacher evaluations. Work samples are usually derived directly from instructional activities, so that products that result from instruction are included. The range of work samples is often extensive, determined to some extent by the subject. For example, in language arts you could use entries from student journals, book reports, audiotapes of oral presentations, workbook assignments, and poetry. In science, you might include lab reports, questions posed by students for further investigation, drawings, solutions to problems, and pictures of projects.

Select categories of samples that will allow you to meet the purpose of the portfolio. If you need to show progress, select tasks and samples that are able to show improvement. If you need to provide feedback to students on the procedures they use in putting together a report, be sure to include a summary of that process as part of the portfolio. Use work samples that capitalize on the advantages of portfolios, such as flexibility, individuality, and authenticity. The categories should allow for sufficient variation so that students can show individual work. This often means giving students choices about what they can include.

To give you a better idea of the types of work samples to include, refer to the examples in Figures 10.5 and 10.6. It is also helpful to consult other sources that include different kinds of portfolios. A number of books on portfolio assessment in specific content areas contain examples.

Determine Student Self-Reflective Guidelines and Scoring Criteria

Before implementing a portfolio assessment, you need to establish guidelines for student self-reflection and the scoring criteria you will use when evaluating student performance. This needs to be done so that both the guidelines and criteria can be explained to students *before* they begin their work. In many cases, students

FIGURE 10.5   Examples of Portfolio Work Samples

Language Arts	Mathematics
• Projects, surveys, reports, and units from reading and writing	• A solution to an open-ended question done as homework
• Favorite poems, songs, letters, and comments	• A mathematical autobiography
• Interesting thoughts to remember	• Papers that show the student's correction of errors or misconceptions
• Finished samples that illustrate wide writing: persuasive, letters, poetry, information, stories	• A photo or sketch made by the student of a student's work with manipulatives or with mathematical models of multidimensional figures
• Examples of writing across the curriculum: reports, journals, literature logs	
• Literature extensions: scripts for drama, visual arts, written forms, webs, charts, time lines, murals	• A letter from the student to the reader of the portfolio, explaining each item
• Student record of books read and attempted	• A report of a group project, with comments about the individual's contribution
• Audiotape of reading	• Work from another subject area that relates to mathematics, such as an analysis of data collected and presented in a graph for social studies
• Writing responses to literacy components: plot, setting, point of view, character development, links to life, theme, literary links and criticism	
• Writing that illustrates critical thinking about reading	• A problem made up by the student
• Notes from individual reading and writing conference	• Artwork done by the student, such as string designs, coordinate pictures, and scale drawings or maps
• Items that are evidence of development of style: organization, voice, sense of audience, choice of words, clarity	• Draft, revised, and final versions of student work on a complex mathematical problem, including writing, diagrams, graphs, charts
• Writing that shows growth in usage of traits—growing ability in self-correction, punctuation, spelling, grammar, appropriate form, and legibility	• A description by the teacher of a student activity that displayed understanding of a mathematical concept or relation
• Samples in which ideas are modified from first draft to final product	
• Unedited first drafts	
• Revised first drafts	
• Evidence of effort—improvement noted on pieces, completed assignments	

PRIMARY

LANGUAGE ARTS PORTFOLIO

Integrated Unit on Spiders

Table of Contents

1. Letter to parents about what students have learned
2. Book review of *Charlotte's Web*
3. Web of characteristics of spiders
4. Water-color picture of spiders
5. Tape of student reading story, about spiders
6. Original short story (first and final drafts) about a spider
7. Science report on "arachnids"
8. Spider rap song
9. Pictures of group project on spiders
10. Self-assessment using a criteria checklist

MIDDLE SCHOOL

GEOMETRY PORTFOLIO

Table of Contents

1. My "Math Phobia" Journal
2. Two geometry tests—corrections included
3. Glossary of geometry terms
4. Drawings of geometric shapes
5. Three problem-solving logs
6. String geometric design
7. Video of group project on angles
8. Essay on video, "Why Math?"
9. Research on math-related careers
10. Self-evaluation of portfolio using rubrics
11. Goal-setting for next quarter

HIGH SCHOOL

BIOLOGY PORTFOLIO

Table of Contents

1. Reports on careers related to the field of biology
2. One lab report
3. One problem-solving log
4. Pamphlet on diabetes (group project)
5. Video of group presentation on the circulatory system
6. Essay on germ warfare
7. Research paper on AIDS
8. Tape-recorded interview with college biology professor about AIDS
9. Self-evaluation of portfolio: using rubric
10. Goal-setting web

HIGH SCHOOL

AMERICAN HISTORY PORTFOLIO

Table of Contents

1. Annotated bibliographies of five books written about the Civil War
2. Reading list of fifty books and articles related to the Civil War
3. One abstract of a research article
4. Tape of interview with local historian
5. Journal entries of trip to Gettysburg
6. Map of the Battle of Gettysburg
7. Video of oral presentation on Pickett's charge
8. Research paper on military tactics used at the Battle of Gettysburg
9. Venn diagram comparing Battle of Gettysburg and Battle of Chancellorsville
10. Critique of TV miniseries *The Civil War*
11. Peer evaluation of portfolio using rubric

FIGURE 10.6 Examples of Portfolio Contents

Source: From *The Mindful School: How to Assess Authentic Learning,* third edition by Kay Burke. Copyright © 1999, 1994, 1993 by Skylight Training and Publishing, Inc. Reprinted by permission of Sage Publications, Inc.

can be involved in the development of self-reflective guidelines and scoring criteria. By working on these together, students will develop greater ownership of the process and will have experience in working collaboratively with you. However, keep in mind that, as the teacher, you have ultimate responsibility to control the process to ensure integrity and high quality. You will also need to be prepared to tell them how their portfolios will be evaluated.

Implementing Portfolio Assessment

Planning is complete. Now you begin the process of actually using the portfolios with your students. This begins with explaining to students what portfolios are and how they will be used. The checklist in Figure 10.7 summarizes the suggestions for effective implementation and use.

Review with Students

Because many students will not be familiar with portfolios, you will need to explain carefully what is involved and what they will be doing. Begin with your learning targets, show examples, and give students opportunities to ask questions. Try to provide just enough structure so students can get started without telling them exactly what to do. Put yourself in the student's place—if you had to do this new thing, what would be your response and what would you like to know?

Supplying Portfolio Content

Who selects the content of the portfolio—the student, teacher, or both? If both the student and teacher supply samples, what should the proportions be? Are the entries prescribed? Answers to these questions depend on the age and previous

---

FIGURE 10.7   **Checklist for Implementing and Using Portfolios**

✓ Are students knowledgeable about what a portfolio is and how it will be used?
✓ Do students know why portfolios are important?
✓ Are students responsible for or involved in selecting the content?
✓ Is there a sufficient number of work samples but not too many?
✓ Is a table of contents included?
✓ Are specific self-evaluation questions provided?
✓ Is the checklist of contents complete?
✓ Are scoring criteria for individual items and entire contents clear?
✓ Are individualized teacher-written comments provided?
✓ Are student–teacher conferences included?

experience of students and the purpose of the portfolio. It is not advisable to have preschool and primary students assume sole responsibility for selecting all the samples for their portfolios, although they certainly can be consulted and play an active role in selection. Older students should assume more responsibility for selection, although even older students who are inexperienced with portfolios will initially need considerable structure. Even if students are primarily responsible for selecting the contents, it will be helpful to provide guidelines about the nature of the works to be included. When the portfolios are used primarily for evaluation, it is best for teachers to make the selections or specifically prescribe what to include.

When deciding who will select the content, you need to consider somewhat conflicting goals. On the one hand, you want to foster student ownership and involvement, which is enhanced when students have input into what to include. On the other hand, you will probably need some degree of standardization so that equitable evidence of student performance and improvement is provided. This is best accomplished with greater teacher control. One effective compromise is for students and teachers to decide together what to include with nonrestrictive guidelines. For example, students can select, in consultation with the teacher, three pieces they believe demonstrate their writing ability and progress for a semester. Another approach is to give students some restrictions and include student explanations of the choices. The teacher might prescribe the categories of writing samples, such as poem, persuasive essay, and technical report, and students would select within each of these categories. Regardless of who makes the selections, however, there needs to be clear guidelines for what is included, when it should be submitted, and how it should be labeled (Green & Johnson, 2010).

Questions about the number of samples also need to be answered. You will find that too many indiscriminate samples become overwhelming and difficult to organize, but too few items will not provide enough information to be useful. A portfolio with more complex products that take a longer time to create will have fewer samples than one that illustrates the growth of a number of relatively simple skills. A general rule of thumb for a documentation portfolio is to add one sample every week or two, for a total of 10 to 15 different items. For showcase portfolios, as few as three samples may be sufficient. Some teachers differentiate between a *working* portfolio, in which students keep most of their work, and a *display* or *final* portfolio, in which selections are made from the working portfolio. Haertel (1990) suggests a value-added approach, in which students include only those samples that contribute to understanding how the student has improved or progressed. That is, the student or teacher might ask, "What value is added by each piece of evidence?" If a piece doesn't contribute something new, it's not included. The fewest number of samples will be contained in an evaluation portfolio, in which only samples that illustrate final performance are included.

To organize the portfolio, it is best to include a table of contents that can be expanded with each new entry. The table, which should be located at the beginning (some are pasted to the back of the front page of the folder), should include a brief description, date produced, date submitted, and date evaluated. A sample table can be provided, but ownership is enhanced if students have some flexibility to develop their own table or overview. Directions to students could be something like, "Suppose some people who don't know you are looking at your portfolio and you are not there to tell them important things. What would you need to tell them so that they could follow and understand your portfolio?" (Collins & Dana, 1993, p. 17).

Student Self-Reflection

One of the most challenging aspects of using portfolios is getting students to the point where they are comfortable, confident, and accurate in analyzing and criticizing their own work. These *reflective* or *self-evaluation* activities need to be taught. Most students have had little experience with reflection, so one of the first steps in using a portfolio is getting students comfortable with simple and nonthreatening forms of self-reflection. One useful strategy to accomplish this is to begin with teacher modeling and critiques. Once students understand what is involved by seeing examples (e.g., using an overhead of work from previous, unnamed students), they can begin to engage in their own reflections orally with each other. After they have engaged in these elementary forms of reflection, are they prepared to proceed to more complex self-evaluations? This can take several weeks.

A good way to introduce students to self-reflection is to have them label various pieces as "Best Work," "Most Creative," "Most Difficult," "Most Effort," "Most Fun," "Most Improved," and so on.

The next step could be the use of such items to structure student evaluations. For example:

> This piece shows that I've met the standard because _____
> This piece shows that I really understand the process because _____
> If I could show this piece to anyone, I would pick _____ because _____
> The piece that was my biggest challenge was _____ because _____
> One thing that I have learned from doing this piece is that I _____

Finally, questions can be asked to give students less structure in how to respond:

What did you learn from writing this piece?

What would you have done differently if you had had more time?

What are your greatest strengths and weaknesses in this sample?

What would you do differently if you did this over?

What problems or obstacles did you experience when doing this? How would you overcome these problems or obstacles next time?

Is this your best work? Why or why not?

What will you do for your next work?

If you could work more on this piece of writing, what would you do?

Which sample would you say is most unsatisfying? Give specific reasons for your evaluation. How would you revise it so that it would be more satisfying?

How did your selection change from rough draft to final copy?

Such reflection is completed for each individual work sample, for groups of pieces, and then for the portfolio as a whole. Student responses are insights into how involved students have been in reaching the learning target, what the students perceive to be their strengths, and how instruction can be tailored to meet needs (sometimes a student's perceived strengths are inaccurate and need to be corrected). Figures 10.8 and 10.9 present examples of student responses to self-reflective prompts. In Figure 10.8, students were asked to select a piece of writing that "is important to them," and explain why they made the selection. In this example, the responses from the same three students are indicated, appearing in

FIGURE 10.8   Middle and High School Student Responses to Self-Reflection Questions

---

Why did you select this particular piece of writing?

"I believe it's my best piece all year. I think it's a very strong piece."
"It's the most thoughtful piece I have written all year."
"I had to use more references to do this writing, and you can see this by how much more details [*sic*] are in it."

What do you see as the special strengths of this paper?

"It shows that I can write a unique piece, different from the rest of the crowd."
"The wording and the form."
"I sense a strong ability to spot details from the text."

What was especially important when you were writing this piece?

"I wanted to write something that would stand out, that people would notice. And it was."
"What I thought friendship was all about."
"My main goal was to defend a thesis with as much information as possible."

What have you learned about writing from your work on this piece?

"I can begin to write something, and end up with something totally different."
"Writing a poem wasn't as hard as it seems."
"I have learned that when you are writing you must always stick to the topic."

If you could go on working on this piece, what would you do?

"I would make it longer, taking off the end, making many more levels of anticipation."
"Be more descriptive."
"I would go into the different ways each of the boys handled their tribes."

What kind of writing would you like to do in the future?

"Short stories, POEMS!"
"Narrative."
"I have always wanted to write a murder mystery."

Source: Figure, "Middle and High School Student Responses to Self-Reflection Questions" from Camp, R. (1992). *Portfolio reflections in middle and secondary school classrooms.* In K. B. Yancey (Ed.), *Portfolios in the Writing Classroom.* Copyright © 1992 by the National Council of Teachers of English. Reprinted and used with permission.

LANGUAGE ARTS PORTFOLIO
STUDENT REFLECTION

Name: _Patricia_ _____   Date: _____

This piece was selected because:

I was very happy with it
My handwritting is good.

This piece is good because:

It shows that I can
write.

One thing I learned from doing this piece was that:

If I try harder I can
do well.

What I would do to make the piece better:

Make it longer.

FIGURE 10.9   Elementary Student Self-Reflection

the same order. The answers, although varied, illustrate what students think about themselves and what they believe they need to work on in the future. Figure 10.9 shows how younger students, in this case third graders, can be involved in self-reflection.

Students often are asked to engage in peer evaluations. These can be very helpful, especially when students are beginning to get used to the idea of self-reflection and the teacher is trying to establish a trusting environment. The focus of peer evaluations is on analysis and the constructive, supportive criticism of strategies, styles, and other concrete aspects of the product. Here are three examples of the type of feedback that you can provide to students. In this situation, students were asked to give advice to one another and to comment on "standout" selections (Lambdin & Walker, 1994):

> When I looked at the portfolio selections with Shawn, I noticed a lot of things I could have done better on. For instance, on my problem-solving section I did not do so good because it was the beginning of the year and I had not really gotten into school yet.
>
> I worked with Jeff today. He helped me see many things about my papers but most of all he helped me pick my best work. This is "How many books are in the library?" This work shows reasoning, estimation, observations, and many other things. This is why this work stands out so well. It shows what my work was. This was also challenging and exciting to me. Even though my estimation was 5,600 and the actual was 19,000 I still think my reasoning and attitude towards this project was very good [*sic*].
>
> Today I worked with Andrew. Helped me see the things I was doing wrong. I had a codecracker which didn't show a lot but he helped me see how to make it work. He told me to add an explanation about it for it to fit. I think a standout piece is my million's project. It shows everything I need. It has the original problem plus it shows all my work. It has an explanation about the problem and what we did. (p. 322)

More comprehensive reflection is done on all the contents of the portfolio, at the end of the semester or year. This evaluation focuses much more on the overall learning target. Notice how the following questions are different from what is asked about a single piece or sample in the portfolio (Camp, 1992):

> *What do you notice about your earlier work?*
>
> *Do you think your writing has changed?*
>
> *What do you know now that you did not know before?*
>
> *At what points did you discover something new about writing?*
>
> *How do the changes you see in your writing affect the way you see yourself as a writer?*
>
> *Are there pieces you have changed your mind about—that you liked before, but don't like now, or didn't like before but do like now? If so, which ones? What made you change your mind?*
>
> *In what ways do you think your reading has influenced your writing?* (p. 76)

Here is how one twelfth-grade student answered these questions (Camp, 1992):

> When I look back at my writing from the beginning of the year I realize that I have changed tremendously as a writer. My earlier work is not as explicit and does not seem like anything I would write now. . . . I know now that revising your work adds a great deal to the quality of the piece. If I may quote [my teacher], "Nothing is ever perfect the first time." Each piece of writing we did made me realize more and more things that could make my writing better. After these changes have been made

I find that I look upon myself as a better and more sophisticated writer. At the beginning of this year I thought my "Lady and the Tiger" piece was the best I could ever do. When I look at it now I see a lot of places in which I could change it to make it 100% better. (pp. 77–78)

A more structured kind of self-reflection is illustrated in Figure 10.10 for a middle school social studies class.

Student self-reflection can also include comments or a review by parents. One of the advantages of using portfolios is that they are well suited to parent involvement. At the beginning of the year, you will need to inform parents about what portfolios are and how they as parents can actively participate to be helpful. Students can consult their parents when selecting work samples, and parents can help students reflect on their work. Informally, parents can continuously provide advice and encouragement. More formally, parents can complete a form or answer a specific set of questions. Students can then incorporate parent comments and suggestions into their own reflection.

Teacher Evaluation

Teachers evaluate the contents of a portfolio in several different ways. These include checklists of contents, evaluations of the overall quality of how well the portfolio has been put together, evaluations of individual entries, and evaluations of learning targets as demonstrated by all the contents. We'll consider each of these types.

Checklists of Contents.   A summary to ensure that the contents of the portfolio are complete is often provided in the form of a simple checklist. The checklist can vary according to the level of specificity desired and by the audience. Some checklists are relatively brief, and others are long and detailed. A student checklist is illustrated in Figure 10.11. Others can be designed for teachers, administrators, or parents. Student checklists tend to be brief, but those for teachers and schools are typically more comprehensive.

Portfolio Structure Evaluation.   Portfolios can be evaluated according to how well students have demonstrated skill in completing the structural requirements, such as the selection of samples, thoroughness, appearance, self-reflection, and organization. These aspects can be evaluated by assigning points to each aspect according to a scale (e.g., 5 = excellent, 1 = poor), by making written comments, or both. When evaluating selections, consider the diversity of the samples, the time periods represented, and overall appropriateness. The quality of student reflection can be judged by the clarity and depth of thought, the level of analysis, and the clarity of communication. Organization can be evaluated by using a checklist to indicate whether required components are included, properly sequenced, and clearly labeled.

FIGURE 10.10   Structured Student Assessment of Portfolio

Personal Assessment of Portfolio

Dear Student: Your portfolio consists of all the writing assignments you have completed in social studies thus far. This form will assist you in monitoring your portfolio and determining the strengths and weaknesses of your writing.

Part I: Read the statements below. Write the number that most honestly reflects your self-assessment. (Scale 1–5: 5 = strong, 4 = moderately strong, 3 = average, 2 = moderately weak, 1 = weak)

_____ **1.** My portfolio contains all of the items required by my teacher.

_____ **2.** My portfolio provides strong evidence of my improvement over the course of the unit.

_____ **3.** My portfolio provides strong evidence of my ability to report factual information.

_____ **4.** My portfolio provides strong evidence of my ability to write effectively.

_____ **5.** My portfolio provides strong evidence of my ability to think and write creatively.

Part II: On the lines below, write the topic of each assignment. Rate your *effort* for each piece. (5 = strong effort, 1 = weak effort). In the space below write one suggestion for improving that piece.

_____ **1.** _____
        _____

_____ **2.** _____
        _____

_____ **3.** _____
        _____

_____ **4.** _____
        _____

_____ **5.** _____
        _____

Part III: In assessing my overall portfolio, I find it to be (check one)

| Very satisfactory | _____ | Satisfactory | _____ |
| Somewhat satisfactory | _____ | Unsatisfactory | _____ |

Part IV: In the space below list your goal for the next marking period and three strategies you plan to use to achieve it.

Goal:

Strategies: 1.

               2.

               3.

Source: From "Portfolio Assessment: A Work in Progress" by D. V. Goerss, *Middle School Journal*, November 1993, Vol. 25(2), 20-24. Copyright © 1993 by National Middle School Association. Reprinted by permission of National Middle School Association.

FIGURE 10.11   Example of Student Portfolio Checklist

Portfolio Checklist
(For Language Arts Class Only)

Name_____   Date_____

By the end of the year, your portfolio must contain the original copies of the following items:

_____ Student Assessment Letter(s)
_____ Reading Log and Book Reviews
_____ Reading Attitude Survey
_____ Writing Samples

Source: From *Portfolio assessment: Getting started,* by Alan A. De Fina. Copyright © 1992 by Alan A. De Fina. Published by Scholastic Professional Books, New York, p. 79. Reprinted by permission of Scholastic.

Evaluations of Individual Entries.   The evaluation of each individual entry in the portfolio can be accomplished with the scoring criteria and rubrics that were discussed in Chapter 9, although often much less standardization is used with portfolios. Many teachers find that more individualized, informal feedback on work samples is effective and efficient, particularly when many items are included in the portfolio. Furthermore, it is likely that not every entry will be evaluated in the same way. However, it is important to provide sufficient feedback so that students know what has been done well and what needs to be improved.

Evaluation of Entire Contents.   The learning targets for the portfolio as a whole are not the same as those for individual entries. Likewise, the criteria for judging progress toward meeting learning targets of all the contents together is different from what is used for each entry. The language of the evaluation reflects the more general nature of the target. The words used also emphasize the developmental nature of learning because the purpose is to focus on student improvement and progress. Thus phrases such as "students demonstrate the ability to understand increasingly complex software programs," "a greater number of self-evaluative criteria applied," "increased understanding of," or "increased ability to" are used. You will also want to be sure to include individualized written comments for each student. This descriptive summary of performance and progress should highlight changes that have occurred, strengths, and areas that need improvement. It's usually best to point out the strengths and improvements first and then use language to address weaknesses that tells clearly what needs improvement but will not discourage students or lead them to a sense of futility. Words such as *improving, developing, partial,* and even *novice* are better than *unacceptable* or *inadequate.*

Overall evaluations can also address effort and the student's willingness to learn. A simple scale can be used (e.g., very willing to learn, somewhat willing to learn, resistant to learning) or individual comments can be written.

Student–Teacher Conferences

The final step in implementing portfolios, before returning them to the student or school file, is conducting a conference with each student to review the contents, student reflections, and your evaluations of individual items and all of the work together as related to learning targets. Conferences with students should be scheduled throughout the year; some suggest having one conference each month at the elementary level. Especially early in the year the conferences can be used to clarify purposes and procedures, answer questions, and establish trust. Although scheduling and conducting these conferences takes time, the sessions provide an important link between students and teachers.

It is best if students are given some guidelines to prepare for each conference. During the conference, allow the student to do most of the talking. Have students compare their reflections with your evaluations and make plans for subsequent work. Although weaknesses and areas for improvement need to be covered, show students what is possible and their progress, rather than what is wrong. Make sure that at the end of the conference there is a plan of action for the future. Limit the conference to no more than 10 or 15 minutes. You may want to have students take notes about what was discussed in the conference and make your own brief notes. Focus on one or two major topics or areas at each conference. This helps ensure a full and thoughtful discussion, rather than a superficial treatment of several areas.

Figure 10.12 summarizes steps in the implementation of portfolio assessment with an emphasis on when certain activities take place and the time needed to

Case Study
for Reflection

Ms. Watson is really frustrated with the progress of her ninth-grade English classes. It's already March and state testing is coming up soon. What if her students aren't ready? It seems as though all she has worked on this year has been the writing portfolios. Last year, when her school district required every student to have one, it sounded like a good idea. Who could have known how much time it would take? Teacher conferencing with students, students' conferencing with each other, and students self-evaluating their own progress has taken time away from teaching.

She promises herself that next year she will develop some strategies to help the whole process run more smoothly.

QUESTIONS FOR CONSIDERATION

1. What mistakes with writing portfolios did Ms. Watson make this school year?
2. Could you help her formulate a list of strategies to try next year so that the process will run more smoothly?

FIGURE 10.12   **Portfolio Implementation Timelines**

Unit	Semester	Yearlong
1. Collect items for three or four weeks.	5. Collect items the entire semester.	10. Collect one to two items each week.
2. Select and reflect on items two weeks prior to the end of the unit.	6. Select seven to ten final items four weeks before the end of the semester.	11. Review all items at the end of each quarter and select three or four items. Date all items.
3. Conduct conferences in the last week.	7. Allow one week for students to select, organize, and reflect on contents.	12. Repeat each quarter. Students write reflections at the end of each quarter.
4. Grade the last week.	8. Allow one week for conferences.	13. Select the final ten to twelve items four weeks before the end of school.
	9. Allow one week for grading.	14. Allow two to three weeks for reflection, organization, and conferencing.
		15. Allow one to two weeks for grading.

Source: From *The Mindful School: How to Assess Authentic Learning,* third edition by Kay Burke. Copyright © 1999, 1994, 1993 by Skylight Training and Publishing, Inc. Reprinted by permission of Sage Publications, Inc.

complete them. Specific timelines will depend on the type of portfolio and the degree of student involvement.

Electronic Portfolios

A relatively new approach to portfolio assessment is to create, store, and report materials electronically. An electronic portfolio (e-portfolio) is a digital collection of evidence, often stored and managed online. This type of portfolio typically can have the same purposes as a hard-copy file, but it allows for some additional analyses to further extend learning and encourages self-directed learning on more authentic topics. As illustrated in Figure 10.13, an electronic format can be used to focus on new learning targets. Students and teachers are able to do more with the results and connect what is stored with other learning activities and goals. Students are encouraged to analyze information, to connect information in new ways, and to collaborate with others. A large amount of information can be stored efficiently and organized in meaningful ways. Students are able to add examples, reflect, and draw conclusions on an ongoing basis.

An obvious advantage of having an electronic portfolio is that is encourages and makes possible the use of multimedia elements. This feature is very motivating

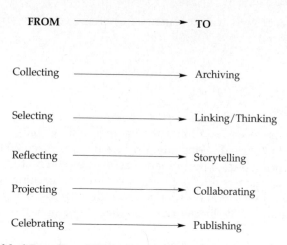

FIGURE 10.13   Added Benefits of Electronic Portfolios[1]

[1]Adapted from Barrett (2007).

for students, promoting the use of unique materials that reflect the individual voices of students. There is more student ownership with opportunities to build self-efficacy and pride. Adding links to Web sites, videos, other students' work, voice recordings, photographs, blogs, audio recordings, and scanned documents, and the ability to synthesize evidence from a variety of sources, engages students in ways that are difficult to achieve with traditional paper-based portfolios. Hyperlinks can be used to quickly access additional material. Students are able to store, refine, and reuse the evidence. For example, electronic portfolios are excellent in showcasing student thinking and creativity for college admissions or selection into specialty high schools.

Of course using electronic portfolios depends on having sufficient hardware and/or online access, adequate teacher and student competence in using computer-based information, and adequate technical support. Storage could be on a network server, CDs, or on classroom computers. There are also a number of options for electronic formats, digitizing, and platforms for presentation of results (Worcester, 2009). For example, original document formats, such as MS Word and PowerPoint, can be used as long as viewers have the same or better software, or PDF or HTML formats can be used. PDF files require Adobe Acrobat, whereas an advantage of HTML is that it can be viewed by any browser. HTML is also easier to use with newer software.

Although there may be a learning curve for both teachers and students (typically more for teachers!) to have the skills necessary to digitize portfolios, electronic formats can be powerful in enhancing student engagement and learning. Because electronic portfolios tend to be unique to individual students, using electronic portfolios for documenting competence and showing growth may be difficult. Electronic portfolios are typically not the best way to document or show growth in achievement; they are excellent for showcasing student work and projects.

Summary

The essence of portfolios is to gather and evaluate, on a continual basis, student products that demonstrate progress toward specified learning targets. By combining principles of performance assessment with student self-reflection, portfolios can be powerful tools to improve student learning. With the flexibility inherent in portfolios, it is possible to individualize assessment so that you can maximize meaningful feedback to each student. Other major points in the chapter include

- Portfolio assessment is systematic and purposeful.
- Portfolio assessment includes student selection of contents and student self-reflection.
- Different types of portfolios include celebration, competence, growth, project, and evaluation.
- Portfolios integrate assessment with instruction by focusing on improvement and progress.
- Portfolios are adaptable to individual students.
- Reliability of scoring is a limitation of portfolios.
- Portfolios require considerable teacher time for preparation and implementation.
- Portfolios may result in limited generalizability.
- Planning for portfolio assessment includes the identification of learning targets and uses, physical structures, sources of content, guidelines for student self-reflection, and scoring criteria.
- Implementing portfolio assessment includes reviewing with students, supplying content, student self-evaluations, teacher evaluations, and student–teacher conferences.
- Students should be meaningfully involved in the selection of work samples.
- Just enough work samples need to be included to meet the purpose of the portfolio.
- A table of contents should be included in the portfolio.
- Student self-evaluation needs to be taught. Students progress to eventually become skilled at analyzing and critiquing their own and others' works.
- The teacher evaluates checklists of contents, the student's ability to put together the portfolio, individual items, and the content as a whole, among other things, which may include scores from rubrics and written comments.
- Student–teacher conferences should be held throughout the year to review progress and establish plans.
- Electronic portfolios offer opportunities to extend and showcase student learning.

Self-Instructional Review Exercises

1. Indicate whether each of the following is an advantage (A) or disadvantage (D) of using portfolio assessment:

   a. Collaboration between student and teacher
   b. Student selection of contents
   c. Scoring
   d. Continuous monitoring of student progress
   e. Training teacher to do portfolios
   f. Generalizability
   g. Student self-evaluation

2. Indicate whether it would be best to use a celebration (CE), competence (CO), growth (G), Project (P) or evaluation (E) portfolio for each of the following purposes:

   a. To show examples of a student's work
   b. For the student to demonstrate his or her best work
   c. To show what students in a class are capable of doing
   d. To indicate the progress of the class on an important target
   e. For grading
   f. To show a student's progress

3. Evaluate the planning that is illustrated by the teacher in the following example. Is what she has planned consistent with what a portfolio is all about? Why or why not? Is her planning adequate? What else does she need to do?

   Ms. Taylor has decided to implement a mathematics portfolio in her sixth-grade classroom. She believes the portfolios will increase student learning. She provides manila folders for the students and tells them that they will keep all their math worksheets and tests in it. She tells the students that they will be talking to her periodically about what is in the folder.

4. Match the description or example with the appropriate step in implementing portfolio assessment. Each step can be used more than once or may not be used at all:

   _____ a. Rubric used to evaluate the sixth writing sample
   _____ b. Mr. Lind meets with students once a week
   _____ c. Students ask questions about how to self-reflect
   _____ d. Teacher prepares an overhead that outlines the basics of portfolio assessment
   _____ e. Table of contents is prepared
   _____ f. Students select three work samples
   _____ g. A checklist includes outline and self-reflection categories

   A. Review with students
   B. Supply content
   C. Student self-reflection
   D. Teacher evaluation
   E. Student–teacher conference

5. The following scenario describes how a middle school social science teacher goes about implementing portfolio assessment in his class. After reading the scenario, review the checklist in Figure 10.7. Use this checklist as criteria to evaluate how well Mr. Trent does in using portfolios.

Gary Trent has read a lot lately about portfolios and decides to use them with his seventh-grade social studies classes. He spends the last week before school fine-tuning what he hopes his students can learn from doing the portfolios. Although he thinks he must give grades to ensure student motivation, he plans to use the portfolios to demonstrate to other teachers what his students are capable of achieving.

Gary decides to ask his students to bring something to class to hold the materials that will go in the portfolio. He explains to his students that they will be selecting one example each week from their work in his class that shows their best effort. Every month students meet with each other to critique what was included, and after the meeting students complete a self-evaluation worksheet. Throughout the semester Gary plans to talk with each student at least once about his or her portfolio.

Near the end of the semester, Gary collects all the portfolios, grades them, and returns them to his students. He makes sure that each student receives individualized comments with the grade.

Answers to Self-Instructional Review Exercises

1. a. A; b. A or D (a disadvantage if students are not provided sufficient direction and supervision); c. D; d. A; e. D; f. D; g. A.

2. a. all; b. CE; c. CO or P; d. G; e. E; f. G.

3. This is not really portfolio assessment, at least not in the way portfolios have been discussed in this chapter. Neither the teacher nor the students select anything (everything is included), and there is no indication that any performance products are included. There is a lack of specification about the purpose of the portfolio. Folders will be used, but we don't know where they will be placed. There is no indication that student self-reflection guidelines and scoring criteria have been developed.

4. a. D; b. E; c. C; d. A; e. B; f. B; g. D.

5. Gary does something right in using portfolios but needs to be more specific and systematic in a number of areas. It's good that he takes time to plan what he wants to do. However, the stated purpose is not one of the major reasons that portfolios should be used. There is only a brief reference to learning targets and no indication that he has prepared specific scoring criteria or student self-reflection guidelines. Simply asking students to select one example of their work per week is probably too vague. Gary needs to be more specific about what kinds of work should be included and about the physical structure of the portfolio. Because he has several classes, it may not be feasible to store each portfolio in the room. It's not clear that students know enough about portfolios for the procedure to work. It's good that

students select the content, and Gary is on target in emphasizing student self-reflection. One problem may be that there will be too many work samples by the end of the semester, making Gary's grading process difficult. It might be better to have students select one work example per week and then at the end of the semester choose a few items from these to demonstrate achievement. Gary's plan to meet with students at least once informally is okay, but there is no provision for a more formal conference near the end of the semester. It's good that he includes individualized written comments.

Suggestions for Action Research

1. Locate two or three examples of portfolios from different teachers. Review the contents of the portfolios carefully, looking for characteristics that have been discussed in this chapter. How are the portfolios alike, and how are they different? Are they being used for different purposes? Is the structure and content appropriate for the intended use?

2. Interview students who have had some experience with portfolios. Ask them what they like and don't like about doing portfolios, how much time it takes them to complete their work, and what the teacher does to help them. Focus on student self-reflection. Ask the students how they have self-evaluated themselves and what they think they have learned from the process.

3. Visit two or three classrooms and see how portfolios are organized and stored. If possible, talk with the teachers to get their views about how to organize portfolios so that they are practical.

4. Devise a student portfolio assignment for students. Include each of the steps in Figure 10.3, and include examples where possible. Then ask two or three teachers to review your assignment and give you feedback on how it could be improved, how much time it would take to implement, how realistic it would be, and what students would probably get out of it.

Assessing Affective Traits, Dispositions, and Beliefs

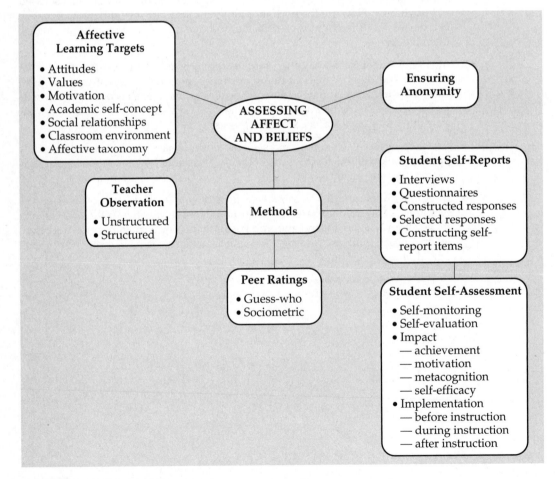

Affective Learning Targets
- Attitudes
- Values
- Motivation
- Academic self-concept
- Social relationships
- Classroom environment
- Affective taxonomy

ASSESSING AFFECT AND BELIEFS

Ensuring Anonymity

Teacher Observation
- Unstructured
- Structured

Methods

Student Self-Reports
- Interviews
- Questionnaires
- Constructed responses
- Selected responses
- Constructing self-report items

Peer Ratings
- Guess-who
- Sociometric

Student Self-Assessment
- Self-monitoring
- Self-evaluation
- Impact
  — achievement
  — motivation
  — metacognition
  — self-efficacy
- Implementation
  — before instruction
  — during instruction
  — after instruction

CHAPTER 11 Concept Map

Chapters 7 to 10 focused on what have traditionally been called *cognitive* learning targets and skills. We now turn to a set of student dispositions, traits, and beliefs that many educators regard as equally important, what have become known as *affective* and student belief outcomes. We'll look at how to define these traits and targets and how, practically speaking, to assess them in the classroom in a way that improves instruction and student cognitive learning.

Are Affective and Student Belief Targets Important?

Research has established clear linkages between affect and learning (Ormrod, 2004; Popham, 2008, 2009; Stiggins, 2008). Students are more proficient at problem solving when they enjoy what they are doing. Students who are in a good mood and emotionally involved are more likely to pay attention to information, remember it, rehearse it meaningfully, and apply it. Too much anxiety interferes with learning, and an optimum level of arousal is needed for maximum performance. Classrooms with more positive "climates" foster student engagement and learning much more than do classrooms with negative climates (Fraser, 1994).

What is interesting about student affect is that despite this research, there is very little systematic assessment of affect in the classroom (McMillan, Workman, & Myran, 1998; Stiggins & Conklin, 1992). Teachers know that students who are confident about their ability to learn, who like the school subjects they study, who have a positive attitude toward learning, who respect others, and who show a concern for others are much more likely to be motivated and involved in learning. At the same time, though, most teachers do not rely on any kind of formal or systematic affective assessment procedures, nor do they state specific affective learning targets for their students. Why? Two reasons seem plausible. First, especially in the higher grades, schooling is organized by subject matter. Cognitive subject matter targets are agreed on as desirable for all students. This puts affect in the position of being important but still secondary to cognitive learning. It also makes coming to an agreement about which affective targets are appropriate for all students difficult. That is, it simply isn't easy to define attitudes, values, and interests.

Second, the assessment of affective targets is fraught with difficulties. The many potential sources of error in measuring affective traits often result in low reliability. Student motivation is a primary concern. Students need to take such assessments seriously to provide accurate results, yet many may be inhibited if their responses are not anonymous. They would find it easy to fake responses on self-report instruments if the results are to be used for grading or some other purpose. They may want to please the teacher with positive responses. Another source of error is that some affective traits are easily influenced by momentary or temporary moods. This is especially true for younger students, who may report much more negative affect after a bad day or session. Teacher bias can also have a significant influence on what may be recorded or perceived.

TABLE 11.1   Relationships Between Learning Success and Affect

Successful Learning	Unsuccessful Learning
Hopeful	Hopeless
Optimistic	Pessimistic
Feels positive	Feels negative
Wants more success	Wants to avoid further failure
Seek out challenges	Avoid challenges
Seeks and uses feedback	Sees feedback as criticism
Empowered	Embarrassed
Confident	Unsure
Engaged	Disengaged
Positive attitudes	Negative attitudes
Values learning	Avoids learning
Seek new ideas	Avoid new ideas

Source: Based in part on Stiggins, 2007.

What cannot be disputed is that affect, in the form of attitudes, self-beliefs, and values, is inexorably intertwined with achievement and student performance. Table 11.1 shows the close relationships between achievement and affect. Students who do well are more positive about themselves and what they are learning, whereas struggling students have much negative affect. As you can no doubt surmise, these affective "feelings" affect student engagement, student motivation, and subsequent achievement.

What are the advantages, then, to systematically setting and assessing affective targets? Positive affective traits and beliefs are essential for:

- Effective learning
- Being an involved and productive member of our society
- Preparing for occupational and vocational satisfaction and productivity (e.g., work habits, a willingness to learn, interpersonal skills)
- Maximizing the motivation to learn now and in the future
- Preventing students from dropping out of school
- Enhancing students' beliefs that they are capable of learning

Most current school and school district mission statements include affective outcomes, and teachers constantly assess affect informally during instruction. The following sections discuss suggestions and techniques for taking affect to a more serious level. What better way can teachers signal to students that clearly defined positive affect is important than by systematically assessing it? This begins with identifying appropriate affect targets, which we consider next.

What Are Affective Traits and Learning Targets?

The term **affective** has come to refer to a wide variety of traits, dispositions, and beliefs that are different from knowledge, reasoning, and skills. The term **affect** has a technical meaning that is rather restrictive: the emotions or feelings we have toward someone or something. However, attitudes, values, self-concept, citizenship, and other traits usually considered to be "noncognitive" involve more than emotion or feelings. In fact, most kinds of student affect involve both emotion and cognitive beliefs. Nevertheless, the literature refers to a range of possible outcomes as affective. I have summarized many of these in Table 11.2. Although there isn't space to consider each of these traits in detail, I do want to look at a few of the more commonly used ones. Because of the general nature of the term *affect*, it is best to use these more specific dispositions when developing your learning targets.

TABLE 11.2   Affective Traits

Trait	Definition
Attitudes	Predisposition to respond favorably or unfavorably to specified situations, concepts, objects, institutions, or persons
Interests	Personal preference for certain kinds of activities
Values	Importance, worth, or usefulness of modes or conduct and end states of existence
Opinions	Beliefs about specific occurrences and situations
Preferences	Desire or propensity to select one object over another
Motivation	Desire and willingness to be engaged in behavior and intensity of involvement
Self-Efficacy	Self-perceptions of capabilities to learn
Self-Esteem	Attitudes toward oneself; degree of self-respect, worthiness, or desirability of self-concept
Locus of Control	Self-perception of whether success and failure is controlled by the student or by external influences
Emotional Development	Growth, change, and awareness of emotions and ability to regulate emotional expression
Social Relationships	Nature of interpersonal interactions and functioning in group settings
Altruism	Willingness and propensity to help others
Moral Development	Attainment of ethical principles that guide decision making and behavior
Classroom Environment	Nature of feeling tones and interpersonal relationships in a class

Attitude Targets

Attitudes are internal states that influence what students are likely to do. The internal state is some degree of positive/negative or favorable/unfavorable reaction toward an object, situation, person, group of objects, general environment, or group of persons. Attitudes do not refer to behaviors, what a student knows, right or wrong in a moral or ethical sense, or characteristics such as the student's race, age, or socioeconomic status. Thus, we always think about attitudes *toward* something. In schools, that may be learning, subjects, teachers, other students, homework, and other objects or persons. Usually, then, you can identify the positive or negative attitudes that you want to foster or at least monitor because they are related to current and future behavior. Some examples are

> **A Positive** *Attitude Toward*
> Learning
> School
> Math, science, English, and other subjects
> Homework
> Classroom rules
> Teachers
> Working with others
> Staying on task
> Taking responsibility for one's acts
>
> **A Negative** *Attitude Toward*
> Cheating
> Drug use
> Fighting
> Skipping school
> Dropping out

Social psychologists, through extensive research, have found that attitudes consist of three elements or contributing factors (Forsyth, 1999):

1. An *affective* component of positive or negative feelings
2. A *cognitive* component describing worth or value
3. A *behavioral* component indicating a willingness or desire to engage in specific actions

The *affective* component consists of the emotion or feeling associated with an object or a person (e.g., good or bad feelings, enjoyment, likes, comfort, anxiety). When we describe a student as liking math or enjoying art, we are focusing on the affective component. The *cognitive* component is an evaluative belief (such as thinking something is valuable, useful, worthless, etc.). In school, students can think history is useless and mathematics is valuable. The *behavioral* component is actually responding in a positive way. A strong and stable attitude is evidenced when all three components are consistent. That is, when Sam likes science, thinks it's important, and reads *National Geographic* at home, he has a very strong positive attitude. But it's likely that for many students these components will contradict one another. Louise may not like English very much but think that it's important. What would her attitude be, in a general sense, toward English? That would depend on what components of the attitude you measure. If you measured only the affective component, the attitude would be negative; a measure of the cognitive component would reveal a positive attitude.

This tripartite conceptualization has important implications for identifying attitude targets. Are you interested in feelings, thoughts, or behaviors? If you want to have a learning target such as "students will have a positive attitude toward school," you need to include all three components in your assessment because the general nature of the target would need to be consistent with the assessment. However, if your target is "students will like coming to school," then the assessment should focus on the affective component.

Value Targets

Values generally refer either to end states of existence or to modes of conduct that are desirable or sought (Rokeach, 1973). End states of existence are conditions and aspects of ourselves and our world that we want, such as a safe life, world peace, freedom, happiness, social acceptance, and wisdom. Modes of conduct are reflected in what we believe is appropriate and needed in our everyday existence, such as being honest, cheerful, ambitious, loving, responsible, and helpful. Each of these values can be placed into categories consistent with different areas of our lives. Thus, you can think about moral, political, social, aesthetic, economic, technological, and religious values.

I recommend that you stick with values that are relatively noncontroversial and that are clearly related to academic learning and school and district goals. Popham (2008) has suggested some values as being sufficiently meritorious and noncontroversial:

- *Honesty.* Students should learn to value honesty in their dealings with others.
- *Integrity.* Students should firmly adhere to their own code of values, for example, moral or artistic beliefs.
- *Justice.* Students should subscribe to the view that all citizens should be the recipients of equal justice from governmental law enforcement agencies.
- *Freedom.* Students should believe that democratic nations must provide the maximum level of freedom to their citizens. (pp. 220–221)

Other relatively noncontroversial values include kindness, generosity, perseverance, loyalty, respect, courage, compassion, and tolerance. Popham also suggests, and I agree, that you should limit the number of affective traits targeted and assessed. It is better to do a sound job of assessing a few important traits than to try to assess many traits superficially.

Motivation Targets

In the context of schooling, motivation can be defined as the extent to which students are involved in trying to learn. This includes the students' initiation of learning, their intensity of effort, their commitment, and their persistence. In other words, *motivation* is the purposeful engagement in learning to master knowledge or skills; students take learning seriously and value opportunities to learn (Ames, 1990; McMillan & Forsyth, 1991). Much research on motivation can be organized according to what is called the *expectancy* x *value* framework (Brophy, 2004; Pintrich & Schunk, 2002). This model suggests that motivation is determined by students' expectations—their beliefs about whether they are likely to be successful and the value of the outcome. Expectations refer to the *self-efficacy* of the student, the student's self-perception of his or her capability to perform successfully. Values are self-perceptions of the importance of the performance. That is, does the student see any value in the activity? Is it intrinsically enjoyable or satisfying? Will it meet some social or psychological need, such as self-worth, competence, or belonging, or will it help the student to attain an important goal? Students who believe that they are capable of achieving success, and that the activity holds value for them, will be highly motivated to learn. If they value the outcome but believe that no matter how hard they try they probably won't be successful, their motivation will be weak. Similarly, we see many very capable students who are unmotivated because the activity holds no importance for them.

I believe your motivation targets should follow from the expectancy x value theory (McMillan, Simonetta, & Singh, 1994). Like attitudes, it is too vague to use the general definition as an outcome because you are unable to pinpoint the source of the lack of effort and involvement. Thus, I suggest that you focus motivation targets on self-efficacy and value, differentiated by academic subject and type of learning (e.g., knowledge, understanding, reasoning). Here are some examples:

- Students will believe that they are capable of learning how to multiply fractions. (self-efficacy)
- Students will believe that it is important to know how to multiply fractions. (value)
- Students will believe that they are able to learn how bills are passed in the U.S. Senate. (self-efficacy)
- Students will believe that it is important to know how bills are passed in the U.S. Senate. (value)

Another important consideration in assessing motivation is why students are learning, the reasons they give for their actions. When students do something because it is inherently interesting, enjoyable, or challenging, they are intrinsically motivated.

In contrast, extrinsic motivation is doing something because it leads to a separate outcome (e.g., reward or punishment; Ryan & Deci, 2000). Similarly, it has been shown that students who are motivated by a need to understand and master the task (mastery orientation) demonstrate more positive behavior and thinking than students who are doing something for the result or outcome (performance orientiation). Mastery orientation students are more engaged, have a natural inclination to generate solutions to difficulties, and generate more positive attributions to success and failure (success attributed to ability and moderate effort; failure to lack of effort).

Academic Self-Concept Targets

There is an extensive literature on self-concept and its cousin, self-esteem. Many educators refer to these characteristics when discussing students who have problems with school and learning (e.g., "Sam has a low self-concept," "Adrianne has a low opinion of herself"). There is no question about the importance of these beliefs, even with the controversy over whether self-concept and self-esteem proceed or result from academic learning. According to my definition of motivation, some level of positive self-efficacy is needed for achievement. It's also likely that this aspect of self-concept is formed, at least in part, when children experience meaningful success with moderate effort.

For setting targets, it is helpful to remember that self-concept and self-esteem are multidimensional (Marsh & Craven, 1997). There is a bodily self, an athletic self, a mathematics self, a social self, and so forth. Each of us has a self-description in each area, which is our self-concept or self-image. In addition, we also have a sense of self-regard, self-affirmation, and self-worth in each area (self-esteem). Thus, a student can have a self-concept that he is tall and thin, but feel very comfortable with that and accept this description. Another student can have the same self-concept but feel inferior or inadequate or have a low self-esteem.

I suggest staying away from global self-concept and self-esteem targets, as well as those that do not differentiate between a self-description and an evaluation of that description. Like attitudes and motivation, measuring general self-concept is simply not that helpful. This is because much of what makes up general self-concept comes from areas not directly related to academic learning. By specifying *academic* self-concept, or self-concept of academic ability, you will obtain a more valid indication of what students think about themselves as learners. If you set targets that are specific to subject areas, the resulting information will be more useful. Also, it's helpful to know where students draw the line between descriptions of themselves and whether they like those descriptions. From the standpoint of more serious mental or emotional problems, a general measure may be needed, but it's best to leave that to a school psychologist or counselor.

Social Relationship Targets

Social relationships involve a complex set of interaction skills, including the identification of and appropriate responses to social cues. Peer relations, friendship, functioning in groups, assertiveness, cooperation, collaboration, prosocial behavior, empathy, taking perspective, and conflict resolution are examples of the nature of social relationships that can be specified as targets. Many of these are important at the elementary level as needed skills for academic achievement. At the secondary level, interpersonal abilities are becoming more important as schools work with the business community to identify and promote the skills needed to be successful in the workplace. Furthermore, social interaction is a key element of knowledge construction, active learning, and deep understanding (Borich & Tombari, 2004). As interaction occurs, students are forced to adjust their thinking to accommodate alternative viewpoints, to defend their ideas, and to debate their opinions. These processes encourage a deep, rather than superficial, understanding and keep students engaged. Also, interaction can promote good reasoning and problem-solving strategies through observation and the give-and-take that ensues.

For each of these broad social relationship areas, specific targets need to be identified. For example, a target concerned with peer relationships might include showing interest in others, listening to peers, sharing, and contributing to group activities. Cooperative skills could include sharing, listening, volunteering ideas and suggestions, supporting and accepting others' ideas, taking turns, and criticizing constructively.

Collaborative skills needed to work in small groups could include four components: (a) basic interaction, (b) getting along, (c) coaching, and (d) fulfilling particular roles (Borich & Tombari, 2004; Hoy & Greg, 1994). Skills for each of the components are summarized in Table 11.3

My recommendation is similar to suggestions about identifying attitude, motivational, and self-concept targets—that it is necessary to be very specific about the target. A general target about "improved social relationships" or "improved collaboration skills" simply does not provide the level of specificity needed to focus your instruction and assessment. Here are some examples of possible social relationship targets:

- Students will contribute to small-group discussions.
- Students will have sustained friendships with two or more other students.
- Students will demonstrate skills in helping other students solve a problem.
- Students will demonstrate that they are able to negotiate with others and compromise.

Classroom Environment Targets

If you have been in many classrooms, you know that each classroom has a unique climate and feel to it; it's as though you can sense the degree to which a class is comfortable, relaxed, and productive, and whether students seem happy, content, and serious. Some classes are warm and supportive, and others seem very cold and rejecting, even hostile. Together, such characteristics make up what is called classroom environment, classroom climate, or classroom culture (Gallego & Cole, 2001).

TABLE 11.3   A Taxonomy of Collaborative Skills

Component	Definition	Skills
Basic Interaction	Students like and respect each other.	Listening Making eye contact Answering questions Using the right voice Making sense Apologizing
Getting Along	Students sustain their respect and liking for one another.	Taking turns Sharing Following rules Assisting Asking for help or a favor Using polite words
Coaching	Students both give and receive corrective feedback and encouragement.	Suggesting an action or activity Giving and receiving compliments or praise Being specific Giving advice Correcting and being corrected
Role-Fulfilling	Fulfilling specific roles creates positive interdependency and individual accountability.	Summarizer Checker Researcher Runner Recorder Supporter Troubleshooter

Source: Authentic assessment in the classroom: Applications and practice by Tombari/Borich © 1999, pp. 191–192. Reprinted by permission of Pearson Education, Inc., Upper Saddle River, NJ.

Obviously, a positive climate promotes learning, so a reasonable affective target would be to establish student feelings, relationships, and beliefs that promote this kind of environment.

Classroom environment is made up of a number of characteristics that can be used as affective targets. These include

Affiliation—the extent to which students like and accept each other
Involvement—the extent to which students are interested in and engaged in learning
Task orientation—the extent to which classroom activities are focused on the completion of academic tasks
Cohesiveness—the extent to which students share norms and expectations
Competition—the emphasis on competition between students

> *Favoritism*—whether each student enjoys the same privileges
> *Influence*—the extent to which each student influences classroom decisions
> *Friction*—the extent to which students bicker with one another
> *Formality*—the emphasis on enforcing rules
> *Communication*—the extent to which communication among students and with teacher is genuine and honest
> *Warmth*—the extent to which students care about each other and show empathy

Fraser (1999) suggests that is useful to compare students' perspectives on classroom environment with those of teachers. For example, it has been demonstrated in many settings that students prefer a more positive classroom environment than they perceive is present and that teachers thought that the environment was more positive than did students. Such a pattern of results helps inform teachers about what needs to be changed to enhance student learning.

Affective Domain of the Taxonomy of Educational Objectives

One of the earliest treatments of affective objectives was called the *Taxonomy of Educational Objectives, Handbook II: Affective Domain* (Krathwohl, Bloom, & Masia, 1964). It was a companion to Bloom's *Taxonomy* of the cognitive domain. The taxonomy arranges affective targets along a five-stage continuum. These stages, with definitions and examples, are summarized in Table 11.4. Let's look at an example that refers to attitudes toward science. At the most basic level, *receiving*, students are merely aware of and perceive science. At the next level, students are able to pay attention to the science (*responding*). Next, the students indicate through their voluntary behavior that science has *value*. Once science is valued, it can be organized with other subjects and other values (*organization*). The highest stage is *characterization*, in which science is so highly valued that it becomes a determining tendency and influence on other aspects of the student's life.

The contribution of the affective taxonomy for classroom assessment of affect is that it helps you determine the standard or level of affect that is part of your target. It also provides good suggestions for using student behaviors as indicators of affect at each of the levels. For example, suppose you want your students to develop an appreciation for classical music. At what level do you want your target? Will students simply be aware of what classical music is and what it sounds like (receiving)? Or do you want them to really *like* classical music (valuing)?

Methods of Assessing Affective Targets

There are really only four feasible methods of assessing students' affective traits and beliefs: teacher observation, student self-report, student self-assessment, peer ratings, and teacher ratings. We will consider each of these.

TABLE 11.4   Affective Taxonomy of Educational Objectives

Category (Level)	Definition	Examples
Receiving (Attending)	Develops an awareness, shows a willingness to receive, shows controlled or selected attention	Student considers reading books for extra credit Student pays attention to teacher lecture about smoking
Responding	Shows a willingness to respond and finds some initial level of satisfaction in responding	Student asks questions about different books Takes pleasure in playing sports
Valuing	Shows that the object, person, or situation has worth Something is perceived as holding a positive value, a commitment is made	Student reads continually, asks for more books Asks for further help in improving writing skills Practices sports all the time
Organization	Brings together a complex set of values and organizes them in an ordered relationship that is harmonious and internally consistent	Student develops a plan for integrating reading and sports Weighs concerns for social justice with governmental size
Characterization	Organized system of values becomes a person's life outlook and the basis for a philosophy of life	Student develops a consistent philosophy of life Reading forms the basis for most everything in the student's life

Source: Adapted from David R. Krathwohl, Benjamin S. Bloom, & Bertram B. Masia. *Taxonomy of educational objectives, handbook II: Affective domain.* Published by Allyn and Bacon, Boston, MA. Copyright © 1964 by Pearson Education. Reprinted by permission of the publisher.

Keep three considerations in mind whenever you assess affect. First, emotions and feelings can change quickly, especially for young children and during early adolescence. This suggests that to obtain a valid indication of an individual student's emotion or feeling, it is necessary to conduct several assessments over a substantial length of time. What you want to know is what the dominant or prevalent affect is, and if you rely on a single assessment there is a good chance that what you measure is not a good indication of the trait.

Second, try to use different approaches to measuring the same affective trait. Reliance on a single method is problematic because of limitations inherent in that method. For example, if you use only student self-reports, which are subject to social desirability and faking, these limitations may significantly affect the results. However, if student self-reports are consistent with your observations, then a stronger case can be made.

Finally, decide if you need individual student or group results. This is related to purpose and will influence the method that you should use. If your purpose is to use assessment for making reports to parents, then obviously you need information on each student. In this case, you should use multiple methods of collecting data over time and keep records to verify your judgments. If the assessments will be used to improve instruction, then you need results for the group as a whole. This is the more common and advisable use of affective assessment, primarily because you can rely more on anonymous student self-reports (Popham, 2008a).

Teacher Observation

In Chapter 4, teacher observation was discussed as an essential tool for formative assessment. Here the emphasis is on how teachers can make more systematic observations to record student behavior that indicates the presence of targeted affective traits.

The first step in using observation is to determine in advance how specific behaviors relate to the target. This begins with a clear definition of the trait, followed by lists of student behaviors and actions that correspond to positive and negative dimensions of the trait. Let's consider attitudes. We can identify the behaviors and actions initially by considering what students with positive and negative attitudes do and say. If we have two columns, one listing behaviors for positive attitudes and one listing behaviors for negative attitudes, we define what will be observed. Suppose you are interested in attitudes toward learning. What is it that students with a positive attitude toward learning do and say? What are the actions of those with a negative attitude? Table 11.5 lists some possibilities. These behaviors provide a foundation for developing guidelines, checklists, or rating scales. The ones in the positive column are referred to as *approach* behaviors; those in the negative column *avoidance* behaviors. Approach behaviors result in more direct, frequent, and intense contact; avoidance behaviors are just the opposite, resulting in less direct, less frequent, or less intense contact. These dimensions—directness, frequency, and intensity—are helpful in describing the behaviors that indicate positive and negative attitudes.

How do you develop these lists of positive and negative behaviors? I have found that the best approach is to find time to brainstorm with other teachers. Published instruments are available that may give you some ideas, but these won't consider the unique characteristics of your school and students. The following characteristics were brainstormed by teachers to indicate a positive student attitude toward school subjects (e.g., mathematics, science, English):

Seeks corrective feedback
Asks questions
Helps other students
Prepares for tests
Reads about the subject outside class
Asks about careers in the subject

TABLE 11.5 Student Behaviors Indicating Positive and Negative Attitudes Toward Learning

Positive	Negative
rarely misses class	is frequently absent
rarely late to class	is frequently tardy
asks lots of questions	rarely asks questions
helps other students	rarely helps other students
works well independently without supervision	needs constant supervision
laughs	Little response to humor
is involved in extracurricular activities	is not involved in extracurricular activities
says he or she likes school	says he or she doesn't like school
comes to class early	rarely comes to class early
stays after school	rarely stays after school
volunteers to help	doesn't volunteer
completes homework	often does not complete homework
tries hard to do well	doesn't care about bad grades
completes extra credit work	never does extra credit work
completes assignments before they are due	never completes assignments before the due date
rarely complains	complains
is rarely off-task	sleeps in class
rarely bothers other students	bothers other students
eyes on work	stares out window

Asks about colleges strong in the subject
Asks other students to be quiet in class
Is concerned with poor performance
Joins clubs
Initiates activities
Stays alert in class and on task

Once a fairly complete list of behaviors is developed, you will need to decide if you want to use an informal, unstructured observation or one that is more formal and structured. These types differ in preparation and what is recorded.

Unstructured Observation.   Unstructured (anecdotal) observation is much like what was discussed in Chapter 4. In this case, however, your purpose is to make summative judgments.

An unstructured observation is usually open ended; typically there is no checklist or rating scale for recording what is observed. However, you do know what affective trait you are focused on, and you have at least generated some guidelines and examples of behaviors that indicate the affective trait. In that sense, you have determined in advance what to look for, but you also need to be open to other actions that may reflect on the trait.

During the observation period, or just after it, record behaviors that reflect the affective trait. Some of what you record may correspond to the guidelines or a list of possible behaviors, but record other actions also—anything that may have relevance to the target. Keep your interpretations separate from descriptions of the behaviors. Take brief anecdotal notes and then make sense of them at a later time. Actually, this is what teachers do regularly in their heads in a way that is even less systemic than these unstructured observations. The difference is in whether there is any predetermined list of behaviors, and whether the teachers record their observations.

Avoid making conclusions or inferences in what you record. You want to describe what you saw or heard, but not what that may mean. Words such as *unhappy, frustrated, sad, motivated,* and *positive* are your interpretations of observed behaviors. It is better to stick to simple descriptions, such as *frowned, asked question, stared out window,* and *kept writing the entire time.* Look for both positive and negative actions. The tendency is to be more influenced by bad or negative behavior, especially if it interferes with other students. Once descriptions from several different times are recorded, then you can look over all of them and come to conclusions about the affective trait. Don't rely on a single observation.

The advantage of the unstructured observation is that it is more naturalistic and you are not constrained by what is in a checklist or rating scale. There is no problem if specific behaviors aren't displayed, and behaviors that were not previously listed can be included. A disadvantage is that it is not practical to record much about student behavior on a regular basis. It's hard to find even 15 or 20 minutes at the end of the day, and it is virtually impossible to find any time during the school day.

Structured Observation.   A structured observation differs from an unstructured one in the amount of preparation needed and the way you record what is observed. In structured observation, more time is needed to prepare a checklist or rating form that is to be used for recording purposes. This form is generated from the list of positive and negative behaviors to make it easy and convenient for you to make checks quickly and easily.

The format of the checklist is simple and straightforward. The behaviors are listed, and you make a single check next to each behavior to indicate frequency. Frequency can be indicated by answering yes or no, observed or not observed; by the number of times a behavior occurred; or by some kind of **rating scale** (*always, often, sometimes, rarely, never; occasionally, consistently*). Rating scales are used to describe behavior over an extended period of time.

Two examples of checklists are illustrated in Figure 11.1 for assessing attitude toward reading. The first, labeled *frequency,* would be used to record the number of times each behavior was observed. The second type is a *rating* in which the teacher estimates how often each behavior occurs as defined by a set scale. Another example is shown in Figure 11.2. In this example the targeted affective trait is participation. A holistic rating scale is used to describe qualitatively different levels

FIGURE 11.1 Checklists for Structured Observations of Reading Behavior

Frequency Method

Student Name: _____ Date: _____ Time Frame: _____

Number of Occurrences	Behavior
	1. Tells others that a book was good
	2. Reads for at least five minutes continuously
	3. Asks questions about what is read
	4. Goes through books on the table

Rating Method

Student Name: _____ Date: _____ Time Frame: _____

Behavior	Never	Rarely	Sometimes	Most of the Time	Almost Always
Tells others that a book was good					
Reads for at least five minutes continuously					
Asks questions about what is read					
Goes through books on the table					

of participation. Notice that several behaviors are included in scores 2–5. This type of rating scale is helpful in providing a general overview of the trait being measured. Your choice of checklist or rating scale depends on the time frame (ratings are better for longer periods of time) and the nature of the behavior. Some behaviors are better suited to a simple checklist, such as "follows instructions" and "completes homework." My experience is that a simple scale, with only three descriptors to indicate frequency (e.g., *usually, sometimes, rarely*), is usually sufficient. Additional rating scales are illustrated in Figure 11.3. If there is a large number of behaviors, organize them into major categories. This will make it easier to record and draw inferences from the results. Other suggestions are listed in Figure 11.4.

FIGURE 11.2   Scoring Criteria for Participation

Participation in Class

Student: _____   Date: _____   Lesson: _____

Criteria	Score
Always listens to instructions. Very actively involved from the beginning. Obviously intent on learning the skill. Leads others. Shares thoughts and ideas.	5
Listens to instructions. Once started, actively involved. Usually intent on learning the skill. Rarely distracted from the task. Often shares thoughts and ideas. Does not usually lead others.	4
Sometimes needs clarification about directions. Hard to get started and stay involved. More passive than active. Sometimes distracted from the task. Rarely shares thoughts and ideas.	3
Does not pay attention to instructions. Distracts others. Needs reminders to stay on task. Passive. Rarely shares thoughts and ideas.	2
Did not participate.	1

Student Self-Report

There are several ways in which students tell us about their affect as a self-report. The most direct way is in the context of a personal conversation or interview. Students can also respond to a written questionnaire or survey about themselves or other students. First, we consider interviews.

Student Interview.   Teachers can use different types of personal communication with students, such as individual and group interviews, discussions, and casual conversations, to assess affect. In some ways this is like an observation, but because you have an opportunity to be directly involved with the students it is possible to probe and respond to better understand. An important prerequisite for getting students to reveal their true feelings and beliefs is establishing trust. Without a sense of trust, students may not be comfortable expressing their feelings. They will tend to say what they think their teachers want to hear, say what is socially acceptable or desirable, or say very little, if anything. Younger students are usually pretty candid about themselves; older students may be more reserved. You enhance trust by communicating warmth, caring, and respect and by listening attentively to what the students communicate.

An advantage of interviewing is that you can clarify questions, probe where appropriate to clarify responses, and note nonverbal behavior. Students have

PRIMARY

SOCIAL SKILLS CHECKLIST

ASSESSMENT OF SOCIAL SKILLS

Dates: 10/21
Class: 3rd Grade
Teacher: Forbes

Rating:
+ = Frequently
✓ = Sometimes
○ = Not Yet

Who	Skill 1 (Listening)	Skill 2 (Using First Name)	Skill 3 (Taking Turns)	Skill 4 (Encouraging)	Skill 5 (Sharing)	Comments
1. Lois	✓	✓	○	✓	✓	
2. Connie	+	+	○	✓	+	Dropped in 2 areas
3. James	✓	✓	✓	✓	✓	
4. Juan	+	+	✓	+	+	
5. Beth	○	○	+	✓	✓	Improved in 2 areas
6. Michele	✓	✓	○	✓	✓	
7. John	✓	✓	○	✓	✓	
8. Charles	+	+	○	✓	+	
9. Mike	✓	✓	✓	✓	✓	Went from 5.0s to this in 2 months
10. Lana	+	+	✓	+	+	

Notes: Work with Lois on a regular basis.
Change her seat and group.

MIDDLE SCHOOL

OBSERVATION CHECKLIST

Student: Denise   Class: Science   Date: 12/5
Type of Assignment: Work Habits

☐ Teacher   Date _____   Signed _____
☐ Peer   Date _____   Signed _____
☒ Self   Date 12/5   Signed Denise Smith

	Not Yet	Sometimes	Frequently
WORK HABITS:			
• Gets work done on time			X
• Asks for help when needed		X	
• Takes initiative		X	
STUDY HABITS:			
• Organize work			X
• Takes good notes			X
• Uses time well			X
PERSISTENCE:			
• Shows patience		X	
• Checks own work	X		
• Revises work		X	
• Does quality work			X
SOCIAL SKILLS:			
• Works well with others		X	
• Listens to others		X	
• Helps others		X	

COMMENTS: I always get my work done on time, and I am really organized. I just need to check my own work and help my group work.

FUTURE GOALS: I need to be more patient with my group and try to work with them more. I worry about my own grades, but I don't do enough to help group members achieve their goals.

FIGURE 11.3   Examples of Rating Scales

Source: From *The Mindful School: How to Assess Authentic Learning*, third edition by Kay Burke. Copyright © 1999, 1994, 1993 by Skylight Training and Publishing, Inc. Reprinted by permission of Sage Publications, Inc.

FIGURE 11.4   Checklist for Using Teacher Observation to Assess Affect

✓ Determine behaviors to be observed in advance.
✓ Record student, time, date, and place.
✓ If unstructured, record brief descriptions of relevant behavior.
✓ Keep inferences separate from descriptions.
✓ Record both positive and negative behaviors.
✓ Make several observations of each student.
✓ Avoid personal bias.
✓ Record as soon as possible following the observation.
✓ Use a simple and efficient system.

Source: From *Assessment Strategies For Self-Directed Learning* by A. L. Costa & B. Kallick. Copyright © 2004. Reprinted by permission of Sage Publications, Inc.

an opportunity to qualify or expand on previous answers. These procedures help avoid ambiguity and vagueness, problems often associated with measuring affect.

It is difficult for some students, even when there is a trusting relationship, to articulate their feelings in a one-on-one interview. They may simply be unaccustomed to answering questions about attitudes and values. A group discussion or group interview is a good alternative for these students. People generally open up more in a group setting, as long as peer pressure and cliques don't interfere. Another advantage of using groups is that it is much more efficient than individual interviews. Also, feelings and beliefs can become clearer as students hear others talk. You can use students as leaders of group interviews. They may be able to probe better because they are familiar with the language and lifestyles of their classmates. Respected student leaders will be highly credible.

Be prepared to record student responses and your interpretations. During an interview it is difficult to write very much, and it's not practical to tape record, transcribe, and analyze the transcription. I suggest that you prepare a brief outline of the major areas that will be covered, leaving space to make brief notes as you interview. As soon as possible after the interview, go back over your notes and fill in enough detail so that what the student said and communicated are clearly indicated. Like observation, be careful to keep your descriptions separate from your interpretations.

Questionnaires and Surveys.   You have probably completed many self-report attitude questionnaires or surveys, so you have a general idea what they are like. However, teachers rarely use such instruments in the classroom (Stiggins & Conklin, 1992). This is primarily because of the time and expertise it takes to construct, administer, and score student responses. Most standardized instruments—there are hundreds of them—are not specific enough to help a teacher in a specific context. What is measured is conceptualized as a general trait, and this usually isn't relevant for teachers to use in planning or delivering instruction.

According to Stiggins (2008b), one key to the successful use of student self-reports is to get students to take the questionnaires seriously. This will happen if students see that what you are asking about is relevant to them and that actions are taken as a result of the findings. You want to help students understand that they have nothing to lose and something to gain by being cooperative.

Another key is using questions to which students are willing and able to provide thoughtful responses. This is accomplished if the wording of the questions is precise, if the format is easy to understand and respond to, and if the response options make sense. These and other suggestions are discussed in reviewing the major types of attitude, value, and self-concept self-report instruments.

Constructed-Response Formats.   A straightforward approach to asking students about their affect is to have them respond to a simple statement or question. Often, incomplete sentences can be used.

Examples

> I think mathematics is . . .
> When I have free time I like to . . .
> The subject I like most is . . .
> What I like most about school is . . .
> What I like least about school is . . .
> Science is . . .
> I think I am . . .

Essay items can be used with older students. These items provide a more extensive, in-depth response than incomplete sentences. You can ask students for reasons for their attitudes, values, or beliefs.

Example

> Write a paragraph on the subject you like most in school. Tell me why. Comment on what it is about the subject and your experience with it that leads you to like it the most. Describe yourself as a student. Are you a good student? What are you good at? How hard do you try to get good grades? Does learning come easy or hard for you?

An advantage of the incomplete sentence format is that it taps whatever comes to mind from each student. You are not cuing students about what to think or suggesting how they should respond, so what you get is what is foremost and most salient in the student's mind. Of course, students need to be able to read and write and take the task seriously. If you use this method, be sure to give students enough time to think and write and encourage them to write as much as they can think about for each item.

There are two disadvantages to constructed-response formats. One is that even if you tell students that their answers are anonymous, they may think you'll recognize their handwriting; hence, faking is a concern. Second, scoring the responses takes time and is more subjective than more traditional objective formats. But this approach offers an excellent way to get a general overview of student perspectives, feelings, and thoughts.

Selected-Response Formats.   There are many different types of selected-response formats to choose from when assessing affective targets. We will look at a few commonly used scales. When you decide to create your own instrument and wonder which of these response formats would be best, try to match the format with the trait. There is no single best response format. Some work better with some traits, and some work better with others, depending on the wording and the nature of the trait. Your job will be to make the best match.

Most selected-response formats create a scale that is used with statements concerning the trait. A widely used format to assess attitudes, for example, is the **Likert scale**. This scale can be adapted to almost any type of affective trait, so it is

Teacher's Corner

Elizabeth O'Brien

National Board Certified Teacher

In the beginning of the year I always have students write a "mathography." I ask them to write about themselves, and their history and relationship with math. I learn a tremendous amount about my students that I would never learn otherwise. This helps to explain some students' attitudes and approaches to the material. It also enables me to understand the situations that students have dealt with in the past, which often affect how they deal with material in the present. In addition, I do a learning style inventory in the beginning of the year with students. I do this as much for them as for myself. Many students have not given any thought to how they learn best or why they often do better for one type of teacher versus another. This instrument allows me and the students to get a better picture of my classroom and the students in it and how I should adapt my teaching to them.

very versatile. Students read statements and then record their agreement or disagreement with them according to a five-point scale (*strongly agree, agree, undecided, disagree, strongly disagree*). The statements are generated from your list of positive and negative behaviors or beliefs and are put in a form that makes sense for the response scale. The statements contain some indication of the direction of the attitude, as illustrated in the following examples. The response scale indicates intensity.

Examples

Mathematics is boring.
It is important to get good grades in school.
It is important to complete homework on time.
Class discussion is better than lectures.
School is fun.
I enjoy reading.
Science is challenging.
Science is difficult.

An advantage of this format is that many such statements can be presented on a page or two to assess a number of different attitudes efficiently (see Figure 11.5). Note that some negatively worded statements are included in the example. These should be used sparingly with younger children, with words such as *not, don't,* and *no* appropriately highlighted or underlined.

FIGURE 11.5   Likert Scale for School Attitudes

Student Opinion Survey

Directions: Read each statement carefully and indicate how much you agree or disagree with it by circling the appropriate letter(s) to the right.

Key: SA – Strongly Agree
A – Agree
NS – Not Sure
D – Disagree
SD – Strongly Disagree

		1	2	3	4	5
1.	Science class is challenging.	SD	D	NS	A	SA
2.	Reading is important.	SD	D	NS	A	SA
3.	I like coming to school.	SD	D	NS	A	SA
4.	I like doing science experiments.	SD	D	NS	A	SA
5.	Homework is hard for me.	SD	D	NS	A	SA
6.	Cheating is very bad.	SD	D	NS	A	SA
7.	Learning about circles and triangles is useless.	SD	D	NS	A	SA
8.	I do *not* like to work in small groups.	SD	D	NS	A	SA
9.	Doing well in school is important.	SD	D	NS	A	SA
10.	I believe that what I learn in school is important.	SD	D	NS	A	SA

The responses to the Likert scale are scored by assigning weights from 1 to 5 for each position on the scale so that 5 reflects the most positive attitude and 1 the most negative attitude (SA = 5, A = 4, NS = 3, D = 2, SD = 1). The scores from all the items assessing the same attitude trait are then totaled, though the percentage of responses to each position is probably more important than summary statistics. In other words, you wouldn't add the scores from items 1, 7, and 8 in Figure 11.5 because they address different traits, though you could add items 3, 9, and 10, which deal with attitudes toward school. When adding items and obtaining average scores of statements that are worded so that a "disagree" response refers to a more positive attitude or belief, the scoring needs to be reversed. Thus, the scoring for items 1, 5, 7, and 8 in Figure 11.5 should be reversed (SD = 5, D = 4, A = 2, SA = 1).

The reliability of overall scores is higher if several items assessing the same trait can be added together. This needs to be balanced with the practical limitation on the total number of items in the questionnaire and with the response of students who feel that they don't need to be answering questions that are just about the same as items they have already responded to.

You can use the principle of the Likert scale to construct any number of different response formats. For younger children, for example, the five-point scale is usually truncated to three responses (*agree, unsure, disagree*), or even two (such as *agree* or *disagree, yes* or *no, true* or *not true*). Many self-report instruments use a Likert-type scale that asks students to indicate *how often* they have engaged in specific behaviors or had particular thoughts. These scales are easier to respond to because they are less abstract. They are best for behaviors and cognitive components of attitudes.

Examples

How often do you believe that most of what you learn in school is important?

   a. Always
   b. Frequently
   c. Sometimes
   d. Rarely
   e. Never

How frequently do you *dislike* coming to this class?

   a. All the time
   b. Most of the time
   c. Sometimes
   d. Rarely
   e. Never

How often do you find the classroom activities interesting?

   a. Almost always
   b. Often
   c. Occasionally
   d. Rarely if ever

Another frequently used variation of the Likert scale is to ask students whether something is true for them. This can be a simple dichotomous item, such as a true/false statement, or you can use a scale.

Examples

How true is each statement for you?

If I want I can get good grades in science.

   a. Very true
   b. Somewhat true
   c. Not at all true

When I really try hard I can do well in school.

   a. True
   b. Untrue

Students try hard to do better than each other in this class.

   a. True
   b. False

I am a good student.

   a. Yes
   b. No

Scales are mixed in some questionnaires so that there are different scales for different items. In these types of items, the response formats are dependent on the terminology and intent of each item. Sometimes the nature of the trait is named in the item; then the scale gives students choices. For other items, the scale defines the trait being measured.

Examples

How important is it for you to be a good reader?

    a. Extremely important   **c.** Somewhat important
    b. Very important   **d.** Not important

Science is:

    a. interesting.
    b. dull.
    c. difficult.

Indicate how you feel about your performance on the test.

_____	_____	_____	_____
Immense pride	Some pride	Some failure	Immense failure

_____	_____	_____	_____
Very happy	Somewhat happy	Somewhat sad	Very sad

Indicate the extent to which you believe your performance on the project was a success or failure.

    a. Extreme success
    b. Somewhat successful
    c. Failure
    d. Extreme failure

Circle the statement that best describes your interest in learning *most of the time.*

    a. I am pretty interested in what we learn.
    b. This class is somewhat interesting, but I find my mind wandering sometimes.
    c. I often find this class pretty boring.

For young students, the response format is often in the form of faces rather than words.

Examples

Learning about science

Reading books

For classroom climate and value targets, self-report questionnaires often ask students to select from several options. The options refer to different traits or values, rather than showing a range of the same trait.

Examples

I did well on this test because I:

   a. studied hard.
   b. got lucky.

Select one of the following:

   a. Students in this class like to help each other out.
   b. There is a lot of bickering between students in this class.

Select the statement that you agree with the most.

   a. People should be required to volunteer to help those less fortunate.
   b. People who find a wallet should give it to the police.

Interests are efficiently measured with checklists, ranking, or simple dichotomous choices.

Examples

Indicate whether you are interested (I) or uninterested (U) in learning about each of the historical topics listed.

_____ **a.** Vietnam War
_____ **b.** World War II
_____ **c.** Holocaust
_____ **d.** Depression
_____ **e.** Stock market crash

Rank the following from most liked (1) to least liked (5).

_____ History
_____ Sports

_____ Science
_____ Music
_____ Art

An advantage of selected-response formats is that they make it easy to ensure anonymity. Anonymity is important when the traits are more personal, such as values and self-concept. It is also a more efficient way of collecting information. However, you don't want to ask too many questions just because it is efficient. It's best to keep self-report questionnaires short. Although you need more than a single item to reliably assess an affective trait, if you have too many items students may lose concentration and motivation. Select only those traits that you will take action on; don't use items simply because it would be interesting to know what students think. It's also not a good idea to include open-ended items such as "Comments" or "Suggestions" at the end of a selected-response questionnaire.

Constructing Self-Report Items. If you need to develop your own self-report items to assess affect targets, begin by listing the behaviors, thoughts, and feelings that correspond to each affective trait, similar to what I suggested earlier for observations. Once you select a response format, write sentences that are clear and succinct, and write direct statements that students will easily understand. You are not trying to assess knowledge, intelligence, reading ability, or vocabulary, so keep items simple and short. You may find that published instruments will give you some good ideas for how to word items, set up response formats, and in general lay out a questionnaire. You may find an existing instrument that meets your purpose very well. Now we move to some specific suggestions, with examples, for those who will be constructing items.

In wording the items, avoid the use of negatives, especially double negatives.

Examples

> *Poor:* There isn't a student in this class who does not like to work with others.
> *Improved:* Students in this class like to work with each other.

If you are interested in present self-perceptions, which is usually the case, avoid writing in the past tense.

Examples

> *Poor:* I have always liked science.
> *Improved:* I like science.

Avoid absolutes such as *always, never, all,* and *every* in the item stem. These terms, because they represent an all-or-none judgment, may cause you to miss the more accurate self-perception.

Examples

> *Poor:* I never like science.
>
> *Improved:* I rarely like science.

Avoid items that ask about more than one thing or thought. Double-barreled items are difficult to interpret because you don't know which of the two thoughts or ideas the student has responded to.

Examples

> *Poor:* I like science and mathematics.
>
> *Improved:* I like science.

These and other suggestions presented in this section are summarized in Figure 11.6. I should point out, however, that classroom teachers rarely have an opportunity to develop sophisticated instruments with strong and well-documented technical qualities. Thus, locally developed items and instruments should be used cautiously and in conjunction with other evidence.

Student Self-Assessment

A particularly effective kind of student self-report occurs when students are engaged in self-assessment. Simply put, student **self-assessment** is a process in which students *monitor* and *evaluate* their learning and performance. Monitoring is an awareness of the thinking and learning strategies that are needed and actual performance. Evaluation involves making a judgment about the quality of their work and their progress toward targeted performance. That is, self-assessment engages students deeply in self-observations and making judgments about their work, identifying discrepancies between current and desired performance (McMillan & Hearn, 2008; Ross, 2006). This aligns closely to what is emphasized in standards-based

**FIGURE 11.6   Checklist for Using Student
Self-Reports to Assess Affect**

✓ Keep measures focused on specific affective traits.
✓ Establish trust with students.
✓ Match response format to the trait being assessed.
✓ Ensure anonymity if possible.
✓ Keep questionnaires brief.
✓ Keep items short and simple.
✓ Avoid negatives and absolutes.
✓ Write items in present tense.
✓ Avoid double-barreled items.

Teacher's Corner

Arleen Rinehart

National Board Certified High School English and Special Education Teacher

Noncognitive assessments help me to determine how effective my activities are, how clear my objectives are, whether students are treated fairly, and whether the classroom environment is conducive to student learning. At the end of each semester, I give students a questionnaire that asks them to evaluate what they have learned, to offer suggestions for my improvement and to comment upon how they feel while in the class. Most students give sincere and helpful comments. In fact, I often learn that students take their learning and time spent in school very seriously. I often use these comments to plan future lessons and to help me build stronger relationships with individual students. Student comments help me to become a better teacher because they force me to reflect upon my teaching.

education because such thinking implies an understanding of performance targets and the criteria that are used to indicate success.

Self-assessment is an excellent strategy for formative assessment, in that students give themselves immediate feedback, based on specific aspects of their performance according to standards and criteria, and make adjustment to how and what they are learning (Crooks, 2007). They improve their performance by taking responsibility for their own learning, gaining an understanding of their strengths and weaknesses. It empowers students to independently guide their own learning (Heritage, 2009).

Successful student self-assessment has a multitude of positive benefits. Perhaps most important, research suggests that self-assessment contributes to higher achievement, especially when students receive direct instruction on self-assessment procedures (Black & Wiliam, 1998; Ross, 2006; Sadler & Good, 2006). The purpose of self-assessment is to involve students deeply in the evaluation of their work so that immediate feedback can be incorporated and used to improve learning. The emphasis is on progress and mastery of knowledge and understanding, which increases confidence and motivation. Students learn to use assessment information to set performance goals, to make decisions about how to improve, to describe quality work, to communicate their progress toward meeting learning targets, and to develop metacognitive skills (Chappuis & Stiggins, 2002).

Theories from three areas of study provide support for concluding that self-assessment is a powerful source of learning: cognitive theories of motivation and learning, metacognition theory, and self-efficacy theory (McMillan & Hearn, 2008). Cognitive and constructivist theories of learning stress the importance of connecting new learning to what they already know and understand. Self-assessment helps this process by providing students with meaningful feedback that is based on their own criteria. Rather than learning in a rote manner, students learn by constantly comparing their understandings with desired learning outcomes. The knowledge that is constructed is meaningful in the sense that it is in the context of students' existing knowledge.

From a motivational perspective, self-assessment is key to establishing a mastery goal orientation. This type of motivation is based on improving knowledge, understanding, and skill, rather than on simply being successful with the outcome. Mastery goals require, to at least some extent, an internal processing of information, whereas for performance goal orientation the monitoring and evaluation is external. Self-assessment contributes to a mastery type of motivation by enabling students to know their progress toward full understanding.

Metacognition involves skills that are directly influenced by self-assessment. Both self-monitoring and self-evaluation are important metacognitive skills. Students learn to manage learning activities and time, check their understanding, and switch to different approaches to learning. They are taught to constantly monitor their progress as well as what is influencing their learning. Students learn how to form internal questions about their learning and performance, to make decisions about what other learning is needed, and to be aware if projected learning plans are not resulting in satisfactory improvement. The emphasis, then, is on self-directed learning, which has powerful implications for motivation and positive attitudes toward learning. Figures 11.7 and 11.8 illustrate rubrics that can be used periodically to remind students about the metacognitive skills they should be using.

Self-efficacy is a student's belief that they are capable of learning a specific task. These are self-perceptions of confidence of obtaining desired tasks. This is accomplished by being able to self-reflect about their ability and opportunities for learning, and self-assessment reinforces this kind of self-reflection. Students estimate what they are able to accomplish and the likelihood of success. Students with a positive self-efficacy are more likely to persist and remain engaged in learning, whereas students with a low self-efficacy tend to give up or avoid what they believe are difficult tasks. Through self-assessment, students build a positive self-efficacy. They are skilled at knowing when they are learning, the degree of effort required for further learning, when they are right or wrong, and which strategies for learning are needed. They are better at knowing when they have mastered the learning target and tend to attribute their success to their ability and effort. These attributions help students have positive self-expectancies about learning in the future.

A good example that shows how student self-assessment can improve learning is reported by Frederikson and White (2004). In their work, students use a process the researchers called *reflective assessment*. The purpose of reflective assessment is to develop students' metacognitive science inquiry knowledge. Students were taught to evaluate their work according to criteria representing "higher-level" cognitive skills, such as reasoning, being inventive, and being systematic. Students evaluated the scientific research they had conducted using these criteria on a five-point scale. They also wrote justifications for their ratings. Based on this approach, experiments comparing students using reflective assessment to a control group

FIGURE 11.7   Rubric for Metacognition

Self-Monitoring, Self-Modifying, and Self-Managing

Criteria	4	3	2	1
Sets goals for work	Independently sets work goals that are realistic and appropriate to the task at hand.	Requires reminders to set work goals. Goals are realistic and appropriate to the task at hand.	Requires reminders. Sets work goals that include some unrealistic expectations for the task at hand.	Requires reminders. Sets minimal goals that indicate minimal expectations for the task at hand.
Monitors progress toward goals	Independently revises and adjusts time-management plans throughout work process.	Requires reminders to make adjustments to work process.	Requires continual reminders to maintain a well-balanced work process.	Requires frequent reminders and shows evidence of poor time management.
Monitors for clarity and under-standing	Independently revises work for depth of meaning. Solicits outside readers to confirm clarity of communication.	Requires suggestion to revise work. Responds to suggestions for outside reader to confirm clarity of communication.	Requires continual reminders to revise work and check for understanding.	Requires frequent reminders and resists revisions and feedback for clarity and meaning.
Monitors for accuracy	Independently checks for accuracy.	Requires sugges-tion to check for accuracy.	Requires continual reminders to check for accuracy.	Requires frequent reminders and resists checking for accuracy.

Source: From *The Mindful School: How to Assess Authentic Learning,* third edition by Kay Burke. Copyright © 1999, 1994, 1993 by Skylight Training and Publishing, Inc. Reprinted by permission of Sage Publications, Inc.

showed that reflective assessment was effective in developing the students' thinking skills and in providing higher-quality products.

A key element in self-assessment is the development of students' reflective habits and skills. This is best accomplished with a clear idea of what the habits and skills are and specific instruction in these dispositions. You will need to be very clear to students about your expectations for them to monitor their work and thinking and to be reflective about their work, describing what you expect them to do in terms they can understand. Examples that illustrate the dispositions are helpful. This may need to be very simple. For example, students can be introduced to self-assessment by asking them to say whether answers to questions are correct or

FIGURE 11.8   Checklist for Metacognitive Skills

Metacognitive Skill	I *Rarely* Do This	I Do This *Some* of the Time	I Do This *Most* of the Time	I *Always* Do This
I make sure I know the criteria for judging my performance before I begin.				
I am willing to share with others and the teacher when I don't understand something.				
I learn from my mistakes.				
I strive for more learning.				
I check my work for mistakes and completeness.				
I know how to evaluate the work of other students.				
I think about what I need to do to perform better.				

incorrect, then answering: Why is the answer incorrect? What tells you specifically that it is incorrect? What can be done to have a correct answer? As students respond to these questions, your focus should be on whether their answers reflect a willingness to apply what they know, so simply showing this kind of engagement needs to be recognized and rewarded.

The goal of self-assessment is to empower students so that they can guide their own learning and internalize the criteria for judging success. This occurs when students first understand the criteria and then evaluate their progress toward attainment of specific achievement targets, as they learn, and to know what further learning is needed to reach the targets. Students give them selves meaningful formative feedback during instruction. This process is individualized for each student, allowing students to obtain specific information rather than relying on general evaluative feedback for the class as a whole. Assessment is integrated with learning as well as with instruction, and when students are judging their own performance the responsibility for learning lies more with them than with the teacher.

There are many kinds of self-assessment activities. Some examples are summarized, which list the activities by when they occur—either before, during, or after instruction (Chappuis & Stiggins, 2002; Costa & Kallick, 2004; Stiggins, 2008b).

Before *Instruction, Students*

- Review with the teacher the table of specifications to discuss what it means.
- Examine samples of student performance in the past to show how criteria can be used to evaluate the samples with reference to the learning goals.
- Suggest how samples of student performance could be improved to meet the targeted performance.
- Share scoring criteria with exemplars of student work illustrating different levels of performance.
- Analyze examples of student work using the scoring criteria.
- Develop a table of specifications.
- Develop assessments and scoring criteria.
- Develop practice test items.
- Match test items to the table of specifications.
- Transform criteria into checklists and other methods of keeping track of progress.
- Practice self-assessment with familiar tasks and easily understood criteria.

During *Instruction, Students*

- Keep track of the match between what is covered and target criteria.
- Keep a log of growth toward meeting the target.
- Signal teacher when milestones are accomplished.
- Indicate level of understanding using cards or electronic clickers.
- Evaluate their own and others' work at the end of each day and show progress toward meeting the target.
- Make predictions about how well they will perform in the summative assessment.
- Ask questions that encourage self-evaluation (e.g., How does your work compare to the exemplars? Have you met the target completely? What additional learning is needed? What can you do to improve your learning? Are you sure that is correct? How do you know? What areas are you having trouble learning? What rating do you deserve? Why? How much more time will be needed to reach this target? What are some ways you can learn to reach the target? What do you need to work on?)

- Rate each other during discussions.
- Predict how well they will perform and the areas in which they will need further learning.
- Identify targets that have been difficult to learn.
- Self-evaluate understanding every 15 to 20 minutes.
- Engage in peer tutoring.
- Maintain learning portfolios.
- Check work in progress.
- List the steps needed to learn the material.

After *Instruction, Students*

- Design practice tests.
- Evaluate the quality of practice test items.
- Participate in scoring the assessments.
- Make suggestions about how to improve the assessment.
- Construct test items and justify how they will measure student performance in relation to learning targets.
- Evaluate their own work and/or others' work according to provided criteria.
- Rate themselves and others.
- Interview each other to judge performance.
- Conduct student-led parent–teacher conferences.
- Provide their own explanations for grades they have received.

Although you won't be able to use all these suggestions, the important point is that you need to find and be comfortable using activities that will use and promote student self-assessment. It's largely a matter of the commitment you make to self-assessment and whether it's something that you are aware of when planning and carrying out instruction as well as end-of-instruction assessments.

Student self-assessment is not without limitations. Perhaps the biggest challenge is to get students used to doing it. This will take time because most students are accustomed to receiving only teacher feedback and appraisal. Some students will self-assess better than others, which will require some individual attention by the teacher. It may also be so time-consuming to have students involved in self-assessment that valuable instructional time is lost. Finally, you may need to develop a strong rationale for using student self-assessment if this is new for your school or department. With the current trend toward standardization of both assessment and instruction, your use of student self-assessment may not fit well with what is required or encouraged.

It will be helpful to students if you provide them with worksheets, checklists, sentence completion, rating scales, and other prepared material to provide structure to self-assessment. Especially for younger students, concepts such as self-assessment, self-monitoring, and self-rating are abstract and difficult to comprehend. Figures 11.9 and 11.10 are examples of the kinds of forms you can prepare and use with your students.

FIGURE 11.9   Student Self-Assessment Rating Form

Student Name: _____   Teacher: _____   Date: _____

Physical Science Standard PS.2:
The student will investigate and understand the basic nature of matter.

Area	Got It—Test Me	Got Most of It—Just Some Fine-Tuning Needed	Got Some of It—Further Work Needed	Don't Get It at All—Help, Please
The particle theory of matter				
Elements, compounds, mixtures, acids, bases, salts, organic, inorganic, solids, liquids, and gases				
Characteristics of types of matter based on physical and chemical properties				
Physical properties (shape, density, solubility, odor, melting point, boiling point, color)				
Chemical properties (acidity, basicity, combustibility, reactivity)				

Source: Virginia Science Standards of Learning from *Standards of Learning for Virginia Public Schools*, 1995, p. 47. Richmond, VA: Virginia Department of Education.

Peer Ratings

Peer appraisal is the least common method of assessing affect. This is due to the relatively inefficient nature of conducting, scoring, and interpreting peer ratings. Also, teachers who are tuned in very much at all in a class can accurately observe what is assessed in peer ratings. However, two primary methods for obtaining peer ratings—the guess-who and sociometric techniques—represent approaches that can be used in conjunction with observation and self-reports to strengthen assessment of interpersonal and classroom environment targets.

FIGURE 11.10 Self-Assessment Rating Form for Reading

Reading Progress Report

Student Name: _____ Teacher Name: _____ Date: _____

I am able to:

	Yes, Let's Go On	Not Quite Yet	Not Yet
Explain the author's purpose			
Pick out fact from fantasy			
Describe how the setting is important to the story			
Describe how the language used is important to the story			
Pick out the main characters of the story			

Guess-Who Approach. In this method, students are asked to list the students they believe best correspond to behavior descriptions. The descriptions may be positive or negative, though usually they are positive to avoid highlighting undesirable behaviors or traits. Typically there are only a few items in this approach so that students can complete it quickly, and scoring is done by simply tallying the number of times each student is listed. One disadvantage is that some shy and withdrawn students may be overlooked, resulting in a lack of information about them. Figure 11.11 illustrates a guess-who form for assessing concern for others.

Sociometric Approach. Sociometric techniques are used to assess the social structure of the class and the interaction patterns among the students. This allows you to learn about the social acceptance and liking patterns of the students. The results can be used for forming small groups of students, targeting interventions with individual students, and identifying cliques, popular students, and social isolates.

Students are asked to nominate students they would like to work or play with. Although this is technically a self-report, the results are used as a way for students to rate each other. The questions would be like the following:

I choose these students to work with.
I would like to sit next to _____.
I would like to have the following students on my team.

It is best to ask about general activities, such as who to work with or sit next to, rather than specific ones (e.g., walking to school or doing a report). It is also advisable to avoid asking negative items (e.g., I would not like to sit next to . . .").

FIGURE 11.11   Example of a Guess-Who Form for Assessing Cooperative Behavior

Student Survey

Directions: Write the names of students in this class who fit the descriptions. No other students will see your answers. Include students who are absent today. The same student can be named in more than one category.

Who is most willing to cooperate with others? _____

Who helps other students the most? _____

Who is asked most for help? _____

Which student is most concerned about others? _____

Which student enjoys working with others? _____

Once the students have made their choices, you need to tabulate the results listing all the students and indicating the number of times each student was selected. This provides a measure of general social acceptance. Second, create a matrix to identify students who have selected each other. Finally, as illustrated in Figure 11.12, construct a **sociogram**. This is a diagram that shows the social structure of the group. In this example, the number of times any student was selected is depicted by the concentric circles (students with more than nine choices in the middle, six to nine choices in the second circle, etc.). Not all choices are shown; lines are used for mutual choices and rejections.

Although this is a very interesting and informative technique, constructing the sociogram takes considerable time. However, often teachers are surprised by the results, so if you intend to assess social adjustment and other interpersonal affect targets in depth, a sociogram would be very beneficial.

Which Method or Combination of Methods Should I Use?

We have covered four approaches to measuring affect and beliefs—observation, student self-report, student self-assessment and peer ratings—and each method has advantages and disadvantages. Your choice of which of these to use depends on a number of factors. Consider the type of affect or belief you want to assess. You can get a pretty good idea of a student's general reaction to something or someone through observation, but to diagnose attitude components you'll need a self-report of some kind. Checklists are effective for self-assessment. Observation can be followed by peer ratings to get at socially oriented affect. If you are interested in group responses and tendencies, which is generally recommended, then a selected-response self-report is probably best because you can ensure anonymity, and it is easily scored. Finally, you need to take into consideration the use of the information. If you intend to use the results for grading (which I do not recommend), then multiple approaches may be

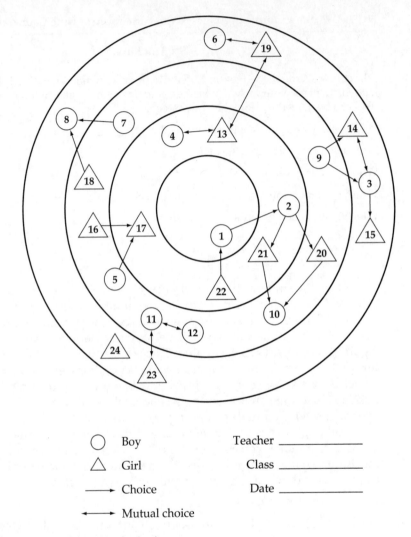

○	Boy	Teacher _____
△	Girl	Class _____
→	Choice	Date _____
←→	Mutual choice	

FIGURE 11.12   Example of a Sociogram

needed, and you'll need to be especially careful about faking on self-reports and even peer judgments. In the end, the choice of method depends most on your context, targets, and level of comfort in using any particular approach.

Ensuring Anonymity

Anonymity has been mentioned several times as a desirable feature when assessing affect. Popham (2008a) makes the argument that anonymity is not only desirable but also essential to obtaining valid results. He has pointed out that several

Case Study
for Reflection

Mrs. Williams is a second-grade teacher at James Elementary School who has had difficulty in her classroom this semester. She has had to spend ever-increasing amounts of time and energy to keep students from verbally or physically abusing each other. She has noticed that many of these students also make disparaging remarks about themselves and call themselves "dumb" or "stupid." She has used anecdotal records and feedback from talking with the school counselor about the situation to help her assess the situation in her classroom. She has decided to take a 15-minute block of time every day next semester to teach appropriate social skills and to allow time for students to air their complaints in a nonviolent atmosphere. The counselor has assured her that these students have low self-esteem and that through classroom discussion and role-play they can learn to appreciate themselves and others. Mrs. Williams also plans to introduce a behavior modification plan for students, which will help her track student progress with improved social behavior. Mrs. Williams is concerned that the principal and parents of her students will not understand her attempts to assess student affective traits to improve the classroom environment.

QUESTIONS FOR CONSIDERATION

1. What should Mrs. Williams do before classes start next semester?
2. What strategies could she use to appropriately assess students to provide data that will be reassuring to the principal and parents?

techniques can be used to enhance perceived anonymity when you are interested in results for the class as a whole:

1. Direct students not to write their names or in any way identify themselves on their self-reports.
2. Use selected-response item formats.
3. Inform students that their responses will be anonymous.
4. Position yourself in the class so that students know you cannot see their answers.
5. Direct students not to write anything other than checking or circling to avoid your recognizing handwriting.
6. Provide a procedure for collecting self-reports so that you won't be able to identify responses (e.g., in a container in the back of the room, not on your desk).
7. Tell students why anonymity is important.
8. Use a response format that minimizes the likelihood that responses can be seen by other students.

Summary

This chapter considered student affect, an important but often neglected area. Sound assessment of affect begins with clear and specific affective targets. Suggestions were made for conceptualizing affective traits that most would consider essential for successful learning. Two methods are used most frequently for measuring affect in the classroom: teacher observation and student self-reports. Observation can be structured or unstructured, and there are many different formats for self-reports. In the end, you'll need to customize the assessment of affect for your students, school, and curriculum. Pick a few most important traits, do a good job of assessing them, and then use the results to improve instruction. Other essential points made in the chapter include

- Positive affective traits influence motivation, involvement, and cognitive learning.
- Although the term *affect* refers to emotions and feelings, affective targets include cognitive and behavioral traits.
- Attitudes are predispositions to respond favorably or unfavorably. They include cognitive, affective, and behavioral components.
- Values are end states of existence or desired modes of conduct.
- Motivation is the purposeful engagement to learn. It is determined by self-efficacy (the student's beliefs about his or her capability to learn) and the value of learning.
- Academic self-concept is the way students describe themselves as learners. Self-esteem is how students feel about themselves. Both are multidimensional; it's best to avoid general measures of self-concept or self-esteem.
- Social relationship targets involve interpersonal interaction and competence.
- Classroom environment is the climate established through factors such as affiliation, involvement, cohesiveness, formality, friction, and warmth.
- The affective domain of Bloom's taxonomy defines different levels of affect in a hierarchical fashion, from attending to something to using something as a determining factor in one's life.
- Four methods are used to assess student affect: teacher observation, student self-report, student self-assessment, and peer ratings.
- Teacher observation can be structured or unstructured. Several observations should be made; recording of behavior should occur as soon as possible after the observation. Inferences are made from what was observed.
- Student self-reports include interviews, questionnaires, and surveys. Trust between the students and the teacher is essential.
- Interviews allow teachers to probe and clarify to avoid ambiguity, though they cannot be anonymous and are time consuming.
- Questionnaires are time efficient and can be anonymous. Proper student motivation to take the questions seriously is essential.
- Constructed-response questionnaires tap traits without cuing students, which indicates what is most salient to students.

- Selected-response formats, such as the Likert scale, are efficient to score and can be anonymous when assessing groups.
- In constructing questionnaires, keep them brief, write in the present tense, and avoid negative and double-barreled items.
- Student self-assessment consists of self-monitoring and self-evaluation.
- Students who self-assess have better achievement, more positive motivation, and a stronger self-efficacy.
- Self-assessment skills, can be taught and implemented before, during, or after instruction.
- Peer ratings can be used to assess interpersonal traits. Frequencies of nominations and sociograms are used to analyze the results.
- Use appropriate techniques for ensuring anonymity.

Self-Instructional Review Exercises

1. What are some reasons that most teachers don't systematically assess affective targets?

2. Match the nature of the learning with the affective target. Each target may be used more than once or not at all.

_____ **(1)** Cooperation and conflict resolution	**a.** Attitude
_____ **(2)** Student expectations and need to do well	**b.** Value
	c. Motivation
_____ **(3)** Honesty and integrity	**d.** Academic self-concept
_____ **(4)** Character education	**e.** Social relationships/ collaboration
_____ **(5)** Cognitive and affective components	
_____ **(6)** Responding and organization	**f.** Classroom environment
_____ **(7)** Warmth in the classroom	**g.** Affective taxonomy
_____ **(8)** Thinking math is important but not liking it	
_____ **(9)** Engagement and involvement	
_____ **(10)** Kindness, respect, tolerance	

3. Critique the efforts of the teachers in the following two scenarios to assess affect. What have they done well and how could they improve?

Scenario 1: Mr. Talbot

Mr. Talbot decided that he wanted to assess his fifth graders on their attitudes toward social studies. He asks students to complete the sentence, "Social studies is. . . ." Also, at the end of each week he summarizes how much students have liked the social studies units. He writes a brief description for each student, then gives each a rating of 1 to 5.

Scenario 2: Ms. Headly

Ms. Headly teaches art to middle school students. Because all the students in the school come through her class, she wants to be sure that students leave the class with a positive attitude toward art and strong aesthetic values. She decides to develop and administer a survey of art attitudes and values at the beginning and end of each semester. She consults other teachers to generate a list of thoughts and behaviors that are positive and negative. She uses a response format of "like me" and "not like me" with the 50 items. Ms. Headley instructs the students not to put their names on the surveys.

4. Identify each of the following as a characteristic of observation (O), constructed-response self-report (CRSR), selected-response self-report (SRSR), or peer rating (PR).

   a. Can take into account nonverbal behaviors
   b. Relatively easy to administer but difficult to score
   c. Subject to teacher bias
   d. Can be anonymous
   e. Very time consuming to gather data
   f. Student explanations for answers can be provided
   g. The method of choice for checking which students are leaders
   h. Can be done without students' knowledge or awareness

5. What are strengths and limitations of student self-assessment?

Answers to Self-Instructional Review Exercises

1. Three reasons were given in the chapter: Affect takes second seat to cognitive outcomes; assessing affect is difficult to do well; and teachers do not want to put up with controversy.

2. (1) e, (2) c, (3) b, (4) b, (5) a, (6) g, (7) f, (8) a, (9) c, (10) b or e.

3. *Scenario 1.* On the positive side, Mr. Talbot has used more than one method to assess attitudes, and he has a fairly narrow trait in mind. It's good that he isolates the affective component of attitudes (likes) and that his observation notes are brief. On the negative, though, his sentence is too broad and may not give him much information about attitudes. There is no indication that he has generated examples of approach and avoidance behaviors. Students could easily respond with answers such as "short" or "in the morning," which wouldn't be much help. He should try to summarize more frequently than once a week, even though trying to write descriptions for each student will take a lot of time. He records his interpretations rather than student behavior.

   Scenario 2. For the most part, this is an example of good affective assessment. Ms. Headly took the time to first list behaviors, then establish a response format that would work, then develop the items. She ensured anonymity, and she looked at attitudes and values before and after her course. However, the survey is pretty long, and she is dependent on a single assessment method. It is possible that her bias would be perceived by students, and it might encourage them to provide positive answers at the end of the semester.

4. a. O and CRSR (interview); b. PR; c. O and CRSR; d. SRSR; e. O and CRSR; f. CRSR; g. PR; h. O.

5. Strengths: promotes better student understanding of learning targets and scoring criteria; promotes student self-reflection and self-evaluation; provides immediate, specific, and individualized feedback; leads to an awareness of progress; increases motivation; enhances self-efficacy. Limitations: self-assessment skills need to be taught; time is needed for self-evaluation; differences between students requires individualized instruction; may not be supported because of other initiatives or alignment requirements; instructional time may be lost.

Suggestions for Action Research

1. Identify some affective targets for students and construct a short questionnaire to assess the targets. If possible, find a group of students who could respond to the questionnaire. After they answer all the questions, ask them about their feelings toward the questions and the clarity of the wording. What do the results look like? Would the teacher agree with the results? How difficult was it to develop the questionnaire?

2. Interview several teachers about affective targets in the classroom. Ask them how they arrived at their targets and whether there is any systematic approach to assessing them. Ask what the advantages and disadvantages would be to using different kinds of assessment techniques, such as observation and student self-reports.

3. Ask a group of students about self-assessment. What do they think about the idea? Do they think it would motivate them? Give them some specific examples of student self-assessment materials. Would they be interested in doing it? What do students see as strengths and weaknesses? Do they think they have the skills to do self-assessment?

Assessing Special Needs and ELL Students

with Yaoying Xu and Seonhee Cho

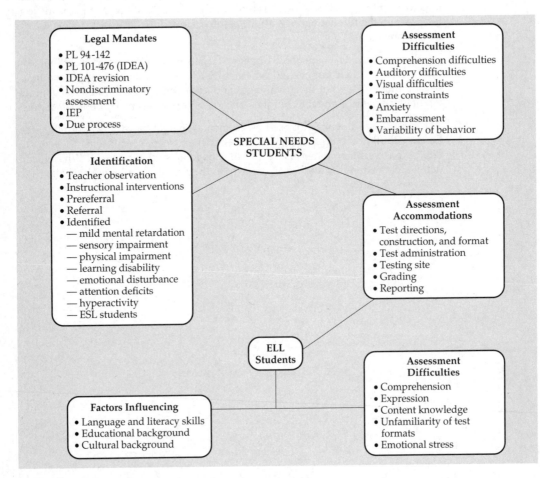

Legal Mandates
- PL 94-142
- PL 101-476 (IDEA)
- IDEA revision
- Nondiscriminatory assessment
- IEP
- Due process

Assessment Difficulties
- Comprehension difficulties
- Auditory difficulties
- Visual difficulties
- Time constraints
- Anxiety
- Embarrassment
- Variability of behavior

SPECIAL NEEDS STUDENTS

Identification
- Teacher observation
- Instructional interventions
- Prereferral
- Referral
- Identified
  — mild mental retardation
  — sensory impairment
  — physical impairment
  — learning disability
  — emotional disturbance
  — attention deficits
  — hyperactivity
  — ESL students

Assessment Accommodations
- Test directions, construction, and format
- Test administration
- Testing site
- Grading
- Reporting

ELL Students

Factors Influencing
- Language and literacy skills
- Educational background
- Cultural background

Assessment Difficulties
- Comprehension
- Expression
- Content knowledge
- Unfamiliarity of test formats
- Emotional stress

CHAPTER 12   Concept Map

One of the most significant challenges for teachers is to accommodate two types of students who are now routinely placed in general education classes⊡ special needs and English language learner (ELL) students. Both groups of students require appropriate assessment accommodations to ensure fairness and accuracy in gathering evidence of student learning. In addition, teachers are responsible for using assessment information to identify students who may need and be eligible for special education services. In this chapter we will consider classroom assessment procedures for both of these groups. First, we will discuss assessment of students with special needs.

Assessing Students with Special Needs

An essential starting point for understanding assessment issues and policies for students with special needs is the legal mandates that have influenced what teachers must do in their assessments of these students.

Legal Mandates

In 1975, the Education for All Handicapped Children Act, Public Law 94-142, was passed to provide free appropriate public education for school-aged individuals with special needs in the least restrictive environment. The act, which was updated in 1990 as the Individuals with Disabilities Education Act (IDEA; P.L. 101-476, and reauthorized in 1997), requires states to establish procedures to ensure that students with special needs are educated, to the maximum extent possible, with students who are not disabled, that is, in the least restrictive environment. The most common procedure for meeting this mandate has been to mainstream students with special needs by placing them in general education classes with appropriate instructional support. Later the term **inclusion** has been used to mean that students with disabilities are served primarily in the general education classroom with individual supports as needed, under the responsibilities of the general education teacher (Mastropieri & Scruggs, 2007). In fact, students can be removed from general classes only when the severity of the disability prevents satisfactory instruction and learning progress. As a result, most classroom teachers must now be familiar with how students are identified as having "special needs" and how assessment procedures used in the course of general education classroom instruction need to be modified to ensure that these students are evaluated fairly.

Another important law was passed in 1986 to extend all rights and protections of PL 94-142 to preschoolers aged 3 to 5 (PL 99-457). The effect of this law has been to encourage states to provide services for individuals from birth through kindergarten, with required services for 3- to 5-year-olds. The Americans with Disabilities Act of 1992 indicates further assurances for persons with disabilities, although these are not focused on schooling. In 1997 IDEA was amended, with final regulations published in 1999. The purpose of the 1997 amendments was to promote the following (Overton, 2003):

- Increased parental participation and involvement
- Ensuring student access to the general curriculum (mainstreaming)
- Preventing inappropriate identification and mislabeling
- Using mediation to resolve disputes and disagreements between parents and educators
- Ensuring the rights of students and their parents through due process
- Enhancement of student learning as determined through accountability mechanisms
- Providing for fair assessment of limited-English-proficiency students
- Using many and varied assessments
- Enhancement of individualized planning in the IEP

One of the most important new provisions under IDEA 1990 was that the law recognized that most students with disabilities spent all or most of their school time in general education settings, and so it included a provision requiring that a general education teacher become a member of the team for the student's individualized education program (IEP).

Thus, the trend is toward increasing governmental involvement in protecting the rights of individuals with disabilities, and you will be responsible for adhering to these regulations with students in inclusive settings.

The most recent reauthorization of IDEA, PL 108-446, also named as the Individuals with Disabilities Education Improvement Act, or IDEIA, was passed in 2004 to provide more educational opportunities for students with disabilities in general education settings (Pierangelo & Giuliani, 2007). According to PL 94-142 and later IDEA, classroom teachers are responsible for gathering and providing the information used to identify students who may become eligible for special education services and for developing and implementing an **IEP.** The IEP is a written plan that serves as a legal document. It is developed by a team of individuals (IEP committee) that specifies the present level of knowledge and skills, annual goals, short-term learning objectives, the initiation and duration of special services, evaluation procedures, and the educational program (Spinelli, 2002).

Some of the significant changes related to IEPs in IDEA 2004 include

- Deleting the requirement that IEPs include short-term objectives, except for students who are assessed using alternative assessment procedures; IEPs must describe how progress will be measured and when reports will be issued.
- Ensuring that states will align their accountability systems for students with disabilities to the No Child Left Behind (NCLB) accountability system, that IEPs specifically address academic achievement of students with disabilities; and giving local school districts greater flexibility in reviewing the progress of a child.

- Including statements that indicate the need for individual accommodations for testing and alternative statewide assessments that must be provided as well as justification for participating in alternative assessments.
- To identify students with learning disabilities or difficulties, schools can use Response to Intervention (RTI) approach to determining eligibility for special education services.

The teacher provides a major role in both determining and implementing the IEP and monitors progress toward mastery of the goals and objectives. Assessments used by teachers provide the information necessary to determine whether students are making satisfactory progress toward meeting learning targets as specified in the IEP. For identification purposes, the law requires that the selection and administration of materials and procedures used for evaluation and placement must be **nondiscriminatory.** At a minimum, the law requires that:

1. Trained personnel administer validated tests and other evaluation materials and provide and administer such materials in the child's native language or other mode of communication.
2. Tests and other evaluation materials include those tailored to assess specific areas of educational need and not merely those designed to provide a single general intelligence quotient.
3. Trained personnel select and administer tests to reflect accurately the child's aptitude or achievement level without discriminating against the child's disability.
4. Trained personnel use no single procedure as the sole criterion for determining an appropriate educational program for a child.
5. A multidisciplinary team assess the child in all areas related to the suspected disability. (Wood, 2002, p. 11)

Essentially, these provisions mean that assessment must be planned and conducted so that the disability does not contribute to the score or result. That is, it would be unfair to use a test written in English to determine that a student whose primary language is Spanish has mental retardation, just as it would be unfair to conclude that a student with a fine-motor disability did not know the answer to an essay question because there was insufficient time to write the answer.

With respect to writing and implementing the IEP, teachers have several responsibilities. As a member of an IEP committee, the regular classroom teacher provides important information because the plan must be based on a clear and accurate documentation of the present level of educational functioning. This includes identification of a student's deficits and weaknesses, as well as the student's strengths.

Another teacher responsibility is setting short- and long-term learning targets and specifying the criteria and evaluation procedures that will be used to monitor progress toward meeting the targets (McLoughlin & Lewis, 2005). Here, it is important to set truly *individualized* targets. Every student needs a customized set of realistic targets that takes into account identified strengths and weaknesses and preferred learning modes and styles. Appropriately delineated evaluation criteria and procedures need to reflect the degree of difficulty in the tasks, the variety of methods that should be employed, and a reasonable timetable.

Finally, teachers are responsible for ensuring that the student will participate in regular classroom activities to the maximum extent possible. This includes both formal and informal classroom assessments. Here, your understanding of what is required with each type of assessment and your knowledge of the specific disabilities of the students are used to ensure that, whenever possible, assessment procedures are not modified.

Assessing Students for Identification

The steps leading to identifying a student as having one or more of the disabilities that qualifies him or her to receive special education services are summarized in Figure 12.1. Identification must adhere to legal requirements and include a multidisciplinary evaluation (MDA) conducted by a multidisciplinary team (MTD; Salvia & Ysseldyke, 2001).

Under IDEA 2004, evaluating a student with a suspected disability must be made by a multidisciplinary team that includes at least one teacher or specialist with knowledge in the area of the suspected disability.

The multidisciplinary team often consists of:

- General education teacher
- Special education teacher
- School psychologist
- Speech and language specialist
- Parents
- Medical personnel whenever appropriate

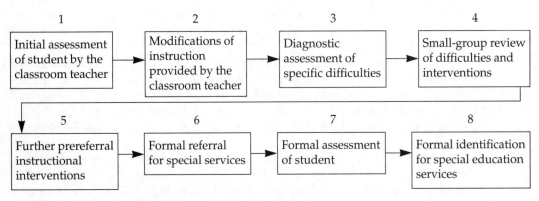

FIGURE 12.1   Steps for Identifying Students for Special Education Services

- Social worker
- School/guidance counselor
- School nurses
- Occupational and/or physical therapists

To examine your role in this process, as related to assessment, we consider two major categories of steps: those done before identification and the actual identification of various disabilities.

Initially, students are observed and evaluated by the classroom teacher, who then tries intervention strategies to see if these changes are sufficient for improving student performance. In effect, you need to be certain that relatively simple changes in teaching methods or materials are not sufficient to improve the student's performance.

If the student continues to have difficulties after you make these instructional interventions, the next step is to more closely analyze the student's ability to perform as expected. This usually includes the diagnostic assessment of specific learning difficulties or deficits using routine, teacher-made assessments. An analysis of errors may pinpoint these difficulties and suggest specific remediation strategies.

Some schools have a formal process of prereferral review for students with continuing difficulties. This may be called the *prereferral committee,* the *child study team,* or the *student assistance team.* The purpose of this group is to provide an external review of your tentative diagnosis and feedback concerning instructional interventions that have been tried. Sometimes members of the committee observe the student in class or conduct individual assessments. Often the committee will recommend additional interventions that may effectively address the problem, or a specific plan will be developed. In the event that the student still struggles, a comprehensive educational assessment is completed.

As a prereferral approach, RTI was proposed by IDEA 2004 and has been used at different levels prior to a referral for special education services. The focus of RTI is to identify students who are experiencing academic and/or behavioral difficulties early in their school life and to provide effective interventions before they fall further behind. RTI is also referred to as *tiered instruction* because of its different levels of intervention. Emerging from prereferral intervention models, the problem-solving approach of RTI requires teamwork of teachers and other school personnel that are formed to identify strategies for adapting instruction and/or the classroom environment to increase the success of students who had academic or behavioral difficulties, prior to referring the student for special education evaluation (Fuchs, Mock, Morgan & Young, 2003; Graner, Fagella-Luby, & Fritschmann, 2005).

Most school districts that are using RTI have implemented a three-tier intervention process. Tier 1 refers to high-quality instructional and behavioral supports for all children in general education settings by measuring the rate of academic growth of all students in comparison to other classes in the school or district or nation. Curriculum-based measurement (CBM) would be used to determine the overall achievement level and growth in achievement for the classroom of the struggling student. When students' rate of progress and performance lag behind those of their grade-level peers, these students will receive more specialized prevention or remediation at the Tier 2 level. Interventions at Tier 2 are still provided within general education settings. If students are not making satisfactory performance with the more intensive, specialized intervention, they will be moved to the Tier 3 level, which is an even more individualized intervention, but not yet special education and related services. This intervention level could occur within general education curriculum but also in a setting outside the classroom that is more appropriate for individualized instruction.

The continuous monitoring of progress (often weekly), measuring how adequately students respond to an intervention, is particularly important in an RTI model. Instead of a fixed period of time for a student staying in a specific tier level, most programs use the rate of progress as a means of determining whether a student should move from one tier to the next. For example, in moving a student from Tier 2 to Tier 3, instead of a 15-week fixed schedule, the student may be moved to a Tier 3 intervention after the ongoing documentation shows consistent nonresponsiveness of the student to a scientific, research-based intervention. After Tier 3, the nonresponsiveness could be cause to suspect that a student has a disability and should be referred for a comprehensive special education evaluation.

Formal referral is a serious step, because it suggests that the student may be eligible for special education services. Consequently, you will need to have specific documentation of the learning or behavior difficulties, interventions that have been tried, and the results of these interventions. It would be inadequate to simply say, for example, "Derek is always causing trouble in class. He likes to bother other students by poking and provoking them. We have tried several different approaches with Derek, each with limited success. He has a lot of trouble with mathematics." Rather, the information needs to be specific. For example:

> Derek physically touched, hit, or poked other students an average of 15 times per day in a way that disturbed or bothered the students. He talks without raising his hand in class discussions 75% of the time. Time out, individual contracts, and sessions with the counselor have been used with limited success that soon dissipates. Derek has turned in homework only 20% of the time. In class, he is unable to complete mathematics assignments that deal with the addition and subtraction of complex fractions. He is off task with mathematics assignments 50% of the time.

A screening committee will review the written referral, and the student's parents will be contacted. Suggestions for additional instructional interventions may be made. If the committee concludes that a formal assessment is needed, parental permission is secured, and a comprehensive evaluation begins. This process includes the assessment of all areas of suspected disability, which is administered and interpreted by specialists in different areas (e.g., a school psychologist to administer intelligence, personality, and projective tests; a physical therapist to evaluate gross motor skills; and an audiologist to evaluate hearing acuity).

Students are tested by a variety of methods, which may include additional informal observation by the regular classroom teacher. In any event, identification is confirmed when classroom teacher evaluations and those of the specialists coincide.

Following formal assessment, the student may be identified as having one or more specific educational disabilities. IDEA includes 13 classifications of disabilities (autism, deafness, deaf-blindness, emotional disturbance, hearing impairment, mental retardation, multiple disabilities, orthopedic impairment, other health impairment, specific learning disability, speech or language impairment, traumatic brain injury, and visual impairment). Each of the disabling conditions is confirmed by applying specific criteria. We will review the assessment criteria and implications of several common mild learning deficits because students with these deficits are the ones most likely to be included in general education classes.

Mild Mental Retardation.   Students are identified as having **mental retardation** on the basis of low scores on a standardized intelligence test and consistent deficits of what are termed *adaptive behaviors* that adversely affect educational performance for their age and/or grade. **Adaptive behaviors** are those that are needed for normal functioning in daily living situations, for example, expressive and receptive communication, daily living skills such as personal hygiene and eating habits, coping skills, and motor skills. The severity of the retardation is indicated in degrees: severe, moderate, and mild.

Although school psychologists will take care of the IQ testing, it may be up to you to provide much of the information regarding adaptive behaviors. Often, you accomplish this with the help of established adaptive behavior scales, such as the Vineland Adaptive Behavior Scale, the Adaptive Behavior Scale, and the Adaptive Behavior Inventory for Children. Teachers, as well as primary caregivers, are interviewed with these types of instruments to document the student's behavioral competence. In addition, it is important for you to confirm findings from these instruments with more informal observations.

You need to keep two cautions in mind when assessing adaptive behavior. First, no single adaptive behavior instrument covers all areas of behavior, and the data for these instruments are gathered from third-party observers. Thus, it is important to select the instrument that will provide the most valid inferences for the situation and to keep in mind that third parties may be biased. Second, you need to be careful that a student's cultural or linguistic background does not cause the student to be inappropriately labeled as having inadequate adaptive behavior. Some students who are perfectly capable of functioning in their day-to-day living environments may have difficulty functioning in the classroom because of the cultural or language differences. Thus, adaptive behavior is best evaluated relative to the context in which it occurs (Witt, Elliot, Daly, Gresham, & Kramer, 1998).

Sensory Impairment.   Students who have vision, hearing, or speech deficits may be identified as sensory impaired. This could include a communication disorder, such as stuttering or impaired articulation; visual difficulties, even with correction, including eye–hand coordination; or a hearing problem that interferes with educational performance. One of the first things you should do with students experiencing difficulty in learning is to check for visual and hearing acuity. Obviously, students who have trouble seeing or hearing will have trouble academically. Your close and careful observation of students will provide clues to these types of impairments.

Physical Impairment.   Other physical disabilities are not sensory, such as an orthopedic impairment (cerebral palsy, amputations) or a physical illness such as epilepsy, diabetes, or muscular dystrophy. Generally, these conditions will be obvious, and resources will be provided to make appropriate accommodations.

Learning Disability.   The IDEA definition of specific learning disability (SLD) has remained constant:

> "Specific learning disability" means a disorder in one or more of the basic psychological processes involved in understanding or using language, spoken or written, which may manifest itself in an imperfect ability to listen, think, speak, read, write, spell, or to do mathematical calculations. (*Federal Register,* 1977, p. 65, 083)

The 2004 reauthorization of IDEA did not change this definition. The student with an average or above-average intelligence who nonetheless has difficulties with academic tasks still must have a disorder that manifests itself in an imperfect ability to listen, think, or speak. The real problem is how to operationalize this definition, that is, how "imperfect" must the student's ability be to be identified as having an SLD? For the past three decades before the IDEA of 2004, a discrepancy approach was applied to answer this question. Under the discrepancy model, a severe discrepancy that is statistically significant between the student's ability and performance must be demonstrated to qualify for SLD. This approach was criticized because of the fact that an IQ-achievement discrepancy cannot be reliably assessed until a student enters the third grade (Shaywitz, Fletcher, Holahan, & Shaywitz, 1992; Stuebing et al., 2002). In other words, educators had to wait for the student to fail before they could reliably detect a specific learning disability.

In response to this criticism, the IDEA 2004 no longer requires the use of discrepancy models for determining SLD (Harris-Murri, King, & Rostenberg, 2006). As an alternative approach, the RTI model was proposed to determine eligibility for special education services. One of the fundamental differences between the RTI and the discrepancy model is in early intervention. Unlike the discrepancy model, which is primarily an assessment system for eligibility requirement, RTI is an intervention delivery system that is provided for all students (Burke, 2006). Instead of looking for within-child deficits as evidence of a disability, RTI targets a broader and more contextual analysis by considering day-to-day interpersonal and institutional factors that may affect student achievement and behavior (Harris-Murri et al., 2006).

Emotional Disturbance.   Also called an *emotional disability* or a *behavioral disorder,* a student identified with **emotional disturbance** consistently exhibits one or more of the following characteristics to a marked degree that clearly interferes with learning: poor academic performance not due to other disabilities; poor interpersonal relationships; inappropriate behaviors or feelings in normal circumstances; unhappiness, melancholy, or depression; or unfounded physical symptoms or fears associated with school or personal problems.

You will need to make systematic observations of a student who may be classified under the category of emotional disturbance. This could include, for example, noting each time the student displays inappropriate behavior, such as crying or yelling, in normal circumstances for no apparent reason. When the inappropriate behavior continues for an extended time, under different conditions, a serious emotional problem may be found. However, final diagnosis will require consultation with a specialist, such as a counselor or school psychologist.

Attention Deficits.   Students with attention deficits have difficulty focusing and staying focused. When inattention is sustained (for 6 months) in different environments and is inconsistent with age-appropriate behavior of the student, one of two disorders is identified: **attention deficit disorder (ADD)** or **attention deficit hyperactivity disorder (ADHD)**. Because ADHD was not listed as a separate disability category under IDEA, a student with ADHD could quality for special education services under "other health impairments (OHI)" of IDEA. In cases when a student with ADHD does not meet the eligibility requirements under OHI category, or who does not have a coexisting disability (e.g., learning disability and attention deficit) that would qualify them for services under IDEA, the student may still qualify under Section 504 of the Vocational Rehabilitation Act of 1973. One essential difference between IDEA and Section 504 is that IDEA emphasizes the educational benefits, whereas Section 504 focuses on accessibility. Therefore, for a student with ADHD to qualify for special education services, it must be documented that the condition (ADHD) has an adverse effect on his or her educational performance. To qualify for special services under Section 504, it must be documented that the condition limits the student's learning substantially, thus the student's access to learning opportunities as well (Mastropieri & Scruggs, 2007).

Students with these disorders are often unable to sustain attention, are easily distracted, have difficulties organizing, make careless mistakes, tend to lose things, and may be forgetful (McLoughlin & Lewis, 2005). Although standardized instruments are used to confirm the presence of these disorders, teacher observations are critical.

Hyperactivity.   Students who fidget excessively, have difficulty sitting, appear restless, and are constantly "on the go" may be identified as **hyperactive**. A related disability, **impulsivity**, occurs when a student has difficulty waiting in turn, "blurts" out answers, and constantly interrupts others. As with attention deficits, hyperactivity must be present for a sustained time, typically 6 months, and must interfere to a significant extent with the ability of the student to learn and demonstrate what he or she understands.

TABLE 12.1 Classroom Teacher's Role in the Assessment Process

Steps in the Assessment Process	Regular Classroom Teacher's Role
Before referral	Use informal assessment methods to monitor daily progress, curriculum-based assessment, and behavioral observations; consult with committee members
	Implement educational interventions
Diagnosis of specific disability	Recognize behaviors and characteristics of specific disabilities so that students can be identified, evaluated, and served if appropriate
	Recognize behaviors and characteristics that indicate cultural or linguistic differences and that do not warrant special education services
Referral	Document educational strengths and weaknesses through data collection of student work samples, behavioral observations, teacher-made tests, and other informal measures
	Consult with committee members
	Consult with parents
	Complete necessary referral forms
	Attend child study committee meeting and present appropriate data collected on student progress and behaviors
	Participate during development and implementation of identification and IEP for students in the regular class setting

Source: Adapted from Wood, J., *Adapting instruction to accommodate students in inclusive settings,* 4th edition, copyright © 2002, p. 36. Adapted by permission of Pearson Education, Inc., Upper Saddle River, New Jersey.

Tables 12.1 and 12.2 summarize the teacher's role in the assessment and identification processes. Table 12.1 summarizes responsibilities for different steps in the assessment process, and Table 12.2 shows a teacher's responsibilities for identification in major categories. Generally, your observations of the student will be used to corroborate the specialists' findings.

Assessment Problems Encountered by Students with Special Needs

Your goal in assessing student learning is to obtain a fair and accurate indication of performance. Because disabilities may affect test-taking ability, you will need to make accommodations, or changes, in assessments when needed to ensure valid inferences and consequences. There are many justifiable ways to alter assessments

TABLE 12.2   Classroom Teacher's Role in the Identification Process

Disability	Teacher's Role	Questions
Mild mental retardation	Document adaptive behaviors; meet with child study committee	How well does the student function with daily life skills? Do deficits in daily living skills affect academic performance? Does cultural or linguistic background contribute to deficits in daily living skills?
Sensory impairment	Document visual, auditory, or speech impairments; meet with child study committee	Can the student see well enough? Is there adequate eye/hand coordination? Is there a problem with the student's hearing? Is there a speech problem of some kind?
Physical disability	Observe effect of disability on academic performance; meet with the child study committee	Does the disability adversely affect academic performance?
Learning disability	Document learning problems and achievement; interpret information in the cumulative folder; meet with the child study committee	Is the student responding to a scientific-based instruction/intervention? Is the student's nonresponsiveness related to environmental factors, cultural situation, or language proficiency?
Emotional disturbance	Document inappropriate behaviors and feelings; meet with child study committee	Does the student have average or above-average intelligence? Is the behavior extreme for the circumstances? Is the behavior fleeting or consistent? Are any other disabilities responsible for the poor performance? How well does the student interact with others? Is the student unhappy, depressed, or withdrawn much of the time?
Attention deficit	Observe and record instances of failing to pay attention	Does the student repeatedly, in many circumstances, demonstrate significant inattention? Is the student easily distracted? Does the student make careless mistakes?
Hyperactivity	Observe and record instances of inappropriate hyperactivity	Is the student constantly restless? Does the student fidget excessively? Is the student always on the go or "wired"?

TABLE 12.3 **Problems Encountered by Students with Special Needs That Impact Classroom Assessment**

Problem	Impact on Assessment
Comprehension difficulties	Understanding directions; completing assessments requiring reasoning skills
Auditory difficulties	Understanding oral directions and test items; distracted by noises
Visual difficulties	Understanding written directions and test items; decoding symbols and letters; visual distractions
Time constraint difficulties	Completing assessments
Anxiety	Completing assessments; providing correct information
Embarrassment	Understanding directions; completing assessments
Variability of behavior	Completing assessments; demonstrating best work

for students with special needs. Before we consider these, it will be helpful to review the problems encountered by students with disabilities in testing situations. These difficulties are summarized in Table 12.3.

Comprehension Difficulties

Many students with mild disabilities have difficulty with comprehension. This means that they may not understand verbal or written directions very well. If there is a sequence of steps in the directions, they may not be able to remember the sequence or all the steps, particularly if the directions are verbal. Lengthy written directions may be too complicated, and the reading level may be too high. There may be words or phrases that the student does not understand. If the directions include several different operations, the student may be confused about what to do. Obviously, without a clear understanding of how to proceed, it will be difficult for these students to demonstrate their knowledge or skills.

Students with mild disabilities have even more difficulty understanding directions or test items that require reasoning skills. These students may respond well to knowledge and understanding questions and deal well with concrete ideas, but they may not respond very well to abstractions. For example, it would be relatively easy for such students to respond to a straightforward short-answer question such as, "What are the characteristics of a democratic government?" but much harder to respond to a more abstract question such as "How is the government of the United States different from a socialist government?"

Auditory Difficulties

Students with auditory disabilities have trouble processing information they hear quickly and accurately. This makes it especially hard for these students to follow and understand verbal directions.

These students may also be sensitive to auditory distractions in the classroom. This could include sound from the hallway or an adjoining classroom, talking among students, outside noise, desk movement, pencil sharpening, questions asked by students, teacher reprimands, school announcements, and so on. Although these sounds may seem "normal" and do not bother most students, those with auditory disabilities will be distracted, and their attention will be diverted from the task at hand.

Visual Difficulties

Students with visual disabilities have difficulty processing what they see. These students may copy homework assignments or test questions from the board incorrectly by transposing numbers or interchanging letters. Often the student has difficulty transferring information to paper. A cluttered board that requires visual discrimination may also cause problems. Visual disabilities also become a handicap on some handwritten tests if the test is not legible and clearly organized. Some students with a visual disability have difficulty decoding certain symbols, letters, and abbreviations, such as $+$, $-$, b and d, $<$ and $>$, and n and m. One symbol may be confused with another, and test problems with many symbols may take a long time for these students to understand.

Some types of objective test items are a problem because of visual perceptual difficulties. For example, lengthy matching items pose particular problems because the student may take a long time to peruse the columns, searching for answers and identifying the correct letters to use. Multiple-choice items that run responses together on the same line make it hard to discriminate among the possible answers.

Visual distractions can also interfere with test taking. For some students, a single visual cue—such as students moving in the classroom when getting up to turn in papers, student gestures, teacher motions, or something or someone outside—disrupts their present visual focus and makes it difficult to keep their concentration.

Time Constraint Difficulties

Time can pose a major problem for many students with disabilities. Frequently visual, auditory, motor coordination, and reading difficulties make it hard for some students to complete tests in the same time frame as other students. Thus, students should not be penalized for being unable to complete a test, especially timed tests that are constructed to reward speed in decoding and understanding questions and writing answers.

Anxiety

Although most students experience some degree of anxiety when completing tests, students with disabilities may be especially affected by feelings of anxiety because they fear that their disability will make it difficult to complete the test. Some students are simply unable to function very well in a traditional test setting because the length or format of the test overwhelms them.

One general strategy to reduce unhealthy anxiety is to make sure that students have learned appropriate test-taking skills. They need to know what to do if they do not fully understand the directions and how to proceed in answering different types of items (e.g., looking for clue words in multiple-choice, true/false, and completion items; crossing out incorrect alternatives in multiple-choice items; crossing out answers used in matching items). They also need to know to skip difficult items and come back to them when they have answered all other questions.

Embarrassment

Students with disabilities may be more sensitive than other students to feelings of embarrassment. They often want to hide or disguise their problems so that they are not singled out or labeled by their peers. As a result, they may want to appear to be "normal" when taking a test by not asking questions about directions and handing in the test at the same time as other students do, whether or not they are finished. They don't want to risk embarrassment by being the only one to have a question or by being the last one to complete their work. Students with special needs may also be embarrassed if they take a different test than others.

Variability of Behavior

The behavior of students with disabilities varies greatly. This means that their disabilities may affect their behavior one day and not the next, and it may be difficult to predict this variability. This is especially true for students with emotional disturbances. For example, a student with a conduct disorder may be very disruptive one day and seem normal the next. Consequently, you will need to be tolerant and flexible in your assessments, realizing that on a particular day the disability may pose extreme difficulties for the student.

Assessment Accommodations

Once you understand how disabilities can interfere with valid assessment, you can take steps to adapt the test or other assessment to accommodate the disability. Thurlow, Lazarus, Thompson, and Morse (2005) reported that all states most commonly allowed accommodations in the areas of presentations, equipment/materials, response, scheduling and timing, and setting. These accommodations can be grouped into three major categories: adaptations in test construction, test administration, and testing site (Wood, 2002).

Adaptations in Test Directions, Construction, and Format

The first component to adapt is the test directions. You can do this for all students, or you can provide a separate set of directions for students with disabilities. Here are some ways to modify test directions:

1. Read written directions aloud, slowly, and give students ample opportunity to ask questions about the directions. Reread directions for each page of questions.
2. Keep directions short and simple.
3. Give examples of how to answer questions.
4. Focus attention by underlining verbs.
5. Provide separate directions for each section of the test.
6. Provide one direction for each sentence (list sentences vertically).
7. Check the students' understanding of the directions.
8. During the test, check student answers to be sure that the students understand the directions.
9. When reading is not the testing purpose, adjust the reading level of the items, or provide assistance with reading if necessary (Mastropieri & Scruggs, 2007).

The general format of the test should be designed to simplify the amount of information that is processed at one time. Accomplish this by leaving plenty of

Teacher's Corner
Susan Pereira
National Board Certified Elementary Teacher

It is critical that the regular education teacher work in collaboration with the special education teacher when assessing children with special needs. The regular education teacher should communicate to the special education teacher the objective or standard that is to be evaluated and, collectively, develop a tool to measure appropriately. Sometimes an evaluation can be used with just a few minor accommodations, perhaps giving the evaluation in a one-on-one settings or asking just a few questions at a time. In order to determine the most effective and appropriate assessment tool, the teacher must look at the child as an individual, keeping in mind the goals and accommodations set forth in their Individualized Education Plan.

white space on each page so that students are not overwhelmed. The printing should be large, with adequate space between items; this results in a smaller number of items per page. The test should be separated into clearly distinguished short sections, and only one type of question should be on each page. The printing should be dark and clear. If bubble sheets are used for objective items, use larger bubbles. Be sure multiple-choice items list the alternatives vertically, and do not run questions or answers across two pages. Number each page of the test. Some students may be aided by a large sheet of construction paper that they can place below the question or cut out to allow a greater focus on a particular section of the test. If possible, design the format of an adapted test to look as much like the test for other students as possible (Salend, 2009).

Other accommodations to the format of the test depend on the type of item, as illustrated in the following examples.

Short-Answer and Essay Items.   Students with disabilities may have extreme difficulty with short-answer items because of the organization, reasoning, and writing skills required. For these reasons, complicated essay questions requiring long responses should be avoided. If you use an essay question, be sure students understand terms such as *compare, contrast,* and *discuss.* To help students better understand your expectations, it is important to define command words and provide examples to demonstrate what you expect for the test items. See Table 12.4 for command words on test items and their definitions. Use a limited number of essay questions, and allow students to use outlines for their answers. Some students may need to record their answer rather than writing it; all students will need to have sufficient time.

TABLE 12.4   **Command Words and Definitions**

Word	Definition
Discuss	Give reasons to support different points of view.
Describe	Give an overall impression of an event or person with examples.
Compare	Show how two or more things are similar with examples of common characteristics.
Contrast	Show how two or more things are different with examples of different characteristics.
Explain	Clarify or simplify with the rationale behind.
Justify	Argue in favor of.
Critique	Argue in opposition of.
List	Give a simple list of elements.
Outline	Organize a list of elements into a system.

Source: Adapted from *The inclusive classroom: Strategies for effective instruction,* by M. A. Mastropieri & T. E. Scruggs, 2007.

Examples

> *Poor:* Compare and contrast the Canadian and U.S. governments.
>
> *Improved:* *Compare* and *contrast* the Canadian and U.S. governments.
>
> I. *Compare* by telling how the governments are *alike*. Give two examples.
> II. *Contrast* by telling how the governments are *different*. Give two examples.

If the short-answer question focuses on recall, you can adapt it in ways that will help students to organize their thoughts and not be overwhelmed.

Example (adapted from *Creating a Learning Community at Fowler High School,* 1993)

> *Poor:*
>
> Directions: On your own paper, identify the following quotations. Tell (1) who said it, (2) to whom it was said or if it was a soliloquy, (3) when it was said, and (4) what it means.
>
> But soft, what light through yonder window breaks?
> It is the east, and Juliet is the sun.
> Arise, fair sun, and kill the envious moon.
> (Include a series of several more quotes.)
>
> *Improved:*
>
> Directions: In the space provided, identify the following for each quotation.
>
> Tell 1. Who said it
> 2. To whom it was said or if it was a soliloquy
> 3. When it was said
> 4. What it means

Who said it; to whom it was said	*When it was said*
Juliet	When Tybalt kills Mercutio
Romeo	When Juliet waits for news from Romeo
Paris	The balcony scene
Mercutio	When Paris discusses his marriage with Friar
The Prince	

1. But soft, what light through yonder window breaks?
It is the east, and Juliet is the sun.
Arise, fair sun, and kill the envious moon.

Who said it	*To whom*	*When*	*What it means*
_____	_____	_____	_____
_____	_____	_____	_____
_____	_____	_____	_____

Multiple-Choice Items.   If the test contains multiple-choice questions, have students circle the correct answer rather than writing the letter of the correct response next to the item or transferring the answer to a separate sheet. Arrange response alternatives vertically, and include no more than four alternatives for each question. Keep the language simple and concise, and avoid wording such as "a and b but not d," or "either a or c," or "none of the above" that weights the item more heavily for reasoning skills. Limit the number of multiple-choice items, and give students with disabilities plenty of time to complete the test. Other students may easily be able to answer one item per minute, but it will take exceptional students longer. Basically, you need to follow the suggestions listed in Chapter 7 and realize that poorly constructed and formatted items are likely to be more detrimental to students with disabilities.

Binary-Choice Items.   True/false and other binary-choice items need to be stated clearly and concisely. Answers should be circled. Negatively stated items should be avoided. Students could be confused when asked to choose "false" to a negative statement, for example, "The office of president is not described in the Constitution" (Salend, 1995). Sometimes students are asked to change false items to make them true, but this is not recommended for students with disabilities. Limit the number of items to 10 to 15.

Completion Items.   These items can be modified to reduce the student's dependence on structured recall by providing word banks that accompany the items.

Teacher's Corner
Andrea Ferment
National Board Certified Elementary Teacher

In general our special needs students who are mainstreamed into the regular classroom complete the same assessments as our regular education students do. However, they are offered multiple accommodations and tools to assist with the completion of assessments. Actually, I make most of these available to all of my students who may benefit from them. These include things like using such aids as highlighters, reading rulers, and colored pencils. I have "flip folders" that students can place a test in and then flip back a strip of the folder to reveal only some of the questions on a test at a time. Students may read aloud to themselves as they test, or if allowed by their IEP, may have the test read to them. They may use cardboard study carrels to help block out other students. Sometimes the special education teacher will "reformat" a test to make it more accessible to special needs students by increasing font size, or limiting the number of items on a page, or by providing a word bank.

The word bank is a list of possible answers that reduces dependence on memory. The list can be printed on a separate sheet of paper so that the student can move it up and down on the right side of the page. Also, provide large blanks for students with motor control difficulties.

Performance Assessments.   Performance assessment is an effective way of measuring all students' deep understanding of academic content such as language, science, math, social studies, music, art, vocational education, and physical education. Performance assessment is especially helpful when testing students who may have word-finding (retrieval) problems, communication disorders, or other skills that limit their verbal communication (Mastropieri & Scruggs, 2007). The first accommodation to performance assessments may need to be in the directions. Students with disabilities need directions that clearly specify what is expected, with examples, and a reasonable time frame. Because these assessments involve thinking and application skills, it is important to be certain that students with disabilities are able to perform the skills required. The steps may need to be clearly delineated.

First, determine exactly what you want your students to be able to do after the instructional unit. Then, include it in the learning objective. After that, set up the materials and provide opportunities for students to perform on the test. Finally, score students' performance by using a scoring rubric that clearly lists test items and scoring criteria (Mastropieri & Scruggs, 2007).

For example,

Draw a picture of an ecosystem. Label all parts.

Score	Scoring Criteria
3	Picture with living and nonliving things that appear to interact in some general way. Living and nonliving things labeled.
2	Picture of living and nonliving things not labeled, or labeled living things, or labeled nonliving things.
1	One of the above or general relevant comment.
0	Nothing relevant.

(Adapted from Mastropieri & Scruggs, 2007).

To score this test item objectively, the scoring rubric needs to be developed with clear and specific criteria:

Obviously, if some aspect of the performance requires physical skills or coordination that the disability prevents or makes difficult, assistance will need to be provided. If the performance requires group participation, you will need to closely monitor the interactions.

Portfolios.   In some ways, this type of assessment is ideal for students with disabilities because the assignments and products can be individualized to show progress. This means that you may need to adapt the portfolio requirements to fit well with what the student is capable of doing. In the portfolio you could include your reflection of how the student made progress despite the presence of the disability to demonstrate how the student was responsible for success.

Portfolio assessment may lack standardization and objectivity; therefore teachers need to ensure that grades or judgments based on portfolio products are reliable and valid (Gelfer, Xu, & Perkins, 2004; Mastropieri & Scruggs, 2007). The following strategies can help reliability and validity of a portfolio assessment.

1. Use multiple measures of the same skills or products.
2. Have multiple individuals independently assess portfolio products.
3. Make comparisons with more traditional measures (e.g., standardized tests, criterion-referenced measurement, or direct observation).

Adaptations in Test Administration

Adaptations during test administration involve changes in procedures that lessen the negative effect of disabilities while the student is taking the test. Most of these procedural accommodations depend on the nature of the disability or difficulty, as summarized in Table 12.5, and are based on common sense. For example, if the student has a visual problem, you need to give directions orally and check carefully to determine whether he or she has understood the questions. For students who are hindered by time constraints, provide breaks and make sure they have sufficient time to complete the test. It may be best to divide a long test into sections and spread the testing over several days, though unlimited time to complete tests should be avoided. A good rule of thumb is to provide students with disabilities 50% additional time to complete a test (Reynolds, Livingston, & Willson, 2006).

In general, it is best to place a Testing—Do Not Disturb sign on your classroom door to discourage visitors and other distractions. You will need to monitor these students closely as they take the test and encourage them to ask questions. It is also helpful to encourage them to use dark paper to underline the items they are currently working on (Lazzari & Wood, 1994).

Adaptations in Testing Site

You may find it necessary to allow students with special needs to take the test in a different location than the regular classroom. This alternative test site is often the resource room in the school or some other room that is quiet with fewer distractions. As long as someone can monitor the testing, the student will have more opportunities to ask questions and feel less embarrassed when asking for clarification or further explanation.

If you are unsure about how you should accommodate students with special needs, check with the special education teacher in your school. This individual can help you more fully understand the strengths and limitations of each student, as well as the appropriateness of specific adaptations.

TABLE 12.5 Adaptations in Test Administration

Disability or Problem	Adaptations
Poor comprehension	1. Give test directions both orally and in writing. 2. Double-check student understanding. 3. Avoid long talks before the test. 4. Allow students to tape-record responses to essay questions or the entire test. 5. Correct open-ended responses for content only and not for spelling or grammar. 6. Provide examples of expected correct responses. 7. Remind students to check for unanswered questions. 8. Allow the use of multiplication tables or calculators for math tests. 9. Read the test aloud for students with reading comprehension difficulties. 10. Give an outline for essay question responses. 11. Give students an audio recording of instructions and questions. 12. Use objective items.
Auditory difficulties	1. Use written rather than oral questions. 2. Go slowly for oral tests, enunciating and sounding out distinctly. 3. Seat students in a quiet place for testing. 4. Stress the importance of being quiet to all students.
Visual difficulties	1. Give directions orally as well as in writing. 2. Give exam orally or tape-recorded on audiocassette. 3. Allow students to take the test orally. 4. Seat the student away from visual distractions (e.g., windows and doors). Use a carrel or place desk facing wall. 5. Avoid having other students turn in papers during the test. 6. Meet classroom visitors at the door and talk in the hallway.
Time constraint difficulties	1. Allow more than enough time to complete the test. 2. Provide breaks during lengthy tests. 3. Give half the test one day, half the second day. 4. Avoid timed tests. 5. Give students with slow writing skills oral or tape-recorded tests.
Anxiety	1. Avoid adding pressure by admonishing students to "Hurry and get finished" or by saying "This test will determine your final grade." 2. Do not threaten to use test results to punish students. 3. Do not threaten to use tests to punish students for poor behavior. 4. Give a practice test or practice items. 5. Allow students to retest if needed. 6. Do not threaten dire consequences if students do not do well. 7. Emphasize internal attributions for previous work. 8. Avoid having a few major tests; give many smaller tests. 9. Avoid norm-referenced testing; use criterion-referenced tests.
Embarrassment	1. Make the modified test closely resemble the regular test; use the same cover sheet. 2. Avoid calling attention to mainstreamed students as you help them. 3. Monitor all students the same way. 4. Do not give mainstreamed students special attention when handing out the test. 5. Confer with students privately to work out accommodations for testing. 6. Do not single out mainstreamed students when returning tests.
Variability of behavior	1. Allow retesting. 2. Allow student to reschedule testing for another day. 3. Monitor closely to determine if behavior is preventing best work.

Source: Adapted from Wood, J., *Adapting instruction to accommodate students in inclusive settings,* 4th edition, copyright © 2002, pp. 567–569. Adapted by permission of Pearson Education, Inc., Upper Saddle River, New Jersey.

Case Study
for Reflection

Mike, an eighth grader with specific learning disability (SLD), received most of his education in general education settings. Mr. Jones was a special education teacher who saw Mike in his middle-class resource room for 45 minutes every day. Although much of the time was devoted to basic skills development, Mr. Jones also allocated time to helping Mike prepare for upcoming tests. Mike had particular difficulty taking tests in his U.S. Constitution and government class, and Mr. Jones also was having difficulty helping him. For 2 days before the test he would work with Mike by reviewing the content and creating practice questions for Mike to answer. However, it seemed that no matter how well prepared Mike appeared to be, he did poorly on the test.

Mr. Jones made appointment to speak to Mike's social studies teacher, Ms. Young. Ms. Young acknowledged that Mike was not doing well on the tests and expressed a willingness to help solve the problem. Mr. Jones and Ms. Young examined the tests together, and Mr. Jones noted that he believed Mike did know the answers to several of the questions that he had answered incorrectly. It appeared that Mike was more likely to answer questions incorrectly when the items contained double negatives, contained potentially confusing options such as "(e) all of the above except (b)," or when the test called for matching two columns of information. Mr. Jones agreed to provide Mike with practice on test-taking skills and to provide practice tests that more closely resembled Ms. Young's tests. Ms. Young agreed to make modifications in her test to make the individual items more understandable. She also asked her class to provide her with some sample items that they thought should be on the test.

With training in test-taking skills and test modifications. Mike's scores increased from an average of D to an average of C. In addition, Ms. Young found that the average score of her entire class seemed to improve.

QUESTIONS FOR REFLECTION

1. If test scores improve, how could you know if your modified tests are more easily understandable, or simply easier?
2. What kind of students would you expect to benefit most from test modifications?
3. How would you determine what aspects of your tests need revision?

Adapted from *The inclusive classroom: Strategies for effective instruction*, by M. A. Mastropieri & T. E. Scruggs, 2007.

Grading and Reporting Accommodations

The purpose of grading is to provide an accurate indication of what students have learned. For students with special needs in inclusive settings, it is necessary to consider some adaptations to the grading procedures used for all students to make sure that student disabilities do not unduly influence the determination of the grade. This may present a dilemma for teachers. On the one hand, is it fair to use different grading standards and procedures for some students? On the other hand, is it fair to possibly penalize students by forcing an existing grading scheme on them that may have detrimental impacts? The ideal solution would be to keep the grading system for students with special needs the same as that used for other students and be sure that appropriate accommodations have been made in the assessment strategies to ensure that the information on which the grade is determined is not adversely affected by the disability. However, depending on the student's IEP, it may be necessary to adapt the grading system that is used.

Grading Accommodations

Several types of grading accommodations are appropriate for students with special needs (Mehring, 1995). These include IEP grading, shared grading, and contract grading.

IEP Grading.   The IEP grading system bases grades on the achievement of the goals and objectives explicitly stated in the student's IEP. The criteria needed to obtain satisfactory progress are stated in the IEP. It is problematic, however, to translate success in reaching IEP objectives to grades. One approach is to use the school district's performance standards to determine grades. For example, if the student has performed at the 90% proficiency level, as required by the IEP to demonstrate competence, and 90% translates to a B letter grade, then the student is assigned a B for that assessment. Another approach is to review the criteria in the IEP and match levels of performance with what other students need to demonstrate for different grades. If you decide, for instance, that the level of mastery a student with special needs demonstrates by achieving but not exceeding all IEP objectives is about the same level as that demonstrated by other students receiving Cs, then the grade for the student with special needs would also be a C. If the student exceeds stated IEP objectives, then a B or A may be appropriate.

Because the goal of inclusion is to make the educational experience of students with disabilities like that of other students, it is best if the grading procedures reflect the same criteria. You should avoid a process whereby the grade is determined merely on the percentage of IEP objectives obtained, because there is a tendency to inadvertently set low or easier objectives to help students obtain good grades (Cohen, 1983).

Shared Grading.   In shared grading, the regular classroom and special education or resource room teachers determine the grade together. The weight that each teacher provides for the grade should be agreed on at the beginning of the marking period. This usually reflects the extent to which each teacher is responsible for different areas of learning. Typically, the classroom teacher will have the most influence on the grades.

One advantage of this type of grading is that the special education or resource room teacher may be able to provide some insight that helps explain some bad grades and other mitigating circumstances related to the student's disability. Using this team approach also helps the classroom teacher determine appropriate criteria and standards for grading.

Contracting.   A contract is a written agreement between the regular classroom teacher and the student that specifies the nature of the work that the student must complete to achieve a particular grade. Teachers frequently use contracts for students with special needs because they can integrate IEP objectives and clearly state for the student and parents the type and quality of work to be completed. For older students, the contract should include options for achieving different grades. Contracts for elementary-level students should be simpler, with more general outcomes at a single level, as illustrated in Figure 12.2. Several components should be included in a contract, such as:

- A description of the work to be completed
- A description of criteria by which work will be evaluated

FIGURE 12.2   Sample Contract for Elementary-Level Students

My Contract

If I . . .

- Take my belongings from my backpack and put them in my desk without being asked,
- Come to my reading group the first time it is called,
- Clean off my desk after snack and put all the garbage in the trash can,
- Raise my hand each time I want to answer, and
- Put all my finished papers in the "done" basket before lunch

. . . then I will receive a "plus" for the morning's work.

If I . . .

- Line up on the playground the first time the whistle is blown,
- Put all the classroom supplies back in the supply boxes after project time,
- Put all my finished papers in the "done" basket before I go home,
- Put my homework papers in my portfolio to take home, and
- Put my belongings in my backpack, get my coat from the cubby, and line up before my bus is called

. . . then I will receive a "plus" for the afternoon's work.

_____   _____
Student   Teacher

                        _____
                        Date

Source: Wood, J., *Adapting instruction to accommodate students in inclusive settings,* 4th edition, copyright © 2002, p. 597. Adapted by permission of Pearson Education, Inc., Upper Saddle River, New Jersey.

- Signatures of the student, teacher, and other involved parties
- A timeline for completion of the work

Reporting Accommodations

Regardless of the grading system that you use, it will probably be necessary to supplement the regular progress report with additional information. This is typically done as a checklist or a narrative summary that interprets achievement in light of the student's disability. A checklist is convenient for showing progress in developmentally sequenced courses and can easily integrate IEP with course objectives to give a more complete report. The checklist states the objectives, and the teacher indicates if each has been mastered or needs further work.

A narrative summary helps you to give the student a still more personalized evaluation. Although such a report takes some time, it more fully explains why the teacher believes the student demonstrated certain skills, which skills were not mastered, and which need special attention. The narrative can also be used to report on behavioral performance, emotions, and interpersonal skills, as well as academic performance. Specific incidents or examples can be described. The following is an example of a progress report for an eighth-grade student with a learning disability (Mehring, 1995). Notice that the teacher has indicated areas of improvement, accommodations (typing), and areas that will be stressed in the future.

> Alphonso has improved his ability to recognize and correct spelling errors. He has mastered the recognition and capitalization of proper nouns, names, titles, and buildings. He is not yet consistent in his capitalization of cities. Punctuation, especially the use of commas, is also an area in which Alphonso needs improvement. He has been using the computer to prepare drafts of his written products. This has made it easier for him to edit since his handwriting is laborious and illegible at times. The overall quality and length of his creative writings has improved significantly since the last reporting period. We will continue to focus on capitalization and punctuation throughout the next grading period. In addition, we will begin working on recognizing and correcting sentence problems (fragments, run-ons, unclear pronoun reference, and awkward sentences). (p. 17)

By focusing a supplemental progress report on the learning process, students will have a better idea about how they need to change to improve their performance. Students and parents need to know if a specific approach to learning needs to be modified or if something else needs to be further investigated.

Another way to report progress of students with disabilities is to graph the student's performance throughout the reported period. Graphs such as bar charts are considered one of the most effective and efficient ways to demonstrate students' learning because it includes the most information with the least explanation, and it is easy for everybody to understand. See Figure 12.3 as an example of using bar charts to illustrate a student's progress.

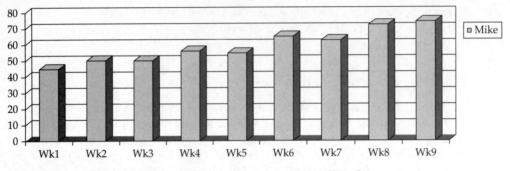

FIGURE 12.3   Mike's Reading Comprehension throughout 9 Weeks

English Language Learners in Inclusive Settings

English language learners (ELL) are the fastest-growing population in United States' public schools, now comprising almost 10% of the entire K–12 school population (Echevarria, Vogt, & Short, 2008). Research has demonstrated that it is best to use an inclusive model in which ELL students have an equal access to grade-level content while they are learning English as a second language (ESL) (Collier, 1989; Cummins, 1996). It typically takes 5 to 7 years for ELLs to demonstrate average grade-level performance in school settings. The earlier students are placed in general education classrooms, the sooner they will become fluent in English.

From a legal perspective, ELLs' right to receive adequate instruction was initiated by the *Lau v. Nicholas* (1974) case. More recently, the No Child Left Behind Act mandates that ELLs demonstrate grade-level content standards. ELLs are not exempted from state-level standardized tests measuring progress in content knowledge under this policy. This has significant implications for general education classroom teachers. They must become familiar with special instructional approaches for ELLs as well as techniques to adequately evaluate learning progress.

Factors Influencing ELL Assessments

Although a variety of factors affect ELLs' performance on assessments, three are most important: language and literacy skills, educational background, and culture (Durán, 2008; Educational Testing Service, 2009). We will look at each of these in greater detail.

Language and Literacy Skill Factors.   Assessments in courses other than English are heavily language dependent and language integrated, which makes it difficult to separate language and content knowledge. It is very likely that the difficulty of ELLs' English language skills will mask their content knowledge, which weakens the validity of the assessments.

English language proficiency is typically identified by ESL specialists through a state- or school district–mandated English language proficiency test and a home language survey. There is a wide range of ELLs' English language proficiency. Some students are nearly fluent, whereas others do not know the alphabet and basic sounds. It is also of note that students who communicate fairly well may struggle with academic English language presented in classes and in the grade-level texts. Furthermore, some ELLs' ability in speaking, listening, reading, and writing have not developed evenly. As a consequence, students who are seemingly fluent in listening and speaking may have difficulty in reading and writing, whereas others show quite opposite strengths and weaknesses.

Educational Background Factors.   Another factor that makes a significant impact on ELLs' learning and assessments is their prior schooling experience pertaining to learning grade-level content (Thomas & Collier, 2002). ELLs have a wide array of schooling experiences in their home countries. Some ELLs received education equivalent to their native English-speaking counterparts, whereas other ELLs have very little or interrupted schooling experiences. The latter group of students is not only far behind in terms of content knowledge but also is not familiar with various school functions, including methods of assessment. It is quite predictable that ELLs who have a general education schooling experience with solid grade-level content knowledge in their home countries tend to do well in tests.

Cultural Factors.   The degree of familiarity with the United States' mainstream culture can have an effect on ELLs' performance on tests, whether classroom or large-scale assessments. Students who are familiar with the norms for taking standarized tests, for instance, will be more comfortable with such assessments. Some cultures may emphasize competition and doing well in tests, but others may not. Also, different cultures have dissimilar perceptions of plagiarism and cheating. Thus, it is crucial to explain explicitly what is expected, why assessment is imperative, and how the results are interpreted and used.

Identifying Difficulties that ELL Students Experience in Classroom Assessment

Typical difficulties that ELLs experience in assessments stem from (a) difficulty in comprehension of test language, (b) difficulty in expressing what they know, (c) lack of content and cultural knowledge in test items, (d) unfamiliarity of test types, and (e) emotional stress.

Difficulty in Comprehending Test Language.   ELL students may struggle with understanding assessment terms and language, especially complex sentence structures, idiomatic expressions, jargons and technical terms, double negatives, and unclear organization. Alvermann and Phelps (2005) suggests teachers check test item readability for ELL students by attending to the following:

- ✓ Vocabulary is intended grade level.
- ✓ Sentence complexity is intended grade level.
- ✓ Sentences are clearly and logically connected.
- ✓ Definitions and glossaries facilitate comprehension.
- ✓ Content of the test items is linked to students' experiences and prior knowledge.
- ✓ Organization of each test item is clear and easy to follow.
- ✓ Examples are clearly provided.
- ✓ Test items include questions of higher-order and critical thinking skills.
- ✓ Test directions are precise, explicit, and understandable.
- ✓ Options of multiple-choice items are reasonable and balanced.

Difficulty in Expressing What Is Known.   Difficulties in expressing what ELLs know can be shown in multiple areas, such as poor spelling, poor grammar, improper word choice, lack of variety in expressions, and poor organization. In general, it takes a considerable amount of time for second language learners to gain sophisticated expressive skills (speaking and writing). Because English is not a phonemic language in which spelling and sound don't always match, this may create more challenges to ELLs. As a result, poor spelling does not necessarily indicate ELLs' lack of comprehension skills. Similar logic applies to grammar, word choice, and organization of writing. Furthermore, it is difficult for ELLs to respond to long essay questions demanding sophisticated persuasive writing.

Lack of Content and Cultural Knowledge in Test Items.   Lack of grade-level content knowledge in test items negatively affects ELL students' ability to understand and respond to questions. Some ELL students, especially those who have little or interrupted schooling, have poor content knowledge foundation. Also, ELL students may have a solid foundation in content knowledge but are simply unable to do well on formal tests that are designed for native speakers. Culturally assumed but not explicitly taught knowledge in the test items can interfere with ELLs' assessment performance. It is best to provide culturally neutral contexts in test items.

Unfamiliarity with Different Types of Tests.   ELL students may not be familiar with commonly used tests. For example, in science classes, students are expected to complete lab reports, which is often integrated into their grades. Students who are not familiar with this type of task may have difficulty or fail to understand why the task is important. In addition, some writing tasks such as explaining how to reach conclusions in problems, writing math problems, writing essays conveying students' own points of view, or conducting research to gather information can present challenges to some ELLs.

Emotional Stress. In addition to difficulties due to a lack of language skills and content knowledge, it is also possible for ELL students' emotional stress, caused by challenges of linguistic and cultural adjustments, to have a negative impact on testing. It may take considerable effort to process information in second language. Timed tests can cause stress, resulting in a short attention span, fatigue, anxiety, and frustration.

Assessment Accommodations and Modifications

Although accommodations for ELLs in large-scale assessments have been largely identified (Rivera & Collum, 2006), less is known about what accommodations are appropriate at the classroom level. We do know, however, that general education classroom teachers can accommodate ELLs' needs by focusing on three assessment-related factors: (a) test format, (b) test-taking procedures, and (c) interpreting and grading ELLs' work. Also, many of the suggestions for accommodating special needs children (Table 12.5).

Test Format. It is helpful to modify test questions and directions by simplifying the language so that it is more comprehensible. This reduces the language burden that can have a negative impact on ELLs' test results. These types of modifications are not intended to dilute or lower the content standards or objectives that students must demonstrate. Rather, it is to help teachers measure ELLs' academic progress more accurately by mitigating the impact of limited English proficiency. It may be appropriate to provide customized dictionaries or a glossary of terms, as well as visual images that help explain concepts and relationships of the content (e.g., maps, graphs, figures, and pictures). In addition, it is helpful to limit the number of selected-response options, to clarify and simplify distracters, to avoid confusing words such as *always* and *never,* and to not use double negatives. For constructed-response assessments, it is beneficial to allow students to submit graphic organizers or outlines as alternative ways to demonstrate their understanding, especially when students' English skills are low. Teachers may also want to consider providing ELL students with a word bank or a model and a few examples. For instance, the following English and Science essay questions provides prompts.

Example. Write a character description of two of the following characters based on the novel *Nothing But the Truth:*

Philip Malloy	Dr. Seymour
Miss Narwin	Mr. Malloy

Philip Malloy is _____. I know this because he _____. I think he would be a _____ friend because in the story he _____. He can also be _____. For example in the story he _____.

Another example is a science lab report prompt that offers clear directions, along with a word bank.

Example. Please write a conclusion for each experiment. The conclusion needs to have three parts:

1. Answer the problem stated at the beginning of the experiment.

2. Accept or reject the hypothesis.

3. Summarize the data collected and explain the results.

Word bank: hypothesis, materials, procedure, data, accept, reject, graph, chart, diagram, summarize, conclusion.

Scaffolding can also be used to reduce language complexity.

Portfolios are effective with ELL students. Becker (2001) suggests conferences, dialogue journals, and learning logs to gather valuable information about student successes as well as difficulties. Opportunities to demonstrate what they know can be communicated by outlining, classifying, graphing, and map reading. Additional examples of materials include exhibits or projects, visual displays, organized lists, tables or graphs, and short answers (O'Malley & Pierce, 1996).

Test-Taking Procedures.   Test-taking procedural accommodations include allowing extra time in test-taking and completion of assignments, flexible scheduling, and a comfortable test-taking environment. ELL students may need extended time because processing information in a second language demands more time and cognitive effort. Breaks between parts of long tests can be beneficial, as is providing a second chance for ELLs to redo assignments or retake the test. In addition, presenting both oral and written test directions will help ELLs comprehend test items. Again, many of these suggestions are consistent with what is included in Table 12.5.

Evaluating Performance and Providing Feedback

Appropriate methods to evaluate ELL student performance are initially framed by whether teachers grade language or content or both. Because most assessments contain embedded English language components, it is important for the teacher to specify what is being weighted for purposes of evaluation. If language is included, it may be best to provide a separate grade for that aspect of the assessment. One useful method of grading is to allow for partial scores, rather than determining grades solely on a correct or incorrect basis. For instance, the ELL student response to the following world history question is neither grammatically correct nor sophisticated. The student's answer, however, displays a good understanding of the concept.

> Question: What was the three field system?
> Answer: This develop in middle Age. Plant two among three fields because of the land need to rest. Each time it was rotate so each field had rest every three year.

Reiss (2005) suggests "focus on content" and "focus on progress," as opposed to "focus on language" and "focus on product" when grading ELLs' work.

Summary

The purpose of this chapter was to introduce you to the assessment adaptations needed to accommodate students with special needs in inclusive settings. Overall, suggestions made in other chapters apply to these students, but you need to keep some additional considerations in mind. In general, it is important to make sure that a student's disability or language limitations do not unfairly influence his or her performance on tests and other types of assessments. Major points in the chapter include the following:

n Legal mandates in IDEA require educational experiences, including assessment, to take place in the least restrictive environment.

- Regular classroom teachers are responsible for gathering information to identify students for special education services.

- The reauthorization of the Individuals with Disabilities Education Act (IDEA) of 1990 required that a general education teacher become a member of the IEP team.

- The evaluation of students for identification must be nondiscriminatory—in the student's native language and not racially or culturally biased.

- The most recent reauthorization of the Individuals with Disabilities Education Act (IDEA) of 2004 proposed that the response to intervention (RTI) model as an alternative approach to determining eligibility for special education services.

- Teacher observation is a major component in identification and writing the student's IEP.

- Teachers are responsible for setting individualized learning targets with appropriate assessments.

- Teachers are responsible for providing specific assessment information for referral and possible identification.

- Procedures are implemented to make identifying a student for special education services difficult.

- Students are identified as having one or more educational disabilities, based in part on careful teacher observation.

- Teachers are responsible for assessing the adaptive behaviors of students referred and identified as having mild mental retardation.

- Comprehension difficulties require adaptations in test directions.

- Auditory and visual difficulties require a minimum of distractions.

- Time constraint difficulties require longer testing time and frequent breaks in testing.

- Anxiety and embarrassment need to be minimized for students with special needs.

- The behavior of students with disabilities varies from day to day; this variation needs to be considered when observing and evaluating student behavior.

- Adaptations may need to be made to test directions, the format of the test, and the construction of different types of items.

- Adaptations may be needed during test administration and to the testing site.
- Grading students with special needs should include consideration of IEP objectives, opinions of other teachers working with the student, and contracting.
- Factors that influence the assessments of ELL students includes language and literacy skills, educational background, and culture.
- Most assessments are heavily language dependent and language integrated, making the distinction between content and language difficult.
- ELL students experience difficulty in classroom-based assessments due to their lack of comprehension, unfamiliarity with different types of assessments, and emotional stress.
- Assessment modifications for ELL students include extra time, simplifying and clarifying test language, use of visual aids, models, examples, prompts and glossaries of terms, graphic organizers, and outlines.
- Alternative assessments can provide ELL students with better opportunities to demonstrate their knowledge, understanding, and skills.
- Partial score, a second chance to take tests or redo assignments, and consideration of efforts and progress are suggested in evaluating ELL student performance.

Self-Instructional Review Exercises

1. According to PL 94-142, what are the two essential responsibilities of regular classroom teachers concerning the assessment of students with special needs who are in inclusive settings?

2. What was one of the most important new provisions added to IDEA 1990 regarding general education teachers' responsibilities?

3. Indicate whether each of the following statements represents nondiscriminatory assessment (Y for yes, N for no):

   a. A single procedure may be used for identification.
   b. Assessment is conducted by a multidisciplinary team.
   c. Assessments are conducted in English.
   d. The disability may not affect the scores students receive.
   e. Racial and cultural discrimination must be avoided.

4. True or False: IDEA 2004 required that response to intervention (RTI) be used to replace the discrepancy approach to identifying a student with specific learning disability.

5. Read the following scenario and indicate whether the teacher has properly followed the steps necessary to refer a student for identification.
   Mrs. Albert was immediately suspicious of Jane, thinking that she might have a learning disability. Jane did not achieve very well on written tests and seemed to have trouble concentrating. She was also distracted very easily. Mrs. Albert tried Jane in another reading group, but this did not seem to help. After looking at Jane's previous test scores, Mrs. Albert decided to refer her for identification.

6. Indicate whether each of the descriptions listed is characteristic of students with mental retardation (MR), emotional disturbance (ED), sensory impairment (SI), physical impairment (PI), attention deficits (AD), hyperactivity (H), or learning disability (LD).

   a. Diabetes
   b. Language deficit
   c. Discrepancy between ability and achievement
   d. Poor adaptive behaviors
   e. Poor eyesight
   f. Slow learning
   g. Restless
   h. Easily distracted

7. Indicate whether each of the difficulties listed is characteristic of students with comprehension difficulties (C), sensory difficulties (SD), time constraint difficulties (TCD), anxiety (A), embarrassment (E), or variability of behavior (VB).

   a. Gets sequence of steps wrong
   b. Worries excessively about performance
   c. Hands in an incomplete test with other students
   d. Has trouble one day finishing a test, no trouble the next day
   e. Takes longer to complete the test

8. Indicate whether each of the following test administration adaptations is considered good practice (Y for yes, N for no).

   a. Making tests with fewer items
   b. Closely monitoring students while they are taking a test
   c. Modifying tests
   d. Giving special attention when handing out tests
   e. Using norm-referenced testing
   f. Emphasizing internal attributions
   g. Giving practice tests
   h. Allowing students to take a written test orally
   i. Using objective rather than essay items
   j. Using normal seating arrangements
   k. Checking student understanding of directions

9. Read the following scenario and indicate what was correct and what was incorrect or lacking in the teacher's assessment accommodations.
   Mr. Parvin was careful to read all the directions aloud, and he gave examples of how the students should answer each item. He prepared a separate set of directions for his students with special needs. He designed the test to make sure as many questions as possible were included on each page. He underlined key words in the short-answer questions and wrote objective items so that the students corrected wrong answers. Mr. Parvin did not permit questions once students began the test. He told students that they had to complete the test in 30 minutes, and he placed a sign on the door indicating that testing was taking place.

10. Ms. Ramirez has a learning-disabled student in her classroom. His name is Tyron. Ms. Ramirez has decided to use a contract grading procedure, and she wants to be

able to report progress on the contract to Tyron's parents. How would Ms. Ramirez begin to develop her contract, and how would she report progress to his parents?

11. Indicate which of the following does **not** help ELL students comprehend test language.

   a. Use simple sentences over complex sentences.
   b. Provide definitions or dictionaries.
   c. Present both oral and written forms.
   d. Avoid test questions containing double negatives, *always*, and *never*.
   e. Avoid jargons and technical terms.
   f. Use idiomatic expressions.
   g. Provide visual images explaining relationships and concepts of test items.
   h. Provide native language translation.

12. Indicate which of the following does **not** help ELL students demonstrate what they already know.

   a. Allow graphic organizers.
   b. Allow outlining or classifying.
   c. Allow illustrations or pictures.
   d. Allow oral responses.
   e. Performance in front of class.
   f. Reduce the length of paper in essay questions.
   g. Provide examples or models.
   h. Provide a word bank and key expressions in essay questions.

13. Mr. Green, an eighth-grade math teacher, did not realize Mei was an ELL student until she failed word problems completely. He was puzzled over why Mei did not do well in word problem questions but she excelled in computation skills. Mei speaks English fluently enough without much difficulty. Mr. Green wonders what he needs to do to help Mei perform better in the math problems. Please discuss the ways that Mr. Green can accommodate Mei's needs in word problems.

14. Ms. Smith is a fifth-grade reading teacher. She noticed that her ELL student, Maria, who seemingly speaks fluently without accents, makes spelling and grammar errors in her writing. Although Maria seems to comprehend grade-level stories quite well, her writing falls short of fifth-grade level work. Ms. Smith feels torn in grading her writing—on one the one hand Maria's idea presented in writing is excellent and deserves an "A," but her poor spelling and grammar are weak. What is the best way to assess Maria's writing?

Answers to Self-Instructional Review Exercises

1. Gathering information for identification and implementing the IEP.

2. One of the most important new provisions added to IDEA 1990 was that the law recognized that most students with disabilities spend all or most of their school time in general education settings, and so it included a provision requiring that a general education teacher become a member of the team for the IEP.

3. a. N, b. Y, c. N, d. Y, e. Y.

4. False. IDEA 2004 *proposed* response to intervention (RTI) as an alternative approach to determining eligibility for special education services. Many states have adopted RTI as an alternative approach under which a severe discrepancy between IQ and achievement was no longer required. However, IDEA did not require that RTI be the only approach.

5. Mrs. Albert did some things right but in general did not do enough to justify formal referral. She seems to have targeted behaviors that are characteristic of students with a learning disability, and she did try one instructional intervention. However, more instructional interventions are needed to be sure that the problems could not be ameliorated in the class without referral. There is no indication that the teacher made any more structured, diagnostic assessments, and there is no evidence of any type of prereferral review. A serious oversight is that Mrs. Albert has not requested that outsiders review the situation.

6. a. PI, b. LD, c. LD, d. MR, e. SI, f. none, g. H, h. AD.

7. a. C, b. A, c. E, d. VB, e. TCD.

8. a. N, b. Y, c. Y, d. N, e. N, f. Y, g. Y, h. Y, i. Y, j. N, k. Y.

9. Correct procedures included reading the directions aloud, giving examples, underlining key words, and placing a sign on the door. Incorrect procedures, from an adaptation perspective, included giving students with disabilities a separate set of directions (which may cause embarrassment), putting too much on each page of the test, asking students to correct wrong answers for objective items, not permitting questions during the test, and giving students what seems like a short time limit.

10. It would be best to begin with a clear indication of the work to be completed and how different grades will be assigned. A specific time line for completing the work should be included. Signatures of the student and parents are needed to ensure that all understand. The teacher's report should not simply indicate what grades are achieved, but should also include some personalized comments and suggestions.

11. f

12. e

13. There is a widespread misconception that math is an universal language and, therefore, ELLs will not experience much difficulty. However, word problems and context-based questions contain inseparable language components, which creates difficulties in understanding questions. Therefore, Mr. Green can simplify test language and/or provide customized glossaries. If possible, using graphs and visual images explaining relationships also helps ELLs demonstrate their math knowledge effectively.

14. First, ELLs do not develop reading and writing skills evenly in an equal pace. Reading is a receptive skill, which is developed prior to writing (expressive) skills. Furthermore, Maria's different native language background, in which spelling and sound match and pronouns are not often used like in the English language, precludes Maria's writing from being error-free. Given this, Ms. Smith should weigh spelling and grammar errors low or not at all, unless her intention is to measure stu-

dents' correct usage of grammar and spelling. Creating a specific analytic scoring rubric will also guide both teacher and students clearly in evaluating her response.

Suggestions for Action Research

1. Interview two or three regular classroom teachers about the accommodations they make for students with special needs or for ELL students who are in their classes. Ask about their experience in gathering information for identification and setting learning targets, as well as about the assessment accommodations they have made. Compare their responses to suggestions in the chapter.

2. Interview two special education teachers. Ask them what they believe regular classroom teachers need to know to accommodate students with special needs in inclusive settings. In their work with regular classroom teachers, what do they see as the teachers' greatest weaknesses when making assessment accommodations?

3. Interview school division central office personnel who are responsible for ELL students. What is the district's approach toward assessing ELL students? What kind of support is provided for the teachers?

4. In a team with one or two other students, devise a plan for how you would accommodate the assessment of one or two students with special needs who have been placed in general education classrooms. You will need as much information about the students as possible, and it would be best if you could observe the students. Once the plan is complete, review it with the students' teacher(s) for feedback and suggestions.

Grading and Reporting Student Performance

with Jesse Senechal

In the past few chapters we have seen how teachers can assess students on a variety of learning targets with different types of assessments. As was pointed out in the model of classroom assessment presented in Chapter 1, now you need to do something with the assessment results. Specifically, you will need to make professional judgments about the quality of student work and translate that into grades

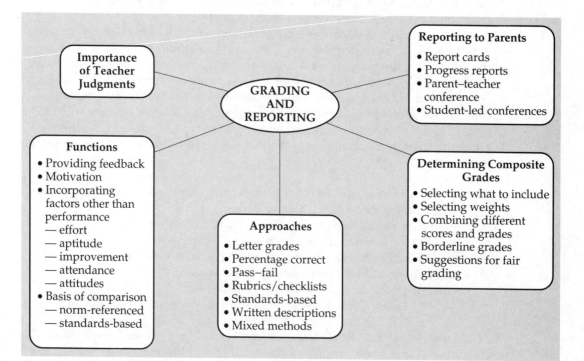

CHAPTER 13   Concept Map

and reports. We begin this chapter with a discussion of the importance of a teacher's professional judgment in the use of assessment, then move on to consider the functions of grading, specific approaches to grading, ideas for determining composite (report card) grades, and finally, a discussion of strategies for reporting progress to parents.

Teachers' Judgments in Grading

For many reasons, it is best practice when grades are seen as an "objective" measure of student performance. When a student receives an A for a course, an objective conclusion is that he/she has mastered the course content, whereas an F represents the student's failure to achieve a minimum level of proficiency. If this is an objectively determined conclusion, there is the expectation that the teacher would be able to produce documentation, in the form of a grade book or a portfolio of student work, to justify the grade. In fact, in certain cases justifying grades becomes a legal requirement (McElligott & Brookhart, 2009). Thus, objectivity is preferred over subjectivity. The preference for objectivity in grading is important because these marks have important uses. School class placements, college admissions, and scholarship awards rely heavily on grades. Grades also affect an individual student's identity and self-esteem. We depend on our grading systems to indicate fairly and accurately the status of the student. Objectivity helps grading meet these goals, but how much "objectivity" is there in grading?

It turns out that teachers' professional judgments are essential in determining what might later be termed objective. Judgments are made before assessment (e.g., the difficulty of test items, what is covered on the assessment, whether extra credit items will be included), as well as after assessments are completed (e.g., scoring short-answer and essay items). Further judgments are made in combining scores of different assessments to determine grades (e.g., how assessments are weighted, how to handle borderline scores). Here are some typical questions teachers ask related to assessment and grading that are answered by using their professional judgment:

> Are my grades supposed to mean the same thing as other teachers' grades?
> Am I grading students too hard or too easy?
> Should effort and improvement be included in the grade?
> Should student participation be included in the grade?
> How should different assessments be weighted and combined?
> What distribution of grades should I end up with?
> What do I do if most of my students fail the test?
> What do I do with students who test well but don't hand in homework?

There are no straightforward or correct answers to these questions. Although certain guidelines may come from school or district guidelines—and the scope and rigidity of these vary widely from school to school—it is always, ultimately, the job of classroom teachers to use their judgment to interpret these guidelines within the unique context of their discipline, grade level, and learning context.

And even when a teacher comes to an understanding of how he or she believes these questions should be answered, there are always individual student situations that demand flexibility to context. Consider the following scenarios (Brookhart, 1993):

> In your seventh grade social studies class, report card grades were based on quizzes, tests, and an out-of-class project which counted as 25% of the grade. Terry obtained an A average on his quizzes and tests but has not turned in the project despite frequent reminders.

> You are a biology teacher of a high school class which consists of students with varying ability levels. For this class you give two exams in each term. As you compute Bernie's grade for this term, you see that on the first exam, he obtained a score equivalent to a B, and on the second exam, a low A. (pp. 131, 133)

What grades would you give? Should Terry get a low grade even though he scores so high on tests? Should Bernie get an A because he showed improvement?

The evaluating and grading process requires you to make many *professional* decisions. These decisions are based on your personal value system toward a number of different issues. In the end, grading is more a reflection of this value system, of perceived importance or perspective, than it is based on following specific correct guidelines or rules.

In some schools, there is substantial professional dialogue around these value systems. For example, the professional learning community model (Dufour, 2005) encourages groups of teachers to develop common understandings of what it means to grade fairly. Advocates of standards-based grading suggest highly structured district guidelines for grading practices (Marzano, 2006; O'Connor, 2009). However, whether it is in the context of district guidelines or in a collaborative or individual setting, as a teacher you will ultimately develop a personal philosophy of grading that translates into what you do. To develop your grading plan, then, you need to consider and answer the following questions (Frisbie & Waltman, 1992):

> What meaning should each grade symbol carry?
> What should "failure" mean?
> What elements of performance should be incorporated in a grade?
> How should the grades in a class be distributed?
> What should the components be that go into a final grade?
> How should the components of the grade be combined?
> What method should be used to assign grades?
> Should borderline cases be reviewed?
> What other factors can influence the philosophy of grading? (p. 210)

These questions are best answered when they are based on an understanding of the different purposes or functions grades serve and the types of comparison standards that are used. In the end, you need to use methods and comparisons that best meet your major purpose. As we will see later in this chapter, grades often serve several purposes, which makes matters more complicated.

We need to make an important point concerning professional judgments. These judgments are *subjective* and *intuitive* in the sense that there is no single correct procedure or set of rules that take professional decision making out of the process. There is no completely objective procedure, nor should there be. You may use a grading scale, score student tests and performances, then mathematically calculate grades, but this is not a procedure that is necessarily correct because it appears to be objective. Think for a moment about a physician making a decision about whether a patient is sufficiently strong to endure an operation. In a sense, this is like grading. The doctor takes many measures, then examines them *in the light of his or her experience and knowledge* before giving a yes or no judgment. Could two physicians differ in their opinions about whether to operate, given the same information? Absolutely. Likewise, two teachers can differ on the meaning of students' performances. One teacher might look at the tests and conclude that the student has mastered a skill, whereas another teacher might conclude the opposite. In the end, it is your value system that makes the difference, and to be an effective teacher you need to understand the issues, make some informed judgments, and then be willing to have confidence in your decisions. Your goal is to use unbiased, thoughtful reasoning (Guskey & Bailey, 2001). One purpose of this chapter is to introduce you to some of the core issues underlying the practice of grading with the hope that this understanding, combined with the experiences and knowledge you gain as you begin to teach, will allow you to practice thoughtful reasoning in your grading decisions.

In Chapter 1 it was pointed out that teachers' assessment and grading decisions are heavily influenced by teacher beliefs and values about enhancing student learning and that these beliefs and values often conflict with external pressures such as mandated statewide testing, parental concerns, and district policies (McMillan, 2002b, 2003; McMillan & Workman, 1999). Teacher internal values and beliefs are essential because they provide a rationale for using grading practices that are most consistent with what is most important in the teaching/learning process. Thus, because teachers want all students to succeed, they may give extra credit to enable students to "pull up" low grades. Because of individual differences in students, teachers may use different types of assessments so everyone has a chance of obtaining a good grade. Performance assessments may be used because they motivate and engage students more effectively than multiple-choice tests and allow teachers to grade participation. Note in the following teacher responses how grading decisions are based on more encompassing beliefs and values about learning:

> To me grades are extremely secondary to the whole process of what we do. I have goals to what I want to teach, and I use assessment so that I know what I need to work on, what students have mastered, and what they haven't.

> I'm always trying to find some ways so that all the children can find success, not just Johnny and Suzy getting the A but also Sally and Jim can get an A.

Then I generally think of their effort, whether I feel they've really tried and whether they've turned in all their work. If they tried to make an effort to improve, I won't give them an F.

When it's borderline, how hard has the child worked during the year?

Recent studies of the ethical dilemmas of assessment show that teachers, in making grading decisions, must often negotiate between several conflicting demands (Pope Green, Johnson, & Mitchell, 2009). For example, it is common in the age of high-stakes tests for teachers to experience pressure to adopt certain grading practices that focus on auditing and reporting student achievement, rather than supporting the teacher's values of promoting learning. Teachers need "objective" evidence of student performance to defend grades to parents, and district policies may restrict the nature and use of different grading procedures. However, the easily audited measures that these pressures require are not always in sync with what teachers know to be quality assessment. Practical constraints such as these limit what teachers can realistically accomplish. Although it might be best to use many different samples of student performance for grades, it might not be feasible in light of other instructional needs. It is best to consider these external factors with your own beliefs and values about teaching and learning in mind. Recognize that tension may exist, but keep your grading decision making based primarily on what is best for student learning.

Functions of Marking and Grading

Why do we grade at all? What do you want your grades to mean to your students? How do you want students to be affected? What might students' grades mean to other stakeholders such as parents or school officials? Although at a basic level all teachers want marks and grades to have positive impact on student learning and motivation, the reality is that grades not only serve a variety of functions, but also have various intended and unintended impacts. For example, suppose Mr. Wren decides to be "fair" to students by using the top score on a test as 100 and adjusts the percentage correct for all other students accordingly (this happened in Jim's son's high school physics class). Would it be fair if the class happened to have one or two exceptionally bright students? What might happen to student motivation in that class? This is one of many factors that will determine how grades are interpreted and thus affect students. Some other important influences include the level of feedback communicated in the grade or mark about the student performance, whether grades are being used to compare students, how grades motivate students, and whether factors other than performance should be included. In this section, we will explore these various functions and effects of grading.

Providing Feedback

Certainly one of the primary functions of assigning and grading work is to collect information about the progress of student learning. This is information that is essential to both the teacher and the student. In the former case, we can understand teaching as a research practice, where every assignment given is an experimental treatment, and every collection of papers, a data set. Teachers analyze and grade collected work to draw conclusions about the effectiveness of their instruction and plan future assignments based on these conclusions. But this information, gained through assessment, is obviously not just for the teacher; equally, if not more important, is what it tells students about their strengths and weaknesses in achieving the learning objectives. This is the logic behind the use of formative assessments as discussed in Chapters 4 and 5. However, one of the most difficult professional decisions you will have to make about grading students is the nature and amount of feedback they will receive about their performance. Let's examine a couple of examples to illustrate this point.

When Ryann was in the sixth grade a few years ago (actually more than a few), she spent several weeks putting together a report on Italy. In looking over the report, her father thought she did an excellent job (of course there may be just a little bias here!). She got the paper back with a B+ on it and a short comment, "Good work." She was somewhat disappointed, but more important, didn't know why she did not get a higher grade. There was no information about how the teacher had come to this conclusion. How did this affect her? She was sad and bewildered, in general a negative effect. An alternative could have been for the teacher to provide her with a detailed summary of how the teacher evaluated each section of the paper, so that she could better understand the strengths and weaknesses.

However, from another perspective, we can say that it is simply not possible for a teacher to give detailed comments to every assignment. For example, say a high school English teacher assigns a three-page paper to five junior-level American Literature classes and 100 papers come back. Does the teacher spend a scant 5 minutes grading and commenting on each paper? If so, that's still over 8 hours of work, and that is for just one assignment. Practically, teachers must make important judgments about what assessments to target for intensive feedback. There is also the issue of what forms of feedback are most useful to students. Some papers could be marked up and commented on extensively, but not in a way that is useful for students. In fact, it has been shown that some forms of feedback can have negative effects on student achievement (Marzano, 2006). This feedback could be too vague or unclear. Additionally, it is easy to understand how "too much red ink"—just like not enough—might discourage students and have a negative effect on motivation.

These examples demonstrate not only the importance of providing appropriate feedback, but also the challenges of doing so. As was stressed in the previous section, this is another instance when your professional judgment as a teacher is essential. We know that in general more detailed feedback has a positive effect on motivation, and it allows students to make more accurate connections between how they studied or prepared and their performance. Through experience, effective teachers learn to develop instructional techniques that give students this consistent, detailed, and useful feedback in ways that are realistic, considering the practical constraints of time and workload.

Basis of Comparison

A second, related, function of grading is to provide a basis of comparison. Typically, when we grade, certain student papers will receive As and others different grades. In a similar fashion, there are also students with high GPAs and others with low. Although we may question its social value, it is hard to argue with the fact that a primary function of grading in our society is comparing and ranking students. As mentioned earlier, these rank orderings—manifested ultimately in the form of GPAs and transcripts—become the basis for access to higher education and job opportunities. However, when we discuss grading as a basis of comparison, an important distinction needs to be made between two types of grading: **norm-referenced** and **standards-based**. Basically, this distinction boils down to the question: "When we assign grades, what exactly are we comparing?" This is an important distinction because it has significant implications not only for how teachers teach and students learn, but also for the issues of educational equity. Let's examine this distinction by a discussion of each method.

Norm-Referenced Grading.   Grading by comparison to the achievement of other students is referred to as **norm-referenced** or *relative* grading. In the classroom, this means that the function of each student's grade is to indicate how the student performed in comparison with the other students in the class (or several classes in middle and high schools). This method is known popularly as grading on the curve. In this approach, certain proportions of students are given designated grades, regardless of the level of performance of the students. That is, a certain percentage of the class will receive As, Bs, Cs, Ds, and Fs. There is no indication of how much students master or what percentage of test items were answered correctly. A student can answer 70% of the items on one test correctly, and if that is the highest score, it will be an A. On another test, a 70 might be relatively low, receiving a C or D. It's also possible for a student to get a C for getting a 95 on a test if others received even higher scores.

Although norm-referenced grading has fallen out of fashion both among the educational research community (Guskey, 2009; Marzano, 2006; O'Connor, 2009) and in the practice of teachers in our schools, it is clear that it has had a significant and lasting impact on the way grading occurs. Because norm-referenced grading is strictly based on comparing students to each other, its major function is to show which are the highest- or best-performing students. In this sense, it provides the conceptual basis for the way our schools sort students. Indeed, a definition of grades that includes C as average and B as above average is a norm-referenced type of comparison. We can also see its influence in how we adjust curves based on student ability (e.g., honors-track classes have a higher percentage of As than general-track classes), by how difficult teachers make their tests, and by how tough teachers are in grading papers, projects, and other products. The idea, common among many teachers, that "if no students fail, I'm not being tough enough," is certainly a remnant of norm-referenced grading.

Another function of relative grading is to foster student competitiveness. It is clear that when students know that their grade is dependent on how others perform, a very competitive environment is created, which in turn usually has a negative impact on student effort, motivation, interpersonal relationships, and teacher communication. The motivation of students who continually score near the bottom is undermined. Student cooperation is reduced. For these reasons, as well as the capriciousness with which some teachers set curves (Jim's son had a teacher who set the curve by the highest score—please don't do that!), most grading is now based on the absolute level of student performance, without any comparison to how others performed.

Standards-Based Grading.   Grading that is determined by what level of performance is obtained is now typically called **standards-based** or **standards-referenced** (*criterion-referenced*). In this method, there is no comparison with other students, but rather with some predetermined standard of performance. This could be as simple as a percentage-based scale of items that must be answered correctly, or as complex as a detailed rubric that presents an analysis of student progress on a list of various content-specific performance standards. In our current era of school reform there is not only a proliferation of national, state, and district standards, but also a pressure to close the achievement gap. In this context the idea of standards-based grading is appealing. When done well, it lays out specific criteria for performance and holds the expectation that all students can meet those goals.

The most common and traditional method of using absolute levels of performance is called *percentage-based* grading. This is typically used for objective tests, for which teachers assign a grade to a specific percentage of items answered correctly. Usually the school system establishes the scale, such as the following:

A   94–100   % correct

B   86–93   % correct

C   75–85   % correct

D   65–74   % correct

F   below 65% correct

The criterion is supposedly set by the percentage of correct items for each grade. Thus, a scale in which 96–100 is an A is often regarded as more stringent or tough than a scale with an A range of 90–100. Some school systems have periodic debates about the relative worth of more stringent versus more lax grading scales. However, this debate is not especially meaningful due to the pressure schools feel to sort students combined with the variability in difficulty on any two assessments. Simply put, a score of 70 on a hard test means something different from a 70 on an easier test. Consequently, what is important is not only the percentage correct, but also how hard it is to get those items correct. Two teachers, given the same learning target, can easily come up with different assessments that are not the same in terms of difficulty.

Standards-based grading is gaining wide support in the research community and is now influencing practices in schools (Guskey, 2009; Marzano, 2006, 2010; O'Connor, 2009). For standards-based grading teachers, schools, and in certain cases, districts develop assessments that spell out in some detail the specific behaviors (standards) students must perform to obtain a grade. The assessments, rather than giving an overall letter or number, use some form of rubric to indicate achievement on specific skills addressed in a given assignment. The scoring rubric and exemplars define the behaviors, and on the basis of the teacher's observations, a grade (or multiple grades) indicates which behaviors were demonstrated and hence which grade is received. Figure 13.1 shows an example of a standards-based assessment rubric. In these systems, students' performances are compared only to the rubrics and exemplars, not to each other. A letter grade may be assigned to different levels, but it is more common to simply indicate the level achieved. As we will see in a later section, this leads to a different type of reporting system from the traditional A, B, C, D, and F.

There are additional advantages to this system. First, because it relies on certain state- or district-determined standards of performance, these assessments will likely be aligned to high-stakes tests. Although there is a consistent and heated

Writing Rubric

Author's Name _____ Title of Piece _____

	1 Does Not Meet	2 Partially Meets	3 Does Not Fully Meet	4 Meets	5 More Than Meets	6 Exceeds
CONTENT/IDEAS	Writing is extremely limited in communicating knowledge, with no central theme.	Writing is limited in communicating knowledge. Length is not adequate for development.	Writing does not clearly communicate knowledge. The reader is left with questions.	Writes related, quality paragraphs, with little or no details.	Writing is purposeful and focused. Piece contains some details.	Writing is confident and clearly focused. It holds the reader's attention. Relevant details enrich writing.
ORGANIZATION	Writing is disorganized and underdeveloped with no transitions or closure.	Writing is brief and underdeveloped with very weak transitions and closure.	Writing is confused and loosely organized. Transitions are weak and closure is ineffective.	Uses correct writing format. Incorporates a coherent closure.	Writing includes a strong beginning, middle, and end, with some transitions and good closure.	Writing includes a strong, beginning, middle, and end with clear transitions and a focused closure.
VOCABULARY/ WORD CHOICE	Careless or inaccurate word choice, which obscures meaning.	Language is trite, vague or flat.	Shows some use of varied word choice.	Uses a variety of word choice to make writing interesting.	Purposeful use of word choice.	Effective and engaging use of word choice.
VOICE	Writer's voice/ point of view shows no sense of audience.	Writer's voice/ point of view shows little sense of audience.	Writer's voice/ point of view shows that sense of audience is vague.	Writer uses voice/point of view. Writes with the understanding of a specific audience.	Writer has strong voice/ point of view. Writing engages the audience.	Writes with a distinct, unique voice/point of view. Writing is skillfully adapted to the audience.
SENTENCE FLUENCY	Frequent run-ons or fragments, with no variety in sentence structure.	Many run-ons or fragments. Little variety in sentence structure.	Some run-ons or fragments. Limited variety in sentence structure.	Uses simple compound, and complex, sentences.	Frequent and varied sentence structure.	Consistent variety of sentence structure throughout.
CONVENTIONS	Parts of speech show lack of agreement. Frequent errors in mechanics. Little or no evidence of spelling strategies.	Inconsistent agreement between parts of speech. Many errors in mechanics. Limited evidence of spelling strategies.	Occasional errors between parts of speech. Some errors in mechanics. Some evidence of spelling strategies.	Maintains agreement between parts of speech. Few errors in mechanics. Applies basic grade level spelling.	Consistent agreement between parts of speech. Uses correct punctuation, capitalization, etc. Consistent use of spelling strategies.	Uses consistent agreement between parts of speech. No errors in mechanics. Creative and effective use of spelling strategies.

FIGURE 13.1   Standards-Based Assessment Rubric

Source: Madison County School District, http://www.madison.k12.ga.us/literacy/rubrics/writingrubric-kindergartennarrative.pdf

debate about the effectiveness of these system standards and standardized tests in improving the quality of education delivered in our schools, when taken on a case-by-case basis it is true that students and schools that do well generally benefit from their high performance. Second, because standards-based grading usually relies on rubrics that give a detailed breakdown of student performance by standard, it is a system that provides a high degree of feedback to the student without being an overly time-intensive method for teachers.

A final note about standards-based grading warrants your attention. Although it is theoretically based on the premise that all students can master learning targets, most teachers simply can't do this. Because we still use school to indicate to others which particular students, from the entire group of students, have performed best, the normative expectation is that teachers (especially middle and high school teachers) will give some As, a lot of Bs and Cs, a few Ds, and even some Fs. To meet this expectation, tests are devised so that not all students will do really well. That is, enough difficulty is built into the test so that not all students will get As. The reality is that most teachers, one way or another, combine absolute performance and sorting in the assigning of grades. This isn't bad or inappropriate, but it needs to be clarified for what it is so that whatever methods are used are fair to students. Recently we have been moving more and more to absolute standards and defining levels of standards in a way that still permits some sorting of students (some call this setting high standards), but sorting is still a function of schooling we need to deal with.

Table 13.1 summarizes differences between norm-referenced and standards-based approaches for marking and grading students.

Motivation

A third primary function of grading is to motivate students. One way or another, your grading practices will enhance or mitigate student motivation. It is fair to assume that all teachers want grades to motivate students to be active learners. It is also important to know that every student enters a class with a particular sense of him- or herself as a learner, whether positive or negative, that has been developed through a personal history of schooling. But as a teacher, one might ask, considering the variable identity of students, how can grades be used to enhance overall motivation to learn? Recent research in student motivation highlights a few key areas of information that are significant for enhancing student motivation (Brookhart, 2004; Marzano 2006). Let's take a look at some important ones.

It is well established that student motivation is enhanced when students believe that their success is due to internal, controllable attributions or beliefs about what caused the success (Covington, 1992; Weiner, 1974). Did they succeed because of something they did (e.g., effort) that can be controlled by them in the future? Or, was success due to something that they can't control, such as luck or help from others? Teachers can help students see the connection between their efforts and the grades they receive to reinforce their self-conception about their ability to be successful. This helps establish a well-grounded belief that they are able to do well,

TABLE 13.1   Characteristics of Norm-Referenced and Standards-Based (Criterion-Referenced) Grading

	Norm-Referenced	Standards-Based (Criterion-Referenced)
Interpretation	Score compared to the performances of other students	Score compared to predetermined standards and criteria
Nature of Score	Percentile rank; standard scores; grading curve	Percentage correct; descriptive performance standards
Difficulty of Test Items	Uses average to difficult items to obtain spread of scores; very easy and very difficult items not used	Uses average to easy items to result in a high percentage of correct answers
Use of Scores	To rank order and sort students	To describe the level of performance obtained
Effect on Motivation	Dependent on comparison group; competitive	Challenges students to meet specified learning target
Strengths	Results in more difficult assessments that challenge students; effective means of sorting students	Matches student performance to clearly defined learning targets; lessens competitiveness
Weaknesses	Grades determined by comparison to other students; some students are always at the bottom	Establishing clearly defined learning targets and setting standards that include mastery is difficult

that they have internalized explanations for success. Students who know that they are capable have a positive *self-efficacy*. Self-efficacy is enhanced when grades are meaningfully connected to internal reasons for success, primarily the belief that students are able to be successful. One implication of this for grading is that grades should not be used to reward mere participation. Rather, grades should be tied to effort exerted to be successful with moderately challenging tasks. When grades are received for tasks that are perceived as very easy, it is simply a verification of already established self-perceptions, with little new information about their ability to do well. This results in lower motivation. The old adage of "making sure students work for their grades" to motivate them is supported by research.

The role of goals in motivating students is also well established (Elliot & Thrash, 2001). Students tend to have one of two types of goals—mastery or performance. As previously discussed, **mastery** or **learning goal** involves students' conceptions of their competence about performing a task or completing a test. The focus is on self-improvement, on being able to demonstrate successfully the knowledge, understanding, or skill. There is an intrinsic reason for learning, for wanting to learn because demonstrating the knowledge or skill is what is important. Students with a mastery goal orientation learn more, prefer more challenging tasks, have more positive attitudes, become more success oriented (rather than failure avoiding), and believe that success depends on internal attributions such as effort and ability (Brookhart, 2004). With a **performance goal,** students are motivated not because of learning for its own sake, but for demonstrating competence, getting a high grade, passing the test, or scoring higher than other students. The motivation is to do well to achieve an extrinsic reward, regardless of the learning that occurs. Good grades are used to impress others, avoid failure, or obtain privileges.

When grades are perceived as feedback pertaining to mastery goals, students are more motivated than when grades are extrinsic rewards. As a classroom teacher, you have a critical role in using grades to relate to mastery goals, especially with the recent emphasis on high-stakes accountability tests and the school culture these tests create. If the meaning of the grade is mostly about "getting a good score" rather than "demonstrating understanding," motivation is transient and less powerful. When grades indicate feedback related to learning, intrinsic motivation results. The implication for grading is that giving grades without accompanying feedback information fosters extrinsic motivation. Grades need to be accompanied by specific feedback—whether in the form of teacher comments, student–teacher conference, or rubric checklists—that students can use to both verify learning and further develop their knowledge, understanding, or skill.

Finally, grades affect motivation most when they are presented while students learn (formatively), not just after learning (summatively). When grades are used to support formative feedback, students are encouraged to be *self-monitoring* and *self-reflecting,* which enhances self-efficacy and intrinsic motivation (Marzano, 2006; McMillan, 2009). When grades are used as a summative judgment, the function tends to focus on extrinsic rewards and management of student behavior (compliance).

Incorporating Factors Other Than Performance

It's fairly obvious that the primary function of a mark or grade is to indicate the academic performance of the student. Simply put, the more a student knows, understands, and can do, the better the grade. However, it's not as simple as it seems. As we have seen, a variety of factors go into the professional decisions teachers must make when assigning grades. In most grading situations, teachers are constantly considering questions about appropriate levels of feedback and effects on motivation. Another element in most teachers' decision-making process is what to do with factors such as student aptitude, improvement, effort, attendance, and attitude. These are aspects of student performance that are important for most teachers, particularly when doing whatever they can to encourage and motivate students. Many studies have documented that teachers tend to award a "hodge-podge" grade of that reflects both academic and nonacademic factors related to achievement (Brookhart, 1993, p. 36; Cross & Frary, 1996; D'Agostino & Welsh, 2007; McMillan, 2001, 2002a; McMillan, Workman, & Myran, 1998). Although most agree that these nonacademic indicators should have little or no bearing on the academic performance grade, they have been recognized in national reports by the business community as important qualities for the preparation of the workforce (Marzano, 2006). A look at several of these factors is warranted. Let's begin with student aptitude.

Aptitude.   One factor that can easily influence grades and marks is student aptitude or ability, which reflects the student's potential or capability for learning. The argument for including aptitude goes something like this: If we can tailor assignments and grading to each student's potential, all students can be motivated and all students can experience success. Rather than grading only on achievement, which favors students who bring higher aptitude for learning, grades reflect how well each student has achieved in relation to his or her potential. High-aptitude students will be challenged, and low-aptitude students will have realistic opportunities for good grades.

An example of this style of grading would be the accommodations and modifications made for special education students (Jung, 2009) and English language learners (Sampson, 2009; see Chapter 12). In these cases, there is a recognition that these populations come to a given curriculum with a lack of requisite skills, and therefore certain adjustments need to be made to give these students a realistic opportunity for success.

However, many problems are also related to the idea of aptitude-based grading. First, this argument is based on knowing what aptitude is and being able to assess it. There has never been a universal, agreed-on definition of aptitude, though it often is used synonymously with general intelligence. Work by Sternberg (1986) and Gardner (1985) has challenged traditional definitions of intelligence and has shown that we are still a long way from adequately understanding something as complex as aptitude for learning. Furthermore, measuring aptitude is fraught with difficulties, not the least of which concerns cultural bias. Even if we had a proper definition and a good measure, there are insurmountable practical difficulties in trying to assess aptitude for each student and grade accordingly. There may be connections between what many see as the low expectations of certain schools and a problematic implementation of aptitude-based grading.

Thus, although there is no question that students do have different levels of ability, and you need to use this knowledge in instruction and for giving students feedback, you don't want to try to factor it into grades and marks. The only exception—aside from special education and ELL (as discussed earlier)—might be for borderline situations when giving semester grades. Even then, it would be better to use prior achievement than to use aptitude. Using prior achievement avoids the conceptualization and measurement problems associated with aptitude. This suggests another factor, improvement, that could be used for grading.

Improvement.   Because learning is defined as a change in performance, why not measure how much students know before and then after instruction? Students who show the most improvement, hence learning, would get the highest grades. Again, there are some serious limitations to this approach. What happens when

Teacher's Corner

Terri Williams

National Board Certified Elementary Special Education Teacher

When determining students' grades, I often consider effort, participation, and improvement. If, when calculating student grades, the numerical percentage is a point or two closer to the next highest letter grade, I consider adding the necessary points to raise that student's grade. Students who put forth effort, participate in class, are motivated, and show improvement over time deserve the better grade. These students often need the extra positive reinforcement to maintain their effort and motivation. By adding the extra points to a final grade increases the chances that motivation and effort will continue.

students score high in the beginning, on the pretest, and don't have an opportunity to show improvement? What about student faking, in which students intentionally receive a low score on the pretest to more easily show improvement. Like trying to incorporate aptitude, keeping track of pre- and postinstruction scores for *each* student would not be very practical. But also like aptitude and effort, improvement can be a positive motivator for borderline situations.

Effort.   There is a commonsense logic to why student effort should be considered when grading. Aren't students who try harder learning more, even if it doesn't show up on a test, paper, or project? Isn't it good to reward low-achieving students who try hard? Don't we need to find something to praise low-achieving students for to keep them engaged? Isn't it true that we value effort in the workplace and as a society, so children should learn the importance of effort by seeing it reflected in their grades?

These may be compelling reasons to include effort in determining grades, but there are a number of good reasons not to. First, different teachers operationalize effort differently, so it is something that varies from one teacher to another. Second, we don't have a satisfactory way to define and measure effort. It's true that we could define effort as "completing homework" or "participating in class discussion" or "being on task," but each of these definitions is problematic. The one that could be easily and accurately measured, completing homework, could also be considered pretty shallow. Participation in class discussion is influenced by many factors, only one of which is controlled by each student. How do you know if a student is on task? Sometimes it seems obvious, though students can fake this pretty well, and most of the time we either can't tell or can't systematically observe and record sufficiently to get a good measure. If students know they will be graded on effort, will they try to make you think that they are trying by how they act, when in fact it's a bluff and they really aren't trying?

Third, does including effort tend to favor more assertive students? What about students who are quiet? Could gender or racial/ethnic characteristics be related to the value of effort or expectations about showing effort? Certainly we would not want our grades to be affected by these characteristics. Fourth, how much would effort count? What amount of a grade or percentage of a score would be reasonable? We really don't know, and how would you keep the level of contribution the same for each student? Finally, are we sending students the wrong message if they learn that they can get by just by trying hard, even if the performance is less than satisfactory?

There seem to be some pretty good reasons for and against including effort. This is one of those areas of professional judgment you'll need to make decisions about. But we do have some suggestions. If you want to include effort, use it for borderline cases. Never allow effort to become a major part of a mark or score. Second, report effort separately from performance. Do this often, and allow students opportunities to disagree with your assessment. Try to define effort as clearly as possible, and stick to your definition. It should be shared with students, with examples. If you include effort for one student, it's only fair to include it for all students. Table 13.2 summarizes arguments for and against the use of effort in grading.

Attendance.   Many schools have specific guidelines related to attendance and grades. That is, in certain schools students become ineligible for credit, or "automatic failures" when they miss a certain number of classes (McElligott & Brookhart, 2009). On a certain level this makes sense. To learn, students need to be in class. If a student misses 15 or 20 classes in a semester, no matter what the reason, it seems that it would be hard to justify giving a passing grade. And similar to the argument for factoring in effort, we can say that school should, as a preparation

TABLE 13.2   Arguments for and against Using Effort in Grading

For	Against
• Students who try hard learn more	• Teachers operationalize effort differently
• Rewards motivation and engagement	• Hard to define and measure
• Rewards lower-achieving students for something	• Can be faked
• Rewards an internal attributional factor that is in control of the student	• Favors more assertive students
• Leads to higher grades	• Lack of consistency in how effort is weighted
	• Teaches students that they can get by with effort and not performance
	• Takes focus away from performance

for the workplace, hold students accountable for their attendance. However, if we punish students academically for nonacademic issues we risk losing focus on the essential purpose of grades. When grades become too closely related to attendance expectations, "just showing up" becomes some students' argument for why they should pass. A better solution for the student with attendance problems would be for the school to develop ways of creating attendance-related consequences, for example, making up class time after school or on Saturdays.

Attitudes.   A final factor to consider in classroom grading and marking is student attitudes. Shouldn't students with a positive attitude be rewarded? Suppose two students perform about the same and both are in between two grades. If one student has a very positive attitude, would that mean that she should get the higher grade? Like student effort, attitudes are important, and it might be helpful if we could efficiently and accurately include this in grading. The reality is that attitudes are difficult to define and measure and are susceptible to student faking. So like the other "nonacademic" factors we have considered, it is generally not a good idea to try to use attitudes in grading. It is best if grades and marks are predominately determined by student performance in relation to learning targets. If other factors are included, their influence should be minimal.

Approaches to Marking and Grading

There are several ways to mark and grade student performance. Each has advantages and disadvantages, which relate to a number of issues, including (a) the degree to which the approach allows for adequate feedback, (b) the flexibility of the approach to various forms of assessment, and (c) the practicality of the approach considering constraints such as limited teacher time. We will consider the most common types of symbols or scores that are used, including letter grades, percentage correct, pass–fail grades, rubrics (checklists), standards-based grades, and written descriptions. Most teachers use a combination of these in the classroom with the hope of trying to achieve a balance between consistency in grading practice and adaptability to a variety of assessments, student learning styles, and school contexts. Of course, ultimately it is the teacher's job to synthesize whatever mixed-approach method of grading is used into a standard district scale. In Table 13.3, we present the advantages and disadvantages of these approaches related to the three issues outlined.

Letter Grades

The most common way most teachers mark student performance on products other than objective tests is to give a letter grade. Traditionally, letter grades correspond to different adjectives, such as excellent or outstanding, good, average or acceptable, poor, and unsatisfactory, and often plus and minus symbols are used to

TABLE 13.3   **Comparison of Different Types of Grading**

Approach	Degree of Feedback	Flexibility to Forms of Assessment	Practical Constraints (Time and skill needed to implement)
Letter Grades	Used alone, provides little feedback to student beyond single indicator of relative performance	Can be adapted for use with multiple forms of assessment	Clarifying meaning of letter grades to students may take time and skill
Percentage Correct	Used alone, provides little feedback to student beyond single indicator of relative performance	Tends to favor assessments that have clearly defined right and wrong answers	Easy to calculate and combine scores; developing appropriate assessments may take some time
Pass–Fail	Used alone, provides almost no feedback of relative performance or achievement on specific skills	Can be adapted for use with multiple forms of assessment	Used alone, it is fairly simple to implement
Rubrics/ Checklists	Gives high degree of feedback related to rubric dimensions; combined dimension scores give feedback for overall performance	Can be adapted for multiple forms of assessment	Developing rubrics takes time; once developed, grading with rubrics is relatively quick
Standards-Based	Gives high degree of feedback related to the identified performance standards	Can be adapted for multiple forms of assessment	Determining appropriate performance standards may be difficult and time consuming; once measures are developed grading is relatively quick
Written Descriptions	Allows a high level of personalized feedback; however, when used alone does not give students measure of relative performance	Designed for qualitative, open-ended forms of assessment; not as appropriate for objective tests with right and wrong answers	Time-intensive grading; not practical for use with all assignments

provide finer distinctions. Letter grades provide a convenient, concise, and familiar approach to marking. In addition, grades are readily understood by students and parents to provide an overall indication of performance.

The major limitation of letter grades is that they provide only a general indication of performance. There is nothing wrong with giving students an overall, summary judgment in the form of a grade. However, such a general mark, by itself, does not indicate what was done correctly or incorrectly. Strengths and limitations are not communicated. There is also a tendency for teachers to be influenced by factors other than performance in coming up with a grade on papers, projects, and presentations (e.g., effort, work habits, attitude). Furthermore, because teachers differ in their value systems, the proportion of students getting each grade can vary. In one class, most students can get As and Bs, whereas in another class, most students receive Bs and Cs.

What you need to make clear to your students about grades is what each letter means, so that their interpretation is accurate, appropriate, and helpful. Does getting an A mean that I did outstanding work, or does it mean that I did best in the class? Does it mean that the teacher thinks I worked hard on this or that I can do it really well? Does getting a C mean that I did about as well as most students or that I did satisfactory work?

As you can see, there are a number of possible interpretations, depending on how much factors other than performance are included and the basis of comparison (norm- or standards-based). In other words, grades can communicate effort, achievement, improvement, achievement in comparison to aptitude (some teachers grade high-aptitude students tougher), relative standing, or level of mastery. If you are clear about what each letter grade means, first to yourself and then to your students, it makes letter grading a much more effective means of enhancing student achievement. Table 13.4 presents different interpretations of letter grades.

Notice that it is possible to combine or mix norm- and standards-based approaches (Terwilliger, 1989). What often occurs is that the higher grades tend to be norm-referenced and the lower ones standards-based. That is, to get an A, students need to perform better than most, but a failure judgment tends to be based on absolute standards. If a purely relative scale were used and the norming group were the class itself, some students would always fail, despite what might be a high level of performance (a better procedure is to use data from previous classes to set the norm from a larger group). Also, some students would always succeed. It is only with absolute scales that all students can either succeed or fail.

Percentage Correct

For objective tests, the most common approach to reporting performance is to indicate the percentage of items answered correctly. Thus, we often characterize our achievement as, say, getting a 75 or a 92 on a test. These numbers refer to the percentage of items or points obtained out of a possible 100. These scores are easy to calculate, record, and combine at the end of the grading period. Usually, letter grades are associated with ranges of scores, so it's really a letter grade system that gives students a finer discrimination in their performance. It is possible, if not very common, to grade everything with percentage correct, even papers and essay items.

One limitation of using percentage correct in marking and grading is that, like a letter grade, only a general indication of performance is communicated. Another disadvantage is that the discriminations that are suggested by a scale from

TABLE 13.4 Different Interpretations of Letter Grades

Grade	Standards-Based	Norm-Referenced	Combined Norm-Referenced and Standards-Based	Based on Improvement
A	Outstanding or advanced: complete knowledge of all content; mastery of all targets; exceeds standards	Outstanding: among the highest or best performance	Outstanding: very high level of performance	Outstanding: much improvement on most or all targets
B	Very good or proficient: complete knowledge of most content; mastery of most targets; meets most standards	Very good: performs above the class average	Very good: better than average performance	Very good: some improvement on most or all targets
C	Acceptable or basic: command of only basic concepts or skills; mastery of some targets; meets some standards	Average: performs at the class average	Average	Acceptable: some improvement on some targets
D	Making progress or developing: lacks knowledge of most content; mastery of only a few targets; meets only a few standards	Poor: below the class average	Below average or weak: minimum performance for passing	Making progress: minimal progress on most targets
F	Unsatisfactory: lacks knowledge of content; no mastery of targets; does not meet any standards	Unsatisfactory: far below average; among the worst in the class	Unsatisfactory: lacks sufficient knowledge to pass	Unsatisfactory: no improvement on any targets

1 to 100 are much finer than what can be reliably assessed. Because of error in testing, there is usually no meaningful difference between scores differentiated by one or two points. That is, scores of 92 and 93 suggest the same level of student performance. In other words, the degree of precision suggested by percentage correct is not justified given the error that exists.

A third limitation is the tendency to equate percentage of items correct with percent mastered. As we have pointed out, items can differ tremendously in level of difficulty, so when students obtain a high percentage of correct answers, mastery may or may not be demonstrated, depending on the difficulty level of the assessment. Thus, it is probably incorrect to conclude that when a student obtains a 100, he or she knows 100% of the learning targets, or that a score of 50 corresponds to mastery of half the targets.

Pass–Fail

The idea of making a simple dichotomous evaluation, such as pass versus fail or satisfactory versus needs improvement, is consistent with mastery learning. In these approaches to learning and instruction, students are assessed on each learning objective. The judgment is criterion-referenced and results in a mastery–no mastery decision. Typically, students work on each objective until they demonstrate mastery, then move on.

There is a certain appeal to this approach, especially at the early elementary level, but unless it is combined with a system of providing clear feedback on specific strengths and weaknesses, it doesn't reflect very well the actual levels of performance that students demonstrate. Used alone, a two-category system is too simple. Most teachers find that at least three categories are needed, something like fail, pass, and excellent, or N (needs improvement), S (satisfactory), and O (outstanding). Also, it is difficult to keep standards high with a pass–fail system. The tendency is to relax the standards so that most students will not fail. This tells students clearly what they need to do to avoid failure, but it doesn't tell them very much about what excellent or outstanding performance is like.

Rubrics/Checklists

A variation of the pass–fail approach is to give students a rubric or a checklist to indicate their performance on each aspect of the learning target. The rubric has two or more categories. In a simple dichotomous rubric, the teacher might prepare a series of statements that describes aspects of the performance that the students need to include and places a check mark next to each one the teacher judges to be demonstrated.

A more elaborate approach provides students with scales of performance with detailed descriptions of each step of the scale. The teacher makes checks on the scale to indicate the level of performance. The rubric that describes the scoring is used as the checklist. The advantage of this type of grading is that the students receive detailed feedback about what they did well and what needs improvement. The detail in the rubric helps students understand more precisely where they need to improve. An additional benefit is that when rubrics are presented at the beginning of an assignment, they give students a specific idea of what they need to do to get the grade they want. The difficulty of this approach is developing the rubrics and keeping the system practical. However, once you develop detailed lists, they are fairly efficient because you only make check marks. This can be done efficiently, even if there are several such statements for each student product. It is certainly more efficient than writing comments on papers, though some individualized comments are important as well.

Standards-Based

Standards-based grading has emerged as a new and highly effective form of providing feedback to students and parents (Guskey, 2009; Marzano, 2006; O'Connor, 2009). Guskey and Bailey (2001) have identified four steps in the development of standards-based grading:

1. Identify major learning goals and standards.
2. Establish performance indicators for the standards.
3. Identify benchmarks that indicate graduated levels of proficiency.
4. Develop reporting forms that indicate progress and final achievement toward meeting the standards.

As discussed earlier and pointed out by Brookhart (2004), standards-based grading is a direct descendent of criterion-referenced grading. Both emphasize the idea of an absolute, established level of performance in a carefully defined domain. In standards-based grading, however, the "criterion" tends to be broad, at a high level, and the same for all students. These domains allow for unidimensionality in grading (Marzano, 2006); that is, each grade on a standards-based assessment reports performance on only one learning goal or standard.

The challenge with identifying the standards is to get them at the right level of specificity. Standards that are too detailed and numerous make reporting cumbersome and time consuming for teachers, and too complex for parent understanding. They also tend to orient assessments—and hence teaching—toward narrowly defined standards, rather than integrated and connected educational outcomes. However, standards that are too general do not provide enough information to show strengths or weaknesses. One effective approach to get standards at the right level is to begin with broad ones (often these are required) and provide more specific standards under each one (see Figure 13.2). This allows parents and students to see overall performance as well as areas of strength and weakness.

The performance indicators are descriptors that indicate the status of student achievement in relation to the standard. The most common form is to use four descriptors: *beginning, progressing, proficient*, and *exceptional*. When the standard is behaviorally oriented, descriptors that indicate how often the standard was reached could be used, such as *seldom, sometimes, frequently*, or *consistently* (Marzano, 2006). It is important for the descriptors to show graduated levels of proficiency to facilitate the reporting of progress as well as current status. By indicating progress, students and parents are able to gauge the amount of learning that has been demonstrated over the marking period. This is key information for understanding the link between student motivation and performance. As we will discuss later in the chapter, the advocates of standards-based grades have suggested the

FIGURE 13.2   **Elementary Reporting Form Illustrating a Grade for Achievement in the Subject Area with Separate Indicators for Process Skills**

Mathematics Grade:	1st B	2nd	3rd	4th
Demonstrates understanding of concepts	3			
Demonstrates mathematical thinking	3			
Makes mental calculations and reasonable estimations	4			
Uses strategies to solve problems	3			
Collects, organizes, and analyzes data	2			
Demonstrates a knowledge of basic facts	3			
Computes accurately	3			
Completes assignments on time	4			

Key to Subject Area Grades:

A = Outstanding (90–100% Mastery of Subject Goals)
B = Very Good (80–89% Mastery of Subject Goals)
C = Satisfactory (70–79% Mastery of Subject Goals)
D = Experiencing Difficulty (Below 70% Mastery of Subject Goals)

Key to Skills Grades:

  4 = Consistently or Independently
  3 = Usually
  2 = Sometimes
  1 = Seldom
NE = Not Evaluated

Source: From page 150 in *Developing Grading and Reporting Systems for Student Learning* by T. R. Gusky and J. M. Bailey. Copyright © 2001 by Sage Publications, Inc. Reprinted by permission of Sage Publications, Inc.

reworking of the traditional report card to reflect the standards-based methodology (Marzano, 2006; Welsh & D'Agostino, 2009).

Written Descriptions

An alternative to giving only a grade or score is to mark students' work with written descriptions. The advantage of this approach is that the comments can be highly individualized, pointing out unique strengths and weaknesses, and can focus attention on important issues. Students appreciate the effort of teachers who take the time to make these comments. Of course, the time needed is a major disadvantage. Most teachers simply do not have sufficient time to give this level of feedback. Then there is the added complication of converting the descriptions into grades or scores for report cards. Here the advantage from one perspective becomes a disadvantage from another because the uniqueness of the descriptions makes it difficult to grade consistently and fairly. In a strict system of written descriptions, the function of grades as a basis of comparison is lost.

Mixed Methods

Recently, assessment experts have focused attention on how marking and grading can improve instruction and student learning (Brookhart, 2004; Guskey, 1994; Guskey & Bailey, 2001). It is clear that detailed checklists, narratives, and marking based on prespecified criteria are preferred. However, for the vast majority of teachers, no one approach to grading is entirely sufficient. Not only do teachers generally use different approaches for different types of assessments in their classes, but they also frequently blend techniques. Obviously, there is overlap between letter grades and percentage correct systems. Rubrics, standards-based grades, and pass–fail systems are often combined with written descriptions. An example is a middle school in Beachwood, Ohio, where the traditional letter grade system was altered to only include the grades A, B, C, and I (for incomplete). This system took the option of failure off the table. Students who did not achieve proficient levels were required to make up the assignment (Guskey, 2009). The best strategy is for a teacher to explore the advantages and disadvantages of each system and experiment with various approaches. The challenge is to incorporate as much detail and reference to learning targets as possible when marking each piece of student work without being overwhelmed. Then you'll need to combine the marks into a final grade for the semester.

Determining Report Card (Composite) Grades

Unit and semester grades are given by teachers to provide a single indicator of student performance. Recognizing that professional judgment is essential for determining final grades as well as marks and grades for individual assessments, you will make some important decisions. These decisions can be summarized in the form of three steps:

1. Select what to include in the final grade.
2. Select weights for each individual assessment.
3. Combine weighted scores to determine a single grade.

Before examining these steps, two points need to be stressed about the process of developing composite grades. One is that it is often at this point that teachers must do the most work, adapting their personal approach of grading to the external pressures of school and district guidelines. These guidelines might include grading formulas that outline what elements need to be included in the final grade. They could specify weights for exams or projects. In certain cases districts have even been known to specify allowable failure rates. These external mandates are often a source of frustration for teachers, who feel their professional judgment is being usurped. The key is to understand these guidelines from the outset and develop ways of negotiating them that don't compromise your values.

Another point about the development of composite grades is how the process has been affected by grade book technology. Although in certain ways electronic grade books are conceptually not too different than the spiral bound books that were the norm in the past, some aspects of the technology have shifted the way we approach the task. This will be discussed in some detail later.

Select What to Include in the Final Grade

Generally, this is where you will have a fair amount of leeway. To some extent, it is up to you to determine which assessments will contribute to the final grade. As we have already suggested, it is best if you base final grades primarily on academic performance. But which performances should be included? Tests? Participation in class? Papers? Quizzes? Homework? Before selecting the assessments, think again about your overall learning goals. Your selection of what goes into the final grade should provide the most accurate information in relation to these goals. If you have done a good job of basing your formal assessments on the learning targets, then each of these assessments will contribute meaningfully to the grade. It is less clear if pop quizzes, participation, and homework should be included.

On the one hand, pop quizzes, participation, and homework do focus on student performance, but can they legitimately serve as documentation of student learning and understanding? If they are primarily formative in nature, to give students practice and feedback, they may be viewed more as instruction than assessment and should not be included in a final grade. Some teachers argue that pop quizzes are not fair to students, and some also contend that homework may not have been completed by the student. Many teachers realize that participation in class is influenced by group dynamics and personality. Other teachers view pop quizzes, participation, and homework as indicators of how much students are paying attention and learning in class and will use them to calculate final grades. The choice of whether to include these student performances is yours, and either choice is legitimate. Just be sure to make clear to students and parents what is going into the grade and why it is fair.

As discussed earlier, you will want to be especially careful in considering factors such as attendance, effort, and personal/social characteristics such as cooperativeness, participation, and work habits in determining grades. Specifically, you don't want nonacademic factors, which probably have little relationship to academic learning, to have much influence on the final grade.

We believe the best rule on these matters is this: If a grade is for academic performance in areas such as reading, science, mathematics, history, and the like, then the grade should be determined primarily by student academic performance on major assessments. This is essentially a matter of maintaining appropriate validity so that your inferences about academic performance are reasonable. If cooperativeness and participation are important targets, consider separate grades for each.

Finally, in planning the assessments that you will include, carefully consider how many are needed to give an accurate overall judgment of each student's performance. Would it be reasonable to base a semester grade on a single exam? How about a 9-week grade—would two tests and a paper be sufficient? Probably most would agree that a single assessment, alone, is definitely not sufficient. In the words of Grant Wiggins, "A single grade hides more than it reveals" (1998, p. 248). Three assessments for a 9-week grade is much better, but even that may not be enough. Often schools using online grade books are able to keep track of the number of assessments teachers record and set guidelines for a minimum number. The rule of thumb with respect to number of assessments needed is the more, the better (Marzano, 2006). Although, one must be sure that assessment time does not interfere significantly with instructional time, there is a danger of overtesting the students. Once again, your professional judgment is needed. We have found that at least one fairly major test or other assessment is needed about every 2 weeks. Many teachers are constrained by a 50-minute or less class period, and it's difficult to sample 2 weeks of content in anything less than an hour of testing time. Besides, children have limited attention spans. If students lose interest or find it hard to concentrate, error is introduced into the assessment.

Select Weights for Each Assessment

Not only do you need to identify the assessments, but you also need to decide how much each one will count in the final grade. Obviously, more important assessments are given greater weight. What determines if an assessment is important? You probably guessed it—more professional judgment! The most significant assessments are those that (a) correspond most closely to the learning goals and targets (content-related evidence for validity), (b) reflect instructional time, (c) are most reliable, and (d) are most current.

Because there are multiple learning targets in a unit or semester, you need to break out the percentage that each target contributes to the whole. We have illustrated this in Figure 13.3 in the form of a pie chart for a unit on the animal kingdom. You can see that different percentages correspond to each topic. In this case, the overall goal is determined mostly by vertebrate animal characteristics and behaviors. Now you need to weigh your assessments to match these percentages so that the final grade reflects the relative contribution of each topic. This will provide good content-related evidence for validity, which is a primary concern. In this example, about 50% of what determines the final grade should be the assessments on vertebrates. This percentage is independent of the length of the book chapters, or assessments, or the instructional time devoted to each topic. What you are determining is solely the value of each of the topics.

Even though instructional time is not a factor in the first consideration of weights, it's still an important barometer of the amount of emphasis given to each topic. For that reason, we think it's only fair to take time devoted to instruction as a factor. As we have already emphasized, students need to know before an assessment is taken what will be covered. Often this includes topics or concepts that have

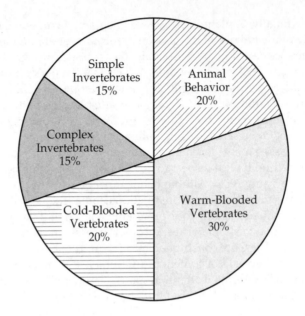

FIGURE 13.3 **Percentage of Each Topic That Contributes to the Final Grade**

not been discussed in class. Although there is nothing wrong with testing students on material they learn on their own, it's best if the weights reflect instructional focus. If you spent 50% of your 9 weeks studying simple invertebrates, it probably wouldn't be fair to weight this topic at only 15%. Similarly, you might determine that you *intend* to weight vertebrates at 50%, but when you look back over the weeks, you figure that only 25% of the students' time was spent learning about vertebrates. This would suggest that a more appropriate weight would be 30–35%, at most. Obviously you don't know for sure how much time you take until the instruction is completed. Although it is good to have guidelines to share with students at the beginning of terms, your final determination of weights needs to be determined close to the end of instruction. Weights should not be set in stone at the beginning of the unit.

Reliability is a factor in weighting because, *other things being equal*, especially validity, we want to put more weight on more accurate assessments. This will reduce the overall amount of error that is included in determining the grade. Generally reliability increases with a greater number of items for each target and for objective items. But it is important to emphasize that the most important concern is validity; highly reliable assessments should never be given more weight than is appropriate, given the validity of the assessment.

If you test the same content more than once, as you would with a cumulative final exam, put more weight on the most current assessment. In fact, a later assessment on the same material might mean that the earlier assessment should be dropped. Although there is a bias toward averaging in most grading systems, it doesn't always make sense pedagogically (Marzano, 2006; O'Conner, 2009). After all, if your goal is to communicate accurately the nature of a student's current performance, wouldn't the more recent assessment be better? From a practical standpoint, however, you'll find that it's difficult to simply discard an earlier test score. The best compromise is to weigh the cumulative exam more than each of the preceding ones so that final performance outweighs what students demonstrate at the beginning or middle of the unit.

Given these considerations, you now need to combine the assessments properly to obtain the final grade.

Combining Different Scores and Grades

Over the past 10 years, most schools and districts have moved toward using electronic grading systems. These systems can take the form of stand-alone grade book software programs that are used on teachers' individual computers, or web-based programs that can be accessed online by teachers, administrators, students, and parents. The advantages of the software-based systems are that you can work offline, and they tend to be quicker for entering grades and making calculations. The main advantage of the online systems is the high degree of communication they allow both within the school and between teachers, students, and parents. Both systems not only save time by allowing teachers to avoid tedious and complex calculations, but also give multiple opportunities for increasing grade feedback with the students and parents.

Although for most teachers grade calculations are now largely a matter of entering scores into the electronic grade book, Guskey (2002) points out that the mathematical precision that is achieved does not necessarily bring greater objectivity, accuracy, or fairness. He points out that these programs do not lessen the challenges teachers face when making decisions about what will be included and how each score or grade contributes to the final grade (e.g., how to handle zeros, averaging, improvement). Professional judgment is still key. In this section we will give a brief overview of what options for combining grades are available when working within a grade book program and then discuss the importance of incorporating the intangibles of teacher judgment. Figures 13.4 and 13.5 illustrate examples of formats that are used with electronic grade books.

Weighted Categories versus Total Points Methods. Traditionally there are two systems for combining grades and computing totals. In the **weighted categories method**, assessments that use different types of scores and grades and tests with different numbers of items are scaled and combined to produce a composite grade. For example, homework assignments, which may be graded on a check plus/check/check minus scale; projects, graded using a rubric; and exams that follow a 100-point objective scale can be weighted by category and combined to develop a final grade. The advantage of the percent correct method is that it allows for some flexibility in the weighting process.

GradeBookWizard.com
Blue Pegasus

Quick Links: Go To...

Gradebook: 4 - Eng. Literature | 45 min | Help | Home | Logout

| Class: | 4 - Eng. Literature | | Gradebook | Website | Setup |
| Dates: | Q2 | 10/26/2009 - 1/22/2010 | Messages | Files | Account |

Home | Gradebook | Students | Assignments | Attendance | Homework | Report Cards | Reports

Class Gradebook | Copy Assignments | Weightings/Worth | Website Handouts

Lock Grades | Create New Assignment | Grade All | Grade All w/Comments | Print Grades | Save to File | Grade Sheet

Sort By: Last Name | Oldest First | Format: Ltr/Score | Set Prefs | Send Email & Message | For Grades Below 80%

<< Previous Week | All weeks in grade period | Next Week>>

Class Gradebook — Select a class and date range from the drop-down lists above. Use the arrow keys to move up/down or left/right in the grid when grading.

Total Points: 800

ID	Name	Grade	#Z	Create New	1. pre-Shakespeare 11/2/2009 (Grp) Class Work ABCDF+- [100]		2. Victorian Literature 12/2/2009 (Grp) Class Work ABCDF+- [100]		3. Shakespeare's Sonatas 12/6/2009 (Grp) Class Work ABCDF+- [100]		4. Shakespeare's Sonatas ch2 12/10/2009 (Grp) Class Work ABCDF+- [100]	
E30055	Albertville, John	A+ 98.8%			A	95	A+	100	A+	100	A	95
01. E29987	Bagginson, Frodo	A+ 97.5%			A+	97	A	95	A+	100	B+	87
03. E29990	Clemens, Samuel	A 94.1%				EXC	A+	100	A+	100	B+	88
04. E155546	Cramer, Al	C+ 77.4%	1		F	MIS 0%	B+	87	B+	88	A	95
02. E30056	Einstein, Albert	A 94.7%			A+	102	D	65	A+	100	A+	100
16. E29992	Gamgee, Samwise	B 85.9%	1		A+	100	F	MIS 0%	A-	90	A+	100
19. E30057	Graves, Suzanne	B- 80.5%			B	85	A	95	A+	100	A+	100
12. E29994	Gray, Gandalf	A 94.7%			A	95	A-	92	B+	88	A+	100
18. E29997	Little, Stuart	C+ 77.4%			C+	78	B-	Late 80	A+	100	D+	68
10. E30058	Nguyen, Dominic	B 84.7%	1		B	85	A	96	A+	100		ABS 0%

ID	Name	Grade	#Z	New Assignment	1. pre-Shakespeare 11/2/2009 (Grp)		2. Victorian Literature 12/2/2009 (Grp)		3. Shakespeare's Sonatas 12/6/2009 (Grp)		4. Shakespeare's Sonatas ch2 12/10/2009 (Grp)	
04. E30003	Perkins, Andy	B 85.7%	1		B	85	A+	100	A+	100		ABS 0%
06. E83808	Simon, Bob	B 86.1%			B+	89	D	63	A-	90	B-	80
17. E30023	Smith, Steven	A- 90.2%			A-	92	B+	87	A+	100	C	75
03. E30004	Springs, Alice	B 86.4%	1		A	93	A+	100	A+	100	C+	77
15. E145913	Svensson, Lars	F 44.6%	3			ABS 0%	A	95	A-	92	B	85
09. E155543	Ypsilon, Delta	A+ 99.0%				EXC	A+	100	A+	100	A	93
	Average Assignment %				91.3%		91.9%		97.3%		90.2%	

FIGURE 13.4   Grading Page Screenshot of an Electronic Gradebook
Source: Courtesy of Blue Pegasus LLC.

Although it is generally important to let students know the weights of categories at the beginning of a class, it is possible that a teacher may want to shift the category weights later in the grading period based on what curriculum was covered or other classroom factors.

With the **total points method,** the teacher gives each assessment a number of points that reflects its weight. The final grade is simply the total points of all assessments added. For example, homework assignments may only count for 5 or 10 points, whereas a test may be weighted for 50 points. The advantage of the total points method is that because the weight is worked into the point value of an

GradeBookWizard.com
Blue Pegasus

Ms. Swanson
GradeBookWizard Demo School

E29990 Clemens, Samuel
Student Progress Report
Grade Period: Q2

Class	Score	Grade
4 - Eng. Literature [Ms. Swanson]	by category	A / 94.1%

4 - Eng. Literature [Enrolled] Ms. Gloria Swanson

Calc Score:	Grade: A / 94.1%

Simple Moving Average (last 4 assignments): 12/2/2009 - 1/12/2010

	A+	A	A-	B+	B	B-	C+	C	C-	D+	D	D-	F	CR
	3			2		1								

Assignment	Due Date	Score	Reported	Class Avg
Test 2 [Class Work]	1/12/2010	80 / 100	B- / 80.0%	96.5%
December Homework [Homework]	12/20/2009	89 / 100	B+ / 89.0%	85.1%
Test 1 [Quizzes and Exams]	12/17/2009	100 / 100	A+ / 100.0%	95.0%
Shakespeare's Sonatas ch2 [Class Work]	12/10/2009	88 / 100	B+ / 88.0%	90.2%
Shakespeare's Sonatas [Class Work]	12/6/2009	100 / 100	A+ / 100.0%	97.3%
Victorian Literature [Class Work]	12/2/2009	100 / 100	A+ / 100.0%	91.9%
pre-Shakespeare [Class Work]	11/2/2009	/ 100	EXC	91.3%

Grades by Category:

Category	Grade	Portion of Grade
Class Work	A- / 92.0% [368 / 400]	60.0%
Homework	B+ / 89.0% [89 / 100]	10.0%
Participation		0.0%
Quizzes and Exams	A+ / 100.0% [100 / 100]	30.0%

Attendance Incidents

Absent:	Excused Absence:	Tardy:	Excused Tardy:

No attendance records are available for the selected date range

PARENT(S)/GUARDIAN(S): Please sign below to indicate that you have read this report.

X_____   X_____

FIGURE 13.5 Electronic Gradebook, Progress Report Screenshot
Source: Courtesy of Blue Pegasus LLC.

assignment, it clearly lets students know the importance of an assignment toward the final grade. The disadvantage of this approach is that the teacher must adjust the number of items to equal the points each assessment should provide, or change the score of an assessment to reflect the points. In most cases this is pretty cumbersome, so if the total points method is used, the assessments are carefully designed to avoid the recalculation of any individual assessment so that they can simply be added. This may constrain the nature of the assessments. Rather than have the method of combining scores drive the assessments, let each assessment be constructed to provide the best measure of student performance, and then combine. In our opinion, the weighted categories approach is much better than total points for this reason. However, in most grade book programs there is a choice when setting up a class between these two methods.

Using Judgment When Combining Grades.   Whether you use the weighted categories or total points method, when you include many different assessments and mathematically combine them, you are essentially taking the average of all the performances. Although averaging is justified as a way to include all the assessments (and keep students motivated), there is a danger that *mindless* averaging, as we have noted, will distort the students' true capabilities. For this reason, it is always important to look at the practice of combining grades as more than just a cold computation. For example, when a student evaluation system is designed to move students from novice to expert on an appropriate skill continuum, it may not make good sense to average performances during the entire period of learning (Wiggins, 1998). If a student begins as a novice and obtains a low score, should that score be averaged with a final "expert" performance to result in an average grade? What is critical is reporting student attainment of the skill in relation to the rubric and scoring criteria at the time of the report, regardless of earlier performances. Obviously this is an instance where adjustments need to be made. This could take the form of shifting weights to emphasize more recent work. Regardless, it is important for teachers to always think critically about the effect of their grading systems.

One approach to this is to consider the use of another, less systematic approach to combining grades: the *eyeball method*. With the eyeball method the teacher simply reviews the scores and grades and estimates an average for them, without performing any calculations, to come up with what seems to be the correct grade. This has obvious disadvantages, not the least of which is the lack of objectivity. This method isn't recommended, but it does have one redeeming quality. With eyeballing, the teacher asks, "All things considered and looking at the whole as more than the sum of each part, what is the most valid grade for this student?" The notion that it's important to consider everything together has some merit because it recognizes that teacher professional judgment is needed to give grades.

Consider the other extreme: teachers who mindlessly calculate averages without any consideration of factors that might be important, such as student absenteeism, effort, and possible testing error. Just because a numeric average comes up with a certain grade doesn't mean that that grade is a valid indicator of student achievement. Just because a test says it's so, does that mean that it is? In some cases, eyeballing grades might be a good first step. The eyeballed grades could then be

Teacher's Corner

Beth Carter

National Board Certified Elementary and Middle School Teacher

I combine several types of grades to get my students' 9 weeks' grades. I break my grade book into categories. One third of my grades collected come from rubrics and class assignments. Another third is from quizzes. These quizzes are typically given on a weekly basis. They can be announced or unannounced. The final third of my grades are from chapter or unit tests. I try to give three per 9 weeks. I also drop one low score in any of the categories to account for a "bad" day.

compared to calculated percentages. This might help teachers identify the inclinations and biases they have that are the root of some of their professional decisions. Another idea is to ask for eyeball grades from students. That is, pass out student portfolios, have students review them and then ask, "Based on what you see in front of you, what grade do you think you deserve? Justify your answer." These student eyeballed grades not only give teachers many insights into the individual student's self-perception as learners, they also lead to very entertaining discussions!

Note in Beth Carter's Teacher's Corner that she combines different types of evidence of learning and gives students the benefit of the doubt if they were not able to demonstrate their learning.

Cheating.   Another issue is the lowering of grades in response to student cheating (Cizek, 1999, 2003). Obviously cheating is a very serious offense, and appropriate disciplinary action is warranted. However, lowering grades is not appropriate discipline if there is an extreme negative impact on the grade. Suppose you give a zero to a student when he or she is caught cheating on a major test. Does this score accurately represent the student's knowledge and performance? Here you are using grades to punish the student. It would be better to find another kind of punishment and retest the student.

Recognizing Teacher Fallibility.   One of the most difficult challenges teachers face, especially when they first start to teach and test students, is to write tests at the appropriate level of difficulty and emphasis. Suppose you prepare a test and the majority of students do very poorly. There are two primary considerations here. One is that the students just didn't get it, didn't understand. The other is that the test is unfair—that the emphasis on some areas does not match instruction. Sometimes when students do poorly it reflects more on inadequacies of your teaching than it does on student achievement! You need to be open to this possibility and make appropriate changes to reflect student achievement more fairly. One option is to give an improved makeup test.

Teacher's Corner

Tami Slater

National Board Certified Elementary Reading Specialist Teacher

I do not use zeros in calculating final grades. Students in elementary school do not get enough grades in one subject, and averaging in a zero as a grade would bring their average down so low, the student would not recover from it. A zero averaged in a final grade would not show a true reflection of what the student can do, and that is what I believe grades need to show.

Finally, it's important to be willing to change grades when justified. In the first place, mistakes are made in calculating grades. A possible hint of this occurs when a final grade for a student doesn't seem right. In this circumstance, go back over the calculations to be sure there are no mistakes. Second, students sometimes have legitimate arguments about a grade. It is possible to overlook things. In fact, this is probable when you grade a lot of assessments. Be willing to admit that you were wrong and record the best, most accurate score or grade.

See Table 13.5 for a summary of what to do and what not to do for effective grading practices.

Case Study for Reflection

By the end of the first 9-week marking period, Ms. Byrd, a new middle school English teacher, had collected and graded a substantial amount of student work, including nine weekly tests, 12 quizzes, nearly 30 homework assignments, a writing journal, a research project, and several in-class assignments. When the time came to turn in student grades, she calculated individual student averages based on all the assignments and tests, the journal, and the research project. She weighted each grade recorded in her grade book the same, but wasn't confident about how to translate journal and research project grades into numbers to get the overall average. Also, as she did the grades, she found several students she thought should have done better and others who probably deserved a lower grade, but she went with the numbers.

QUESTIONS FOR CONSIDERATION

1. What suggestions do you have for Ms. Byrd to improve her grading practices?
2. What kind of parent reaction do you think she might get when the grades are sent home?

TABLE 13.5 Do's and Don'ts of Effective Grading

Do	Don't
Use well-thought-out professional judgments	Depend entirely on number crunching
Try everything you can to score and grade fairly	Allow personal bias to affect grades
Grade according to preestablished learning targets and standards	Grade on the curve using the class as the norm group
Clearly inform students and parents of grading procedures at the beginning of the semester	Keep grading procedures secret
Base grades primarily on student performance	Use effort, improvement, attitudes, and motivation for borderline students
Rely most on current information	Penalize poorly performing students early in the semester
Mark, grade, and return assessments to students as soon as possible and with as much feedback as possible	Return assessments weeks later with little or no feedback
Review borderline cases carefully; when in doubt, assign the higher grade	Be inflexible with borderline cases
Convert scores to the same scale before combining	Use zero scores indiscriminately when averaging grades
Weight scores before combining	Include extra credit assignments that are not related to the learning targets
Use a sufficient number of assessments	Rely on one or two assessments for a semester grade
Be willing to change grades when warranted	Lower grades for cheating, misbehaving, tardiness, or absence

Reporting Student Progress to Parents

An important function of marks and grades is to provide information that can be shared with parents. Parents are critical to student learning, and effectively reporting student progress can help them better understand their children and know what they can do to provide appropriate support and motivation. Reporting to parents can take many forms, including weekly or monthly grade reports, phone calls, e-mails, letters, newsletters, conferences, and of course, report cards. For teachers, schools, and districts that use them, online grade books have also become important means of reporting and communicating about progress. Although report card grades are the most common way by which parents keep abreast of student progress, what those grades communicate is usually limited and therefore needs to be supplemented with additional forms of communication.

Report Cards

The foundation for most reporting systems is the report card. This simple form is constructed to communicate to parents the progress of their children. Typically, grades, checklists or numerical scores are provided, along with teacher comments or observations that relate to effort, cooperation, and other behaviors. For report cards to be effective, parents must be able to understand what the grades and comments mean. The information needs to be accurately interpreted, and parents need to learn enough to guide improvement efforts.

Most report cards indicate only current status in different subjects, and they do not provide the detail needed for parents to know what to *do* with the information (see Azwell & Schmar, 1995; Brookhart, 2004; Guskey, 1996; Guskey & Bailey, 2001; Wiggins, 1998, for alternatives to traditional report cards). Consequently, you'll probably need to supplement report cards with other forms of communication.

Progress Reports

One approach to reporting student progress is to provide some type of periodic progress report. This could be done weekly, biweekly, or monthly. The advantage of progress reports is not only that they help ensure that there are no surprises at the end of the term, but they have also been shown to have a significant and positive effect on student learning (Marzano, 2006). The problem they present is that they take time to put together. However, with electronic gradebooks, it is now possible to quickly create grade reports for entire classes. These reports can be customized by the teacher to show not only student grades on class assignments and averaged totals, but also summaries of performance by category, graphs, connections between assignments and standards, and student attendance information. Additional information you may want to include would be learning targets for the period, copies of rubrics and scoring criteria, descriptions of student motivation and affect, and written suggestions for helping the student. You will want to be sure to include some positive comments. It may be helpful to identify two or three areas that the parents could focus on until the next report. If possible, provide specific expectations for what you want parents to do at home to help. Be clear in asserting that parents need to be partners in the learning process. If these expectations can be individualized for each student, so much the better, but even a standard list of expectations is good.

It is important to note that when using online grade applications this information is always available to students and parents. All they need to do is log in to the system and review the grade book to see their progress. This fundamental change in the method of grade reporting has clear implications for the teacher. A grade book that from day one of the term is open to students and parents changes the nature and degree of professional judgment the teacher may use. Once a score is published—in this case by simply entering it in the program—it would be harder to think about going in and changing weights and scores.

Another type of written communication is the informal note or letter. Taking only a minute or two to write a personal note to parents about their child is much appreciated. It shows concern and caring. Begin such a note with something positive, then summarize progress and suggest an expectation or two for improvements.

Parent–Teacher Conferences

The parent–teacher conference is the most common way teachers communicate with parents about student progress. This is typically a face-to-face discussion, though phone conferences and calls can also be used. In fact, brief phone calls by the teacher to talk with parents, like informal notes, are very well received and appreciated, especially when the calls are about positive progress and suggestions rather than for disciplinary or other problems.

There are two types of parent–teacher conferences, based on two primary purposes. Group conferences, such as what occurs at back-to-school or open-house nights, are conducted to communicate school and class policies, class content, evaluation procedures, expectations, and procedures for getting in touch with the teacher. Individual conferences are conducted to discuss the individual student's achievement, progress, or difficulties. Parent–teacher conferences may be initiated by either the teacher or the parent, based on these purposes.

Parent–teacher conferences are required in most schools. Although the format for middle and high school conferences are different than elementary because of the number of students, the goals are basically the same. Whether the conference is in the context of a one-on-one meeting or a back-to-school night, most of the suggestions in Figure 13.6 apply.

It is essential to plan the conference and to be prepared. This means having all the information well organized in advance and knowing what you hope to achieve

---

FIGURE 13.6   Checklist for Conducting Parent–Teacher Conferences

✓ Plan each conference in advance.
✓ Conduct the conference in a private, quiet, comfortable setting.
✓ Begin with a discussion of positive student performances.
✓ Establish an informal, professional tone.
✓ Encourage parent participation in the conference.
✓ Be frank in reviewing student strengths and weaknesses.
✓ Review language skills.
✓ Review learning targets with examples of student performances that show progress.
✓ Avoid discussing other students and teachers.
✓ Avoid bluffing.
✓ Identify two or three areas to work on in a plan of action.

from the conference. This will probably include a list of areas you want to cover and some questions to ask parents. If possible, you may be able to find out what parents would like to review before the conference. Examples of student work should be organized to show progress and performance in relation to learning targets. The conference is an ideal time for pointing out specific areas of strength and weakness that report card grades cannot communicate.

You want the conference to be a conversation, not a lecture. Listening to parents will help you understand their child better. Even though it is natural to feel anxious about meeting with parents, it's important to take a strong, professional stance. Rather than being timid, take charge. This should be done with a friendly and informal tone that encourages parents to participate. You'll want to be positive, but you need to be direct and honest about areas that need improvement. Keep the focus on academic progress rather than student behavior.

We think it's always important to discuss student performance in reading, writing, and speaking, regardless of the subject matter of the class. These language skills are essential and should be reviewed. Avoid discussing other students or teachers, and be willing to admit that you don't know an answer to a question. By the end of the conference you should identify, in consultation with the parents, a course of action or steps to be taken at home and at school.

Student-Led Conferences

A new kind of reporting to parents involves students as the leader in their own conferences (Stiggins, 2008b). In a student-led conference, students lead parents through a detailed and direct review of their work. Teachers take the role of facilitator by creating a positive environment in which the conferences can take place, and by preparing students. For students to take responsibility for leading a conference with their parents, they need to have reflected on and evaluated their performance. This is usually accomplished by some kind of portfolio assessment. In addition to promoting student responsibility, parents tend to be more involved.

In a student-led conference, students are essentially telling a story about their learning. This helps parents see progress over time from the perspective of the student. In preparing for the conference, students must learn to describe and evaluate their work. This self-reflection promotes additional learning (Marzano, 2006) and gives students confidence that they are able to understand their capabilities and achievements. A sense of pride and ownership is developed in the student.

Summary

This chapter stressed the importance of a teacher's professional judgment when implementing a grading and reporting system. There is no completely objective procedure for grading. Grading is professional decision making that depends on the teacher's values and beliefs, experience, external pressures, and best subjective judgments. We reviewed the different functions of marking and grading and took a close look at how factors other than academic performance affect grades. The chapter examined the basis of comparison used in grading, as well as approaches to marking and grading. Approaches to combine assessments were presented, along with reporting procedures to parents. Important points include the following:

- In the classroom, the major function of marking and grading is to provide students with feedback about their academic performance.
- Although teachers should strive for a high degree of objectivity in grading, it is important to understand the role of professional judgment.
- When grading, teachers must negotiate between external constraints (e.g., grade policies, limited time) and their professional values related to assessment.
- Teachers need to provide a sufficient level of detail for marking to be informative for students.
- In general, use nonacademic factors such as effort, attendance, student aptitude, improvement, and attitudes only in borderline cases.
- Grades communicate comparison between student performance and the performance of other students (norm-referenced) or between student performance and predetermined standards (standards-based).
- The major function of norm-referenced systems is to rank and sort students. Student competitiveness is fostered; most teachers find they must do some degree of sorting.
- The major function of standards-based systems is to judge students in relation to established levels of performance.
- Percent correct is the most common type of standards-based grading. Percentage correct depends on item difficulty.
- Motivation is enhanced when grades are used formatively as well as summatively to communicate internal attributions, self-efficacy, progress on mastery goals, and intrinsic value.
- Approaches to grading include using letters, percent correct measures, pass–fail tests, rubrics, checklists, standards-based, and written descriptions.
- Determining report card grades requires professional decisions about what to include, how to weight each assessment, and how weighted assessments are combined.
- Provide a sufficient number of assessments to obtain a fair and accurate portrait of the student.
- Weight each assessment by the contribution to the goal, instructional time, and reliability. Give more recent, comprehensive assessments more weight.
- Consider variation of each assessment if combining relative comparisons.
- Be flexible with borderline cases; don't let numbers make what should be professional decisions, subjective decisions.
- Do not use zeros indiscriminately when averaging scores.
- Grades should not be determined by inappropriate student behavior or cheating.

- Grades should be changed when warranted to reflect the most fair and accurate record of student performance.
- Reporting student progress to parents can be done by phone, e-mail, with written materials, and in teacher–parent conferences.
- Reports to parents should be well prepared with samples of student work to illustrate progress and areas that need further attention.
- Teacher–parent conferences are informal, professional meetings during which teachers discuss progress with parents and determine action steps to be taken.
- Student-led conferences with parents promote student self-evaluation and parent involvement.

Self-Instructional Review Exercises

1. Indicate whether each of the following refers to norm-referenced (NR) or standards-referenced (SR) grading.

   a. Used to show which students are the worst in a group
   b. Average test scores are typically lower
   c. Easily adapted from scoring rubrics
   d. Uses percentile rank
   e. Uses percent correct
   f. Items tend to be easier
   g. Determination of standards is subjective
   h. Fosters student competitiveness

2. In what ways is teacher professional judgment important in determining the actual standard employed in grading and marking students?

3. What major limitation do most approaches to grading have in common? What can teachers do to avoid this limitation?

4. Shaunda is a sixth grader. She is the oldest in a low-income family of six. Because her parents are not home very much, Shaunda takes on responsibilities with her brothers and sisters. The family lives in a small home, so it's hard for Shaunda to get the privacy she needs to do her homework. Consequently, she often does not hand in any homework. She has a very positive attitude toward school, and she is very attentive in class and tries hard to do well. Your class uses the following grading policy: in-class work accounts for 25% of the final grade; homework, 25%; and 50% for tests and quizzes. The grading scale in the school is 95–100, A; 85–94, B; 75–84, C; 65–74, D; <65, F. Shaunda's averages are in-class work, 85%; homework, 30%; and tests and quizzes, 70%. What overall composite percent correct would Shaunda have? What grade would you give her? Does the grade reflect her academic performance? Should the grading policy be changed?

5. Suppose Greg is a very capable student who does very well on tests (e.g., 95s) but very poorly on homework. He just doesn't want to do work he sees as boring. His homework scores pull his test scores down so that the overall average is B−. What final grade would you give? How is motivation affected?

Answers to Self-Instructional Review Exercises

1. a. NR, b. NR, c. SR, d. NR, e. SR, f. SR, g. SR, h. NR.

2. The standard is set by how difficult the teacher makes the assessment items; scores essay, short-answer, and performance-based assessments; and sets the criterion level (e.g., the percentage correct).

3. The major limitation of letter grades, percent correct, and pass–fail approaches is that they provide only a general overview of performance. Supplemental information that details the strengths and weaknesses of the students is needed.

4. Shaunda's composite score would be figured as $(85 \times .25) + (30 \times .25) + (70 \times .5) = 21.25 + 7.5 + 35 = 63.75$. According to the grading scale, she would receive an F. This reflects the relatively high contribution of homework and the fact that she was not able to get much of it finished. However, her classwork and performance on tests tell a different story, and a more accurate grade would be a D. Suppose homework was 10% instead of 25% and classwork was 40%. Then her composite would be a 72, almost 10 points higher. Given her home situation, she certainly should not fail, and the grading scale needs to be changed to put more weight on academic performance. The relatively high percentage for in-class work, 25%, is subject to teacher bias and should be reduced.

5. Actual test performance should not be affected negatively by nonacademic factors such as effort and compliance. We suggest a policy that homework won't hurt a grade, but could improve it, and give the student an A. Motivation is negatively affected because homework is obviously too easy and does not help Greg learn. The final grade has little meaning with respect to his self-efficacy. The goal orientation is on performance rather than mastery, and the final grade of B− does not accurately indicate his level of competence. There is no indication that grades have been used formatively.

Suggestions for Action Research

1. Create a grading plan that would make sense for a class you plan to teach. Include a statement of purpose and explain what would be included, how weights would be established, and the final grading scale. Then give the plan to other students and ask them to critique it. If possible, give the plan to a classroom teacher and see how realistic it is.

2. Interview teachers on the subject of grading. Do they use a norm-referenced or criterion-referenced approach or a combination? Ask them about the areas that require professional judgments, like what to do with borderline students, how zeros are used, how to apply extra credit, and the like. Ask them how they use grades to motivate students. Have them tell the story of some especially difficult professional judgments they had to make.

3. Observe a class when graded tests or papers are returned to students. What is their reaction? What do they seem to do with the information? If possible, speak with the students afterwards and ask them how they feel about the grading.

4. Conduct an experiment by giving some students just grades and other students grades with comments and suggestions for improvement. See if the students react differently. Interview the students to determine if the nature of the feedback affected their motivation.

5. Talk with some parents about their experiences with parent–teacher conferences. What did they get out of it? How could it have been improved? Were the suggestions in Figure 13.6 followed?

6. Write a personal history of your experiences of being graded as a student. Discuss a time that you felt you were graded unfairly. Tell the story of a teacher who you thought did a good job encouraging learning through good grading practices.

Administering, Interpreting, and Using Standardized and State Standards-Based Tests

In this chapter, we are concerned with important uses of standardized tests by classroom teachers, including year-to-year program evaluation and interpreting standardized and standards-based test scores to parents. This will include a review of different types of standardized tests and scores to better understand students' initial levels of achievement and aptitude, strengths and weaknesses, and deficiencies to establish learning targets and plan an effective instructional program. We will also discuss your role in administering standardized tests and preparing students to do their best. First we need to review the statistical terms and numerical indices that are commonly used in creating and reporting standardized test scores.

Fundamental Descriptive Statistics

Descriptive statistics are used to describe or summarize a larger number of scores. The nature of the description can be in the form of a single number, such as an average score, a table of scores, or a graph. You have seen and read many of these kinds of descriptions (e.g., the average rainfall for a month, the median price of new homes, a baseball batting average). Descriptive statistics efficiently portray important features of a group of scores to convey information that is essential for understanding what the scores mean. For standardized tests, descriptive statistics are used as the basis for establishing, reporting, and interpreting scores.

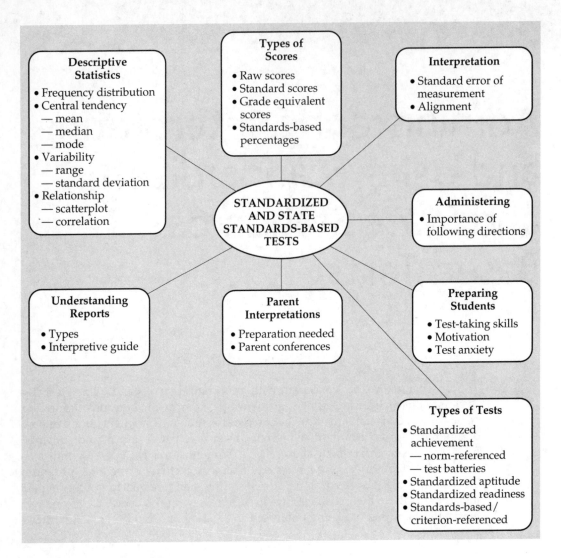

CHAPTER 14   Concept Map

Frequency Distributions

The first step in understanding important characteristics of a large set of scores is to organize the scores into a frequency distribution. This distribution simply indicates the number of students who obtained different scores on the test. In a simple **frequency distribution,** the scores are ranked, from highest to lowest, and the number of students obtaining each score is indicated. If the scores are organized into intervals, a *grouped frequency distribution* is used. Suppose, for example, that a

FIGURE 14.1   Frequency Distributions of Test Scores

Student	Score	Simple Frequency Distribution		Grouped Frequency Distribution	
		Score	f	Interval	f
Austin	96				
Tyler	94	96	1	92–96	3
Tracey	92	94	1	86–91	4
Karon	90	92	1	80–85	7
Hannah	90	90	2	74–79	3
Lanie	86	86	2	68–73	3
Allyson	86	84	3		
Felix	84	80	4		
Tryon	84	78	1		
Freya	84	74	2		
Mike	80	70	2		
Mark	80	68	1		
Ann	80				
Kristen	80				
Laura	78				
Megan	74				
Michelle	74				
Kathryn	70				
Don	70				
Jim	68				

test had 80 items. Figure 14.1 illustrates the scores received by 20 students, as well as simple and grouped frequency distributions that show the number of students obtaining each score or interval of scores.

Often the scores are presented graphically as a frequency polygon or histogram to more easily explain important features (Figures 14.2a and 14.2b). The **frequency polygon** is a line graph, which is formed by connecting the highest frequencies of each score. The **histogram** is formed by using rectangular columns to represent the frequency of each score.

For a relatively small number of scores, a frequency polygon is usually jagged, as shown in Figure 14.2a. For a large number of scores and test items, the line looks more like a smooth curve. The nature of the curve can usually be described as being *normal, positively skewed, negatively skewed,* or *flat.* Typically, for standardized tests, the curve very closely approximates a normal distribution (a symmetrical, bell-shaped curve) for a large group of students (e.g., for the norming group). If the distribution is **positively skewed,** or skewed to the right, most of the scores are piled up at the lower end, and there are just a few high scores. For a **negatively skewed** distribution, it is just the opposite—most of the scores are high

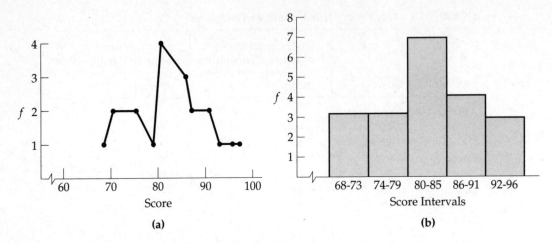

FIGURE 14.2 **Frequency Polygon of Scores (a) and Histogram (b) from Figure 14.1**

with few low scores (skewed to the left). In a flat distribution, each score is obtained with about the same frequency. Figures 14.3a–14.3d illustrate each of these types of curves.

Measures of Central Tendency

A measure of central tendency is a single number that is calculated to represent the average or typical score in the distribution. There are three measures of central tendency commonly used in education: the mean, median, and mode. The mean is the

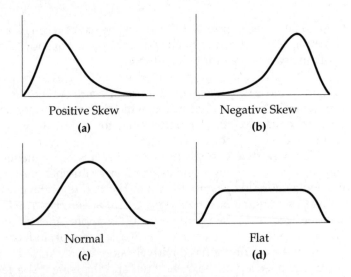

FIGURE 14.3 **Types of Frequency Distributions**

arithmetic average. It is calculated by adding all the scores in the distribution and then dividing that sum by the number of scores. It is represented by $\overline{X}$ or M. For the distribution of scores in Figure 14.1 the mean is 82.

$$\overline{X} = \frac{\sum X}{N}$$

where

$\overline{X}$ = the mean
Σ = the sum of (indicates that all scores are added)
X = each individual score
N = total number of scores

for Figure 14.1:

$$\overline{X} = \frac{1,640}{20}$$

$$\overline{X} = 82$$

The **median,** represented by *mdn,* is the midpoint, or middle, of a distribution of scores. In other words, 50% of the scores are below the median, and 50% of the scores are above the median. Thus, the median score is at the 50th percentile. The median is found by rank ordering all the scores, including each score even if it occurs more than once, and locating the score that has the same number of scores above and below it. For our hypothetical distribution, the median is 82 (84 + 80/2; for an uneven number of scores it will be a single existing score).

The **mode** is simply the score in the distribution that occurs most frequently. In our distribution, more students scored an 80 than any other score, so 80 is the mode. It is possible to have more than one mode; in fact, in education, distributions are often described as *bimodal.*

In a normal distribution, the mean, median, and mode are the same. In a positively skewed distribution, the mean is higher than the median (hence skewed positively), and in a negatively skewed distribution, the mean is lower than the median. This is because the mean, unlike the median, is calculated by taking the value of every score into account. Therefore extreme values affect the mean, whereas the median is not affected by an unusual high or low score.

Measures of Variability

A second type of statistic that is essential in describing a set of scores is a measure of variability. Measures of variability, or dispersion, indicate how much the scores spread out from the mean. If the scores are bunched together close to the mean, then there is little or a small amount of variability. A large or great amount of variability is characteristic of a distribution in which the scores are spread way out from the mean. Two distributions with the same mean can have very different variability, as illustrated in Figure 14.4.

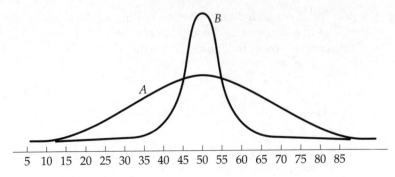

FIGURE 14.4   Distributions with the Same Mean, Different Variability

To more precisely indicate the variability, two measures are typically used, the range and standard deviation. The **range** is simply the difference between the highest and lowest score in the distribution (in our example 28; 96 − 68). This is an easily calculated but crude index of variability, primarily because extremely high or low scores result in a range that indicates more variability than is actually present.

A more complicated but much more precise measure of variability is standard deviation. The **standard deviation** (*SD*) is a number that indicates the *average* deviation of the scores from the mean. It is calculated by employing a formula that looks difficult but is relatively straightforward. These are the essential steps:

1. Calculate the mean of the distribution.
2. Calculate the difference each score is from the mean (these are called deviation scores).
3. Square each difference score (this makes all the deviation scores positive).
4. Add the squared difference scores.
5. Divide by the total number of scores in the distribution.
6. Calculate the square root of the result of step 5.

These steps are illustrated with our hypothetical set of test scores in Figure 14.5. Essentially, you simply calculate the squared deviation scores, find the *average* squared deviation score, and then take the square root to return to the original unit of measurement. In this distribution, one standard deviation is equal to 7.92. Unless you are using a normative grading procedure, standard deviation is not very helpful for classroom testing. However, because of the relationship between standard deviation and the normal curve, it is fundamental to understanding standardized test scores.

With a standardized test, the frequency distribution of raw scores for the norming group will usually be distributed in an approximately normal fashion. In a normal distribution, the meaning of the term *one standard deviation* is the same in regard to percentile rank, regardless of the actual value of standard deviation for that distribution. Thus, +1*SD* is always at the 84th percentile, +2*SD* is at the 98th percentile, −1*SD* is at the 16th percentile, and −2*SD* is at the 2nd percentile in every normal distribution. This property makes it possible to compare student scores to the norm group distribution in terms of percentile rank and to compare relative

FIGURE 14.5   Steps in Calculating Standard Deviation

Score	(1) Deviation Score	(2) Deviation Score Squared	(3) Squared Deviation Scores Added	(4) Added Scores Divided by N	(5) Square Root
96	$96 - 82 = 14$	$14 \times 14 = 196$	+196		
94	$94 - 82 = 12$	$12 \times 12 = 144$	+144		
92	$92 - 82 = 10$	$10 \times 10 = 100$	+100		
90	$90 - 82 = 8$	$8 \times 8 = 64$	+ 64		
90	$90 - 82 = 8$	$8 \times 8 = 64$	+ 64		
86	$86 - 82 = 4$	$4 \times 4 = 16$	+ 16		
86	$86 - 82 = 4$	$4 \times 4 = 16$	+ 16		
84	$84 - 82 = 2$	$2 \times 2 = 4$	+ 4		
84	$84 - 82 = 2$	$2 \times 2 = 4$	+ 4		
84	$84 - 82 = 2$	$2 \times 2 = 4$	+ 4		
80	$80 - 82 = -2$	$-2 \times -2 = 4$	+ 4		
80	$80 - 82 = -2$	$-2 \times -2 = 4$	+ 4		
80	$80 - 82 = -2$	$-2 \times -2 = 4$	+ 4		
80	$80 - 82 = -2$	$-2 \times -2 = 4$	+ 4		
78	$78 - 82 = -4$	$-4 \times -4 = 16$	+ 16		
74	$74 - 82 = -8$	$-8 \times -8 = 64$	+ 64		
74	$74 - 82 = -8$	$-8 \times -8 = 64$	+ 64		
70	$70 - 82 = -12$	$-12 \times -12 = 144$	+144		
70	$70 - 82 = -12$	$-12 \times -12 = 144$	+144		
68	$68 - 82 = -14$	$-14 \times -14 = 196$	+196 = 1,256	$1,256/20 = 62.8$	$\sqrt{62.8} = 7.92$

standing on different tests. For instance, suppose a norm group took a standardized test, and on the basis of their performance a raw score of 26 items answered correctly was one standard deviation above the mean for the norm group (84th percentile). When a student in your class gets the same number of items correct (26), the percentile reported is the 84th. Obviously, if the norm group were different and 26 items turned out to be at +2SD, then the student's score would be reported at the 98th percentile. You would also know that a score at one standard deviation on one test is the same in terms of relative standing as one standard deviation on another test. Most important for standardized tests, standard deviation is used to compute standard scores and other statistics that are used for interpretation and analysis.

Measures of Relationship

It is often helpful, even necessary, to know the degree to which two scores from different measures are related. Typically, this degree of relationship is estimated by

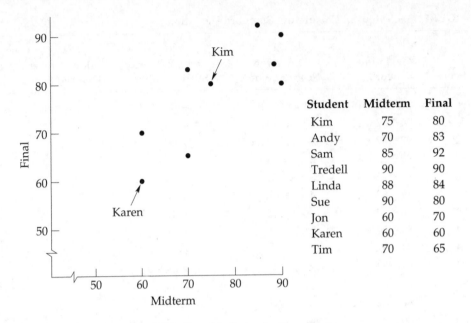

FIGURE 14.6 Scatterplot of Relationship between Two Tests

what is called a *correlation coefficient*. Correlations are reported in standardized test technical manuals for validity and reliability. Also, an important principle in interpreting test scores, standard error of measurement, is determined from correlation.

Scatterplot. The **scatterplot,** or *scattergram,* is a graphic representation of relationship. When used in education, a scatterplot can give you a descriptive picture of relationship by forming a visual array of the intersections of students' scores on two measures. As illustrated in Figure 14.6, each measure is rank ordered from lowest to highest on a different axis. The two scores from each student are used to establish a point of intersection. When this is completed for all students, a pattern is formed that provides a general indication of the direction and strength of the relationship. The direction of the pattern indicates whether there is a positive, a negative, a curvilinear, or no relationship. It is positive if scores on one variable increase with increases in the other scores, and it is negative (inverse) if scores on one variable increase as scores on the other measure decrease. If the pattern looks like a U shape, it is curvilinear; and if it is a straight line or no particular pattern at all, there is little if any relationship.

Scatterplots help to identify intersections that are not typical, which lower the correlation coefficient, and to identify curvilinear relationships. However, these scatterplots are rarely reported in standardized test manuals. Typically, these manuals report the correlation coefficients.

Correlation Coefficient. The **correlation coefficient** is a number that is calculated to represent the direction and strength of the relationship. The number ranges between −1 and +1. A high positive value (e.g., +.85 or +.90) indicates a high positive relationship, a low negative correlation (e.g., −.10 or −.25) represents a low negative relationship, and so forth. The *strength* of the relationship is independent from the *direction*. Thus, a positive or negative value indicates direction, and the value of the correlation, from 0 to 1 or from 0 to −1, determines strength. A perfect correlation is designated by either +1 or −1. As the value approaches these perfect correlations, it becomes stronger, or higher. That is, a correlation is stronger as it changes from .2 to .5 to .6, and also as it changes from −.2 to −.5 to −.6. A correlation of −.8 is stronger (higher) than a correlation of +.7.

There are several different types of correlation coefficients. The most common one is the Pearson product-moment correlation coefficient. This is the one most likely to be used in test manuals. It is represented by *r*.

Four cautions need to be emphasized when interpreting correlations. First, correlation does not imply causation. Just because two measures are related, it rerely means that one *caused* the other. Other factors may be involved in causation, and the direction of the cause is probably not clear. Second, be alert for curvilinear relationships, because most correlation coefficients, such as the Pearson, assume that the relationship is linear. Third, also be alert to what is called **restricted range.** If the values of one measure are truncated, with a small range, it will in all likelihood result in a low correlation. Given a full range of scores, the correlation would be higher. Fourth, relationships expressed as correlation coefficients generally are less precise than the number would suggest. That is, a very high correlation of .80 does not mean that 80% of the relationship is accounted for. If you think of correlation as predicting one score from another score, you will see how relatively imprecise this can be. Examine the scatterplots of various correlations in Figure 14.7. You will see that in a moderate relationship (c), if you try to predict the value of variable *B* on the *y* axis, say, from a score of 10 for variable *A*, a range of approximately 5 to 20 is predicted.

Types of Standardized Tests

Standardized tests have been much criticized as having few positive implications for teaching. The argument is made that because of broad coverage and infrequent testing, heavy reliance on selected-response formats, encouragement to "teach to the test," cultural bias, and inappropriate ranking and comparing students, the information from these tests is not very helpful. Despite these criticisms, however, standardized testing will continue, if for no other reason than it has traditionally been used to provide the public with information for accountability. Standards-based tests, based on principles of standardized tests, are required for accountability. If anything, we will see greater emphasis on standardized tests as Common Core Standards and common assessments for groups of states are developed, as well as a need to judge teachers using student achievement. As this book is going to press the federal government is supporting the development of "new" large-scale assessment systems that will integrate with and support curriculum, instruction,

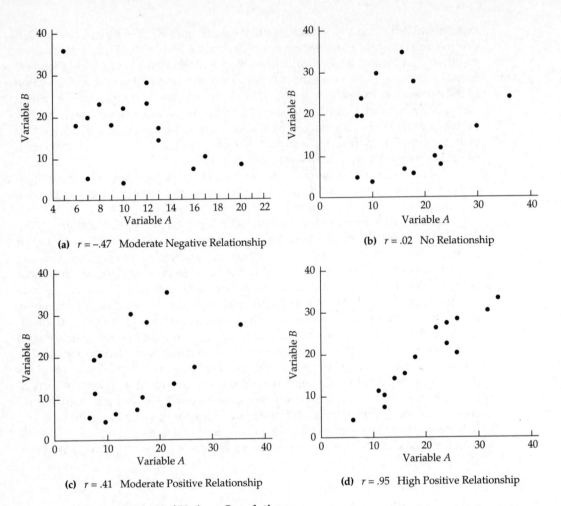

FIGURE 14.7   Scatterplots of Various Correlations

and student achievement. There is a focus on the measurement of student growth and use of results as data in accountability systems to ensure that students are making progress toward success in higher education and/or in careers. There is also an emphasis on assessing a greater number of high-end intellectual skills. Google the *Center of K–12 Assessment and Performance Management* for recent updates and developments.

Standardized test results, when used appropriately, can provide helpful information for instructional planning. The key is being able to understand the scores that are reported as well as the limitations on how scores should be interpreted. As long as results from these tests are not used as the *sole* criterion, scores can be used to form conclusions about the ability or prior achievement of students.

Norm-Referenced Achievement Test Batteries

Norm-referenced achievement test batteries are characterized by qualities shared by other types of large-scale standardized tests, including high technical quality, precise directions for administration, uniform scoring procedures, equivalent or comparable forms, and test manuals for interpretation of the scores. When standardized tests are **norm-referenced,** national samples of students have been used as the *norming* group for interpreting relative standing. Close inspection of the objectives and types of test items is needed to determine how well the test matches the emphasis in the local curriculum. Increasingly, norm-referenced tests are designed to give information about student achievement on specific knowledge and skills, often tied directly to state standards.

When comparing an individual's performance to the norm group, the overall competence of this group is critical in determining relative position. Ranking high with a low-performing group may indicate, in an absolute sense, less competence than ranking low in a high-performing group. Thus, the exact nature of the norming group is important, and several types of norms can be used.

Norms are sets of scores. Each type of norm differs with respect to the characteristics of the students who comprise the norm group. The most commonly used type are *national norms.* These norms are based on a nationally representative sample of students. Generally, testing companies do a good job of obtaining national samples, but there is still variation from one test to another based on school cooperation and the cost of sampling. Also, most testing companies oversample minorities and other underrepresented groups. Thus, one reason that national norms from different tests are not comparable is that the sampling procedures do not result in equivalent norm groups. For example, you should never conclude that one student has greater knowledge or skill than another because her reading score on the Stanford Achievement Test is at the 90th percentile, compared to another student

Teacher's Corner

Arleen Rienhart

National Board Certified High School English Teacher

The Stanford 9 was a test that my county used to give that enabled me to understand more fully the reasons for a student's difficulty. I was able to help my parents and students understand why they struggled more in one area than in another. As a result, I was able to suggest strategies and use strategies in my classroom that helped me individualize instruction for students more quickly. Although this test was, of course, only one type of assessment, it offered a good starting point for me to better understand my students' strengths and weaknesses.

who scored at the 80th percentile on the Metropolitan Achievement Test (there would also be differences in the content of the items). On the other hand, most testing companies use the same norm group for both achievement and aptitude batteries, which allows direct achievement/aptitude and subtest score comparisons.

There are also many different *special group norms*. These types of norms comprise subgroups from the national sample. For example, special norms are typically available for large cities, high- or low-socioeconomic-status school districts, suburban areas, special grade levels, norms for tests given at different times of the year (usually fall and spring), and other specific subgroups. Whenever a special group norm is used, the basis for comparison changes, and the same raw score on a test will probably be reported as a different percentile rank. For instance, because both achievement and aptitude are related to socioeconomic status (higher socioeconomic status, higher achievement), school districts that contain a larger percentage of high-socioeconomic-status students than is true for the population as a whole (and hence the national norm group) almost always score above the mean with national norms. Conversely, districts with a high percentage of low-socioeconomic-status students typically have difficulty scoring above the mean. However, if the high-socioeconomic-status district is compared to suburban norms, the percentile ranks of the scores will be lower; for low-socioeconomic-status districts, the percentiles will be higher if the norm group is low-socioeconomic-status districts. Understandably, then, suburban districts almost always want to use national norms.

Another type of norm is one that is for a single school district. These are called *local norms*. Local norms are helpful in making intraschool comparisons and in providing information that is useful for student placement in appropriate classes. These different types of norms make it very important for you to examine standardized test reports and know the type of norm that is used to determine percentile rank and standard scores.

For a **test battery** several individual tests are normed on the same national sample. This allows a comparison of proficiency in different areas to determine students' strengths and weaknesses. Such comparisons are possible only when the tests have used the same national sample and cannot be done with different standardized tests that have different norming groups.

The results of test batteries are reported by objective or skill area. Some tests, such as the *Metropolitan Achievement Tests*, the *Stanford Achievement Tests*, the *Terra-Nova*, and the *California Achievement Tests*, have diagnostic batteries. These batteries have more items in each area than the survey forms of the tests. Each battery is identified with a descriptive title, such as *spelling, punctuation, letter recognition, fraction computations, graphs,* and so on, but the best way to be sure about the match between what the battery says it is testing and your learning targets or standards is to examine the objectives and the type of test items that are used.

Aptitude Tests.   Standardized **aptitude tests** measure a student's cognitive ability, potential, or capacity to learn. This ability is determined by both in-school and out-of-school experiences. Thus, aptitude tests are less specifically tied to what is taught in school than are achievement tests.

Aptitude tests provide a measure of current developed ability, not innate capacity that cannot change. This level of ability is helpful in planning instruction in two ways: knowing the general capabilities students bring to the class in different areas and knowing the discrepancies between aptitude and achievement.

An understanding of the general ability levels of your students will help you design instructional experiences and group students appropriately. Suppose one class has an average aptitude score of 83 (below average) and another a score of 120 (above average). Would you use the same teaching materials and approaches in each of these classes? Similarly, would you give the same assignments to individual students who differ widely in ability? Student achievement is maximized when the method of instruction or learning activity matches the aptitude. For example, low-ability students may need remediation, and high-ability students would benefit most from enrichment activities. For cooperative learning, it is best to form groups that have mixed levels of aptitude.

Aptitude tests are also used for determining *expected* learning by examining any discrepancy between ability and achievement. If there is a large discrepancy and if other information is consistent, a student may be an underachiever. Many standardized test services provide a report that includes both aptitude and achievement test score results and presents predicted scores. This makes the determination of discrepancy easier.

Readiness Tests.

Readiness tests are actually a specialized type of aptitude test. However, readiness tests, because of the high number of items from specific skill areas, can also be used diagnostically to determine the skills students need to improve if they are to be successful in school. Thus, readiness tests both predict achievement and diagnose weaknesses.

Most readiness tests are used in early elementary grades and for reading. The tests are helpful in identifying particular skills and knowledge to plan instruction and in designing remedial exercises. For example, the *Boehm Test of Basic Concepts Third Edition,* assesses student comprehension of the basic verbal concepts that are needed for comprehension of verbal communication (e.g., concepts such as many, smallest, nearest). Reading readiness tests are helpful in identifying skills that need to be mastered, such as visual discrimination of letters, auditory discrimination, recognition of letters and numbers, and following instructions. Readiness tests should not be used as the sole criterion for determining whether a child has the skills and knowledge to begin kindergarten or first grade. Scores from these tests should always be used with other information to provide a comprehensive evaluation of readiness.

Standards-Based State and District Tests.

Now that all states are required to have standards-based achievement tests, you will very likely have access to the performances of your past and/or current students on these tests from the previous year.

Analyzing scores of students from the previous year is helpful in confirming their progress and determining weaknesses in curriculum or teaching that should

FIGURE 14.8   Suggestions for Interpreting Students' Standards-Based Test Scores

1. Review the specific standards that were tested, along with sample items if possible, and know which standards are included in each subscale.

2. Determine the number of items that measure each standard or set of standards; be wary of results based on just a few items.

3. Base your interpretation on how scores are verified by other data or observations.

4. Be wary of individual item scores, even if aggregated to the entire class.

5. Do not try to analyze each item for each student. What is most important is what is true for groups of students and standards that are represented by more than a few items.

6. Get some help aggregating results if a lot of paperwork or detailed item reports are distributed. Work with central office and school personnel to aggregate the data in a meaningful way.

be addressed in the current year. Scores of current students at the end of the previous school year are helpful as long as the interpretation takes into account several factors (see Figure 14.8). First, these scores are usually reported in categories or subscales as well as for the total test, and these groupings of items refer to student performance in the corresponding domains of knowledge and skills. Although some standards-based test reports show results for each item, it is not what the individual items measure but what is represented by the items as a group that is important. The tests sample from the larger domains. Thus, it is important to generalize from the group of items to the standards they represent. An example of the kind of data that can be provided is illustrated in Table 14.1 for fourth-grade mathematics on Virginia's Standards of Learning test. You will see that there are five reporting categories (subscales) on the test. Each reporting category is represented by specific standards, and there are a few items that measure each reporting category. Unlike most standards-based tests, results for individual items are reported.

TABLE 14.1   Example of Data Provided by State Standards-Based Tests; Virginia Grade Four Mathematics Standards

Reporting Category	Standards	Number of Test Items
Number and Number Sense	4.1–4.4	8
Computation and Estimation	4.5–4.9	12
Measurement and Geometry	4.10–4.18	12
Probability and Statistics	4.19, 4.20	8
Patterns, Functions, and Algebra	4.21, 4.22	10

Source: Adapted from Virginia Department of Education (2003). Retrieved October 10, 2009, from http://www.pwcsmath.com/sol/blueprints/Gr4Blueprint.pdf.

The report shows which standard the item tested, however, not the item itself. This means that there may well be one or two items that assess a standard, which is not sufficient for a reliable interpretation. Even at the subscale level there are relatively few items, and yet the subscale score is what would be most informative about the level of knowledge and skills that your students are bringing to your class.

Second, these scores should be disaggregated, if possible, by groups of students. This allows for more specific probing of certain students to confirm what is suggested by the test scores. In doing this, be careful of using the average score because this value is distorted by a few high or low scores. Third, consider possible sources of error or student motivation issues that could affect student performance. Fourth, be wary of comparing the percentage of items answered correctly for different subscales or domains. Because items differ in difficulty, such comparisons are usually not warranted. Fifth, keep interpretations at the level of groups of students rather than individual student, unless there are unusually high or low scores. Finally, as with other types of assessments, consider these as barometers of student performance that could be quite different with changes over the summer; always verify with other information.

The scores from these tests are reported by indicating how many items and/or the percentage of items that were answered correctly. The interpretation is based on what percentage correct indicates a satisfactory level of performance. How students' performances compare to others is not emphasized. Some tests will report whether "mastery" has been demonstrated. If pass–fail information is provided, be sure that you understand what has been done to determine that a specific percentage correct of test items is reasonable. Difficult items, for instance, can make a relatively low percentage correct indicate a high level of performance.

Benchmark Assessments.   Benchmark, or *interim*, assessments were introduced in Chapter 4 as tests that are given every 6 or 9 weeks, based on what has been taught during these weeks, hopefully aligned to standards that will be assessed on end-of-year accountability tests. The purpose of using these tests is to determine student status on achieving learning targets, to design appropriate instruction, such as remediation for certain students or whole class review of specific content, and to predict performance on end-of-year tests (Perie, Marion, & Gong, 2009). But as pointed out by Shepard (2009), benchmark assessments are very new and not well researched. The quality of items is sometimes wanting, and there may be no estimates of reliability or evidence for validity. This is especially true for benchmark test items that are written by district personnel. Although having teachers develop test items does contribute to validity, it is still likely that there will be weak items and sometimes wrong "correct" answers.

Teachers usually get benchmark test results by item for each student. This kind of data requires careful consideration by teachers when examining the results for their class. It is very helpful for teachers to get together and discuss their results. When students do poorly, it is necessary to probe about the quality and difficulty of the item and to determine if the content was taught (Abrams, Wetzel, & McMillan, 2010).

Types of Derived Standardized Test Scores

Raw scores are simply the number of items answered correctly. Raw scores, by themselves, however, are not as versatile for standardized tests as other scores that are *derived* or *transformed* from these raw scores. One easily understood derived score, for example, is percent correct, which is used ubiquitously for standards-based tests. Percentile rank and grade-equivalent scores are also derived in the sense that they are computed from raw score distributions.

Standard Scores

Standard scores are derived from raw scores in units based on the standard deviation of the distribution. They are obtained by using a linear transformation, which simply changes the value of the mean and one standard deviation, or a nonlinear, normalizing transformation based on the percentiles of the normal curve. Most standard scores reported with standardized tests are normalized. The term *standard* in this context does not mean a specific level of performance or expectation. Rather, it refers to the standard normal curve as the basis for interpretation. Standard scores have equal units between different values, which allows for additional statistical procedures.

Z-Score.   The simplest and most easily calculated standard score is the **z-score,** which indicates how far a score lies above or below the mean in standard deviation units. Because $1SD = 1$, a z-score of 1 is one standard deviation unit above the mean. The formula for computing z-scores is relatively straightforward if you know the value of one standard deviation:

$$z\text{-score} = \frac{X - \overline{X}}{SD}$$

where
$$X = \text{any raw score}$$
$$\overline{X} = \text{mean of the raw scores}$$
$$SD = \text{standard deviation of the raw score distribution}$$

For example, a z-score for 90 in our hypothetical distribution would be 1.01 $(90 - 82/7.92)$. If the raw score is less than the mean, the z-score will be negative (e.g., the z-score for 70 in our distribution of twenty students would be -1.01 $(70 - 82/7.92)$.

If the z-score is a linear transformation, the distribution of z-scores will be identical to the distribution of raw scores. It is also possible to normalize the raw score distribution when converting to z-scores. This transforms the distribution to a normal one, regardless of what the raw score distribution looked like. If the raw score distribution is normal, then using the formula will also result in a normal distribution of z-scores. For most standardized tests, the standard scores are normalized.

Thus, a z-score of 1 is at the 84th percentile, a z-score of 2 is at the 98th percentile, and so forth.

Because the z-score distribution has a standard deviation equal to 1, these scores can easily be transformed to other standard scores that will only have positive values.

Normal Curve Equivalent.   The **normal curve equivalent (NCE)** is a normalized standard score that has a mean of 50 and a standard deviation of 21.06. The reason for selecting 50 for the mean and 21.06 for the standard deviation was so that NCE scores, like percentiles, would range from 1 to 99. The percentiles of 1, 50, and 99 are equivalent to NCEs of 1, 50, and 99. However, at other points on the scale, NCEs are not the same as percentiles. For example:

NCE	Percentile
90	97
75	88
25	12
10	3

It is fairly easy to confuse NCEs with percentiles because they convert the same range of scores (1–99), especially for someone who is not familiar with measurement principles. Thus, you need to be careful when explaining what NCEs mean to parents. So why are NCEs used at all? Because they are standard scores (percentiles are not), they can, like other standard scores, be used statistically for research and evaluation purposes.

Stanines.   One popular type of standard score for standardized tests is the *stanine*. A **stanine** indicates about where a score lies in relation to the normal curve of the norming group. Stanines are reported as single-digit scores from 1 to 9. A stanine of 5 indicates that the score is in the middle of the distribution; stanines 1, 2, and 3 are considered below average; 7, 8, and 9 are above average; and stanines of 4, 5, and 6 are about average. Although there is a precise, statistically determined procedure for determining stanines, it is practical to use the range from 1 to 9 as a simple, easily understood way to indicate relative standing. Each stanine covers a specific area of the normal curve in terms of percentiles:

Stanine	Percentile Rank	Stanine	Percentile Rank
9	96 or higher	4	23 to 39
8	89 to 95	3	11 to 22
7	77 to 88	2	4 to 10
6	60 to 76	1	Below 4
5	40 to 59		

Notice that there is a different percentage of scores in stanines 5, 6, 7, 8, and 9. This is because the width of the stanine is the same in relation to the curve of the normal distribution. Another way you can think about stanines is that they have a mean of 5, with a standard deviation of 2. Because they are normalized, stanines from conceptually similar but different tests can be compared, such as aptitude and achievement tests. Remember that meaningful differences in performance are indicated when the scores differ by at least two stanines.

A disadvantage of the stanine is that even though you know the area of the normal curve the score lies in, you don't know what part of this area the score is in. In this sense, stanines are less precise than percentile rank. For example, percentile scores of 42 and 58 have the same stanine score of 5. However, when stanine scores differ by more than 1, it is probable that there is a meaningful difference between achievement in those areas. That is, if the reading stanine score is 5 and the mathematics stanine is 7, the student is demonstrating stronger achievement in mathematics.

Scaled Score. Most standardized achievement tests use what is called a **scaled score** (also called the *scale level*, or *growth score*) to show year-to-year progress in achievement and to compare different levels of the same test. Each test publisher uses a different scale. Higher scores are associated with higher grade levels. For example, the Iowa Test of Basic Skills uses a score of 200 to indicate the median performance of students in the fourth grade, 150 as the median for first graders, and 250 as the median for eighth graders. The complete scale, across grade levels, is as follows:

Grade:	K	1	2	3	4	5	6	7	8	9
SS:	130	150	168	185	200	214	227	239	250	260

Thus, the median performance for third graders is assigned a score of 185, and so on. These median and mean scores, and associated standard deviations, provide anchors against which a student's progress can be compared. This makes it possible to use developmental standard scores to plot performance from year to year.

Deviation IQ Scores. For many years, the results of IQ and general ability testing have been reported on a scale that has a mean of 100 and a standard deviation of 15 or 16. Originally, IQ scores were actual intelligence quotients, calculated by dividing mental age by chronological age and multiplying this ratio by 100. Today, IQ scores are determined like other derived standard scores. For each age group in a norming sample, the raw scores are converted to z-scores, then to deviation IQ scores by multiplying the z-score by 15 or 16 and adding that product to 100. Most test publishers refer to the student's "ability," "aptitude," or to "standard age" scores rather than IQ because *intelligence* today refers to many other traits besides academic ability or reasoning.

Other Standard Scores. The advantage of standard scores—being able to convert raw scores to scores directly related to the normal curve and percentile rank—is also a disadvantage from the standpoint that there are so many different standard scores. Once you understand the nature of the scores, you can readily interpret the results. For example, in Virginia, a unique scale of 0–600 is used for reporting results, even though there are only about 50 questions on each test.

Grade Equivalent Scores

Grade equivalents (GEs) are much like scale scores, except that the unit is expressed in grade levels and months. GEs are useful only in indicating growth or progress; they should not be used for grade placement. In addition, most GEs are determined by interpolation. That is, a test may be given to beginning fourth graders, and the median score for that group will be assigned a grade equivalent of 4.0. The same test might be given to a beginning group of fifth graders, with the median score given a GE of 5.0. No other tests are given, but scores are still reported in months (e.g., 4.2 or 4.8). If the students in grades 4, month 2 and month 8 were not given the test, how was the median of each group determined? The answer is that the medians were interpolated, estimated, from existing scores. This means that the reported scores of, say, 4.1 or 4.6, are only estimates. For some tests, GEs are extrapolated beyond the grade levels actually tested. Thus, a test may be given to students in grades 3, 4, and 5, but GEs may range from 2.0 to 7.0 and beyond. Extrapolated scores are less accurate than interpolated ones, and they should be interpreted cautiously.

Interpreting Standardized and State Standards-Based Test Scores

Armed with a basic knowledge of important descriptive statistics and types of scores, you can accurately understand, interpret, and use your students' standardized test scores. We begin our discussion of interpretation of scores with two more technical issues—standard error of measurement and alignment of the test with curriculum, teaching, and classroom assessments. Then we will look at issues involved in norm- and standards-referenced/criterion-based interpretation before examining some actual standardized test score reports.

Standard Error of Measurement

As I have stressed throughout this book, every test has some degree of error. Chapter 3 introduced the relationship between error and reliability. Basically, as error increases, reliability decreases. But we can directly measure reliability only in a test; we cannot know what type or amount of error has influenced a student's score. Therefore we estimate the degree of error that is probable, given the reliability of the test. This degree of error is estimated mathematically and is reported as the **standard error of measurement (SEM).**

SEM is determined by a formula that takes into account the reliability and standard deviation of the test. If a student took a test many times, the resulting scores would look like a normal distribution. That is, sometimes the student would get "good" error and get a higher score, and sometimes the student would get "bad" error, resulting in a lower score. If we assume that the student's *true* score is the mean of this hypothetical distribution, then we can use this as a starting point for estimating the *actual* true score. From what we know about the normal curve and standard deviation, 68% of the time the actual true score would be between one standard deviation of the student's normal curve of many testings, and 96% of the time the actual true score would fall within two standard deviations of this distribution. We call the standard deviation of this hypothetical normal distribution the *standard error of measurement*.

For example, if a student's GE score on a test were 3.4, and the test had a standard error of measurement of .2, then we would interpret the student's true performance, with 68% confidence, to be 3.4 ±.2; and with 96% confidence, we would interpret the student's true score to be 3.4 ±.4. In other words, the standard error of measurement creates an interval, and it is within this interval that we can be confident that the student's true score lies. Different degrees of confidence are related to the number of standard errors of measurement included; these intervals can be thought of as **confidence bands.** Of course, we do not know *where* in the interval the true score lies, so we are most accurate in interpreting the performance in terms of the interval, not as a single score.

The idea of interpreting single scores as bands or intervals has important implications. If you are drawing a conclusion about the performance of a single student, your thinking should be something like this: "Trevor's performance in mathematics places him between the 86th and 94th percentiles," rather than, "Trevor's score is at the 90th percentile." This will give you a more realistic and accurate basis for judging Trevor's real or actual level of performance. When comparing two scores from the same test battery, a meaningful difference in performance is indicated only when the intervals, as established by one standard error of measurement, do not overlap. Thus, it would be wrong to conclude that a student's language achievement score of 72 is higher than the reading score of 70 if the standard error is two or more. The same logic is needed for comparing ability with achievement or for comparing the scores of different individuals on the same test. That is, if the bands do not overlap, then you should conclude that there is no difference between the scores.

Fortunately, test publishers report standard errors of measurement to help you interpret the scores properly, and often they are displayed visually in the form of a shaded band surrounding the score. Unfortunately, there is usually a slightly different standard error of measurement for each subtest and for different ranges of scores. Thus, in the technical manual, there are tables of standard errors of measurement. I don't want to suggest that you consult these tables for each student and for each score. However, it may be helpful to use this information in decisions regarding referral for identification for special education, and for placement into special programs. Many standardized test reporting formats display the appropriate standard error of measurement on each student's report, although you will need to look at a key to know the exact nature of the band. Some tests use one SEM; others use the middle 50 percent.

Alignment

As pointed out in Chapter 3, one of the most critical aspects of interpreting standardized test scores is to determine the extent to which the test content is aligned with the curriculum, with your teaching, and with your classroom assessments.

If the content, emphasis, and cognitive level of the standardized or standards-based test match well with your instruction, the curriculum, and classroom assessment, then there is strong alignment. With strong alignment, the test scores serve as a check on the effectiveness of the instruction. With weak alignment, scores on standardized tests have some implications, but because of a lack of emphasis on the same content and cognitive level, these implications are not as clear. For example, if we know that there is a good match, and the scores are low, there is reason to learn why. High test scores with a good match are validation that students are indeed learning the content as intended.

Standards-Based/Criterion-Referenced Interpretations

As we previously discussed, standards-based/criterion-referenced interpretations compare student performance to established standards rather than to other students. Some standardized tests are only criterion-referenced (they may also be called objectives based, absolute, domain referenced, or content referenced, though the technical meaning may differ). These tests are designed to provide a valid measure of skills and knowledge in specific areas. Most norm-referenced tests also provide criterion-referenced information by indicating the number of items answered correctly in specific areas, but because the primary purpose of these tests is to compare individuals, they typically do not provide information as meaningful as what standards-based/criterion-referenced tests provide. Thus, you need to keep in mind that there is a difference between a standards-based/criterion-referenced standardized test and standards-based/criterion-referenced *interpretations.*

It is important for each skill or area for which a score is reported to be described in detail. With delimited and well-defined learning targets, the score can more easily be interpreted to suggest some degree of mastery. Without a clearly defined target, such interpretation is questionable at best.

Your judgment concerning the degree of a student's mastery is usually based on the percentage of correctly answered items that measure a specific target. The meaning that is given to the percentage of correct answers is generally made by the teacher, based on a review of the definition of the target and the difficulty of the items. This involves your professional judgment; at the state level and in some districts standards may be set by a team, a group of educators, or parents. An important aspect of making this decision is having a sufficient number of items to adequately measure the trait.

Although results are not reported as percentile ranks or standard scores, there may be information in the technical manual about the difficulty of items or average scores of various groups. This information is helpful when deciding the correspondence between the percentage of items answered correctly and mastery of the skill or content area. One approach to doing this is to set in your mind a group of "minimally competent" students in reference to the target, then see how many items these students answer correctly. If the mean number of correct answers is, say, 7 of 10, then your "standard" becomes 70% of the items. It may be that the level is set in relation to a goal for students by the end of the year, or you may set standards based on how others have performed in the past. Regardless of the approach, the interpretation is largely a matter of your professional judgment, so think carefully about the criteria you use.

With NCLB and adequate yearly progress (AYP) requirements, state testing results are reported simply by indicating the percentage of students that "passed" or "met or exceeded" established targets. For example, if students need to obtain a scaled score of 400 to pass, which is what is used in Virginia, the result reported for a specific class or school is the percentage of students tested that scored 400 or above. This simple statistic is helpful to the public and satisfies federal reporting requirements, but it is not very helpful to teachers, especially if the result is for an extensive amount of material. Obtaining a "pass" or "proficient" score is standards-based in the sense that a standard has been used to report results, but such information is not diagnostic or criterion-referenced. To fully interpret the results, teachers need to know how the test was designed, what subscales are used, and how the standard was determined. Disaggregating results to specific targets provides information most likely to be used by teachers in their instruction.

With these recommendations, keep the following suggestions in mind when making standards-based/criterion-referenced interpretations from standardized tests (summarized in Figure 14.9):

1. Determine the Primary Purpose of the Test—Is It Norm- or Standards-Based/Criterion-Referenced? Standards-based/criterion-referenced tests are designed for standards-based/criterion-referenced interpretations. As long as the descriptions of the traits match your learning targets, these types of tests will provide the best information. Be wary of using norm-referenced tests for standards-based/criterion-referenced interpretations.

FIGURE 14.9   Checklist for Using Criterion-Referenced/Standards-Based Test Scores

✓ Is the primary purpose of the test norm- or criterion-referenced/standards-based?
✓ Are measured targets delimited and clearly defined?
✓ Are there enough items to measure each target adequately?
✓ Is the difficulty level of the items matched with the learning targets?

2. Examine the Clarity and Specificity of the Definitions and Traits Measured.   For each score that is reported, there needs to be an adequate definition of what is being measured. Norm-referenced tests tend to define what is measured more broadly, standards-based/criterion-referenced tests more specifically. You may need to consult the technical manual to get sufficient detail of the definition to make a valid judgment about the match between what the test says it is measuring and what you want measured. There should be good content-related evidence of validity to demonstrate an adequate sampling of content or skills from a larger domain.

3. Be Sure There Is a Sufficient Number of Items to Make a Valid Decision.   The general rule is to have four to six different test items for each target. For learning targets that are less specific, more than 10 items may be needed. In some norm-referenced tests you may see skills listed with as few as three or four items. This is too few for making definite conclusions, though this may suggest a need for further investigation.

4. Examine the Difficulty of Items and Match This to Your Standards.   Norm-referenced tests may not use easy items because they do not discriminate among students, whereas standards-based/criterion-referenced tests tend to have easy items so that most students will do reasonably well. This means that the difficulty of the items may differ considerably with the same definition for the target. Inspect the items carefully and use your knowledge of their difficulty in setting standards.

Understanding Standardized and Standards-Based Test Score Reports

When you first look at test score reports, they may seem to be very complicated and difficult to understand. This is because they are designed to provide as much information as possible on a single page. For a comprehensive battery, scores are often reported for each skill as well as each subskill. The best approach for understanding a report is to consult the test manual and find examples that are explained. Most test publishers do a very good job of showing you what each part of the report means.

There are also many different types of reports. Each test publisher has a unique format for reporting results and usually includes different kinds of scores. In addition, there are typically different formats to report the same scores. Thus, the same battery may be reported as a list of students in your class, the class as a whole, a skills analysis for the class or individual student, individual profiles, profile charts, growth scale profiles, and other formats. Some reports include only scores for major tests; others include subskill scores and item scores. Different norms may be used. All of this means that each report contains somewhat different information, organized and presented in dissimilar ways. You need to first identify what type of report you are dealing with, then find an explanation for it in an interpretive guide.

After you have become acquainted with the types of standardized tests and reports used in your school, you will be in a position to routinely interpret them in accurate and helpful ways.

Figures 14.10 and 14.11 illustrate different test score reports. In Figure 14.10 norm-referenced scores are reported for one class of students. Five major areas are illustrated, with many items measuring each area. The results show that student achievement in reading, compared to national norms, is stronger than language. Figure 14.11 is from the same standardized test, the *TerraNova*, Third Edition, but this time gives standards-based/criterion-referenced information. More specific skills are reported for a single student. Notice the bands presented to indicate margin of error, and the key to a level of mastery of each area, at least as determined by the testing company, CTB McGraw-Hill. For this student, science is obviously weak and two areas of social science strong.

A different kind of report is illustrated in Figure 14.12. This report shows the standards-based achievement of a class of students for a single teacher. Note that there are "reporting categories" for each student. These groups of items represent subscales, and they are shown to indicate overall strengths and weaknesses of students in this class. Although there is a note on the report that a score of 30 or less indicates that the "student may benefit from additional instruction," and that "a score of 30 or above indicates strength," it would be helpful to also have information about margin of error.

Using Standardized and Standards-Based/ Criterion-Referenced Test Scores

Teachers typically use several sources of information to plan their instruction, including student records, previous teacher recommendations, informal observation, pretests, structured exercises, formative assessments, benchmark assessments, results of summative classroom assessments, and results of standardized and standards-based test results. This can be thought of as "sizing up" assessment (Airasian & Russell, 2008), used to identify levels of knowledge, understanding, and skills that will influence instructional decisions. It is essentially what was described in Chapter 1 as preassessment. This requires getting to know about not only the entire class, but individuals as well. Given the current emphasis on helping every child to be successful, it is important to spend enough time sizing up each student prior to each instructional unit. Effective instruction is targeted to the class as a whole; it is also structured to be tailored to small groups and individual students. The data from sizing up assessments are helpful in answering questions such as:

Do students have the content knowledge and intellectual skills to handle the material?
How can instruction be planned so that students will be motivated?
What are the implications of individual differences among the students?
Do I need to review certain topics before moving ahead with new material?

TerraNova™, Third Edition

TERRANOVA

COMPLETE BATTERY

Group List Report, Part I

Class: JONES

Grade: 6.7

Simulated Data

Purpose
This report summarizes achievement data for a specified group. Part I provides a variety of norm-referenced scores for the group; Part II provides the individual scores for each student. Together with classroom assessments and classwork, this information can be used to identify potential strengths and needs in the content areas shown.

Number of students: 30
Number of students using accommodations: 2

Form/Level: G-16

Test Date: 04/24/07   Scoring: PATTERN (IRT)
QM: 31   Norms Date: 2007

School: WIDE VISTA
District: GREEN VALLEY

City/State: ANYTOWN, U.S.A.

CTBID: 0032180934860001-03-00001

Page 1

Mc
Graw **CTB**
Hill **McGraw-Hill**
The *McGraw-Hill Companies*

Norm-Referenced Scores

	No. of Stdnts	No. using Accomm	MNS	GME	MNCE	MSS	MDNP	Low/ High NP
Reading	30	2	6.9	10.8	65.8	688.8		54-90
Language	30	2	6.1	8.5	57.1	670.1		28-81
Mathematics	30	2	6.8	8.6	63.9	687.9		52-93
Total Score	30	2	6.7	9.2	62.3	682.3		40-83
Science	30	2	6.9	9.4	65.1	690.1		46-93
Social Studies	30	2	6.5	9.3	60.7	682.4		33-90

*Based on locally reported data.
**Total Score consists of Reading, Language, and Mathematics

Key: MNS = Mean National Stanine   MSS = Mean Scale Score
      GME = Grade Mean Equivalent   MDNP = Median National Percentile
      MNCE = Mean Normal Curve Equivalent Accomm = Accommodations

National Percentile Scale

National Stanine Scale

Key: Low NP ├────◆────┤ High NP
                 Median

Observations

Displayed on the left are the norm-referenced scores for every content area tested. The Median National Percentile (MDNP) score, and the lowest and highest National Percentile (NP) scores of the group are shown in the last two columns. Displayed on the right is a graph of the MDNP scores. The MDNP is indicated by the diamond. The width of the band running through the diamond represents the range (low to high) of the students' scores. The shaded area on the graph represents the average range of scores, defined as the middle 50 percent of the students' scores. Four of the group's six MDNP scores are in the average range. Scores in the area to the right of the shading are above the average range. Scores in the area

to the left of the shading are below the average range. Two MDNP scores are above the average range and no MDNP scores are below the average range. In Reading, for example, the MDNP score is 78, which is above the average range. The lowest Reading score in the group is 54 and the highest is 90. (This information is shown both on the graph and in the "Low/High NP" column.)

Additional information about the interpretation of these scores and the use of test results can be found at CTB's Web site, www.ctb.com/TerraNova3.

FIGURE 14.10 Standardized Norm-Referenced Test Score Report

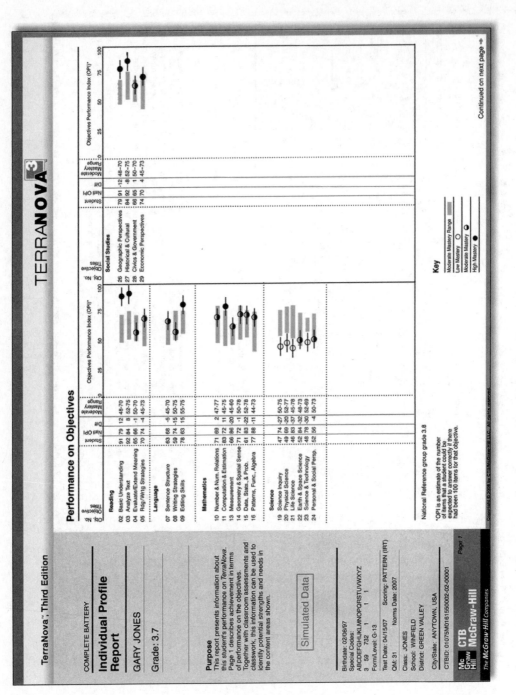

FIGURE 14.11   Standardized Individual Student Criterion-Referenced Test Score Report

Before school begins in the fall, there is no lack of information that is available on students. The decisions about what to teach at this point are influenced primarily by curriculum guides, teacher experience, and student performance on previously administered standardized and standards-based tests. Prior to the beginning of the year student scores from previously administered standardized and standards-based tests are available, which require skill in interpretation and application. During the year, unit, chapter, and benchmark summative test results can be used to help plan subsequent instruction.

I need to point out, however, that initial impressions from previously gathered data should be treated as hypotheses that need to be confirmed or disproved with subsequent assessments. This is especially true during the first week or so of school as teachers learn more about students on a firsthand basis. During that time informal observation, pretests, and structured exercises are needed to confirm results from previously taken standardized and standards-based assessments. In some cases, teachers target individual students or groups of students during the first week to confirm suspected weaknesses. In this sense, then, summative assessments are used formatively to influence the gathering of additional information. This could be called *differentiated assessment* (Chapman & King, 2009).

Interpreting Test Reports for Parents

Most teachers interpret the results of standardized tests for parents, although research has shown that nearly half of our teachers feel unprepared to do this (Nolen, Haladyna, & Haas, 1989). Because you are in contact with students daily and are aware of their classroom performance, you are in the best position to communicate with parents regarding the results of standardized tests. You can determine what level of detail to report and how the results coincide with classroom performance. This is done most effectively face-to-face in the context of a teacher–parent conference, though many schools send written reports home without scheduling a conference. In such a conference, you can point out important cautions and discuss the results in a way that will make sense. Before the conference, you should review available information and prepare it to show student progress and areas of strength and weakness that may need specific action at home and school. This should include other examples of student work, in addition to the test results, to lessen the tendency to place too much value on test scores.

In preparing for the conference, keep in mind that most parents are interested in particular types of information. These include some indication of relative standing, growth since earlier testing, performance compared to standards, weaknesses, and strengths. For each of these areas you should present the relevant numbers, but be sure to include a clear and easy-to-understand narrative—using plain, everyday language—that explains the numbers. You should always include some explanation of norms, standards, and the standard error of measurement. It is important for parents to realize that, for most reports, the scores do not represent comparisons with other students in the class. Parents obviously don't need an extended explanation of error, but it's important for them to understand that the results represent *approximate* and not absolute or precise performance.

Of the different types of scores to report to parents, percentiles from norm-referenced tests are most easily understood, even though some parents will confuse percentile with percentage correct. They may also think that percentile scores below 70 are poor because they are accustomed to grading systems in which 70 or below may mean failure. In fact, for most standardized tests, students will score in the average range if they answer 60 to 70% of the items correctly. Grade equivalents are commonly reported but easily misunderstood. Parents often think that GEs indicate in which grade a student should be placed. You will need to be diligent in pointing out that GEs are only another way of comparing performance to the norm group.

Some standardized tests have special reports that are prepared for parents. Although these are very informative, it is still important to supplement the scores with a note from the teacher indicating a willingness to confer with the parents, by phone or in person, to answer any questions and clarify the meaning of the results.

In summary, the following suggestions will help you interpret standardized test reports confidently and in a way that will accurately inform parents and help the student:

1. **Understand the Meaning of Every Score Reported to Parents.**   It is embarrassing, not to mention unprofessional, not to know how to interpret each score on the report.

2. **Examine Individual Student Reports Comprehensively before a Conference with Parents.**   This will prevent you from trying to understand and explain at the same time.

3. **Gather Evidence of Student Performance in the Classroom That Can Supplement the Test Scores.**   This demonstrates your commitment to the preparation and careful analysis of each student's performance, and it provides more concrete examples of performance that parents can easily understand.

4. **Be Prepared to Address Areas of Concern Most Parents Have, Such as Standing, Progress, Performance Compared to Standards, Strengths, and Weaknesses.**   This may require you to review the student's previous performance on other standardized tests.

5. **Be Prepared to Distinguish between Ability and Achievement.**   Many parents want to know whether their child is performing "up to their ability." You might even have a short written description of the difference to supplement your verbal explanation.

6. **Explain the Importance of Norms and Error in Testing for Proper Interpretation.**   This could include your knowledge of any extenuating circumstances that may have affected the student's performance.

7. **Summarize Clearly What the Scores Mean.**   Don't simply show the numbers and expect the parents to be able to understand. You will need to summarize in language that the parents can comprehend.

Case Study
for Reflection

Mrs. Jones called right after the standardized test score reports were sent home. She wanted to know how her daughter, Ellen, could be scoring so high yet not be getting very good grades. In reviewing Ellen's scores, it turns out that she scored on the 80 and 90 national percentile range for most subjects, but her grades were Cs and Bs.

QUESTIONS FOR CONSIDERATION

1. How would you explain the meaning of Ellen's national percentile scores to her mother?
2. How would you explain the discrepancy between her grades and test score? What other information might be important in providing a reasonable explanation?
3. How would you prepare for a meeting with Mrs. Jones to discuss the scores and Ellen's grades?

8. Try to Create a Discussion with Parents, Rather Than Making a Presentation to Them. Ask questions to involve parents in the conference and to enhance your ability to determine whether they in fact understand the meaning of the scores.

Preparing Students to Take Standardized Tests

You want your students to perform as well as possible on standardized tests, and with high-stakes testing accompanying increased demands for accountability, it is important for every student to have a fair opportunity to do his or her best work. This is accomplished if students are properly prepared before taking the test, and this preparation will probably be your responsibility.

One area to address is making sure that students have good test-taking skills. These skills help to familiarize the students with item formats and give them strategies so that the validity of the results is improved. Students should be proficient with the test-taking skills listed in Table 14.2.

You also want to set an appropriate classroom climate or environment for taking the test. This begins with your attitude toward the test. If you convey to students that you believe the test is a burden, an unnecessary or even unfair imposition, then students will also adopt such an attitude and may not try their best. Be happy with the test, convey an attitude of challenge and opportunity. Discuss with your students the purpose and nature of the test. Emphasize that it is most important for students to try to do their best, not just to obtain a high score. Tell the students how the tests will be used in conjunction with other information; this will reduce anxiety. You want to enhance student confidence by giving them short practice tests. These tests help to acquaint students with the directions and the types of items they will answer. Also provide students opportunities for instruction and assessment that is different from the specific test format. Using "varied-format" preparation increases overall knowledge and improves performance (Popham, 2008a).

Student motivation is an important factor. Motivate your students to put forth their best effort by helping them understand how the results from the test will

TABLE 14.2 Test-Taking Skills and Strategies

Skill or Strategy	Description	Purpose	Components
Tuning In	Using and following oral directions	To listen for rules and directions To hear the time limits	Be alert for a cue to begin listening Stop what you are doing Look at the speaker Tune in to the directions Concentrate, focus, listen Follow directions
Following Written Directions	Learning to read, interpret, and do	To know what to do To know steps and procedures To understand the task To gather instructions	Read all directions thoroughly and carefully Check, highlight, underline, or circle the words that tell you what to do Number the directions Visualize the steps Go over directions again when the task is completed
Bubbling In	Learning to fill in the answer sheet quickly and accurately	To know how to fill in a small circle correctly that matches the right answer for each question To be sure the test is scored accurately To allow you to show what you know	Use a number two pencil Using the hand you do not write with, point to the correct answer on your test booklet so that you don't lose your place Use other hand to fill in the bubble next to the correct number on the answer sheet Fill in completely Stay inside the bubble Erase all marks outside the bubble

Skill or Strategy	Description	Purpose	Components
Know and Go	Learning to trust your instincts about an answer and move on	To recognize the "aha" or intuitive feeling when you know the answer To learn to mark the answer quickly and move on To avoid analyzing a question too much	Read the question Read the answers If you know an answer is right, mark it If you know it, do not change your answer Move on to the next question
Be Back	Learning to answer easy questions first and mark difficult ones to revisit later	To answer all the questions you know first To answer easy questions first and quickly To prevent you from getting "stuck" on an item To know to return to a question if there is time	Answer questions and move on If the answer does not come quickly, think "I'll be back" If permitted, jot down the numbers of any items you want to check Return to marked items and complete the test Guess if there is no penalty for guessing
When in Doubt, Try It Out	Learning to make educated guesses	To consider each choice as the correct answer To eliminate incorrect answers To narrow your choices to two possible answers To mark one answer when you are in doubt	Read questions carefully Eliminate clearly wrong answers Try out remaining answers For math questions, first try the middle option as correct Make smart guesses and move on If you have no idea which answer is correct, guess
Take a Double Take	Learning to check your work and avoid careless errors	Find and correct mistakes To realize that if you know the answer but accidentally fill in the wrong circle, you lose points	Quickly review each answer, testing it against the question See if the number of the response matches the question

(Continued)

TABLE 14.2 continued

Skill or Strategy	Description	Purpose	Components
		To remember to always check your work	Look for spaces not completed then guess the answers
		To be sure you don't lose points for a simple error	Scan the answer sheet for stray marks and erase as needed
Set the Pace	Learning to control the time spent on each task	To develop an awareness of time segments for pacing	When starting a question, decide if it is easy or hard
		To adjust the speed of your work	Speed up for easy questions
		To know when to use fast versus slow reading	Slow down for hard questions
		To develop a feel for pacing	Adjust reading speed to the purpose
		To keep from running out of time	Practice fast-pace tips such as knowing facts, formulas, and terms; how to read graphs and charts; knowing when to use a calculator; knowing when to move on (after 2 minutes)
Keep On Keeping On	Learning to try different approaches and be persistent	To get past difficult spots and do your best	Try educated guesses when the answer is unknown
		To avoid wasting time	Read the passage for thorough understanding
		To learn to apply different approaches or strategies for difficult questions	Try various strategies to answer the question
			Keep working in each section until finished
			Use deep breathing if feeling frustrated, defeated, or hopeless

Source: Adapted from Chapman and King, 2009.

benefit them. Show how results can be used to improve learning and essential life skills, their knowledge of themselves, and planning for the future. Avoid comments that might make students concerned or anxious.

Reassure your students that some anxiety is normal and can provide energy to help them perform better. Some of your students may be so anxious about the test that their anxiety seriously interferes with their performance. If you suspect that a student's performance is adversely affected by test anxiety, after you have done all you can to alleviate the fears, then you may want to have the student examined by a counselor to determine the extent of the problem. If necessary, appropriate counseling and desensitization exercises can be explored. At the very least, incorporate your awareness of the anxiety when interpreting the results of the test. See Cizek and Burg (2006) for further detail on test anxiety.

Emphasize the importance of a good night's sleep and a healthy breakfast or lunch to students to stay alert and at their best for the test. Of course, be sure that the physical environment for taking the test is appropriate. There should be adequate work space and lighting as well as good ventilation. The room should be quiet, without distractions, and the test should be scheduled to avoid events that may disturb the students. Students should be seated to avoid distractions and cheating. Morning testing is preferred. One of the important ways to prepare students for testing is do everything you can to make students comfortable, self-confident, and in control. Students need to be familiar with the nature of the test and know what to expect. Likewise, teachers need to be confident about the way students will perform on the test. This is communicated to students when the teacher knows directions, guidelines, and procedures and demonstrates confidence by being calm and businesslike (Flippo, 2008). It is best to remove any visual aids that could assist students and to place a sign on the outside of the door, such as Testing—Do Not Disturb.

The key to successful student performance on standards-based tests is to focus more on the standards and student learning than on test performance. This requires an in-depth understanding of the nature of the standards and the kind of mental operations needed to answer test questions. Teachers achieve this in-depth understanding by "unpacking" standards, breaking them down to know the specific levels of knowledge and skills that are required (Tileston & Darling, 2008). Is the knowledge declarative or procedural? Is the emphasis on knowing, applying, or problem solving? What mental operation is needed to answer the types of questions on the standards-based tests?

It is particularly important to maximize teaching time and learning and familiarize students with the test format and item type just enough to help them develop the self-confidence they need to be successful. The worst practice, seen more and more with standards-based education, is to drill students over and over by taking tests similar to the standards-based ones. There is no compelling evidence that such strategies improve test scores. Some familiarity is important, but in many schools there is simply way too much time taken to test, test, and then test some more, often with multiple-choice items that are commonly used in standards-based tests.

Poor test performance is caused by many different factors, though the following are most prevalent (Chapman & King, 2009):

- Distractions that prevent clear thinking, caused by lack of sleep, noise, hunger, physical discomforts, interruptions, teacher pressure
- Inadequate preparation, caused by poor study and test-taking skills, inattention, lack of confidence, unfamiliarity with the test format and procedures

Figure 14.12   Do's and Don'ts of Standardized Test Preparation

Do	Don't
Improve student test-taking skills	Use the standardized test format for classroom tests
Establish a suitable environment	Characterize tests as an extra burden
Motivate students to do their best	Tell students important decisions are made solely on the basis of test scores
Use released items	
Explain why tests are given and how results will be used	Use previous forms of the same test
Give practice tests	Teach the test
Tell students they probably won't know all the answers	Have a negative attitude about the test
Tell students not to give up	Use items with a format that is identical to the test
Allay student anxiety	Limit instruction and classroom assessments to be aligned only with the test
Have a positive attitude about the test	

- Lack of internal readiness, promoted by negative self-talk, fear of failure, panic, low motivation, nervousness.
- Confusion, caused by unfamiliarity with types of items, unclear directions, lack of strategies for completing the test (p. 90)

Figure 14.12 lists some do's and don'ts regarding the test preparation practices of teachers.

Administering Standardized and Standards-Based Tests

Because most standardized and standards-based tests are given in the classroom, you will most likely be responsible for administering them to your students. The most important part of administering these tests is to *follow the directions carefully and explicitly.* This point cannot be overstated. You must adhere strictly to the instructions that are given by the test publisher. The procedures are set to ensure standardization in the conditions under which students in different classes and schools take the test. The directions indicate what to say, how to respond to student questions, and what to do as students are working on the test. Familiarize yourself with the directions before you read them to your students, word for word as specified. Don't try to paraphrase directions or recite them from memory, even if you have given the test many times.

During the test you may answer student questions about the directions or procedures for answering items, but you should not help students in any way with an answer or what is meant by a question on the test. Although you may be tempted to give students hints or tell them to "answer more quickly" or "slow down and think more," these responses are inappropriate and should be avoided. You need to suspend your role as classroom teacher for a while and assume the role of test administrator. This isn't easy, and you may well catch yourself with minor variations from the directions.

While observing students as they take the test, you may see some unusual behavior or events that could affect the students' performance. It is best to record these behaviors and events for use in subsequent interpretation of the results. Interruptions should also be recorded.

Summary

The purpose of this chapter was to introduce you to the principles of standardized and standards-based testing to enable you to administer such tests and interpret your students' scores. The results of these tests, when used correctly, provide helpful information concerning the effectiveness of your instruction and progress of your students. Important points in the chapter include the following:

- Frequency distributions show you how scores are arrayed: normal, positively skewed, negatively skewed, flat.
- Measures of central tendency include the mean, median, and mode.
- Measures of variability, such as the range and standard deviation, provide numerical values for the degree of dispersion of scores from the mean.
- Standard scores are converted from raw scores into units of standard deviation.
- Grade equivalency scores indicate performance related to norming groups and should be cautiously interpreted.
- Scatterplots show relationships graphically as being positive, negative, or curvilinear.
- Correlation coefficients are numbers from −1 to 1 that indicate direction and strength of the relationship.
- Correlation does not imply causation.
- Standard error of measurement (SEM) expresses mathematically the degree of error to be expected with individual test scores; test results are best interpreted as intervals defined by the SEM.
- Percentile rank, standard scores, and grade equivalents for students are based on comparisons with the norming group.
- Alignment of the content, emphasis, and cognitive level of a test with instruction is needed for proper interpretation.
- Norm-referenced test scores provide external measures and help identify relative strengths and weaknesses.
- Different types of norms, such as national norms, special group norms, or local norms, influence the reported percentile ranks and other comparative scores.

- Proper interpretation of scores from norm-referenced standardized tests depends on the nature of the norm group and on understanding relative standing as indicated by percentile rank and grade equivalent.
- Norm-referenced standardized achievement test batteries can indicate strengths and weaknesses.
- Norms are not standards or expectations; they should be recent, appropriate to your use, and based on good sampling.
- Aptitude and readiness tests measure capacity to learn.
- Standards-based/criterion-referenced interpretations depend on the difficulty of the items and professional judgments to set standards.
- Good standards-based/criterion-referenced judgments depend on well-defined targets and a sufficient number of test items to provide a reliable result.
- Standardized test reports vary in format and organization; consult the interpretive guide to aid in understanding.
- Adequate interpreting of standardized test scores to parents depends on your preparation, your full understanding of the meaning of the scores, your ability to translate the numerical results into plain language, and placing the scores in the context of classroom performance.
- Prepare your students for taking standardized tests by establishing a good environment, lessening test anxiety, motivating students to do their best, avoiding distractions, and giving students practice tests and exercises.

Self-Instructional Review Exercises

1. For the following set of numbers, calculate the mean, median, and standard deviation. Also determine linear z-scores for 18, 20, and 11.

   10, 17, 18, 15, 20, 16, 15, 21, 12, 11, 22

2. If you have a normal distribution of scores with a mean of 80 and a standard deviation of 6, what is the approximate percentile rank of the following scores: 86, 68, 83, and 71?

3. What kind of information would lead one to conclude that a student has clear weaknesses in a particular skill?

4. How is it possible for all school districts in a state to be above the 50th percentile on a standardized norm-referenced test?

5. Indicate whether each of the following characteristics refers to a norm-referenced (NR), standards-based criterion-referenced (SB), aptitude (A), or state standardized (S) test. More than one may apply to each characteristic.

   a. Reports scores as percentage of items correct
   b. Shows capacity to learn
   c. Reports grade equivalents
   d. Reports percentile scores
   e. Readiness test

6. Given the following standardized test scores for Mary, an eighth grader, her mother believes that Mary is in the wrong grade. She believes Mary would be better off in the ninth grade. She also believes that the test scores seem to indicate that Mary is stronger in science than in language arts, mathematics, or social science. How would you respond to Mary's mother?

Test	NATL PR	Stanine	GE
Mathematics	75	6	9.2
Science	87	7	9.7
Social studies	80	7	9.4
Language arts	63	6	8.5
Study skills	72	6	9.0

7. Indicate whether each of the following suggested activities help or hinder student performance on a standardized test:

   a. Tell students their futures depend on their scores.
   b. To avoid making students anxious, do not tell them very much about the test.
   c. Make sure the room temperature is about right.
   d. Arrange desks so that students face each other in groups of four.
   e. Give students a practice test that is very similar in format.
   f. Tell students they probably won't be able to answer many of the questions.
   g. Teach to the test.
   h. Tell students you think the test is taking away from class time and student learning.

Answers to Self-Instructional Review Exercises

1. $\overline{X} = 161/11 = 16.09$; $mdn = 16$. Rounding the mean to 16, the SD is 3.83. The z-scores are as follows: 18: $z = 18 - 16/3.83 = .53$; 20: $20 - 16/3.83 = 1.05$; 11: $11 - 16/3.83 = -1.31$.

2. The score of 86 is one standard deviation above the mean, so the percentile is the 84th; 68 is two standard deviations below the mean, so the percentile is the 2nd; 83 is one half of a standard deviation above the mean, so the percentile rank is between 50 (mean) and 84 (one SD); because 34% of the scores lie in this range, one half of 34 is 17, so 83 is at about the 67th percentile (50 + 17) (actually it would be a little greater than 17 because of the curve of the distribution, but 67 is a good approximation); using the same logic, 71, which is one and one-half standard deviations below the mean, would be at approximately the 8th percentile (50 − 34 + 8).

3. When the information from several different sources suggests the same conclusion, when there is a pattern of performance for several years, and when your own informal assessment coincides with what is in school records.

4. Because norms are established in one year (e.g., 2004) and then used for several more years, and current scores (2006) are compared to the 2004 norms. Before new norms are established, all the school districts may target skills assessed on the test.

5. a. clearly SB, some NR and S, not A; b. A; c. NR; d. NR, A, maybe S; e. A.

6. Mary's mother is probably looking at the GEs and thinking that this means Mary should be in the ninth grade. This is not true. It's very possible that most of the students in the eighth grade have GEs of 9 or higher. It's true that Mary's science score is her highest, but given a normal standard error of measurement that is about 6 percentile points, the confidence interval overlaps suggest that there is no meaningful difference between science (81–93) and social studies (74–86), but it could be concluded that the science score is definitely higher than the language arts (57–69). The stanines give you the impression that the scores on all the tests are about the same, which is somewhat misleading. Yes, they are all well above the norm, but the science percentile score is at the top of stanine 7, whereas the language arts percentile is at the bottom of stanine 6.

7. a. hinder, b. hinder, c. help, d. hinder, e. help, f. hinder, g. help, h. hinder.

Suggestions for Action Research

1. Observe a class in which students take a standardized test. If possible, take a copy of the test administration guidelines with you and determine how closely the teacher follows the directions. What has the teacher done to motivate the students and set a proper environment? Observe the students as they are taking the test. Do they seem motivated and serious? How quickly do they work?

2. Sit in on two or three teacher–parent conferences that review the results of standardized tests. Compare what occurs with the suggestions in the chapter. How well, in your opinion, does the teacher interpret the scores? Is the teacher accurate?

3. Interview some parents about standardized tests. What did they get from the reports? Which types of scores were most meaningful to them? Did the results surprise them? Were the results consistent with other performance, such as grades?

4. Interview some teachers about standardized testing. Ask them how they use the results of standardized tests to improve their instruction. Ask them to recall situations in which parents did not seem to understand the results of the test very well. Looking back, what could the teacher have done differently to enhance parent understanding?

The Scope of a Teacher's Professional Role and Responsibilities for Student Assessment

The scope of a teacher's professional role and responsibilities for student assessment may be described in terms of the following activities. These activities imply that teachers need competence in student assessment and sufficient time and resources to complete them in a professional manner.

Activities Occurring prior to Instruction

a. Understanding students' cultural backgrounds, interests, skills, and abilities as they apply across a range of learning domains and/or subject areas
b. Understanding students' motivations and their interests in specific class content
c. Clarifying and articulating the performance outcomes expected of pupils
d. Planning instruction for individuals or groups of students

Activities Occurring during Instruction

a. Monitoring pupil progress toward instructional goals
b. Identifying gains and difficulties pupils are experiencing in learning and performing
c. Adjusting instruction
d. Giving contingent, specific, and credible praise and feedback
e. Motivating students to learn
f. Judging the extent of pupil attainment of instructional outcomes

Activities Occurring after the Appropriate Instructional Segment
(e.g., lesson, class, semester, grade)

a. Describing the extent to which each pupil has attained both short- and long-term instructional goals
b. Communicating strengths and weaknesses based on assessment results to students and parents or guardians
c. Recording and reporting assessment results for school-level analysis, evaluation, and decision making
d. Analyzing assessment information gathered before and during instruction to understand each student's progress to date and to inform future instructional planning
e. Evaluating the effectiveness of instruction

    f. Evaluating the effectiveness of the curriculum and materials in use

*Activities Associated with a Teacher's Involvement in School Building and
School District Decision Making*

    a. Serving on a school or district committee examining the school's and district's strengths and weaknesses in the development of its students
    b. Working on the development or selection of assessment methods for school building or school district use
    c. Evaluating school district curriculum
    d. Other related activities

Activities Associated with a Teacher's Involvement in a Wider Community of Educators

    a. Serving on a state committee asked to develop learning goals and associated assessment methods
    b. Participating in reviews of the appropriateness of district, state, or national student goals and associated assessment methods
    c. Interpreting the results of state and national student assessment programs

Source: Standards for Teacher Competence in Educational Assessment of Students. (1990). American Federation of Teachers, National Council on Measurement in Education, National Education Association.

Standards for Teacher Competence in Educational Assessment of Students

Standard	*Skills*
1. Teachers should be skilled in *choosing* assessment methods appropriate for instructional decisions.	**a.** Use concepts of assessment error and validity. **b.** Understand how valid assessment supports instructional activities. **c.** Understand how invalid information can affect instructional decisions. **d.** Use and evaluate assessment options considering backgrounds of students. **e.** Be aware that certain assessment activities are incompatible with certain instructional goals. **f.** Understand how different assessment approaches affect decision making. **g.** Know where to find information about various assessment methods.
2. Teachers should be skilled in *developing* assessment methods appropriate for instructional decisions.	**a.** Be able to plan the collection of information needed for decision making. **b.** Know and follow appropriate principles for developing and using different assessment methods. **c.** Be able to select assessment techniques that are consistent with the intent of the instruction. **d.** Be able to use student data to analyze the quality of each assessment technique used.

Standard	*Skills*
3. The teacher should be skilled in administering, scoring, and interpreting the results of both externally produced and teacher-produced assessment methods.	**a.** Be skilled in interpreting informal and formal teacher-produced assessment results, including performances in class and on homework. **b.** Use guides for scoring essay questions, projects, response-choice questions, and performance assessments. **c.** Administer standardized achievement tests and interpret reported scores. **d.** Understand summary indexes, including measures of central tendency, dispersion, relationships, and errors of measurement. **e.** Analyze assessment results to determine student strengths and weaknesses. **f.** Use results appropriately and do not increase students' anxiety levels.
4. Teachers should be skilled in using assessment results when making decisions about individual students, planning teaching, developing curriculum, and making recommendations for school improvement.	**a.** Use accumulated assessment information to organize a sound instructional plan. **b.** Interpret results correctly according to established rules of validity. **c.** Use results from local, regional, state, and national assessments for educational improvement.
5. Teachers should be skilled in developing valid pupil grading procedures that use pupil assessments.	**a.** Devise, implement, and explain a procedure for developing grades. **b.** Combine various assignments, projects, in-class activities, quizzes, and tests into a grade. **c.** Acknowledge that grades reflect their own preferences and judgments. **d.** Recognize and avoid faulty grading procedures. **e.** Evaluate and modify their grading procedures.
6. Teachers should be skilled in communicating assessment results to students, parents, other lay audiences, and other educators.	**a.** Understand and be able to give appropriate explanations of how to interpret student assessments as moderated by student background factors such as socioeconomic status. **b.** Explain that assessment results do not imply that background factors limit a student. **c.** Communicate to parents how they may assess a student's educational progress. **d.** Explain the importance of taking measurement errors into account when making decisions based on assessment. **e.** Explain the limitations of different types of assessments. **f.** Explain printed reports of assessments at the classroom, school district, state, and national levels.

(continued)

Standards for Teacher Competence in Educational Assessment of Students (*continued*)

Standard	Skills
7. Teachers should be skilled in recognizing unethical, illegal, and otherwise inappropriate assessment methods and uses of assessment information.	**a.** Understand laws and case decisions that affect their classroom, school district, and state assessment programs. **b.** Understand the harmful consequences of misuse or overuse of various assessment procedures such as embarrassing students or violating a student's right to confidentiality. **c.** Understand that it is inappropriate to use standardized student achievement test scores to measure teaching effectiveness.

Source: Standards for Teacher Competence in Educational Assessment of Students. (1990). American Federation of Teachers, National Council on Measurement in Education, National Education Association.

The Student Evaluation Standards

Propriety

P   Propriety Standards   The propriety standards help ensure that student evaluations will be conducted legally, ethically, and with due regard for the well-being of the students being evaluated and other people affected by the evaluation results. These standards are as follows:

P1   **Service to Students**   Evaluations of students should promote sound education principles, fulfillment of institutional missions, and effective student work, so that educational needs of students are served.

P2   **Appropriate Policies and Procedures**   Written policies and procedures should be developed, implemented, and made available, so that evaluations are consistent, equitable, and fair.

P3   **Access to Evaluation Information**   Access to a student's evaluation information should be provided, but limited to the student and others with established legitimate permission to view the information, so that confidentiality is maintained and privacy protected.

P4   **Treatment of Students**   Students should be treated with respect in all aspects of the evaluation process, so that their dignity and opportunities for educational development are enhanced.

P5   **Rights of Students**   Evaluations of students should be consistent with applicable laws and basic principles of fairness and human rights, so that students' rights and welfare are protected.

P6   **Balanced Evaluation**   Evaluations of students should provide information that identifies both strengths and weaknesses, so that strengths can be built upon and problem areas addressed.

P7   **Conflict of Interest**   Conflicts of interest should be avoided, but if present should be dealt with openly and honestly, so that they do not compromise evaluation processes and results.

Source: The Joint Committee on Standards for Educational Evaluation. (2003). *The Student Evaluation Standards*. Thousands Oaks, CA: Corwin Press.

Utility

U   Utility Standards   The utility standards help ensure that student evaluations are useful. Useful student evaluations are informative, timely, and influential. Standards that support usefulness are as follows:

U1   **Constructive Orientation**   Student evaluations should be constructive, so that they result in educational decisions that are in the best interest of the student.

U2   **Defined Users and Uses**   The users and uses of a student evaluation should be specified, so that evaluation appropriately contributes to student learning and development.

U3   **Information Scope**   The information collected for student evaluations should be carefully focused and sufficiently comprehensive, so that evaluation questions can be fully answered and the needs of students addressed.

U4   **Evaluator Qualifications**   Teachers and others who evaluate students should have the necessary knowledge and skills, so that evaluations are carried out competently and the results can be used with confidence.

U5   **Explicit Values**   In planning and conducting student evaluations, teachers and others who evaluate students should identify and justify the values used to judge student performance, so that the bases for the evaluations are clear and defensible.

U6   **Effective Reporting**   Student evaluation reports should be clear, timely, accurate, and relevant, so that they are useful to students, their parents/ guardians, and other legitimate users.

U7   **Follow-Up**   Student evaluations should include procedures for follow-up, so that students, parents/guardians, and other legitimate users can understand the information and take appropriate follow-up actions.

Feasibility

F   Feasibility Standards   The feasibility standards help ensure that student evaluations can be implemented as planned. Feasible evaluations are practical, diplomatic, and adequately supported. These standards are as follows:

F1   **Practical Orientation**   Student evaluation procedures should be practical, so that they produce the needed information in efficient, nondisruptive ways.

F2   **Political Viability**   Student evaluations should be planned and conducted with the anticipation of questions from students, their parents/guardians, and other legitimate users, so that their questions can be answered effectively and their cooperation obtained.

F3   **Evaluation Support**   Adequate time and resources should be provided for student evaluations, so that evaluations can be effectively planned and implemented, their results fully communicated, and appropriate follow-up activities identified.

Accuracy

A   Accuracy Standards   The accuracy standards help ensure that a student evaluation will produce sound information about a student's learning and performance. Sound information leads to valid interpretations, justifiable conclusions, and appropriate follow-up. These standards are as follows:

A1   Validity Orientation   Student evaluations should be developed and implemented, so that interpretations made about the performance of a student are valid and not open to misinterpretation.

A2   Defined Expectations for Students   The performance expectations for students should be clearly defined, so that evaluation results are defensible and meaningful.

A3   Context Analysis   Student and contextual variables that may influence performance should be identified and considered, so that a student's performance can be validly interpreted.

A4   Documented Procedures   The procedures for evaluating students, both planned and actual, should be described, so that the procedures can be explained and justified.

A5   Defensible Information   The adequacy of information gathered should be ensured, so that good decisions are possible and can be defended and justified.

A6   Reliable Information   Evaluation procedures should be chosen or developed and implemented, so that they provide reliable information for decisions about the performance of a student.

A7   Bias Identification and Management   Student evaluations should be free from bias, so that conclusions can be fair.

A8   Handling Information and Quality Control   The information collected, processed, and reported about students should be systematically reviewed, corrected as appropriate, and kept secure, so that accurate judgments can be made.

A9   Analysis of Information   Information collected for student evaluations should be systematically and accurately analyzed, so that the purposes of the evaluation are effectively achieved.

A10   Justified Conclusions   The evaluative conclusions about student performance should be explicitly justified, so that students, their parents/guardians, and others can have confidence in them.

A11   Metaevaluation   Student evaluation procedures should be examined periodically using these and other pertinent standards, so that mistakes are prevented or detected and promptly corrected, and sound student evaluation practices are developed over time.

Glossary

Absolute grading a criterion-referenced type of grading in which grades are based on performance compared to set standards.

Adaptive behavior being able to meet independence and social responsibility expectations for the age and context in which the behavior occurs.

Adequate yearly progress (AYP) a provision of NCLB legislation requiring schools to show improvements each year in student participation and performance.

Affect *see* Affective.

Affective emotional feelings.

Alignment extent to which instructional activities and classroom assessments cover tested material.

Alternative assessment refers to a number of different kinds of assessments that are not traditional paper-and-pencil tests, such as performance and portfolio assessments.

Alternatives refers to possible answers in a multiple-choice item.

Analytic scale type of scoring in which separate scores are provided for each criterion used.

Anchor examples of student responses, products, and performances that illustrate specific points on a scoring criteria scale.

Anecdotal observation brief written notes or records of student behavior.

Aptitude test type of standardized test that measures cognitive ability, potential, or capacity to learn.

Assessment the process of gathering, evaluating, and using information.

Attention deficit disorder (ADD) a classification of special needs in which the student is unable to sustain attention while being easily distracted.

Attention deficit hyperactivity disorder (ADHD) a classification of special needs in which the student is inattentive, hyperactive, and/or impulsive.

Attitude a predisposition to respond favorably or unfavorably to something; consists of affective, cognitive, and behavioral components.

Authentic assessment assessments that mirror tasks carried out in actual, naturally occurring settings.

Authenticity describes instruction and assessment that are characterized by tasks that are similar to what is done or accomplished in real life.

Benchmark content standard for particular grade levels or developmental levels.

Benchmark test regular testing of students during the school year to monitor progress toward achieving end-of-year state standards.

Binary-choice item type of selected-response item in which the respondent selects one of two possible answers.

Blueprint *see* Test blueprint.

Central tendency error Scoring bias in which students tend to be rated in the middle of the evaluation scale.

Classroom assessment the collection, evaluation, and use of information for teacher decision making.

Cognitive mental processing that includes knowing, understanding, and reasoning.

Confidence bands show the standard error of measurement for obtained scores.

Constructed-response format type of item in which students create or produce their own answer or response.

Construct-related evidence type of evidence for validity that focuses on the meaning and definition of constructs that are assessed.

Content-related evidence type of evidence for validity in which judgments are made about the representativeness of a sample of items from a larger domain.

Content standards   describe what students should know and be able to do.

Correlation coefficient   a number between −1 and +1 that indicates the direction and strength of relationship between two measures.

Criteria   categories of specific behaviors or dimensions used to evaluate students.

Criterion-referenced   type of test score interpretation in which performance is compared to levels of established criteria.

Criterion-related evidence   type of evidence for validity in which scores from an assessment are related to other measures of the same trait or future behavior.

Developmental standards   describe what students should know and be able to do at each grade level.

Distractors   Incorrect alternatives in a multiple-choice item.

Educational goal   a general statement of what students should know and be able to do.

Educational objective   a relatively specific statement of what students should know and be capable of doing at the end of an instructional unit.

Electronic portfolio   a systematic collection of materials in digital format.

Emotional disturbance   consistent, inappropriate behaviors and feelings not attributed to other disabilities that interfere with academic work.

Essay   type of item in which students provide an extended or restricted written response to a question.

Evaluation   interpretation of gathered information to make the information meaningful.

Exemplar   *see* Anchor.

Expectation   level of performance communicated to others.

Extended-type task   a performance assessment task that may last days or weeks in which students provide extensive answers to tasks.

Feedback   indicating verbally or in writing the correctness of an action, answer, or other response.

Formative assessment   assessment that occurs during instruction to provide feedback to teachers and students.

Frequency distribution   indicates the number of individuals receiving each score.

Frequency polygon   shows the number of individuals receiving each score as a line graph.

Generosity error   scoring bias in which teachers rate students higher than their performance deserves.

Goal   *see* Educational goal.

Grade equivalent (GE)   type of standardized test score that indicates performance in units of year and month of school as compared to the norm group.

Grade-level standards   describe age-appropriate standards that reflect changes over time.

Halo effect   general impression influences scores or grades on subsequent assessments.

High-stakes tests   tests that students must perform adequately on for graduation, promotion in grade, school accreditation, and other important implications.

Histogram   graphic illustration of a frequency distribution, using bars to represent the frequency of each score or groups of scores.

Holistic scale   type of scoring in which a single score is given for overall performance.

Hyperactive   excessively active behavior sustained in many situations.

Impulsivity   responding quickly, without time for reflection.

Inclusion   educational approach in which students with disabilities are taught in classrooms with students who do not have disabilities.

Individualized education program (IEP)   plan for providing appropriate services to students with disabilities.

Instructional validity   judgment of the extent of the match between what is taught and what is assessed.

Item analysis   review of pattern of responses to an objective item to determine the quality of distractors, discrimination, and difficulty.

Learning disability   mental processing deficit that manifests as a significant discrepancy between aptitude and achievement.

Learning goal   student desire to understand and learn with positive self-conceptions of competence.

Learning target   a description of performance that includes what students should know and be able to do and what criteria are used to judge the performance.

Likert scale   rating scale in which a respondent indicates the extent to which there is agreement or disagreement among a series of statements.

Mastery goal   *see* Learning goal.

Mean   arithmetic average of all scores in a distribution.

Measurement   a systematic process of differentiating traits, characteristics, or behavior.

Median   the midpoint of a distribution, dividing it into an equal number of scores.

Mental retardation   poor aptitude and adaptive behaviors that result in slow learning.

Mode   the most frequently occurring score in a distribution.

Negatively skewed   a distribution in which the mean is lower than the median.

Nondiscriminatory   assessment in which the nature of the materials, questions, and procedures do not influence the results.

Normal curve equivalent (NCE)   derived normalized score with a mean of 50 and a standard deviation of 21.06.

Norm-referenced   a type of test interpretation in which relative standing is identified by comparing performance to how others (norm group) performed.

Objective   see Educational objective or Teaching objective.

Oral questioning   type of assessment in which the teacher asks questions orally.

Percentile rank   indicates the percentage of scores at or below the specified score.

Performance assessment   type of assessment in which students perform an activity or create a product.

Performance criteria   *see* Criteria.

Performance goal   motivation for doing well is to pass or obtain a score rather than primarily to understand.

Performance standard   a set of criteria designated to signify qualitatively different levels of performance.

Personal communication   student interactions with the teacher to provide assessment information.

Portfolio   a systematic collection of student products to assess progress.

Positively skewed   a distribution in which the mean is higher than the median.

Preassessment   gathering information about students prior to instruction.

Range   the difference between the highest and lowest score in a distribution.

Rating scale   a scale that contains gradations of the trait being assessed.

Readiness test   type of standardized aptitude test that identifies strengths and weaknesses of specific skills.

Reasoning   mental operation in which cognitive skills are combined with knowledge to solve a problem, make a decision, or complete a task.

Reliability   the consistency, stability, and dependability of scores.

Restricted range   a small range of scores.

Restricted-type task   performance assessment task in which the student provides a limited response to a task that is completed within a day, hour, or minutes.

Rubric   a scoring guide that uses criteria to differentiate between levels of student proficiency on a rating scale.

Scaled score   derived scores used in standardized testing to indicate growth in years.

Scatterplot   visual array of scores from two measures that illustrates possible relationships.

Selected-response format   type of item for which students select a response from possible responses that are provided.

Self-assessment   students' self-report evaluations of their work.

Severity error   scoring bias in which teachers rate students lower than they should.

Sociogram   pictorial graph that shows how members of a group relate to one another.

Speeded tests   type of test in which students have a set, minimal amount of time to answer all questions.

Standard deviation   a number that indicates the average distance of scores from the mean.

Standard error of measurement (SEM)   estimate of the degree of error in obtained scores.

Standards   *see* Performance standards *or* Content standards.

Standards-based   *See* Criterion-referenced.

Stanine   derived score that indicates the approximate location of a score on the normal distribution.

Stem   question or phrase in a multiple-choice item that is answered by selecting from given alternatives.

Student self-assessment   students reporting on or evaluating themselves.

Summative assessment   assessment that occurs at the end of an instructional unit to document student learning.

Table of specifications   *see* Test blueprint.

Target   *see* Learning target.

Teacher expectation   beliefs about what students are capable of knowing, understanding, and doing.

Teacher observation   method of gathering assessment information in which the teacher systematically or informally observes students.

Teaching objective   a description of the instructional plan.

Test   a formal, systematic procedure for assessment in which students respond to a standard set of questions.

Test battery   several standardized tests that are normed on the same sample.

Test blueprint   systematic presentation of the learning targets and nature of items in an assessment.

Test-retest   a stability estimate of reliability in which a group answers the same questions twice.

Total points method   approach to grading in which points for each product are summed.

Validity   the appropriateness and legitimacy of the inferences, claims, and uses made from test scores.

Values   end states of existence or desirable modes of conduct.

Weighted categories method   approach to grading in which each product is assigned an emphasis toward the final grade.

z-score   derived scores with a mean of 0 and a standard deviation of 1.

References

Abrams, L. M., Wetzel, A., & McMillan, J. H. (2010, May). *Teachers' formative use of benchmark test data*. Paper presented at the annual meeting of the American Educational Research Association, Denver.

Ainsworth, L., & Viegut, D. (2006). *Common formative assessments: How to connect standards-based instruction and assessment*. Thousand Oaks, CA: Corwin Press.

Airasian, P. W., & Russell, M. K. (2008). *Classroom assessment: Concepts and applications* (6th ed.). New York: McGraw-Hill.

Alonzo, A., & Gearhart, M. (2006). Considering learning progressions from a classroom assessment perspective. *Measurement, 4*, 99–104.

Alvermann, D. E., & Phelps, S. F. (2005). Assessment of students. In P. A. Richard-Amato & M. A. Snow (Eds.), *Academic success for English language learners: Strategies for K–12 mainstream teachers.* (pp. 311–340) White Plains, NY: Longman.

American Educational Research Association. (2003). Standards and tests: Keeping them aligned. *Research Points, 1(1)*, 1–4.

Ames, C. A. (1990). Motivation: What teachers need to know. *Teachers College Record, 91*, 409–421.

Anderson, L. W., & Krathwohl, D. R. (2001). *A taxonomy for learning, teaching, and assessing: A revision of Bloom's taxonomy of educational objectives*. New York: Longman.

Arter, J., & McTighe, J. (2001). *Scoring rubrics in the classroom: Using performance criteria for assessing and improving student performance*. Thousand Oaks, CA: Corwin Press.

Arter, J. A. (1996). Establishing performance criteria. In R. E. Blum & J. A. Arter (Eds.), *Handbook for student performance assessment in an era of restructuring* (pp. VI-1: 1–VI-2:8). Alexandria, VA: Association for Supervision and Curriculum Development.

Azwell, T., & Schmar, E. (1995). *Report card on report cards: Alternatives to consider*. Portsmouth, NH: Heinemann.

Barrett, H. C. (2007). Researching electronic portfolios and learning engagement: The REFLECT Initiative. *Journal of Adolescent & Adult Literacy, 50(6)*, 436–449.

Becker, H. (2001). *Teaching ESL K–12*. Boston: Heinle & Heinle.

Billups, L. H., & Rauth, M. (1987). Teachers and research. In V. Richardson-Koehler (Ed.), *Educator's handbook*. White Plains, NY: Longman.

Black, P., & Wiliam, D. (1998). Assessment and classroom learning. *Assessment in Education, 5(1)*, 103–110.

Black, P., & Wiliam, D. (2004). The formative purpose: Assessment must first promote learning. In M. Wilson (Ed.), *Towards coherence between classroom assessment and accountability*. 103rd Yearbook of the National Society for the Study of Education. Chicago: University of Chicago Press.

Bloom, B. S. (Ed.) (1956). *Taxonomy of educational objectives: The classification of educational goals. Handbook 1. Cognitive Domain*. New York: David McKay.

Borich, G. D., & Tombari, M. L. (2004). *Educational assessment for the elementary and middle school classroom* (2nd ed.). Upper Saddle River, NJ: Pearson Education Inc.

Brookhart, S. M. (1993). Teachers' grading practices: Meaning and values. *Journal of Educational Measurement, 30*, 123–142.

Brookhart, S. M. (2001). Successful students' formative and summative uses of assessment information. *Assessment in Education, 8(2)*, 153–169.

Brookhart, S. M. (2004). *Grading*. Upper Saddle River, NJ: Pearson Education Inc.

Brookhart, S. M. (2005, April). *Research on formative classroom assessment: State-of-the-art*. Paper presented at the annual meeting of the American Educational Research Association, Montreal.

Brookhart, S. M. (2007). Expanding views about formative classroom assessment: A review of the literature. In J. H. McMillan (Ed.), *Formative classroom assessment: Theory into practice*. New York: Teachers College Press.

Brookhart, S. M. (2008). *How to give effective feedback to your students*. Alexandria, VA: Association for Supervision and Curriculum Development.

Brophy, J. E. (2004). *Motivating students to learn* (2nd ed.). Boston: McGraw-Hill.

Brophy, J. E., & Alleman, J. (1991). Activities as instructional tools: A framework for analysis and evaluation. *Educational Researcher, 20*, 9–23.

Brown, R. S., & Coughlin, E. (2007). *The predictive validity of selected benchmark assessments used in the Mid-Atlantic Region*. Washington, DC: U.S. Department of Education, Institute of Educational Sciences, National Center for Educational Evaluation and Regional Assistance, Regional Educational Laboratory Mid-Atlantic. Available at http://ies.ed.gov/ncee/edlabs.

Burke, K. (1999). *The mindful school: How to assess authentic learning* (3rd ed.). Arlington Heights, IL: SkyLight Professional Development.

Burke, K. (2006). *From standrds to rubrics in six steps: Tools for assessment student learning. K–8*. Thousand Oaks, CA: Corwin Press.

Camp, R. (1992). Portfolio reflections in middle and secondary school classrooms. In K. B. Yancey (Ed.), *Portfolios in the writing classroom*. Urbana, IL: National Council of Teachers of English.

452

Carlson, M. O., Humphrey, G. E., & Reinhardt, K. S. (2003). *Weaving science inquiry and continuous assessment: Using formative assessment to improve learning.* Thousand Oaks, CA: Corwin Press.

Chapman, C., & King, R. (2009). *Test success in the brain-compatible classroom* (2nd ed.). Thousand Oaks, CA: Corwin Press.

Chappuis, S., & Stiggins, R. J. (2002). Classroom assessment for learning. *Educational Leadership, 60*(1), 40–44.

Cizek, G. J. (1999). *Cheating on tests: How to do it, detect, and prevent it.* Mahwah, NJ: Erlbaum.

Cizek, G. J. (2003). *Detecting and preventing classroom cheating: Promoting integrity in assessment.* Thousand Oaks, CA: Corwin Press.

Cizek, G. J., & Burg, S. S. (2006). *Addressing test anxiety in a high-stakes environment: Strategies for classrooms and schools.* Thousand Oaks, CA: Corwin Press.

Cohen, S. B. (1983). Assigning report card grades to the mainstreamed child. *Teaching Exceptional Students, 15,* 86–89.

Collier, V. (1989). How long? A synthesis of research on academic achievement in a second Language. *TESOL Quarterly, 23,* 509–531.

Collins, A., & Dana, T. M. (1993). Using portfolios with middle grades students. *Middle School Journal, 25,* 14–19.

Conley, M. W. (2005). *Connecting standards and assessment through literacy.* Boston: Allyn & Bacon.

Cooper, H., Lindsay, J. J., Nye, B., & Greathouse, S. (1998). Relationships among attitudes about homework, amount of homework assigned and completed, and student achievement. *Journal of Educational Psychology, 90,* 70–83.

Costa, A. L., & Kallick, B. (2004). *Assessment strategies for self-directed learning.* Thousand Oaks, CA: Corwin Press/Sage Publications.

Covington, M. V. (1992). *Making the grade: A self-worth perspective on motivation and school reform.* New York: Cambridge University Press.

Creating a learning environment at Fowler High School. (1993). Syracuse, NY: Inclusive Education Project, Syracuse University.

Crooks, T. (2007, April). *Key factors in the effectiveness of assessment for learning.* Paper presented at the Annual Meeting of the American Educational Research Association, Chicago.

Cross, L. H., & Frary, R. B. (1996). *Hodgepodge grading: Endorsed by students and teachers alike.* Paper presented at the annual meeting of the National Council on Measurement in Education, New York.

Cummins, J. (1996). *Negotiating identities: Education for empowerment in a diverse society.* Ontario, CA: California Association for Bilingual Education.

D'Agostino, J., & Welsh, M. (2007). *Standards-based progress reports and standards-based assessment score convergence.* Paper presented at the annual meeting of the American Education Research Association, Chicago.

DiRanna, K., Osmundson, E., Topps, J., Barakos, L., Gearhart, M., Cerwin, K., Carnahan, D., & Strang, C. (2008). *Assessment-centered teaching: A reflective practice.* Thousand Oaks, CA: Corwin Press.

Doyle, W. (1986). Classroom organization and management. In M. C. Wittrock (Ed.), *Handbook of research on teaching* (3rd ed.). New York: Macmillan.

Dufour, R., Eaker, R., & Dufour R. (2005). *On common ground: The power of professional learning communities.* Bloomington, IN: Solution Tree Press.

Durán, P. R. (2008). Assessing English language learners' achievement. *Review of Research in Education, 32,* 292–327.

Earl, L. M. (2003). *Assessment as learning: Using classroom assessment to maximize student learning.* Thousand Oaks, CA: Corwin Press.

Echevarria, J., Vogt, M., & Short, D. J. (2008). *Making content comprehensible for English language learners: The SIOP Model.* Boston: Pearson Education.

Educational Testing Service. (2009). *Guidelines for the assessment of English language learners.* Retrieved June 1, 2009, from http://www.ets.org/Media/About_ETS/pdf/ELL_Guidelines.pdf

Ekman, P., & Friesen, W. V. (1969). The repertoire of nonverbal behavior: Categories, origins, usage, and coding. *Semiotica, 69,* 49–97.

Elliot, A. J., & Thrash, T. M. (2001). Achievement goals and the hierarchical model of achievement motivation. *Educational Psychology Review, 13*(2), 139–156.

Ennis, R. H. (1987). A taxonomy of critical thinking dispositions and abilities. In J. B. Baron & R. J. Sternberg (Eds.), *Teaching thinking skills: Theory and practice.* New York: W. H. Freeman.

Evertson, C., & Green, J. (1986). Observation as inquiry and method. In M. C. Wittrock (Ed.), *Handbook of research on teaching* (3rd ed., pp. 162–213). New York: Macmillan.

Federal Register. (1977, December 29). *Procedures for evaluating specific learning disabilities.* Washington, DC: Department of Health, Education, and Welfare.

Flippo, R. F. (2008). *Preparing students for testing and doing better in school.* Thousand Oaks, CA: Corwin Press.

Forsyth, D. R. (1999). *Our social world* (3rd ed.). Belmont, CA: Wadsworth.

Fraser, B. J. (1994). Research on classroom and school climate. In D. Gabel (Ed.), *Handbook of research on science teaching and learning.* New York: Macmillan.

Fraser, B. J. (1999). Using learning environment assessments to improve classroom and school climates. In H. J. Freiberg (Ed.), *School climate: Measuring, improving and sustaining health learning environments.* London: Falmer Press.

Frederiksen, J. R., & White, B. Y. (2004). Designing assessments for instruction and accountability: An application of validity theory to assessing scientific inquiry. In M. Wilson (Ed.), *Toward coherence between classroom assessment and accountability.* 103rd Yearbook of the National Society for the Study of Education. Chicago: University of Chicago Press.

Frey, B. B., Schmitt, V. L., & Bowen, A. (2009, April). *Dimensions of authenticity in authentic assessment.* Paper presented at the Annual Meeting of the American Educational Research Association, San Diego.

Frisbie, D. A., & Waltman, K. K. (1992). Developing a personal grading plan. *Educational Measurement: Issues and Practice, 11,* 35–42.

Fuchs, D., Mock, D., Morgan, P. L., & Young, C. I. (2003). Responsiveness intervention: Definitions, evidence, and implications for the learning disabilities construct. *Learning Disabilities Research & Practice, 18*(3), 157–171.

Furtak, E. M. (2009). *Formative assessment for secondary science teachers.* Thousand Oaks, CA: Corwin Press.

Gagne, E. D., Yekovich, C. W., & Yekovich, F. R. (1993). *The cognitive psychology of school learning* (2nd ed.). New York: HarperCollins.

Gallavan, N. P. (2009). *Developing performance-based assessments: Grades 6–12.* Thousand Oaks, CA: Corwin Press.

Gallego, M. A., & Cole, M. (2001). Classroom cultures and cultures in the classroom. In V. Richardson (Ed.), *Handbook of research on teaching* (4th ed.). Washington, DC: American Educational Research Association.

Gardner, H. (1985). *Frames of mind: The theory of multiple intelligences.* New York: Basic Books.

Gelfer, J. I., Xu, Y., & Perkins, P. (2004). Developing portfolios to evaluate teacher performance in early childhood education. *Early Childhood Education Journal, 32*(2), 63–68.

Glatthorn, A. A. (1998). *Performance assessment and standards-based curricula: The achievement cycle.* Larchmont, NY: Eye on Education.

Goertz, M. E., Oláh, L. N., & Riggan, M. (2010). *From testing to teaching: The use of interim assessments in classroom instruction.* Consortium for Policy Research in Education Research Report RR-65.

Good, T. L., & Brophy, J. E. (2008). *Looking in classrooms* (10th ed.). New York: Longman.

Gordon, M. (1987). *Nursing diagnosis: Process and application.* New York: McGraw-Hill.

Graner, P.S., Faggella-Luby, M.N., & Fritschmann, N. S. (2005). An overview of responsiveness to intervention: What practitioners ought to know. *Topics in Language Disorders, 25*(2), 93–105.

Green, S. K., & Johnson, R. L. (2010). *Assessment is essential.* Boston: McGraw-Hill.

Groeber, J. F. (2007). *Designing and using rubrics for reading and language arts, K–6.* (2nd ed.). Thousand Oaks, CA: Corwin Press.

Gronlund, N. E. (1995). *How to write and use instructional objectives* (5th ed.). New York: Macmillan.

Gullickson, A. R. (2003). *The student evaluation standards.* Thousand Oaks, CA: Corwin Press.

Guskey, T. R. (1994). Making the grade: What benefits students? *Educational Leadership, 52,* 14–20.

Guskey, T. R. (Ed.). (1996). *Communicating student learning: 1996 ASCD Yearbook.* Alexandria, VA: Association for Supervision and Curriculum Development.

Guskey, T. R. (2002). Computerized gradebooks and the myth of objectivity. *Phi Delta Kappan, 83*(10), 775–780.

Guskey, T. R. (2005, April). *Formative classroom assessment and Benjamin S. Bloom's theory, research, and implications.* Paper presented at the annual meeting of the American Educational Research Association, Montreal.

Guskey, T. R. (2007). Formative classroom assessment and Benjamin S. Bloom: Theory, research, and practice. In J. H. McMillan (Ed.), *Formative classroom assessment: Theory into practice.* New York: Teachers College Press.

Guskey, T. R. (2009). *Practical solutions for serious problems in standards-based grading.* Thousand Oaks, CA: Corwin Press.

Guskey, T. R., & Bailey, J. M. (2001). *Developing grading and reporting systems for student learning.* Thousand Oaks, CA: Corwin Press.

Haertel, E. (1990). *From expert opinions to reliable scores: Psychometrics for judgment-based teacher assessment.* Paper presented at the annual meeting of the American Educational Research Association, Boston.

Harlen, W. (2003). *Enhancing inquiry through formative assessment.* San Franciso: Institute for Inquiry, Exploratorium.

Harris-Murri, N., King, K., & Rostenberg, D. (2006). Reducing disproportionate minority representation in special education programs for students with emotional disturbances: Toward a culturally responsive response to intervention model. *Education and Treatment of Children, 29*(4), 779–799.

Hattie, J., & Timperley, H. (2007). The power of feedback. *Review of Educational Research, 77,* 81–112.

Hebert, E. A. (1998). Lessons learned about student portfolios. *Phi Delta Kappan, 79,* 583–585.

Heritage, M. (2007). Formative assessment: What do teachers need to know and do? *Phi Delta Kappan, 89*(2), 140–145.

Heritage, M. (2008). *Learning progressions: Supporting instruction and formative assessment.* Los Angeles, CA: National Center for Research on Evaluation, Standards, and Student Testing.

Heritage, M. (2009). Using self-assessment to chart students' paths. *Middle School Journal, 40*(5), 27–30.

Heritage, M., & Anderson, C. (2009, April). *Laying the groundwork for formative assessment.* Paper presented at the 2009 Annual Meeting of the American Educational Research Association

Heubert, J. P., & Hauser, R. M. (Eds.). (1999). *High stakes testing for tracking, promotion, and graduation.* Washington, DC: National Academy Press.

Hill, B. C., Ruptic, C., & Norwick, L. (1998). *Classroom based assessment.* Norwood, MA: Christopher-Gordon.

Hill, D. (2007). *Emotionomics.* Edina, MN: Beavers Pond Group.

Horowitz, F. D., Darling-Hammond, L., Bransford, J., Comer, J., Rosebrock, K., Austin, K., & Rust, F. (2005). Educating teachers for developmentally appropriate practice. In L. Darling-Hammond & J. Bransford (Eds.) *Preparing teachers for a changing world.* Hoboken, NJ: Wiley.

Hoy, L., & Greg, M. (1994). *Assessment in special education.* Pacific Groves, CA: Brooks/Cole.

Individuals with Disabilities Education Improvement Act of 2004. P. L. 108-446. Washington DC: U.S. Government Printing Office.

Individuals with Disabilities Education Act (1997). P. L. 105-117. Washington DC: U.S. Government Printing Office.

Jackson, P. W. (1990). *Life in classrooms.* New York: Holt, Rinehart, and Winston.

Jung, L. A., (2009). The challenges of grading and reporting in special education: An inclusive grading model. In T. R. Guskey (Ed.), *Practical solutions for serious problems in standards-based grading.* Thousand Oaks, CA: Corwin Press.

Keeley, P. (2008). *Science formative assessment: 75 practical strategies for linking assessment, instruction, and learning.* Thousand Oaks, CA: Corwin.

Kendall, J. S., & Marzano, R. J. (1997). *Content knowledge: A compendium of standards and benchmarks for K–12 education.* Aurora, CO: Mid-continent Regional Educational Laboratory.

Kingore, B. (2008). *Developing portfolios for authentic assessment, prek–3: Guiding potential in young learners.* Thousand Oaks, CA: Corwin Press.

Kluger, A. N., & DeNisi, A. (1996). The effects of feedback interventions on performance: A historical review, a meta-analysis, and a preliminary feedback intervention theory. *Psychological Bulletin, 119*(2), 254–284.

Knapp, M. L., & Hill, J. A. (2009). *Nonverbal communication in human interaction* (7th ed.). Florence, KY: Wadsworth Cengage Learning.

Krathwohl, D. R., Bloom, B. S., & Masia, B. B. (1964). *Taxonomy of educational objectives, handbook II: Affective domain.* New York: David McKay.

Lambdin, D. V., & Walker, V. L. (1994). Planning for classroom portfolio assessment. *The Arithmetic Teacher, 41*, 318–324.

Lazzari, A. M., & Wood, J. W. (1994). *Test right: Strategies and exercises to improve test performance.* East Moline, IL: LinguiSystems.

Leathers, D. G., & Eares, M. H. (2008). *Successful nonverbal communication: Principles and applications* (4th ed.). New York: Macmillan.

Marsh, H. W., & Craven, R. (1997). Academic self-concept: Beyond the dustbowl. In G. D. Phye (Ed.), *Handbook of classroom assessment: Learning, adjustment, and achievement.* San Diego, CA: Academic Press.

Marsh, J., Pane, J., & Hamilton, L. (2006). *Making sense of data-driven decision making in education: Evidence from recent RAND research.* Washington, DC: RAND Corporation.

Martin-Kniep, G. O., & Cunningham, D. (1998). *Why am I doing this? Purposeful teaching through portfolio assessment.* Portsmouth, NH: Heinemann.

Marzano, R. J. (2006). *Classroom assessment and grading that work.* Alexandria, VA: ASCD.

Marzano, R. J. (2010). *Formative assessment & standards-based grading: Classroom strategies that work.* Bloomington, IN: Marzano Research Library.

Marzano, R. J., & Kendall, R. S. (1996). *A comprehensive guide to designing standards-based districts, schools, and classrooms.* Aurora, CO: Mid-continent Regional Educational Laboratory.

Marzano, R. J., & Kendall, J. S. (2007). *The new taxonomy of educational objectives* (2nd ed.). Thousand Oaks, CA: Corwin Press.

Marzano, R. J., Pickering, D., & McTighe, J. (1993). *Assessing student outcomes: Performance assessment using the dimensions of learning model.* Alexandria, VA: Association for Supervision and Curriculum Development.

Mastropieri, M. A., & Scruggs, T. E. (2007). *The inclusive classroom: Strategies for effective instruction* (3rd ed.). Upper Saddle River, NJ: Pearson/Merrill Prentice Hall.

Matese, G. (2005, April). *Cognitive factors affecting teachers' formative assessment practices.* Paper presented at the annual meeting of the American Educational Research Association, Montreal.

Mayer, R. E., (2002). *The promise of educational psychology: Vol. II. Teaching for meaningful learning.* Upper Saddle River, NJ: Merrill/Prentice Hall.

McElligot, J., & Brookhart, S. M. (2009). Legal issues of grading in the era of high stakes accountability. In T. R. Guskey (Ed.), *Practical solutions for serious problems in standards-based grading.* Thousand Oaks, CA: Corwin Press.

McLoughlin, J. A., & Lewis, R. B. (2005). *Assessing students with special needs* (6th ed.). Upper Saddle River, NJ: Pearson Education, Inc.

McMillan, J. H. (2001). Secondary teachers' classroom assessment and grading practices. *Educational measurement: Issues and Practice, 20*(1), 20–32.

McMillan, J. H. (2002a). Elementary school teachers' classroom assessment and grading practices. *Journal of Educational Research, 95*(4), 203–214.

McMillan, J. H. (2002b). *The impact of high-stakes external testing on classroom assessment decision-making.* Paper presented at the annual meeting of the American Educational Research Association, New Orleans.

McMillan, J. H. (2003). Understanding and improving teachers' classroom assessment decision making. *Educational Measurement: Issues and Practices, 22*(4), 34–43.

McMillan, J. H. (2008). *Assessment essentials for standards-based education.* Thousand Oaks, CA: Corwin Press.

McMillan, J. H. (2009). Synthesis of issues and implications for practice. In T. Guskey (Ed.), *Practical solutions for serious problems in standards-based grading.* Thousand Oaks, CA: Corwin Press.

McMillan, J. H. (2010). The practical implications of educational aims and contexts for formative assessment. In H. L. Andrade & G. J. Cizek (Eds.), *Handbook of formative assessment* Oxford, England: Routledge (pp. 41–58).

McMillan, J. H., & Forsyth, D. R. (1991). What theories of motivation say about why learners learn. In R. J. Menges & M. D. Svinicki (Eds.), *College teaching: From theory to practice.* San Francisco: Jossey-Bass.

McMillan, J. H., & Hearn, J. (2008). Student self-assessment: The key to stronger student motivation and higher achievement. *Educational Horizons, 87*(1), 40–49.

McMillan, J. H., Simonetta, L. G., & Singh, J. (1994). Student opinion survey: Development of measures of student motivation. *Educational and Psychological Measurement, 54*, 496–505.

McMillan, J. H., & Tierney, R. D. (2009). *Reconceptualizing fairness for classroom assessment.* (Unpublished Manuscript).

McMillan, J. H., & Workman, D. (1999). *Teachers' classroom assessment and grading practices: Phase 2.* Richmond, VA: Metropolitan Educational Research Consortium.

McMillan, J. H., Workman, D., & Myran, S. M. (1998). *Teachers' classroom assessment and grading practices: Phase 1.* Richmond, VA: Metropolitan Educational Research Consortium.

McTighe, J., & Ferrara, S. (1998). *Assessing learning in the classroom.* Washington, DC: National Education Association.

McTighe, J., & Wiggins, G. (2005). *Understanding by design: Professional development workbook.* Alexandria, VA: Association for Supervision and Curriculum Development.

Mehrabian, A. (1981). *Silent messages* (2nd ed.). Belmont, CA: Wadsworth.

Mehring, T. A. (1995). Report card options for students with disabilities in general education. In T. Azwell & E. Schmar (Eds.), *Report card on report cards: Alternatives to consider.* Portsmouth, NH: Heinemann.

Miller, M. D. Linn, R. L., & Gronlund, N. E. (2009). *Measurement and assessment in teaching* (10th ed.). Upper Saddle River, NJ: Pearson Education Inc.

Moskal, B. M. (2003). Recommendations for developing classroom performance assessments and scoring rubrics. *Practical Assessment, Research & Evaluation, 8*(14). Retrieved June 1, 2005, from http://PAREonline.net/getvn.asp?v=8,n=14

Mottet, T. P., & Richmond, V. P. (2000). *Student nonverbal communication and its influence on teachers and teaching: A review of literature.* Paper presented at the Annual Meeting of the National Communication Association.

National Council on Measurement in Education. (1995). *Code of professional responsibilities in educational measurement.* Washington, DC: Author.

National Forum on Assessment. (1995). *Principles and indicators for student assessment systems.* Cambridge, MA: National Center for Fair and Open Testing (FairTest).

National Research Council. (2001). *Knowing what students know: The science and design of educational assessment.* Washington, DC: National Academy Press.

Newmann, F. M. (1997). Authentic assessment in social studies: Standards and examples. In G. D. Phye (Ed.), *Handbook of classroom assessment: Learning, adjustment, and achievement.* San Diego, CA: Academic Press.

Nilsen, B. A. (2008). *Observation and assessment.* Clifton Park, NY: Thompson Delmar Learning.

Nolen, S. B., Haladyna, T. M., & Haas, N. S. (1989). *A survey of Arizona teachers and administrators on the uses and effects of state-mandated standardized achievement testing* (Tech. Rep. No. 89–2). Phoenix, AZ: Arizona State University, West Campus.

O'Connor, K. (2009). *How to grade for learning K–12.* Thousand Oaks, CA: Corwin Press.

O'Malley, J. M., & Pierce, L. V. (1996). *Authentic assessment for English language learners: Practical approaches for teachers.* White Plains, NY: Longman.

Ormrod, J. E. (2004). *Human learning* (4th ed.). Upper Saddle River, NJ: Merrill/Prentice Hall.

Overton, T. (2003). *Assessing learners with special needs: An applied approach.* Upper Saddle River, NJ: Merrill/Prentice Hall.

Parke, C. S., Lane, S., Silver, E. A., & Magone, M. E. (2003). *Using assessment to improve middle-grades mathematics teaching and learning: Suggested activities using QUASAR tasks, scoring criteria, and students' work.* Reston, VA: National Council of Teachers of Mathematics.

Perie, M., Marion, S., & Gong, B. (2009). Moving toward a comprehensive assessment system: A framework for considering interim assessments. *Educational Measurement: Issues and Practice, 28*(3), 5–13.

Pierangelo, R., & Giuliani, G. A. (2007). *Special education eligibility: A step-by-step guide for educators.* Thousand Oaks, CA: Corwin Press.

Pierangelo, R., & Giuliani, G. A. (2008). *Assessment in special education: A practical approach* (3rd ed.). Boston: Pearson Education, Inc.

Pintrich, P. R., & Schunk, D. H. (2002). *Motivation in education: Theory, research, and applications.* Upper Saddle River, NJ; Columbus, OH: Merrill/Prentice Hall.

Pope, N., Green, S. K., Johnson, R. L., & Mitchell, M. (2009). Examining teacher ethical dilemmas in classroom assessment. *Teaching and Teacher Education, 25,* 778–782.

Popham, W. J. (2007). The lowdown on learning progressions. *Educational Leadership, 64*(7), 83–84.

Popham, W. J. (2008b). *Transformative assessment.* Alexandria, VA: Association for Supervision and Curriculum Development.

Popham, W. J. (2009). Assessing student affect. *Educational Leadership, 66*(8), 85–86.

Popham, W. J. (2011). *Classroom assessment: What teachers need to know* (5th ed.). Boston: Allyn & Bacon.

Quellmalz, E. S., & Hoskyn, J. (1997). Classroom assessment of reasoning strategies. In G. D. Phye (Ed.), *Handbook of classroom assessment: Learning, adjustment, and achievement.* San Diego, CA: Academic Press.

Reeves, D. B. (2003). *Making standards work: How to implement standards-based assessments in the classroom, school, and district.* Englewood, CO: Advanced Learning Press.

Reiss, J. (2005). *Teaching content to English language learners.* White Plains, NY: Pearson Education.

Reynolds, C. R., Livingston, R. B., & Willson, V. (2006). *Measurement and assessment in education.* Boston: Pearson Education Inc.

Rivera, C., & Collum, E. (Eds.). (2006). *State assessment policy and practice for English language learners: A national perspective.* Mahwah, NJ: Erlbum.

Rokeach, M. (1973). *The nature of human values.* New York: Free Press.

Ross, J. A. (2006). The reliability, validity, and utility of self-assessment. *Practical Assessment, Research & Evaluation, 11*(10). Available online at http://pareonline.net/getvn.asp?v=11&n=10

Roth, W. M. (2001). Gestures: Their role in teaching and learning. *Review of Educational Research, 71*(3), 365–392.

Ruiz-Primo, M. A., & Furtak, E. M. (2007). Exploring teachers' informal formative assessment practices and students' understanding in the context of scientific inquiry. *Journal of Research in Science Teaching, 44*(1), 57–84.

Ryan, A. M., & Deci, E. L. (2000). Self-determination theory and the facilitation of intrinsic motivation, social development, and well-being. *American Psychologist, 55,* 68–78.

Sadler, P. M., & Good, E. (2006). The impact of self- and peer-grading on student learning. *Educational Assessment, 11,* 1–31.

Salend, S. J. (1995). Modifying tests for diverse learners. *Intervention in School and Clinic, 31,* 84–90.

Salend, S. J. (2009). *Classroom testing and assessment for ALL students: Beyond standardization.* Thousand Oaks, CA: Corwin Press.

Salvia, J., & Ysseldyke, J. E. (2001). *Assessment* (8th ed.) Boston: Houghton Mifflin.

Sampson, S. O. (2009). Assigning fair, accurate, and meaningful grades to students who are English language learners. In T. Guskey (Ed.), *Practical solutions for serious problems in standards-based grading.* Thousand Oaks, CA: Corwin Press.

Schunk, D. H. (2004). *Learning theories: An educational perspective* (4th ed.). Upper Saddle River, NJ: Pearson Education Inc.

Schwartz, J. L., & Kenney, J. M. (2008). *Tasks and rubrics for balanced mathematics assessment in primary and elementary grades.* Thousand Oaks, CA: Corwin Press.

Section 504 of the Rehabilitation Act of 1973.

Seitz, H., & Bartholomew, C. (2008). Powerful portfolios for young children. *Early Childhood Education Journal, 36,* 63–68.

Shaywitz, B. A., Fletcher, J. M., Holahan, J. M., & Shaywitz, S. E. (1992). Discrepancy compared to low achievement definitions of reading disability. *Journal of Learning Disabilities, 25,* 639–648.

Shepard, L. A. (2000). The role of assessment in a learning culture. *Educational Researcher, 29*(10), 4–14.

Shepard, L. A. (2004). Curricular coherence in assessment design. In M. Wilson (Ed.), *Towards coherence between classroom assessment and accountability.* 103rd Yearbook of the National Society for the Study of Education. Chicago: University of Chicago Press.

Shepard, L. A. (2009). Commentary: Evaluating the validity of formative and interim assessment. *Educational Measurement: Issues and Practice, 28*(3), 32–37.

Shute, V. J. (2008). Focus on formative feedback. *Review of Educational Research, 78*(1), 153–189.

Smith, J. K., Smith, L. F., & De Lisi, R. (2001). *Natural classroom assessment: Designing seamless instruction & assessment.* Thousand Oaks, CA: Corwin Press.

Smith, T. E. C., Polloway, E. A., Patton, J. R., & Dowdy, C. A. (2006). *Teaching students with special needs in inclusive settings* (4th ed). Englewood Cliffs, NJ: Merrill.

Spinelli, C. G. (2002). *Classroom assessment for students with special needs in inclusive settings.* Upper Saddle River, NJ: Merrill/Prentice Hall.

Sternberg, R. J. (1986). The future of intelligence testing. *Educational Measurement: Issues and Practice, 5,* 19–22.

Stiggins, R. J. (2002). Assessment crisis: The absence of assessment for learning. *Phi Delta Kappan, 83*(10), 758–765.

Stiggins, R. J. (2007). Assessment through the student's eyes. *Educational Leadership, 64,* 22–26.

Stiggins, R. J. (2008a). *A call for the development of balanced assessment systems.* Princeton, NJ: Educational Testing Service.

Stiggins, R. J. (2008b). *Student-involved assessment FOR learning.* Upper Saddle River, NJ: Pearson Merrill Prentice Hall.

Stiggins, R. J., Arter, J., Chappuis, J., & Chappuis, S. (2007). *Classroom assessment for student learning: Doing it right—using it well.* Upper Saddle River, NJ: Pearson.

Stiggins, R. J., & Conklin, N. F. (1992). *In teachers' hands: Investigating the practices of classroom assessment.* Albany: State University of New York Press.

Strickland, K., & Strickland, J. (1998). *Reflections on assessment: Its purposes, methods, and effects on learning.* Portsmouth, NH: Heinemann.

Stuebing, K. K., Fletcher, J. M., LeDoux, J. M., Lyon, G. R., Shaywitz, S. E., & Shaywitz, B. A. (2002). Validity of IQ-discrepancy classifications of reading disabilities: A meta-analysis. *American Educational Research Journal, 39,* 469–518.

Terwilliger, J. S. (1989). Classroom standard setting and grading practices. *Educational Measurement: Issues and Practice, 8,* 15–19.

Thomas, W. & Collier, V. (2002). *A national study of school effectiveness for language minority students' long-term academic achievement.* Santa Cruz, CA: Center for Research on Education, Diversity and Excellence.

Thurlow, M. L., Lazarus, S. S., Thompson, S. J., & Morse, A. B. (2005). State policies on assessment participation and accommodations for students with disabilities. *Journal of Special Education, 38,* 232–240.

Tierney, R. D. (2008, May). *Fairness in classroom assessment: Multiple and conflicting interpretations.* Paper presented at the Canadian Society of Studies in Education.

Tileston, D. W., & Darling, S. K. (2008). *Teaching strategies that prepare students for high-stakes tests.* Thousand Oaks, CA: Corwin Press.

Tittle, C. K., Hecht, D., & Moore, P. (1993). Assessment theory and research for classrooms: From Taxonomies to constructing meaning in context. *Educational Measurement: Issues and Practices, 12,* 13–19.

Tomlinson, C. A. (1999). *The differentiated classroom: Responding to the needs of all learners.* Alexandria, VA: Association of Supervision and Curriculum Development.

Wayman, J., & Cho, V. (2009). Preparing educators to effectively use student data systems. In T. Kowalksi & T. Lasley, II (Eds.), *Handbook of data-based decision making in education* (pp. 89–104). New York: Routledge.

Weiner, B. (1974). *Achievement motivation and attribution theory.* Morristown, NJ: General Learning Press.

Wiggins, G. P. (1993). *Assessing student performance: Exploring the purpose and limits of testing.* San Francisco: Jossey-Bass.

Wiggins, G. P. (1998). *Educative assessment: Designing assessments to inform and improve student performance.* San Francisco: Jossey-Bass.

Wiggins, G. P., & McTighe, J. (2005). *Understanding by design* (2nd ed.). Washington, DC: Association for Supervision and Curriculum Development.

Wiliam, D. (2010). An integrative summary of the research literature and implication for a new theory of formative assessment. In H. L. Andrade & G. J. Cizek (Eds.). *Handbook of formative assessment.* New York: Routledge (pp. 18–40).

Wiliam, D., & Leahy, S. (2007). A theoretical foundation for formative assessment. In J. H. McMillan (Ed.), *Formative classroom assessment: Theory into practice.* New York: Teachers College Press.

Wilson, M., & Bertenthal, M. (Eds.). (2005). *Systems for state science assessment.* Washington, DC: National Academies Press.

Witt, J. C., Elliott, S. N., Daly, E. J., III, Gresham, F. M., & Kramer, J. J. (1998). *Assessment of at-risk and special needs children* (2nd ed.). Boston: McGraw-Hill.

Wolf, D. P. (1989). Portfolio assessment: Sampling student work. *Educational Leadership, 46,* 35–39.

Wood, J. W. (2002). *Adapting instruction to accommodate students in inclusive settings* (4th ed.). Upper Saddle River, NJ: Prentice Hall.

Worcester, T. (2009). *Portfolio planning sheet.* Accessed September 29, 2009, from http://www.tammyworcester.com/TWHandouts/HandoutsPresentationsTW/Entries/2022/1/1_Electronic_Portfolios_files/electronic portfolio.pdf

Wright, P. W. D., & Wright, P. D. (2005). *Wright's law IDEA 2004: Parts A & B.* Hartfield, VA: Harbor House Law Press.

Index

Attitude targets, 288–89
Attributes to be scored, 211
Audience, feedback and, 141
Auditory difficulties,
    of special needs
    students, 339
Authentic assessment, 220
Authenticity, 16, 228
Authentic tasks, 234–35
Avoidance behaviors, 296
Azwell, T., 396

B

Backward design, 8
Bailey, J. M., 366, 383, 384,
    385, 396
Balance, 89
Bar Average Task
    scoring criteria, 206
    student response to, 207,
    208
Barrett, H. C., 279
Barrow, Michelle, 3
Bartholomew, C., 263
Becker, H., 356
Behavioral disorder, 334
Behavioral objectives, 30
Behavior variability, of special
    needs students, 340
Benchmark assessments,
    125–26, 417
Benchmarks, 34
Bias
    avoiding, 82–84
    cultural, in test items, 354
    in observations, 111
    personal, 249
    teacher, 285
Billups, L. H., 5
Bimodal distribution, 407
Binary-choice items, 63, 165,
    181–85
    adaptation for special
    needs students, 344
    advantages and
    disadvantages of, 183–84
    assessing deep
    understanding and
    reasoning, 184–85
    clues, avoiding, 184
    negative statements,
    avoiding, 184
    writing, 183
Black, P., 99, 118, 119, 311
Blackboard, 124
Bloom, B. S., 38, 148, 149, 294,
    295
Bloom's taxonomy, 53
    of objectives, 38–40
    revision of, 40, 46, 49, 53
Blueprint. *See* Test blueprint

Body language, 107–8
Boehm Test of Basic
    Concepts, Third
    Edition, 415
Borich, G. D., 47, 238, 259,
    261, 292, 293
Bowen, A., 234
Bransford, J., 137
Brookhart, S. M., 14, 100, 134,
    135, 142, 364, 365, 372,
    374, 377, 383, 385, 396
Brophy, J. E., 50, 126, 147, 290
Brown, R. S., 125
Burg, S. S., 435
Burke, K., 258, 267, 278,
    301, 334

C

California Achievement
    Test, 414
Camp, R., 271, 273
Carlson, M. O., 102
Carter, Beth, 108, 393
Carter, M. A., 266
Celebration portfolios,
    258, 259
Central tendency, measures
    of, 406–7
Central tendency error, 249
Chapman, C., 429, 434, 435
Chappuis, J., 239, 258
Chappuis, S., 311, 315
Chapter tests, administration
    of, 167–68
Cheating, 393
Checklists, grading with, 379,
    382–83
Child study team, 331
Cho, V., 125
Cizek, G. J., 167, 393, 435
Classification, of assessment
    methods, 63
Classroom assessment,
    9–12, 15
    components of
    implementing, 9–12
    decision making, 21–23
    high-quality, 60–97
    model of fairness in, 84–86
    purpose of, 9–10
    recent trends in, 15–19, 19
Classroom environment
    targets, 292–94
Classroom response systems,
    124
    examples of, 124
*Code of Professional
    Responsibilities in
    Educational Measurement*
    (NCME), 24
Cognitive dimension, 44

Cognitive learning theory,
    13, 15
Cohen, S. B., 349
Cole, M., 292
Collaborative assessment, 259
Collaborative skills,
    taxonomy of, 293
Collier, V., 352, 353
Collins, A., 270
Collum, E., 355
Command words and
    definitions, 342
Communication skills, 224–26
Comparison, in grading,
    369–72
    norm-referenced, 369–70
    standards-based, 370–72
Competence, teacher, 442
Competence portfolios, 258,
    259
Completion items, 198–215
    adaptation for special
    needs students, 344–45
    assessing deep
    understanding
    and reasoning, 202–4
    short-answer items,
    200–202
    writing, 198
Complex overt response, 227
Comprehension
    assessment of, 176–77,
    182–84, 190–91
    difficulties for special
    needs students, 338
Comprehension
    dimension, 39
Conferences, 257
    parent-teacher, 397–98
    student-led, 398
    student-teacher, 277–78
Confidence bands, 422
Conklin, N. F., 285, 302
Conley, M. W., 32
Constructed-response
    assessment, 64, 65,
    197–218
    completion items, 198–215
    essay items, 204–15
    portfolios, 256–83
    self-report, 302–3
Constructivist learning
    theory, 14, 15
Construct-related evidence,
    69, 72–73
Content, of portfolios, 265,
    267
    checklists of, 274
    supplying, 268–70
Content-related evidence,
    69–71
    professional judgments
    in establishing, 71

Content standards, 32
Continuous assessment, 102
Contracting, 350–51
Cooper, H., 122
Cooperative behavior,
    guess-who approach
    for, 319
Correlation coefficient,
    410–11
Cost, of assessments, 93
Costa, A. L., 313, 315
Coughlin, E., 125
Covington, M. V., 372
Craven, R., 291
Criteria, 11, 34–35, 239
    for ensuring high-
    quality classroom
    assessments, 62
    performance, 34
    scoring, 34
    for selecting learning
    targets and standards,
    53–55
    specifying, 35
Criterion-referenced grading,
    370
    characteristics of, 373
Criterion-referenced tests
    interpretations, 423–25
    using test scores, 426–29
Criterion-related evidence,
    69, 71–72
Crooks, T., 311
Cross, L. H., 374
Cultural differences, 83–84
Cultural factors, ELL
    and, 353
Cultural knowledge,
    in test items, 354
Cummins, J., 352
Curriculum-based
    measurement
    (CBM), 332
Curriculum guide, 48, 50
Curriculum research, 13–14
Curriculum standards, 32
Curriculum theory, 14

D

D'Agostino, J., 374, 384
Daly III, E. J., 333
Dana, T. M., 270
Darling, S. K., 435
Darling-Hammond, L., 137
Deci, E. L., 291
Decision consistency,
    evidence based on, 80
Declarative knowledge, 44,
    176
    understanding and, 45
Deductive reasoning, 203